Territory Beyond Terra

Geopolitical Bodies, Material Worlds

This series publishes studies that originate in a range of different fields that are nonetheless linked through their common foundation: a belief that the macro-scale of geopolitics is composed of trans-local relations between bodies and materials that are only understandable through empirical examination of those relations. It is the interaction of these elements that produces the forces that shape global politics, often with outcomes that differ from the predictions of macro-scaled theories. This world poses questions: how do materialities such as the built environment and the body reproduce global power structures, how are they caught up in violent transformations and how do they become sites of resistance? How do assemblages of human and non-human elements both fortify and transform political space? What possibilities for political change are latent within the present?

Series Editors:

Jason Dittmer, Professor of Political Geography
at University College London

Ian Klinke, Associate Professor in Human Geography
and Tutorial Fellow at St John's College, Oxford

Series Titles:

The Geopolitics of Real Estate: Reconfiguring Property, Capital and Rights
Dallas Rogers

Choreographies of Resistance: Mobilities, Bodies and Politics
Tarja Väyrynen, Eeva Puumala, Samu Pehkonen, Tiina Vaittinen and
Anitta Kynsilehto

Life Adrift: Climate Change, Migration, Critique
Andrew Baldwin and Giovanni Bettini

Forthcoming:

The Politics of Bodies at Risk: The Human in the Body
Maria Boikova Struble

Micropolitics on the Line: Excavating Earth and Nature in Ecuador
Joe Gerlach

Chemical Bodies: The Techno-Politics of Control
Alex Mankoo and Brian Rappert

Territory Beyond Terra

Edited by Kimberley Peters,
Philip Steinberg and Elaine Stratford

ROWMAN &
LITTLEFIELD
━━━━━━━━━INTERNATIONAL

London • New York

Published by Rowman & Littlefield International Ltd
Unit A, Whitacre Mews, 26–34 Stannary Street, London SE11 4AB
www.rowmaninternational.com

Rowman & Littlefield International Ltd. is an affiliate of Rowman & Littlefield
4501 Forbes Boulevard, Suite 200, Lanham, Maryland 20706, USA
With additional offices in Boulder, New York, Toronto (Canada), and Plymouth (UK)
www.rowman.com

British Library Cataloguing in Publication Data
A catalogue record for this book is available from the British Library

ISBN: HB 978-1-7866-0011-0
         PB 978-1-7866-0012-7

Library of Congress Cataloging-in-Publication Data

Names: Peters, Kimberley A., editor. | Steinberg, Philip E., editor. |
   Stratford, Elaine, editor.
Title: *Territory beyond terra* / edited by Kimberley Peters, Philip Steinberg
   and Elaine Stratford.
Description: London; New York : Rowman & Littlefield International, 2018. |
   Series: Geopolitical bodies, material worlds | Includes bibliographical
   references and index.
Identifiers: LCCN 2018001910 (print) | LCCN 2018002857 (ebook) |
   ISBN 9781786600134 (electronic) | ISBN 9781786600110
   (cloth) | ISBN 9781786600127 (pbk.)
Subjects: LCSH: Environmental geography—Case studies. |
   Geopolitics—Case studies.
Classification: LCC G143 (ebook) | LCC G143 .T47 2018 (print) |
   DDC 304.2—dc23
LC record available at https://lccn.loc.gov/2018001910

Contents

List of Figures

Foreword

Stuart Elden

In the opening lines of *Genesis*, the Bible distinguishes the earth from two other terms. On the first day, there is the division between the heavens and the earth. In the Vulgate, the terms used are *caelum* compared to *terram*, the accusative case of *terra*. The earth, here, appears to be the planet, the globe (*Genesis* I, i). But only a few verses later, on the third day, the earth is itself divided into the arid or dry, *aridam*, and the water, *aquarum*. The water is gathered together to form what in the Bible is called the sea, *maria*; the dry area is described as the earth, *terram* (*Genesis* I, x). So, the earth in the first sense is divided into two: earth (in the second sense) and sea. The second sense of earth is perhaps more commonly thought of as land, but the Latin words are the same. In Hebrew the phrase for earth in the first sense is הָאָרֶץ; and in the second אֶרֶץ שָׂה. The term would transliterate as *eretz* – often used to describe the land or country. There is a minor grammatical difference in the Hebrew – the earth to this earth – but the choice of translating both the words with the same Latin word, *terra*, is crucial for the formation of the Western tradition. The dry area, יַבָּשָׁה or *yabasha*, is uncovered, rather than simply created, by the gathering of the waters. *Yabasha* is a word in modern Hebrew to describe a continent. That tension between the general and differentiated sense of the term *terra*, the Earth and earth, is at the heart of some of the issues today that structure our understanding of what should be the object of geopolitics and the scope and limits of territory.[1]

The English language has three roots for words connected to earth, territory, and geopolitics. The term 'earth' can be traced back to Anglo-Saxon roots. The word *eorð* is found in the *Beowulf* poem, for instance, in phrases such as *eorðsele*, an earth-hall, and *eorðdraca*, an earth-dragon (Swanton ed., lines 2410, 2712, 2825). There is a range of related terms in Germanic languages – *eorþe* in Old English; *erthe* in Old Frisian, *ertha* in Old Saxon; *erda* in Old High German, from which we get the English *earth*, German *Erde*, and Dutch *aarde*. But English is not simply formed from Germanic roots. The importance of the Norman Conquest is linguistic, among other political, social, and economic considerations, and indeed the marks in the language can help understand some of the other factors. At the beginning of Sir Walter Scott's *Ivanhoe*, for instance, a Saxon peasant is told that there is reason for the difference between the names given to animals and to their meat. Swine, ox, and calves are tended by Saxons, but are eaten, as pork, beef, and veal, by Normans. The first set of words are of Anglo-Saxon origin, the latter from Norman French (Scott 1996 [1820], 31–32).[2]

The words deriving from the French, with Latin antecedents, pertaining to 'earth' revolve around the *terr-* root, which is the word used in the Vulgate. Frantz Fanon's *The Wretched of the Earth*, for example, is Les damnés de la terre (1961, 1965). Interestingly, the French *terre* has a dual sense of land and earth – terms that are distinct in vocabulary in English. The French *terre* and Latin *terra* form the root of many English words – terrestrial, terrain, and even terrier, as well as the words or phrases we have taken directly into the language such as *terra firma*, *terra incognita*, and *terra nullius*. There is another Latin root to words that appear similar, *terrere*, meaning to frighten or scare away. While directly the root of terror, terrorism, terrify, and so on, there is a debate as to whether the root of territory is *terra*, land, or *terrere*, to frighten, and whether a territory, which derives from *territorium*, is place around a place, or a place from which people are warned off. I have discussed the relation between terror and territory elsewhere (Elden 2009), suggesting that the relation is stronger in practice than etymology, but it is worth noting that the suffix of territory, from *territorium*, is at least as interesting as the prefix.[3] We find that suffix in other words of Latin origin taken into English – crematorium, a place of death; sanatorium, a place of health; and auditorium, a place for hearing.

It is not unusual in modern English to have Anglo-Saxon, and therefore Germanic, words in the language alongside Latin, Norman-French ones. But there is a third set of words in English, deriving from the Greek root: ge, Γη. This set includes, of course, all the words like geography, geology, geometry, and geopolitics. However, as I have argued elsewhere (Elden 2017a), in those disciplines we are perhaps today losing the element of the *geo*, as earth, and replacing it with other ideas. In those terms, contemporary work on geopolitics is not far from critical work on global politics or international relations; geometry is abstract, a branch of mathematics that has little to do with actual earth-measuring; while geography is no longer earth-writing but a loose spatial sensibility to work that could equally have been done in international relations, in sociology, in cultural studies. It might be argued that only geology retains the etymological sense of the *logos* of the *geo*. In a fascinating study of the philosophical sense of this discipline, Robert Frodeman (2003, 3) suggests that the term "geology", which was 'once identified exclusively with the study of the solid Earth . . . has lost ground to "Earth sciences" . . . meant to highlight the need for an integrated study of air, water, soil, rock, ice, and biota'. This collection develops that broad understanding by looking at the political aspects of such expanded earth questions.

As well as the threefold root of words concerning earth, there is, as the passages from *Genesis* indicated, an ambiguity about the specificity of the term. What is the earth? The philosopher John Sallis (2000, 176) explores this question:

> But what is the earth? Is the earth even such that it has a *what*, a τί εςτι? Or does it have a sense only in some other sense? How is one to delimit the sense of the word? What kind of word is *earth*? Is it a proper noun, the name of a unique individual: *Earth*? Or is it a common noun, a word that signifies a universal sense but that happens to refer only to a single individual, to what is called *the earth*? Is that to which the word refers by way of its sense not also something else distinguishable from this individual? For there are occasions in which one says, not *the earth*, but simply *earth*, as one says also *water, fire,* and *air*, designating what within the schema of production would be identified as material and conceptualized philosophically as matter but, now, outside the schema, would be reconfigured monstrologically as elemental.

Thus, the word functions as an index of three kinds: of the individual (Earth); of the universal and only secondarily, through this, of the individual (the earth); and a third kind that has been thought as materiality but is now, outside the schema of production, to be thought as elemental (earth).

As the third instance of the term shows, "earth" can be understood in the narrow sense, the elemental, which today would suggest the physical substance of dry land. For the Greeks the geo had a special significance. In the *Metaphysics*, Aristotle tells us that it was Empedocles who first spoke of four material elements, though he contrasted three of them, earth [*ge*], air and water, to the fourth, fire (985a30–985b2). Aristotle later tells us that Hesiod 'expressly says that earth was the first of bodies to come to be' (989a10–11). In the *Physics*, Aristotle himself suggests that the reason that heavy things fall downwards is that they are earthy, whose natural place is below (208b20–22). But the other meanings both indicate a wider sense, which encompasses the planet with its much wider set of geophysical features. When we shift from geophysics to geopolitics we should confront a similar question. Of course, geopolitics means the politics of the "geo", but does the "geo" here signify earth as land, or *the* earth, planet, or world? If we, rightly, put the stress on the second alternative, how do we understand the relation between the earth, planet, or world, and how does each relate to the global? Geopolitics has long been understood to include analysis of the sea, even if it is sometimes understood as structured by a clear distinction between that and the land. And is territory, which is so often assumed to be rooted in the *terra*, the earth or land, something that is solely grounded in that way?

This collection provides an essential reorientation to such debates. Through a rich set of analyses that are both theoretically sophisticated and empirically rich, the contributors develop a multifaceted approach to the question of territory. Several of the uncritical assumptions of work in international relations and political geography are examined, pushed further, and opened up in a range of productive ways. The analysis of territory here offers a way for political geography – understood as a set of questions rather than just an academic subfield – to better account for the dynamics of our changing planet. It offers a way for political geography to be adequate to the challenge of the Anthropocene.

The chapters that follow outline this reorientation in a range of ways. Beginning with four chapters on the classical elements, Marijn Nieuwenhuis, Weiqiang Lin, Jon Phillips, and Nigel Clark show how the Earth in its general sense is made up of earth, water, air, and fire, even today. In the book's second part, Environments, Clayton Whitt further develops the notion of terrain to think about the fluid materiality of mud, a land-water dynamic which is also explored by Stephanie C. Kane and Ross Exo Adams. Johanne Bruun and Philip Steinberg look in detail at ice, a solid form of water that similarly complicates any straightforward division of geophysical state and geopolitical regime. In the final part, Edges, Elaine Stratford and Thérèse Murray, Kate Coddington, Leah Gibbs, and Rachael Squire further develop implicit themes from the earlier chapters, bringing in bodies, lives, the human, and the more-than-human. The geo-corporeal, the geo-physical, and the geo-political are shown to relate in significant and underexplored ways. Powerfully, these chapters discuss the complex interrelations of these lived bodies in such fluid and dynamic spaces.

Multiple themes come through in the collection. Striking is the stress on the vertical or volumetric way we need to think about these spaces, freed from the two-dimensional cartographic imagination. Whether it is airspace, the subterranean, or the submarine, the book's contributors think productively about height and depth, space not just area. They imagine these territories as in flux, dynamic, indeterminate, and changeable, rather than static and fixed: territory as process rather than product of political-social-geophysical transformation. In that, they recognise the limits of human agency, individual or collective. While pushing against some of the traditional understandings of the relation between politics and space, and developing the concepts to make sense of this, the contributors establish their arguments on detailed empirical and historical material.

In my own recent work I have been trying to develop my theory of territory to take better account of some themes that I neglected in previous work. In my forthcoming book *Shakespearean Territories* I use readings of several of Shakespeare's plays to examine different aspects of the question of territory (Elden forthcoming). As well as exploring themes which have been important in my previous work on territory – the political-economic, strategic, legal, and technical – I use Shakespeare to push me further: I explore the colonial, corporeal, and geophysical aspects as well. In other work I am trying to analyse territory in terms of its physical and political materiality, as the notion of terrain. Terrain, like *terra* and conventional understandings of territory, might be seen as too tied to dry land, to the form rather than the process, the static rather than the indeterminate or the dynamic. But in the way I am trying to develop a political theory of terrain, I want to contribute to debates that push us beyond the simple land-sea-air divide of international law, international relations, and political geography. Geophysical state and geopolitical regime are rarely so clearly demarcated. In trying to make sense of rivers, mountains, river deltas, coastlines, glaciers, deserts, swamps, marshes, airspace, the subterranean, and the sub-marine, I have tried to broaden the way we understand terrain. It is work that draws upon the use of the notion of "terrain" in physical geography and military geography, yet tries to push beyond some of their understandings (Elden 2017c; see 2013b, 2017b).[4]

My work on territory, especially now that I am exploring it as terrain, has been in dialogue with many of this book's authors. I am very pleased to see that several of the contributors here use, engage with, critique, and develop some of my own previous work on territory. I am sure that my future work on territory and terrain will make use of the contributions to this essential collection. In all it is clear that the Earth is more than earth: the *eretz* or *terram* of *Genesis* needs to be understood in its twofold sense. Territory, as this collection clearly shows, is air, water, ice, as well as land, earth; it has height and depth rather than just surface; it is dynamic rather than fixed. Territory beyond *terra* indeed.

Stuart Elden

NOTES

1. I am grateful to Moriel Ram for his help with the Hebrew text.

2. Scott's editor Ian Duncan notes (p. 533) that this follows a passage in Fuller 1850 [1622], Vol. I, p. 193.

3. Some of this is explored in Elden (2013a).

4. For physical geography, see, for example Mitchell (1991), Wilson and Gallant (2000); for military geography see Winters et al. (1998); Doyle and Bennett (2002); Rose and Nathanial (2000). For related developments of the notion of terrain to my work, see Squire (2016b) and Gordillo (forthcoming a, forthcoming b).

Acknowledgments

This collection first took shape at the Annual Association of American Geographers conference in Chicago, 2015, where two sessions titled; 'Territory beyond Terra' were convened. It was a fascinating conference not least because, in addition to these sessions, others spoke closely to how processes and practices of territorialisation were occurring beyond earthly, or grounded, parameters. Sessions that considered the politics of the air, pyropolitics, Arctic sovereignty, and terrain were also speaking to such ideas, and this collection joins together work by some of the scholars who presented at the original 'Territory beyond Terra' sessions and selected contributors to other panels.

As session convenors and now as editors we are grateful for the commitment and enthusiasm shown by the contributors in bringing this book into being. We would also like to express our thanks to those with whom we shared the vision of the book at the outset: notably Stuart Elden and Gastón Gordillo. We add further thanks to Jason Dittmer and Ian Klinke, series editors of 'Geopolitical Bodies, Material Worlds' for their support of the project and helpful feedback as we finalised the manuscript.

Finally our thanks go to all those at Rowman and Littlefield International and affiliates – past and present – who have provided assistance from the writing to production stage. Our particular thanks go to editorial assistant Natalie Bolderston, production editor Lisa Whittington, marketing manager Guy Sewell, project manager Brindha Thirumoorthy, and our indexer, Gabrielle Sale.

Chapter 1

Introduction

Kimberley Peters, Philip Steinberg and Elaine Stratford

As Stuart Elden (2013a, 3) writes in *The Birth of Territory*, 'it is generally assumed that territory is self-evident in meaning'. Because territories are typically understood as the bounded units that result from efforts by humans and their institutions to control space, most academic inquiry has failed to approach the concept directly. Instead, scholars have tended to focus either on the borders that define the limits of territories or on the processes of territoriality by which territories are constructed. Literatures in both areas have advanced considerably over the past few decades. The field of border studies, for instance, has advanced from the empirical study of why borders are where they are to the development of conceptual work on how enforcing and crossing borders intersect with identity, citizenship, and governmentality (Jones 2016; Mezzadra and Neilson 2013; Newman and Paasi 1998; Paasi 1998). Studies of territoriality, similarly, have expanded from work that roots territorial behaviour in animal instincts to claim space (Ardrey 1966; Dyson-Hudson and Smith 1978), to research that associates changes in territorial practice with social change (Sack 1986; Soja 1971), to scholarship that conceptualises territorialisation as a social construct, a discursive strategy, or a process that is continually articulated amid competing tendencies of deterritorialisation and reterritorialisation (Agnew 1994; Albert 1998; Gottman 1973; Kratochwil 1986; Ruggie 1993). However, in these literatures, whether one focuses on the borders that define territories or on the territorial behaviours and institutions that create them, attention is diverted from understanding how space is transformed into *territory*, a specifically modern innovation that, according to Elden (2013a), must occur prior to its bounding.

Delving further, Elden identifies territory as a "political technology". Territory, for Elden (2013a), is a complex bundle of political, geographical, economic, strategic, legal, and technical relations that joins a particular perspective on *land* – wherein one conceives of land as a series of points whose difference and distance can be calculated with another on *terrain* – wherein Earth's substance is understood as a material resource that can provide value, whether by providing a surface for mobility or elevations for surveillance, or as a source of soil or minerals. Elden's formulation is provocative. Indeed, the political materialism that lies at the heart of his approach is taken up throughout this book. However, his choice of terms for the two fundamental aspects of territory – *land* and *terrain* – suggests limits to his perspective. In everyday usage, *land* is often understood as a synonym for solid earth, and *terrain* is frequently used solely to refer to that earth's surface and its morphology. These assumed meanings pervade Elden's text, as Elden himself has subsequently acknowledged (Elden 2013b, 2017c). This collection seeks to advance an understanding of territory beyond the geophysical limits implied by conventional understandings of *land* and *terrain*.

THINKING BEYOND SOLID LAND

In some respects, the landward (or terrestrial) bias underpinning histories of territory is not surprising, whether these histories focus on the development of territorialising practices (Sack 1986) or on the development of a political technology that links notions of *land* with those of *terrain* (Elden 2013a). In writing of the seas, Steinberg (1999, 368) notes that the land bias of the social sciences can be credited to the fact that watery spaces are not 'permanent spaces of sedentary habitation'. Much the same could be said of the skies, the underground, or marginal intersectional spaces such as tidal flats and swamps. In other words, we focus our attention on the land because this is where most of us reside. Land's assumed stability, as well as the ways in which it is amenable to visible striation by humans, has led to its elevation as the paradigmatic space of partition and control (Schmitt 2006). Here, on solid earth, we can erect walls, build fences, insert checkpoints (Weizmann 2002). This assumed correspondence of territory with land is countered by anthropological research on cultures that have different systems for inserting the social into non-terrestrial matter – for instance, island societies that integrate water into their daily livelihoods and, in the process, produce more fluid notions of territory (Anderson and Peters 2014; Hastrup and Hastrup 2015). However, the use of these societies to support calls for alternative notions of spatial order illustrates that these are outside the modern world's terracentric normative ideal (Hau'ofa 2008; Stratford, Baldacchino et al. 2011).

Challenging the land bias of our understanding of territory means asking questions that cut to the core of received assumptions about both geopolitics and geophysics: Is territory always a process related to the classic element of "earth"? What other elements or geophysical manifestations might territory and territorialising processes function through? Where might these processes of territory occur? Are they always landed or – as Elden (2013b) notes in alerting us to "volumes" of territory – might the making and contestation of territory occur at height and depth: in the skies or under the seas; in environments as varied as mudflats or ice islands, coasts or boats; and at edges or interfaces between spaces? And most crucially, if the concept of territory can be thought of beyond land, what might we learn of the concept applied to these settings; and of a process of territory that is (re)worked through elements other than earthly, solid matter? These questions are central to this book.

Modern social institutions are increasingly extending their geopolitical reach to what we might think of as "ungrounded" spaces whose properties differ from that of solid land. We need only think of recent instances of chemical warfare played out through the air; of contestation over deep-sea mining in our oceans; of debates concerned with the creation of artificial islands in the South China Sea. Indeed, these spaces "beyond *terra*" might include (but are not limited to) airspace, the underground, the ocean, the seabed, swamps, deserts, islands, and the polar regions: spaces notable for their indeterminacy, dynamism, and fluidity (Steinberg and Peters 2015). They have height and depth, are often difficult to apprehend, and frequently change form (Elden 2017c; Gordillo 2014; Lash 2012). These properties challenge territorial norms that have been developed with reference to an idealised world of solid, static land masses, controlled at surface level. Put another way, if territory is realised through the qualities of *terrain* – the geophysical properties of territory – it is prudent to ask if territory may work not just through terrains of earthly matter but also through liquid, aeriated, and "hybrid" matters (mud, swamps, or ice, for example). Investigations that explore the "ungrounded" workings of territory are needed to interpret the spatial politics of our changing world. Building upon a rich legacy of historical and anthropological work on the topic, as well as on more recent theoretical explorations, this book seeks to advance understandings of a key principle of political geography and international relations, adding a critical new dimension to conceptual thinking about territory.

This opening chapter sets the scene for this project of investigating, writing about, and developing ways of thinking territory beyond *terra*. To be clear, by highlighting the term "beyond" we are not arguing for a theory or practice of territory that positions land as irrelevant to discussions of geopolitical power. Territory in relation to land remains relevant. Indeed, the chapter that follows is specifically about land, broken down into its constitutive grains of sand. However land, like the other three elements (air, water and fire) and the environments and intersections in which they occur, is never static and never exists only at the surface (even if it is experienced that way). If *terra* implies static points arrayed on an abstract surface, then earth too – an assemblage of shifting plates, lively molecules, and constitutive elements – is also, always, "beyond *terra*".

As our explorations take us to conceptions of land beyond *terra*, it also takes us to surfaces and spaces beyond land: oceans in which "places" are continuously re-formed; air that can never be fully contained; watercourses that obtain their value by transcending boundaries; wetlands, estuaries, and archipelagos that (in very different ways) challenge received fundamental divisions between land and water; frozen environments that undergo dramatic seasonal transformations of physical state. In approaching these environments, we ask how a consideration of politics in these spaces can inform our understanding of the challenges that are emerging in an increasingly dynamic world that renders contestable all of these spatial categories, as well as the ideal of solid, stable, surficial land against which they are each counterpoised.

For three reasons it is imperative that understandings of territory be extended beyond the facile surface of an earthly plane. First, a land-based perspective on territory limits our understanding of both power and nature. Increasingly, economic activity and political power are exercised in spaces that are neither static nor "grounded" surficial units of land. The extension of mechanisms of production, trade, and governance into the atmosphere, outer space, the ocean, and the underground, as well as on to the indeterminate spaces where these elements meet and change form, requires us to engage new ways of understanding the territorial practices by which power is constructed and contested.

Second, we now live in an era of unprecedented anthropogenic change that is altering the environment (Crutzen 2002; Crutzen and Stoermer 2000; Whitehead 2014). The rise of geoengineering technologies, for example, allows for intentional manipulation of planetary and extra-planetary matter to create new territories (for example, land reclamation to create new, inhabitable islands, most notably in the South China Sea). Such developments are combined with unintentional geophysical transformation resulting from human-induced climate change (for instance, other islands disappearing into the ocean, most notably in the Pacific). Together, these changes are opening up new frontiers for capital investment and state power, and mandate new ways of thinking of nature as always emergent, in creative tension with the human activities that turn landscapes and seascapes into resources and environments. Increasingly, the frontiers of human activity are beyond, or on the edge of, or cut across, continental land masses. Today's political technologies of territory, which emerged in the context of continental (and specifically European) land masses, are inadequate for the spaces that increasingly are subjected to modern forms of governance. As a result, these spaces – of sea, air, or ice, for example – are frequent venues of intense political struggle. In some cases, they are seized upon for their alterity in offering possibilities for alternate social futures; in others, they are normalised through creative adaptation. In all cases, however, they present challenges for both theorising and implementing the practice of territory as they remind us that territory can no longer be understood as occurring solely in an environment of static, surficial points on land.

Third, as scholarly attention has turned to territory, this literature has engaged with others the central concern of which is the material foundation of political power. Alternately called "geo-politics" by political geographers (Dittmer 2014; Dodds 2009) and "new materialism" by political theorists and international relations scholars (Coole and Frost 2010; *Millennium* 2013), advocates of this movement acknowledge that political institutions are not purely of human extent but rather emerge through continual engagements with the non-human and the more-than-human. Scholars who have merged such perspectives with the study of territory have typically focused on the land forms that constitute Earth's surface, as well as on the vectors of verticality that bring the Earth's surface in contact with the skies above and the sub-surface beneath (Bridge 2013; Elden 2013b). However, some of the most recent writings on territory have noted that to appreciate fully the ways in which territory is constructed and exercised attention must be directed to the complex, dynamic environment of a changing planet (Lehman 2013a; Steinberg and Peters 2015). Thus, the terrains of territory need to be understood as voluminous, elemental, fluid, and indeterminate: as spaces that challenge the "grounded", static world of solid surface (*terra*) that typically has informed political thought (Elden 2013b, 2017c; Squire 2016b; Steinberg and Peters 2015). This conceptual shift directs attention to the material elements, environments, and edges that constitute the planet's surfaces, volumes, and atmospheres.

MAPPING THE WAY AHEAD

To extend thinking about territory beyond the limits of land, this book is divided into three parts. In Part I, the focus is on the four elements that classically are seen as constituting the planet's matter: earth, air, water, and fire. In each of the four chapters that constitute this part, authors discuss how efforts to construct territory out of one of these elements are alternately confounded and enabled by ontological perspectives that assume both determinate boundaries (within and between elements) and containable surfaces. In chapter 2, Marijn Nieuwenhuis examines the materiality of sand to show that the territory of earthly *terra* is not fixed and static but fluid and dynamic.

The chapter analyses the relationship between sand and territory by considering two different ways in which sand is imagined, used, and experienced, drawing on case study examples from China: the Silk Road project, which is intended to reimagine and reinvent the old trade route between China and Europe, and the country's infamous dust storms, sometimes called "yellow winds". By investigating these examples, Nieuwenhuis demonstrates both how territorial representations, experiences, and geo-politics relate to sand, and how the specific material make-up of sand opens up new spatial understandings that unhinge notions of territory from their association with properties of timelessness and immobility.

In chapter 3 Weiqiang Lin examines air as both a tool and object of governance. This chapter unpacks the ways in which state actors have attempted to create specific territorial knowledges about the air in civil aviation. The chapter frames this discussion in an in-depth analysis of the various specialised laws governing navigation for air sovereignty, air traffic management, and air traffic services oversight. Lin demonstrates the unequal nature of air territory, and shows how elemental forces, idiosyncrasies, and recalcitrant natures of air interfere with and inform each of these endeavours in territory-making.

From the air to the seas, Jon Phillips takes on the task of thinking through the workings of territory in relation to water. In chapter 4, he explores territorialising, de-territorialising, and re-territorialising processes that have occurred in relation to the control and use of resources located in waters adjacent to Ghana. The chapter analyses the establishment of two offshore zones for the protection of oil industry assets: the West Africa Gas Pipeline and an oil production vessel. These infrastructures, Phillips argues, rely on a historically contingent set of political relations that are shaped by human activity, non-human life, and the biophysical characteristics of the oceans, all of which complicate the exercise of control over space that is beyond *terra*.

Chapter 5 is the last in Part I, and there Nigel Clark engages in a novel analysis of fire. Blazing fire and its environmental effects, Clark contends, have little respect for the ordering devices and securing measures through which the logic of territory is performed. Drawing on the example of Indonesia and the member states of the Association of Southeast Asian Nations (ASEAN), the chapter explores the work of the ten ASEAN countries and the Agreement on Transboundary Haze Pollution (2002), which came into being following the effects of land and forest fires. This chapter addresses the complex issues associated with fire as a force that simultaneously plays across the surficial boundaries between nation-states and the sub-surface junctures between geological epochs. The chapter *unearths* the complex ways in which fire can be conceived as both a deterritorialising and "destratifying" force, and this poses profound challenges to conventional understandings of territory.

Part II takes up where Part I leaves off, working from the recognition that territory is not so much accomplished through control of individual elements but in *environments* where different elements interact with and transform each other. In a sense, it is posited that the space of territory is more-than-elemental. To this end, the four chapters of Part II investigate environments – mudflats, floodplains, cities, and ice islands – where elements come together and are separated in surprising ways that confound commonplace understandings of territory as surficial land. Earth as an element is ever-present in all of these environments, but narratives about the ways in which territory is being constructed simultaneously force us to think beyond the limits of an earth-informed understanding of territory.

In chapter 6, Clayton Whitt shows how earth-based territory can be challenged by the material properties of specific environmental terrains: in this case the terrain of mud, where water and earth mix. Whitt draws on thirteen months of fieldwork conducted in 2013 and 2014 in an agricultural village in the Bolivian highlands to explore how climate change is experienced as a fluid materiality and how this materiality translates into political disputes that challenge the perceived stability of territory. The chapter investigates these disputes in terms of the presence of mud, the absence of roads, and the removal of mud/earth for national road building projects elsewhere. It also considers the entanglements between the body and mud in these contestations, where resistance is instigated because of the impacts of mud (on the ability to move or work, for example). Expanding on Elden's conceptualisation of territory as a political technology, the chapter draws attention to the subtle political effects of climate change that are mediated through material transformations of territorial terrains.

In chapter 7, Stephanie C. Kane explores how the well-being and safety of inhabitants of Winnipeg, Canada depends upon the infrastructural logistics that govern the unstable boundaries between water and land at the confluence of two major flood-prone rivers. Employing the concept of the "technozone", a space of intersection spanning technology, culture, and nature, the chapter weaves together a series of threads to tell a richly critical story of how state power is extended and challenged by logistical and infrastructural projects that are, in turn, a consequence of territorial attempts to constrain, constrict, reshape, and challenge the forces of nature over the landscape.

Also exploring the specificity of environments for challenging territorial knowledge, Ross Exo Adams focuses on the city. In chapter 8, Adams argues that the conventional territorial norm of the landed state has always been beyond *terra*, due to the long-standing influence of the sea on the land – or, what he calls the "maritimisation" of the land. Turning to the writings of nineteenth-century engineer Ildefonso Cerdá, Adams locates the city within maritime conceptions of network (*réseau*) and circulation. Adams thus uses his exploration of Cerdá's imaginative urban futures to open up new questions about the status of the city vis-à-vis both land and ocean.

In the final chapter of Part II, Johanne Bruun and Philip Steinberg turn to T-3, an Arctic ice island that was occupied by the US military during the Cold War. Chapter 9 first focuses on how the scientific research programme on T-3 brought an entire environment within reach of the United States, extending territorial control far beyond 'official' state boundaries and establishing a basis for its further extension. However, the chapter also offers a counter-narrative wherein the US government became concerned about the impact that this extension might have on the nation's interests as a global power. The chapter draws out the complexities encountered when one attempts to construct territory in environments that are neither solid land nor liquid water, and in spaces that can be occupied but that can never be possessed.

Part III turns to the *edges* in which elements and environments meet, and which pose specific challenges for the establishment of territory. In particular, a focus on edges leads to consideration of the negotiations and interpretations made by individual subjects as they encounter and construct territory. The chapters in this part explore contact points – bodies, boats, shores, and seabeds – wherein territory is simultaneously reproduced and challenged through engagements with the dynamic materiality of space. Elaine Stratford and Thérèse Murray begin this part with chapter 10, where they explore the ways in which indentured, convict, and slave labour has been fundamental to the practice of territory. Existing on the very edges, characterised as sub-human, dysfunctional, or diminished, the bodies that constitute the labour-making of territory are shown to be mobilised manifestations of territories that are also entangled in the developmental push to keep territory for sovereign ends. Focusing on the *Waterloo*, a convict ship bound for Van Diemen's Land (Tasmania) that shipwrecked in 1842, this chapter explores actual and metaphorical processes of drowning to make sense of bodies in the construction of territory beyond *terra*.

In chapter 11, Kate Coddington moves to the edge of land and to law, and investigates Australia's attempts to regulate asylum seeker mobilities offshore. In focusing on the case of asylum seeker boats pushed back from Australian waters, she demonstrates how territory becomes fluid – existing beyond defined national space as boats become extensions of national space when towed by Australian naval vessels through international waters; yet *beyond* territory once abandoned off the coast of Indonesia. Exploring how territory is produced through asylum seeker mobilities within the Australian settler colonial context, Coddington argues that the pushed-back vessel represents a continuation of the colonial frontier spaces beyond Australia's continental borders.

In chapter 12, Leah Gibbs shifts from the sea to the liminal shore zone, and from human to non-human life, to explore the complex interpretations of territory that occur when animals are enlisted in territorialising practices. Focusing on the threat of shark attacks in New South Wales, Australia, Gibbs analyses the Shark Meshing (Bather Protection) Program (SMP) as a method to govern near-shore ocean spaces adjacent to popular swimming beaches. She examines the contestation over territory in edge-spaces – between land and sea, between human and shark – where there is an assertion that sharks establish and defend territory in the near-shore ocean, which is likewise defined as an area of human territory. She shows both how policies privilege anthropocentric territorialisation, and how state government must negotiate federal and international agreements for the protection of marine environments and threatened species while enlisting non-human animals as territorialising agents in the shifting space of the shore-zone.

In Part III's final chapter, Rachael Squire focuses on underwater territory using a case study of the Sealab projects, a series of pioneering attempts to live and work on the continental shelf beneath the sea during the Cold War. Squire challenges the surficial nature of studies of territory, urging scholars to open up the very volumes of space through which politics are played out. While the sea is not permanently inhabited, she contends, "habitable" versus "uninhabitable" are labels that further bifurcate the land/sea divide and conceal a host of embodied territorial practices that take place beneath the edges of surface, under the sea. By moving deeper, she suggests, we can unearth new understandings of territory as a three-dimensional construct that is immersive (Adey 2015) rather than calculable (Elden 2013a).

TERRITORIES BEYOND *TERRITORY BEYOND TERRA*

The cover of this book depicts an aerial, possibly extra-planetary, environment with mountains and water – a landscape as diverse as it is fantastic. It speaks to a fantasy of multiplicity. Indeed, the diversity of the world's environments is not merely incidental to the proliferation of territories. Notwithstanding normative notions of territory that operate through a conceptual flattening of the universe's multiple environments, the construction of territory has thrived on difference. Lauren Benton's (2010) historical analysis of the making of sovereignty, for example, beautifully examines the uneven creation of European territories in the spatial particularities of mountain regions, rivers, oceans, and islands. Given the ways in which territory leverages the multiplicity of nature, a limitless number of environments – physical and imaginary, material and atmospheric – could and *should* be studied.

And yet this book, like any, is necessarily limited in its scope. The constitutive concepts around which the book is organised – elements, environments, and edges – provide a framework for understanding territory's multiplicity, but they are just a framework. To conclude this introduction, and suggest further lines of inquiry for the inquisitive reader, we suggest three territories beyond *terra* that are particularly pertinent in the present age and that receive relatively little attention in this volume: mediated, artificial, and extraplanetary spaces.

Mediated Spaces

When the first underwater cable was successfully laid across the Atlantic in 1866 to enable wired telecommunications between the United Kingdom and the United States, it was a feat that crossed territories in both the financing of the endeavour and the physical laying of the cable. Using Brunel's ship, the *SS Great Eastern*, several attempts to lay the cable failed when its weight in relation to its strength and the depth of water caused it to snap. On one occasion, this happened over 1,000 km into the process (Gordon 2002). Cross-territorial mediated communication would not be easily achieved. In a media-saturated world, it is difficult to comprehend the dogged determination of this effort to span the Atlantic Ocean using a technology of communication that could send approximately eight words a minute from one side of the ocean to the other. Yet the eventual success of the project, and subsequent underwater cables that were laid following this, changed the way in which the world was connected (Malecki and Wei 2009).

People (particularly those in the Global North and Southeast Asia) still rely heavily on the submarine cable for reliable communications. Even as communication technologies have advanced, the cable structure inherited from the nineteenth century remains relevant, its infrastructure reflecting patterns of colonial domination while still shaping communication networks and the territories that these networks support (Starosielski 2015). Even as technologies and their 'spray' transcend natural and political borders (Keough 2010, 80), the geography of world communications reproduces a territorial tension that encompasses, but is also more complex than, a simple neologism of mobile information crossing seemingly impermeable borders (Steinberg and McDowell 2003). Notwithstanding the considerable work that has already been done on the variegated geography of what McDowell et al. (2008) call the "infosphere", expanding such efforts to directly examine the world of electronic communications in the context of territory could assist in further exploring the limits of both territory and *terra* as conceptual frameworks (see also Adams et al. 2014; Graham 1998; Kitchin 1998). By seriously considering the *geo*politics of these technologies and asking how media create environments or territories beyond *terra*, one can challenge grounded conceptions of territory by linking people together in new formations, forging new political communities that contest traditional notions of territory as bounded land (see, for example, Peters 2017).

Artificial Spaces

While the world of electronic communications is a virtual environment, this move beyond *terra* and into the virtual also suggests a further move into *artificial* environments. To be clear, we do not foresee an era where territory is constituted by a turn *away* from nature. Rather, we are pointing to a world where nature is increasingly mediated. When we break nature into the elemental or the molecular, as the contributing authors do in most of the chapters in this book, the division between the natural and the artificial becomes blurred (Anderson and Wylie 2009; McCormack 2007; Romero et al. 2017). We live in a world where we can manufacture "artificial" materials, but the underpinning constitution is still material, atomic nature. For instance, plastics are typically made from base elements such as hydrogen and carbon. Through the reconstitution of elements into new "artificial" materials, new "artificial" environments and, subsequently, new territories become possible. Think, for example, of the Great Pacific Garbage Patch or gyre, floating in the ocean, estimated to be twice the size of the US state of Texas (NOAA n.d.). Here, "trash" environments have formed as waste materials, discarded to the ocean, move from territorial boundaries to the open ocean, driven by ocean currents. Eventually, these forge new spaces of concern that ultimately may be managed as territories. Or, thinking of the term artificial as a *reproduction* of something "real", consider the combination of materials in the building of seasteads (Steinberg et al. 2012) or "artificial" islands (Woon and Dodds 2017), where societies are forming new, sometimes mobile territories of inhabitation offshore. What questions of territory beyond *terra* might these environments raise?

This problematisation of a received division between "artificial" and "natural" environments thus suggests that more attention needs to be directed to the substances that root *all* environments in underlying matter. Elements have a significant presence in this collection; indeed each chapter in Part I is devoted to an investigation of one of the four classical elements – earth, air, water, and fire. However, each of these elements exists as a combination of base elements, and a close examination of those can go far in aiding our understanding of the ways in which elements are entangled with the lived experiences of environments. What of the politics bound-up with mercury or lead (in relation to poisoning, for example); or magnesium, calcium, and others (in relation to health)? What of the character of these elements in respect of their usage for territorial politics where "strong" elements are embraced for defence or where "softer" elements create opportunities and vulnerabilities? What also of the different isotopic qualities of atomic elements, where the make-up of the element itself permits particular usages? In short, we ask how can we meld science, social science, politics, and geography to deepen our understandings of territory in contemporary times, and we ask how such elemental understandings may also help unlock historical practices of territory.

Moreover, while the base elements can independently act as useful materials through which to interrogate practices of territory, it would also be useful to think of combinations of elements fundamental to planetary life, where common (and also less common) substances have a particular molecular form (see McCormack 2007). As a classical element, water is a compound of hydrogen and oxygen, for example. And the very air around us is a compound of oxygen and nitrogen, with small amounts of argon and carbon. Earth may consist also not of compounds but *layers* of various elements. So, just as the classical elements often combine (for, as the chapters in this collection show, as air, fire, water, earth, and so on entwine), so too do the atomic elements, creating with them different compounds vital, or threatening, to life. It may be prudent in exploring a territory beyond *terra* then, to also explore the "compound" politics of territory, where practices are played out through atomic combinations that are more-than, and that *exceed* land alone (to borrow from Anderson and Wylie 2009).

Extra-Planetary Spaces

While a conception of territory that exceeds land leads us to the elemental and the molecular (and to the ways in which these categories are mediated through notions of the "natural" and the "artificial"), it also leads us to the extra-terrestrial and the extra-planetary. As the book cover hints, a comprehensive consideration of territory beyond *terra* would require us to think extra-terrestrially, or at the very least vertically to the parts of the earthly atmosphere that are mostly beyond current examination. The chapters in this book stay firmly on Earth, (as in planet Earth), notwithstanding ventures into airspace and the ocean's depths by Lin and Squire, respectively. Extra-planetary territory connects with the earlier discussion of territory in virtual environments, since significant portions of the infosphere's environment are located in outer space. As others have begun to explore, efforts to control the limited space of geospatial orbit are characterised by efforts that alternately reproduce and push against the limits of territorial norms that were developed for *terra* (Beery 2016; Klinger 2015; Lehman 2016; MacDonald 2007).

Beyond the relatively near-Earth world of satellite communications, territory is being formed at still higher altitudes, for other purposes. An early extra-planetary construction of territory occurred in 1969, when the Apollo 11 mission planted an American flag on the moon. This flag-planting did not establish territory in the legal sense; the United Nations Outer Space Treaty would not allow it and the United States had no interest in extending its sovereign territory in such a way. Nonetheless, it raised questions related to territorial practices beyond planetary space (Platoff 2014). In relation to spaces ever more distant and different from *terra*, these questions remain, as scholars consider how hypothetical extra-planetary activities would require constructions of territory as a political technology, if not in the formal legal sense as sovereign and bounded space – not least among them activities such as moon mining (Cole 2017), asteroid mining (Rowan 2017), or the settlement of Mars (Tutton n.d.).

We conclude by highlighting these three environments – mediated spaces, artificial spaces, and extra-planetary spaces, as well as the complex interplay of the classical and atomic elements that underpin them – not to apologise for any limits in the book's scope but rather to stress that the book is necessarily a beginning. The construction of territory beyond *terra* is an exploratory endeavour, stretching the limits of political categories and institutions as it stretches the space of politics beyond the limits of land. When one frees territory from the constraints of *terra*, the sky is *not* the limit.

Part I

ELEMENTS

Preface

Kimberley Peters

To begin to think about territory beyond *terra* requires thinking of the planet – and the sociocultural and political partitions of space that constitute it – as more than, and other than, solid, grounded materialities. The material 're-turn' of geography over the past two decades has enlivened the discipline (Whatmore 2006) – and also the wider social sciences – with a focus on living and non-living entities and things, challenging the anthropocentric leanings of social, cultural, political, and even environmental studies (see Bennett 2010). Yet while a materialist approach offers much potential, there is an enduring problematic in working with the term "materiality" and, indeed, directly with worldly *matter* (Anderson and Wylie 2009, 318). As Ingold notes (2012), our perspectives on what materiality is and what it can do are hindered by a philosophical understanding of it as finished: as typically non-lively and, notably, as grounded. As Anderson and Wylie (2009, 319) confirm, it is often assumed 'that materiality has properties of shape, consistency and obduracy that are assumed to define the state of a solid or the *element of earth*' (emphasis added). This understanding of materiality as solid earth stems from the hylomorphic model proposed by Aristotle, where all things are 'a compound of matter (*hyle*) and form (*morphe*)', where matter is formed to create an artefact (Ingold 2012, 432), a physical *thing*, or even, we may argue, a territory.

Indeed, in geopolitical studies of territory, where the *geo* is taken seriously to refer to the geologic and geophysical properties bundled up with boundary-making and nation-building processes, the onus is often on a 'vocabulary of ground' and of a world configured of solid, earthly materials (Anderson and Wylie 2009, 319; see also Jackson and Fannin 2011). However, as outlined in the Introduction, it is necessary to start thinking beyond a world where geopolitics is a process wrought through the "earth" or *terra* (land) alone.

Certainly geographers, political theorists, and others have already started this work (see Adey 2010; Elden 2013b; Ingold 2012; Steinberg 2001). They have done so primarily through processes of elemental gerrymandering – where the boundaries of traditional studies of territory have been reshaped by opening up a thoroughly materialist way of conceiving of the shape and form of the world (to follow Anderson and Wylie), alert to how territorial practices work through airspace (Adey 2010; Lin 2016); seas and oceans (Steinberg and Peters 2015) or islands (Stratford 2016, 2017); processes of slash and burn, cultivation and combustion (Clark and Yusoff 2014); and a conception of earth that is ungrounded (Forsyth 2016; Gordillo 2014). Such studies are alert to the force of things (to follow Bennett 2004) – in particular, the *geo* and *bio* (Whatmore 2006) – where material forces have political capacities and the capacity to be harnessed politically. Territory, then, may be (re) worked through the range of classical elements – earth, air, water, fire.

The chapters in this part are inspired by these classical worldly elements as defined by the ancient Greek philosopher Empedocles, a rogue figure known for magic and miracle work. He and other early philosophers were driven by a curiosity about the one *prote hyle* or first matter from which all things derive (Ball 2002, 6–7). Although acknowledging that this single substance may be 'too unknowable' or 'too remote', Empedocles's four foundational elements were largely accepted at the time. Even as Empedocles's typology of matter constituted as earth, air, wind, and fire was superseded by atomic studies that recognised the 118 or so base elements of the modern periodic table, thinking with the "classic four" has endured (Ball 2002, 7). As just one example, the philosopher Gaston Bachelard, originally a natural scientist, reached (back) beyond atomistic understandings to Empedocles's classical elements to suggest that each element sparked a specific poetic that expressed the 'material imagination' and that preceded dreams and contemplation (Bachelard 1983 [1942], 4; see also, Bachelard 1984 [1961], 1988 [1943]).

Following from Anderson and Wylie's (2009, 319) provocation that materiality 'far exceeds any invocation of ground or physicality', the chapters that follow show that the materials imbricated in processes and practices of territory also far exceed a physical, solid, "earthly" form. *Geo*politics is played out on earth and also in the skies (Lin), at sea (Phillips), and through the transboundary movement of fire (Clark). Even when the focus remains on earth, the solidity of this substance is challenged. As Nieuwenhuis stresses, earth is more than a singular dense, solid form; it is also loose, light, shifting, mobile, and fragile. Accordingly, the chapters in Part I show how perspectives that assume determinate boundaries are challenged when attention is directed away from presumptions about a solid and unchanging landscape to conjectures about other-worldly material spaces of unstable earth, surrounding air, deep waters, and insatiable fires. Traces of such thinking move beyond Part I to later chapters that help us rethink the stability of elements (see, for instance, the chapter by Bruun and Steinberg on the liminal category of the ice island or Whitt's examination of earth that lacks solidity, becoming slippery as mud).

Although each of Part I's chapters is paired with a classical element, the authors do not conceive of the elements in isolation. As the work of Empedocles posited, the elements 'blend' and 'mix', together forging and forming our world (Ball 2002, 7), and each chapter here demonstrates the melding of classical elemental materialities and the 'flows of energy' and 'circulations' and connections between earth, air, water, and fire (Ingold 2012, 427). Fire, as Clark shows, is driven by oxygen (air) and extinguished by water and solid earth. Sand, as Nieuwenhuis demonstrates, is a solid earthly material that is picked up and moved by air, creating huge dust storms that surround us as volume, even as earth is fundamentally conceived as the horizontal layer below our feet (Ingold 2011). The chapters show, when thinking of the elements in such a way, that different, often transboundary modes of governing space emerge (as Lin demonstrates with respect to air, and Phillips does with water). Indeed, these chapters move beyond narratives of traditional, humanly constructed, and imposed boundaries (Nieuwenhuis and Clark), alerting us to the imaginations, affinities, and affects of these materials of territory (see Bachelard 1983 [1942]; Adey 2015; Anderson and Wylie 2009, respectively), which, in turn, demand new forms of governance (Clark, Lin, and Phillips).

Yet there is further work to do. This part paves the way for the chapters to follow and sets an agenda for future "elemental" work. While the classical elements and their blendings and mergings help us to think anew about territory, we might also ask questions of territory beyond *terra* by shifting our attention to the atomic elements catalogued in the periodic table, alluded to earlier. As Jackson and Fannin (2011, 436) note, we are 'still elementally prejudiced to a metaphysics which enframes the geo as a crust from which we raise our constructions'. Arguably, we may better understand contemporary *geo*politics by upending traditional "earthly" obsessions and examining the *122* elements that underscore and constitute planetary life: that is, the 118 of the periodic table, alongside earth, air, wind, and fire. There is already work in this vein considering copper and gold and geopolitical mining practices (Bridge 2004; Emel et al. 2011); the geographies of carbon usage (Bergmann 2013; Bridge 2011); and other chemical geographies (Romero et al. 2017). This part should therefore be read in the spirit of the classical elements – as open and processual – insofar as work is now embracing these materials to rethink territory, and where new materialist approaches may yet emerge and follow.

Chapter 2

EARTH

A Grain of Sand Against a World of Territory: Experiences of Sand and Sandscapes in China

Marijn Nieuwenhuis

Before checking my emails, I start my working day by browsing the Internet for news stories that contain the word "sand". I do so a bit secretly, so as not to look suspiciously "unproductive" to my colleagues, but also because I want to keep my fascination with sand a little bit to myself. I discover beautiful stories about black sand in San Francisco, which 'is always coming and going, depending on storms, currents, the waves, the tides, the movement of the ocean', or 'strange buildings in the sand' in the Egyptian desert, or 'puzzling sand dunes on Mars' (respectively, SF GATE 2016; Tech Times 2016; Science 2016). These are just some of the stories I discovered before writing the introduction to this chapter. Fortunately for me, little attention is paid to sand in the discipline of human geography and so it remains a bit of a secret, one which I do not mind sharing.

Sand is everywhere, but it is difficult to account for what we actually mean by it. It is 'somewhat like beauty – we know it when we see it, or touch it, but it seems difficult to describe' (Welland 2009, 6). If sand has a defining characteristic, it must be sought by exploring its emergence from the source of its origins. Sand is conventionally held to spring from various processes of rock weathering, biological precipitates, and mineral solutions (Greenberg 2008). However, it is not the origins that define sand, at least not in the material sciences. It would otherwise be difficult to separate sand from other sediments such as silt and gravel. It is, rather, differentiated by its size. The Udden-Wentworth scale measures a grain of sand between 1/8 mm and 2 mm (Udden 1914; Wentworth 1922), although some geologists (such as Pettijohn, Potter, and Siever 1987) point out that limiting sand to a mere standard of measurement denies the diversity and heterogeneity of its provenance. Restricting sand to a matter of size also detaches it from its origins and travels, and its relationship to the more general environment.

Instead of abstractly looking at sand as part *of* the environment, this chapter thinks *with* sand in its transient-becoming-environment. This task means perceiving sand as part of a perpetual process of becoming that blurs the horizon of separation between sky and earth. It is no coincidence that Gilles Deleuze and Felix Guattari (2004, 421–22) have ice and sand deserts in mind when they write about the 'smooth spaces of the rhizome type'; this is, they explain, an extraordinarily 'fine typology that relies not on points or objects but rather on haecceities, on sets of relations (winds, undulations of snow or sand, the song of the sand or the creaking of ice, the tactile qualities of both)'. Sand's haecceity is characterised by a mode of material fluidity and shaped by a perpetual process of becoming rather than rooted being. It is difficult to capture, locate, position, or define. Its disorganised and disorganising relationality positions it against any myth of *terra* as fixed, solid, or grounded, and unhinges it from these stable associations. A single grain of sand invites us to rethink or, indeed, join in thinking *with* material flows and movements.

The British desert explorer and geologist Ralph Alger Bagnold, who served as a commander and founded the British Army's Long Range Desert Group during the Second World War, developed during his service an intimate fascination for desert sand.[1] His *Physics of Blown Sand and Desert Dunes* (2005 [1941]) argued for sand's specificity by focusing on its distinctive behavioural characteristics in the interaction with wind movements. Of note, the work 'encouraged the British adoption of a new form of covert warfare in WWII' (Forsyth 2016, 231). "Mastery" of and control over sand was of strategic importance, with Isla Forsyth (2016, 231–32) describing how Bagnold's 'science of sand' helped in making the '"encrypted space" [of the] desert knowable and to some extent controllable'. The *Physics of Blown Sand* remains a seminal text that revolutionised scientific understandings of the physics of sand and dust particles.[2] Bagnold's work continues to be the key source for understanding geomorphology of deserts and dunes by accounting for sand's unique propensity for self-accumulation.

While modern scientific explorations into the nature of sand go back as far as those provided by Antoni van Leeuwenhoek (1632–1723), in the social sciences and humanities sand is significantly less well explored. When the subject *is* mentioned, it is often done in a casual or unreflective manner, and used either as a metaphor or as a scenic backdrop. An exception to this general rule is the anthropological work of geologists such as Michael Welland (2009), whose *Sand: the Never-Ending Story* is an important source of inspiration to challenge the oft-supposed homogeneity and general silence on the subject of sand. Other works on sand tell us more about imaginations and materiality – things never too far apart when it comes to sand – of larger "sandscapes": beaches, dunes, islands and, of course, deserts (see Squire 2014, for example). Contributions to the "imaginative geography" of the desert include the lucid writings by Roslynn Haynes (1998) on the Australian desert, the oriental imaginings in Western romanticisms in Hsu-Ming Teo's (2012) *Desert Passions*, and stories about the desert's history as a spiritual site for philosophers, poets, authors, religious followers, and other wanderers (for example, Jasper 2006; see also Haynes 2013, chapter 5; Welland 2015).

Of course, there is a larger body of especially European travel literature that relates experiences of desert landscapes to colonialism (for example, see Brower 2009). French Legionnaires in Algeria referred to "desert fever" [*le cafard*] as the condition when sand had seized the body and mind of a person and was now hiding within (Rosen 1910). Many of these postcolonial geographies of sand continue to haunt contemporary European thought. Kaplan (in Beck 2001, 76) observes that the

> desert symbolises the site of critical and individual emancipation in Euro-American modernity; the nomad represents a subject position that offers an idealised model of movement based on perpetual displacement. Euro-American recourse to the metaphors of desert and nomad can never be innocent or separable from the dominant orientalist tropes in circulation throughout modernity.

This insight means that we have to be careful not to blindly accept 'popular European poststructuralist models of smooth space that take the idea of the desert as a trope of unregulated, unmappable freedom' (Beck 2001, 77).[3] Instead, I take heed of a call for an expanded 'understanding of the co-constitution of visuality and materiality' made by Gillian Rose and Divya Tolia-Kelly (2012, 4). I neither wish to assume the solidity of the object of my research nor take for granted the fixity of its meaning in the sources I cite: one must take seriously the underlying politics of the co-constitution between representational culture and materiality.

My contribution considers two stories of sand and sandscapes, and reads them not exclusively as representational places of identity, belonging, and becoming, but also as deeply political materialities. Sand is both a powerful representational and physical component of territory. It moves materially from one politically defined territory to another, and also swirls around in our imaginations and associations with it, carrying with it new ways of thinking about what territory even is. To paraphrase Nigel Clark (2011, xvii), sand is of 'defining interest of the physical sciences – dominions devoid of human imprint – [but has *always been*] a topic of importance for all of us'.

I will be exploring sand on the basis of two stories encountered during my daily online searches. These stories are situated in China, a country known for its deserts and dust storms, and each brings out a different way of thinking about and relating to sand. The stories do not account for a conclusive or complete account of sand and merely constitute a small segment of its never-ending story.

I start my exploration with reference to China's New Silk Road project, which is connecting China with Western Europe by rail. Orientalised sandscapes feature prominently in the representational politics of what already has been called the largest infrastructural project since the Second World War. Rather than focusing on the starting or end point of the project, I am interested in official representations of the imaginative sandscape "in-between". By focusing on the representation of sand rather than its experienced materiality by "sand dwellers", it is possible to discover how things and people in the desert's sandscape become imagined and identified as subjects of sand. I show that the project's orientalising geographic imagination, and its attempt to associate the inhabitants with sand, take inspiration from established historical imaginative geographies existing in both European and Chinese imaginations of sand and sandscapes.

The second story revolves around China's notorious dust storms which, during each spring period, plague large parts of, especially, the country's northern and western territories. These so-called Yellow Dust storms blow dust, silt, and sand particles from China's harsh deserts into clean and orderly cities. This transboundary movement of swirling desert materialities challenges the capacity of the territorial state to govern its own *terra*. A focus on the materiality of travelling sand allows us consider the things (that is, *geo*politics) and life forms (that is, *bio*politics) transported every year to nearby and faraway lands on the millions of tons of sand. That focus further enables us to destabilise our understandings of territory as somehow fixed and static even while, at the same time, reaffirming territory's elemental 'earthiness'.

Both these stories, neither of them complete, reveal something unique about the relationship between the *terra* of sand and its relationship to territory. Sand is both a transient component of the ever-changing earth, through and by which territory is formed and consolidated, but it is also something that can move freely and without territorial interference or constraints.[4] A simple grain of sand forms part of the materiality of territory but will also always move beyond it. Sand can slowly creep, compelling aeolian bedforms to change shape, but wind can also force grains fervently to dance in leaps of saltation. It is the little-discussed, but vital ingredient of asphalt and concrete, the fuel of modern urbanisation, but it also can easily crystallise and turn into dust. By foregrounding sand as a fleeting materiality with an agency of its own it is possible to enter into an intimate dialogue with the transient materiality from which territory is made of. Such an approach, similar in purpose to work on water and oceans by Philip Steinberg and Kimberley

Peters (2015, 261), asks for an attentiveness to 'a world of fluidities where place is forever in formation and where power is simultaneously projected on, through, in, and about space'.

SAND AND DESERT

I want to foreground this discussion about sand by graining the smooth and unproblematic relationship commonly shared towards sandscapes and sand. A grain of sand is both part of a cosmically large multitude and always a singularity. Its multitude translates into the materiality of sandscapes.

It is especially the vastness of deserts that, historically, has been the preferred site of metaphysical encounters between gods and wandering prophets (Jasper 2006). References to deserts as holy places go back at least as far as the early Christian "Desert Saints" who moulded 'a spiritual landscape that transcended the everyday realities of desert life' (Goehring 2003, 438). The desert sandscape is also the imagined postcolonial virgin land where the "Western" Self confronts and continues to encounter the "Eastern" Other.

While Western religions are said to have moved on and out of the desert, Islam is popularly condemned as being stuck in the "Garden of Allah" (Welland 2015) and continues to be punished for this geographical association. The image of the desert continues to play a harmful role in Western imaginations of Islam as an Eastern religion. W.T.J. Mitchell (2002, 272) describes imaginations of the desert in the colonial settlements in Palestine where the desert similarly was (and still is) imagined as a '"land of opportunity" . . . to be opened up, developed' so that it can bloom into a small garden of Europe in the midst of a wild and barren desert wasteland.

Chinese imaginations of the desert are certainly no less politically suspect than Western ones. Yi-Fu Tuan (2013, 85) writes that 'Chinese poetry, where it touches the steppe and desert, is filled with desolation, melancholy, and death'. In both Europe and China, the metaphorical desert is imagined as if harbouring an unmediated and uncomfortable metaphysical truth that either invokes images of devastation or makes them visible. The trope of the desert as a zone of death is commonly deployed in names such as the *Taklamakan*, which literally translates into the "place of no return", or in *Death Valley*, the "most hostile" desert in the American Southwest. The German noun for destruction and devastation is literally "desertification" [*Verwüstung*] and is used in philosophical thought (see, for example, Heidegger 2004, especially pages 29–30). In English, *to desert* means to abandon one's regiment, cause or loved one, and a *deserter* is one who violates an oath of allegiance.

The idea of the desert is deeply ingrained in the popular imagination as 'the enemy, the "Other" to both the individual and civilisation' (Haynes

2013, 153), but that understanding is not equally shared by all peoples (see Myers 1991; Watson 1997; and especially Green 2014). Nothing about the desert is in itself frightening, empty, intimidating, or undifferentiated. The desert is neither singular nor static and is 'as varied in age as . . . in appearance' (Haynes 2013, 11). It harbours a rich array of wild life, offers vastly heterogeneous landscapes and is in perpetual geomorphological change. The Arabic word for "desert", *ashara*, 'means to enter the desert, for there, if one knows where to look, there are springs and wells of water and places of life' (Jasper 2006, 3).

The desert, then, is more than temporary points of location. Yet, as it shifts its topology – depending on changes in weather and climate – its embodying sand, perpetually *becomes* rather than *is*. The project of graining common perceptions of the desert thus also entails a fine-graining of the materials this moving sandscape consists of. The micro-photographic artist Gary Greenberg (2008) shows, for example, how heterogeneous and beautiful this supposedly undifferentiated mass looks in three-dimensions, his detailed photographs of sand from sandscapes around and beyond the Earth demonstrating the unlimited variety and colourful diversity of the (microscopic) grains.

Furthermore, developments in dating techniques have created the possibility of uncovering hundreds of thousands years of geological, geographical, and biological history in single grains of sand, thereby unsettling the myth of sand's homogeneity and monotonous timelessness (Vermeesch et al. 2010). Today's technologies help to determine sand's places of birth and the travels that follow from these sites of "genesis". Every second, a billion grains of sand are born, and the birth of each 'signifies the death of a mountain' (Welland 2009, 5). Every grain is a unique piece in the puzzle of Earth's restless becoming. A single grain constitutes an archive filled with information about the geophysical and meteorological conditions that helped shape it. The grain's evolution does not occur outside of the realm of biological life but blurs the distinction between biological life and inorganic materiality. In this sense, sand is host to a rich organic cosmos and is, in its "biogenic" form, itself composed by a universe of past life (Barboza and Defeo 2015). Consider, for example, that beaches contain on average roughly 25 per cent of biogenic debris and, in some cases, are themselves almost entirely constituted by previous life.

Sand thus speaks to the imagination of the very small and the very large.[5] Its physicality has been used to address metaphysical questions of both time and space. The tenth-century scholar Al-Biruni 'mentioned sand as preferable to water for time measurers' (Turner 1982, 165), while Joseph Needham et al. (1986) recount Ming dynasty (AD 1368–1644) experiments with wheels rotated by sand. In relation to medieval Europe, Nigel Thrift (2009, 92) shows that sand in the hourglass made working people 'aware of passing moments, silently and without a numerical rhythm . . . Yet in the hands of Death the sandglass reminded them of their final hour and urged them to make of the moment for as long as there was still time' (see also Cohen 2014). Gerhard Dohrn-van Rossum (1996) describes how sand's falling materiality helped standardise the hour as a temporal unit in the everyday context of court proceedings, school classes and clock towers. Clearly, a dedicated history of fleeting sand in glass deserves to be written.

Moreover, the story of sand is as much about understandings and representations of time as it is about questions of space. More resistant to changes in movement and temperature, sand's physics allowed it to replace water in *clepsydrae* as the primary element for Renaissance European sailors in their navigating of the seas. Columbus, Magellan, and their contemporaries all depended on the reliability and accuracy of sand to measure their ships' speeds in knots while using them also to regulate the crew's shifts in thirty-minute long "watches" (Welland 2009). The physics of sand served a navigational purpose and helped regulate everyday life on ships. It is no exaggeration to say that sand helped Europeans to travel the waters into Asia.

Sand and sandscapes enjoy equal historical importance in China. This status is apparent in historical representations of Chinese identity in which both the yellow colour of sand and frontier sandscapes have played crucial roles in distinguishing the Self from the Other. Frank Dikötter (2015, 35) explains that the colour yellow [*huangse*],

> one of the five 'pure' colours in China, was regarded favourably, since it symbolised fame and progress. Yellow was coupled with the concept of the middle [*zhongqu*], probably because the annual deposit of loess from the Gobi desert [*hanhai*, literally 'vast sea']⁶ turned the plains of north China yellow. It also became the colour of the Emperor of the Middle Kingdom, ancestral home of the descendants of the Yellow Emperor. The Yellow River [yellow for its loess sediments] is still regarded in China as a symbol of the country.

While China developed into the "yellow centre" [*huangzhong*], with an imagined, racially homogeneous Han population, the desert sandscape came to be imagined as a barren, uncultivated borderland [*huangfu*] known in ancient Confucian texts to be 'fit only for savages [*yidi*] and exiles' (*Shangshu* translated in Goldin 2015, 43). That is to say, the 'location from the imperial centre was determined not only by [the] degree of savagery but by [the] quality of the land you occupied' (Merserve 1982, 51). Dikötter (2015, 4) notes that the very name of this barren outer zone invoked 'a dreadful imagery of drought and famine, of barrenness and desolation'.

In China, the Othering and racialisation of the desert and its peoples served ends similar to those in colonial Europe – here was a radical outside confirming the ethnocentric idea of a cultivated inside. The desert was an environmental-cultural barrier surrounding and preserving what Jonathan Skaff (2012) has called the Han-centred "culture island". Those living in the sand were labelled as culturally and racially inferior, and associated with the backward materiality of sand. A case in point is the sandscape of the Gobi Desert, perceived as an arid borderland that keeps the "barbarians" at bay. A decision to translate the term "Gobi" to mean a sand desert (*shamo*) had immediate consequences for the peoples, animals, and things inhabiting and existing in it, who unknowingly were to become part of a broader desert imagination. Yet *Gobi* is a Mongolian noun and refers not to a desert as such but rather to a 'low-lying and arid [area] . . . with sparse vegetation' (Lattimore in Cane 2014, 80). Martha Avery (2003, 79) explains that Gobi 'refers to habitable land, land that offers some pasture for sheep goats and camels' (cf. Haynes 2013, 24). And Claire Sermier (2002, 71) clarifies that 'Mongols do not talk of a single Gobi but of many *gobis*. They list thirty-three different *gobis*, according to soil composition and colour'. Isabel Cane (2014, 80) argues that the closest linguistic equivalent to the concept of the desert is the Mongolian word *tsol*, 'and this is only used to describe a few areas within the [Gobi] region that are without water and [thus considered] uninhabitable'.

The Taklamakan in China's Tarim Basin has also been the object of exotic historical imagining as a "wild" and barren borderland in need of constant taming. The ancient Chinese poem *Zhao hun* ("Summons of the Soul") describes how the 'west was a thundering abyss, a vast wasteland *huangye* where red ants were like elephant and wasps were like bottle-gourds' (in Meserve 1982, 52–53). Long-standing imaginings of a barbarous hinterland helped in the mid-eighteenth century the Qing's colonial conquest of the region, which resulted in its territorial integration and the extermination of indigenous nomadic Mongolian tribes. The colonised space served for China's last dynasty as a strategic frontier territory and later, in the second half of the nineteenth century, was fully integrated as a political province. It received and still bears the telling name *Xinjiang* (or new frontier). Soon after its conquest, the region and the people living in it – now collectively identified as "Uyghur" – were subjected to elaborate domestication policies that range from mass assimilation policies to political repression, and to ethnic repopulation strategies. This postcolonial geography has recently been the representational target of the 'largest infrastructure undertaking ever built' (Cohen 2015, n.p.). China's New Silk Road project shows how imaginations of sand are closely interwoven with the material mobilisation of sand as territory: it is from within the materiality of sand that the potential for creating new worlds is imagined.

THE NEW SILK ROAD

China plans to pump US$900 billion into the New Silk Road development project (*China Daily* 2015). The initiative officially follows a two-track logic consisting of a so-called "Silk Road Economic Belt" and a "Maritime Silk Road Belt" forming what has popularly been dubbed the "One Belt, One Road" project. The idea behind the revival is the revitalising of the trade route between Western Europe and East Asia along the illustrious path once taken by Marco Polo. This time, however, it is not silk and silver being transported but 'oil from Kazakhstan; natural gas from Turkmenistan, Kazakhstan, and Uzbekistan; uranium from Kazakhstan . . . gold [from] Kyrgyzstan and Tajikistan [and] rare earths in Tajikistan' (Putz 2015, n.p.).

What Marco Polo once did on horseback is anticipated soon to be possible using the US$161 billion railway network that links China to Europe (Knowler 2015). What happens in the imagined geographic "void" in-between is, for me, more interesting than the arrival and departure points of capital. The materiality of Central Asia's dusty plains and the geographic imagination of the desert perform interesting roles in representations of the project. They define the project in a similar manner as water and the ocean did for the British Empire. The Empire both "ruled the waves" and transformed the very meaning of them by using a "nautical language" of coordinates that penetrated these now-emptied spaces on the map (Carroll 2015).[7]

In the Chinese project, sand is imagined in ways similar to water – as an element that one can sliver *through*, rather than as an obstacle one has to step over or dig under. Like the ocean, constructed as a 'formless transport surface' (Steinberg 2001, 16), the desert cannot be crossed by foot, but requires an infrastructure that striates space. Technology compels the layered, dynamic, and resilient nature of the desert into the same regime of submission and domestication that is imposed onto the ocean. Desert and ocean became belt and road – almost indistinguishable and dematerialised smooth terrains ready to be crossed. As much as sharp vessels are necessary to slice through ocean waves, trains are needed to carve a way into the body of the desert. The train becomes a sophisticated weapon, a "bullet train" that 'slices past the edge of the Gobi Desert, through gale-swept grasslands and past snowy peaks' (*Guardian* 2014, n.p.). The abstraction of the desert is imagined as the ocean; no longer as impeding movement but rather as facilitating it – when equipped with the right tools. The desert can be transformed into a channel that allows capital to circulate from one end to another.

The materiality of the space in-between is conceived as something that needs to be tamed as quickly and effortlessly as possible. It bears remembering that slicing through sand is faster than cutting through water. While it takes over a month for a ship to sail from China to Europe, trains would 'enable door-to-door transport from almost anywhere in China to most European cities in 19 to 22 days'. Indeed 'rail often is twice as fast as ships and a fraction of the cost of air' (*China Daily* 2013a, n.p.). The priority granted to the acceleration of movement becomes visible in official documentation, in which speed and connectivity play dominant roles in capital's overcoming and elimination of obstructive sand (see also Xinhua 2015). There is a certain geographic absence in the imagining of the places between Europe and China. In a more-than-geomorphological sense, the region is "desertified" and imagined as lacking in something; it is transformed into a barren ocean of dry sand devoid of speed and (civilised) life.

Imaginations of the desert as empty and monotonous are, then, nothing new in either European or Chinese imaginative geographies. (It should come as no surprise that the Taklamakan was the site of China's thirty-two-year-long programme of nuclear testing. The spread of cancer and the ecological destruction that ensued expose the myth of an empty desert.) In official propaganda for the New Silk Road project, the anonymised and "deadened"desert is portrayed as being inhabited by a group of burdened camels guided by a single nomad under a burning sun ploughing, rather than cutting, through the heavy sand. The slowness of movement and absence of habitation are far removed from the pace, modernity, and sense of achievement used to portray the eastern and western ends of the region. The vast sea of sand constitutes the intermediary plane where nothing worthy of reflection seems to reside. There, the only time the bullets of the trains are expected to halt is when capital feels the need to remove and replace the anonymous fluidity of sand with the solidity of stone and steel. Already, the ancient city of Kashgar has gone through a relentless programme of modernisation, and a destructive urban "renovation" programme has seen many of its 13,000 Uyghur families relocated (see *Time* 2009). By 2020, the city will have been subject to a last phase in the realisation of the Chinese government's Special Economic Zone plan. Moulded after the example of Shenzhen – once a small southern fishing village, now a ten-million megacity of concrete steel – Kashgar is expected to become the ' "next booming hub" of China' (Sandano 2013, n.p.).

Imagined as a "virgin" land ready for modernisation, the desert simultaneously performs the negation of existing life and the condition for creating new life. Fused into the imaginative sandscape of the desert, its people are not recognised as sedentary or civilised enough to fit into the dominant narrative of progress. And their identification with sand positions them as being, on the one hand, outside history and, on the other hand, without roots to a specific territory. Their loyalty and fidelity is not to the state but to the looseness of sand. People from the sand or "sand people" often do not have passports or are denied them, as in the case of the Uyghur. They are left in a region in-between, the undifferentiated desert that, in ways akin to the ocean, is not a location but an imagined medium for those from elsewhere. In the political imagination, sand people are thus seen as drifting nomads who belong to what is seen by others as the uprooted and treacherous shifting sand of the desert: terrorism, we have long been told, 'is always born in the desert' (Mitchell 2005, 202). Thus, when 'Uyghurs travel beyond Xinjiang, they are often unable to check into hotels as ethnic Han staff view them as potential terrorists and call police to check their papers' (*USA Today* 2014, n.p.). In this way, everything about the desert is suspect and subject to securitisation; even the traditional dress of the desert has become 'associated with extremist ideas' (*Express Tribune* 2015, n.p.), and wearing it is now punishable by law. Beards and Islamic clothing are also considered topographical warning signs; Chinese government officials are trying hard to criminalise key characteristics of Islamic Uyghur traditions in an attempt to exorcise the desert and modernise (see Hayes and Clarke 2016). In the process, sand needs to be removed, emptied-out or, at very least, transformed into submissive, indestructible, and predictable steel before it can be trusted and become productive. The need to tame the desert is more than a metaphor for disciplining sand people as it speaks to the threatening qualities of sand's swirling distinctiveness.

DUST STORMS

Sand has a tendency to slow things down, and slowness is dangerous because it impedes the propensity of capital to flow and obstructs efficient governance. Sand's temporality is paradoxical and treacherous: sometimes slowly sifting away without beginning or end (Borges 1998, 481), but at other times as powerful and devastating as sandstorms. For example, in 1993 the notorious '*Black Storm*' that hit China on 5 May drove 'fine soil particles . . . into the atmosphere and revolved around the Earth three times with atmospheric currents' (Zheng 2009, 11). By such means, sand "worlds" through processes of temporal acceleration and deceleration; it has a movement of its own.

Consider, then, how dust storms and volcanic eruptions have a shared capacity to reveal the fragility of the material and social structures of territory. Some time ago, a farmer in China's dust and silt storm-stricken Hebei province told a reporter, 'Sometimes I dream of the sand falling around me faster than I can dig away. The sand chokes me. I worry that in real life, the sand will win' (in Gluckman 2000, n.p.). Dust storms and sand storms neither halt at the windows of apartment blocks, nor at the borders of territory. The dancing of sand, known as "saltation" (from *saltus*), signified that the natural earth is not predisposed to territory's imagined *terra firma*. Loose silt and dust seep through cracks and crevasses, and travel far beyond national boundaries. More recently, Peter Adey et al. (2011) have written about the 2010 volcanic eruption of Eyjafjallajökull, which emitted a large 100 million m³ cloud of airborne tephra that forced cancellation of 95,000 flights in the space of a week. They also note that the affect and effects of the mushroom cloud revealed the 'fragility of a tightly coupled, complex and quite fragile network of airline movements, logistics chains, insurance products and the complex supra-national organisation of European air-space' (p. 338).

Thus, sand grains and dust disrupt and clog up fine and well-oiled technologies of power. The complex physics of these bio- and authigenic bits of "dirt" contrast sharply with the imagined smooth pace of life in the concrete and dust-free terrain of the city. Dust, a particle that enjoys its own distinct physics, 'is about circularity, the impossibility of things disappearing, or going away, or being gone. Nothing *can be* destroyed . . . Nothing goes away' (Steedman 2001, 164, original emphasis). In contrast, solid stone and steel are instruments of permanency and linearity over circularity and disruption. They are the preferred elements of modern progress, while the movement of sand and dust seems, in contrast, to exist in an alternative, rebellious dimension of real time. In this respect, Gary Fine and Tim Hallett (2003, 11) note that dust 'is a metaphor of destruction and simultaneously of resoluteness and inspiration'. To paraphrase William James on the irrationality of dirt, dust, and sand are 'matter out of place' (in Douglas 2008, 203).

Only children and artists make sandcastles, living in other times, creating entirely other universes. The temporality of desert sand and dust has a different rhythm, resilient to and entirely out-of-step with the "unmoveable" and trustworthy steel of the city. Perhaps that is why people 'easily forget the universal swirl of particles. . . . Even when human beings have written the obituaries of minuscule things past and embraced infinitesimal and virtual new, they will still fear dust's final requiem for all life. They will still dread the infinite granularity of all things' (Amato 2000, 176–77). When sand meets steel, when "Asian Dust" forces machines to a halt, airports to close, schools to shut, then the desert takes over, causing traffic standstills, electricity blackouts, weather changes, reduced visibility, forcing the pace of everyday life to adjust to the desert's own erratic temporality (figure 2.1). The annual 'Sand-ageddon [that hits China] feels like it is the end of the world . . . it feels like we are living in a desert. I wonder how we can survive such bad weather' (*Russia Today* 2015, n.p.). A great wall of yellow haze swallows the sky, while 'the howl of the wind seems amplified by its cargo of sand. The air is filled with flying sand, unbreathable' (Welland 2009, 146).

Such conditions are not, in fact, new: as Jianguo Liu and Jared Diamond (2005, 1183) note, between AD 300 and 1949 dust storms containing "Yellow Sand" [*huangsha*] from the Gobi Desert and the Taklimakan occurred on average only once every thirty-one years. Since 1990, however, there has been one almost every year and, as Chinese deserts continue to expand

Figure 2.1   A storm sweeps down an empty street in Hongsibao (Ningxia, PR China). *Source:* Reproduced with permission from Benoit Aquin, photographer, https://thewalrus. ca/the-chinese-dust-bowl

annually, this number is likely to increase in the future. It is probably 'the largest conversion of productive land into sand anywhere in the world' (Alleyn 2012, n.p.). Mitigating the effects of desertification has become a top priority for the Chinese government which, in 1978, launched a decades-long project popularly dubbed the 'Green Great Wall'. At 4,500 kilometres in length, it is meant to reduce 'the detrimental economic and social impact of the dust storms' (Tratt et al. 2001, 18; see also *China Daily* 2013b). The 'largest human-made forest in the world' has done little, however, to stop the imperceptibly small from polluting and harming the very large (Moxley 2010, n.p.).

Of course, the state is not in control of its swirling *terra* body, which threatens the health and subsistence of roughly 400 million people (Wilkening 2006) and is said to cost the Chinese economy around US$6.5 billion each year. But besides their obvious social and economic costs, dust storms also have an effect on existing atmospheric conditions, climatological states, biogeochemical cycles, and ecological equilibria (Goudie 2009; Goudie and Middleton 2006). The "becoming-atmospheric" (Choy and Zee 2015) of dust and sand brings with it a 'synthesis of environmental states, including climate, ecosystem and soil' (Wang et al. 2005, 510). That synthesis blurs distinctions between social and material realities, and organic and inorganic matter, and also between vertical and the horizontal, things in the air and on the ground. As Joseph Amato (2000, 5) notes in his history of dust, it is 'part of the earth's continual making and unmaking. Desert storms fill the skies for thousands of miles and change seasons, vegetation, and landscapes'. Change, not stasis, is the natural state of being.

To understand the magnitude of the challenges that whirling *terra* poses to the imagined fixity of territory – and earthly materiality – it is worth considering that storms carry two billion metric tons of dust annually into the Earth's atmosphere (Griffin et al. 2002). Traces of China's modernisation project have been found in places as far away as New Zealand (Zheng 2009). Elsewhere, Dale Griffin et al. (2002) estimate that large dust storms are responsible for carrying 4,000 metric tons of Asian desert sediments to the Arctic each hour. Each gram of airborne sediment, they remind us, contains hundreds of thousands of microorganisms such as bacteria, fungi, and virus-like particles that physically alter landscapes by modifying the biology and ecology of receiving ecosystems. The inhalation of trespassing dust has, besides its societal and geological impacts, immediate consequences for human health. For example, desert 'dust collected in Kuwait . . . was found to cause cellular membrane and DNA damage' (Athar et al. in Griffin and Kellogg 2004, 288), while Asian dust in northern China has been associated with silicosis, respiratory hospitalisation, and hypertension (Meng and Lu 2007; Norboo et al. 1991). In Korea, dust may be a possible source of foot-and-mouth virus (Griffin 2007, 467).

Such possibilities raise a broader concern about a 'proliferation of airspaces filled with danger' (Choy and Zee 2015, 211). Peter Sloterdijk (2011, 245) predicts that the 'future era will be climate-technical, and as such technologically oriented. . . . The air that, together and separately, we breathe can no longer be presupposed'. Of course, atmospheric governance is not something new (see, for instance, Whitehead 2009), but today's rampant air pollution certainly confirms the urgency to think atmospherically. Aptly, Timothy Choy and Jerry Zee (2015, 211) write that the 'wrong air of the Anthropocene trains our attention to the mechanics of suspension, to how things lift and settle in mediums, to how things exist in atmospheres'. Sand moves in-between earth and air, (trans)forming them, but also becoming itself with them. It lives in both, while always existing in a process of change. A grain of sand or dust defies easy definition but has the potential to challenge a world of territory.

CONCLUSION

Fleeting sand provides an ephemeral vision of solidity but sooner or later creeps into a different shape or dances away altogether. With swirling ease, it challenges the material ground and static imagination of territory and its 'solid' earthliness. As the desert grows in size, yellow sand travels through borders as if they do not exist, transporting organic and inorganic materialities that reshape existing ecologies and micro- and macro-biologies in nearby and remote territories. Fine granular particles block the sophisticated machineries that control the rhythm and speed of everyday urban life, while desertification transforms fertile soil into the stark nakedness of desert sand. Despite its attempt to securitise *terra*, the state seems oftentimes unable to control the fluidity of the material body that it claims as its own but never possesses. Sand's behaviour offers a reminder of the necessity to think beyond timeless and unshakable conceptualisations of the territory that is "beyond terra".

By inviting sensitive attention to the macroscopically small, sand opens up a world that enables us to imagine materiality differently. Each grain of sand 'carries the equivalent of the DNA of its parentage and develops a character through its life that is moulded partly by its parentage, partly by its environment' (Welland 2009, 3); each is equipped with a different story to tell.

NOTES

1. Forsyth (2016, 234) explains how Bagnold's role as a geomorphologist, an explorer and a soldier aided the British military development of a 'new method of warfare designed for desert covert operations behind enemy lines'. Bagnold wrote about his experiences of working in-between the military and science in his memoirs *Sand, Wind and War: Memoirs of a Desert Explorer* (1990).

2. Fine grained sand is sometimes categorised as dust.

3. Beck's intervention echoes that by Kaplan (1996, 87, original emphasis), who writes that in Deleuze and Guattari's work, 'the site of the desert is *sidéreal* space: empty, liberatory, and a margin for linguistic, cultural, and political experimentation'.

4. Welland (2009, 6) writes that 'perhaps half of all sand grains have been through six cycles [of lithification and weathering]'.

5. Perhaps the first-ever "scientific" text (Serres 2000), Archimedes's *Sand-Reckoner* used the multitude of sand to estimate the size of the universe.

6. It should be remembered that the Gobi Desert hosts one of the Earth's largest amounts of fine dust.

7. The space of the Ocean came to be transformed from an unfathomable and mythical imaginary to a standardised geometric space that would form the 'foundation of Britain's maritime empire' (Carroll 2015, 15).

Chapter 3

AIR

Spacing the Atmosphere: The Politics of Territorialising Air

Weiqiang Lin

The vertical realm of the air has been a source of fascination in the social sciences in recent years. On one hand, scholars are recognising how this amorphous space is replete with entanglements and reciprocal relations with *terra firma*, rendering life "above" and life "on earth" impossible to separate (Adey 2010). On the other hand, they are increasingly realising that the air is a sinister zone of ascent for the military terror it is capable of unleashing, when its high platform is combined with flying technologies, distanced forms of surveillance, and aerial ordnance (Gregory 2011; Shaw 2013). These observations concerning the potentials and fears of the air have inspired new perspectives on how modern lives are irrevocably sutured to, and sometimes held hostage by, this ethereal domain – for mobility, for war, for trade. Yet, for better or worse, they have also signalled the advent of a profound reorganisation in the way society knows, uses, politicises, and ultimately territorialises its spaces, from the ground up.

Certainly, this chapter is not the first to highlight these "new" spatial logics pertaining to the air's vertical affordances. Rather, building on existing literatures, the chapter will examine a specific instance of the imbrication between air as an elemental state and air as a territorialised entity. This examination is achieved by interrogating the organisation of the sky, or airspace, for civil air navigation – an increasingly widespread practice among state actors that has supported and given shape to the world's uneven air infrastructures and aeromobile geographies. I do not presume that such aerial organisation for commercial flying is, by any means, paradigmatic of the air's territorialisation in total. Rather, I seek to use this planetary-scale example as a foil to relate to other pressing forms of aerial control of our time, including the spatio-legal governance of drones (Kindervater 2017), territory-based transmissions of telecommunication signals (Ash 2013), and transboundary air pollution – together with the associated punitive actions taken against violators in certain territories (Hirsch 2016).

Other authors have made strong assertions about how the air's occupation has precipitated unprecedented social realities, rationalities, and reformations. Writing about aerostatic experiences, Derek McCormack (2009, 27) elevates 'air and atmosphere as zones in which a range of important disciplinary concerns might be addressed', from novel affective sensations to new notions of the self (see also Engelmann 2015). On the visualities afforded by the air, Lucy Budd (2009, 80–81), in contrast, equates air's vertical extension from earth with the 'ability to see places from above . . . [and] to gain a sense of proportion and appreciate the relationships between human settlement and topography' (see also Powell 2007). Yet, while these are astute renderings of how the use of the air has given rise to new practices and ways of parsing space, little is said about the implications and outcomes of when air is, itself, practiced on and parsed *as* space. As I argue elsewhere, the air is not simply a domain for habitation, or a high ground to resist (see Williams 2013); rather, in its own right it is 'an eventful space to divide and manage through particular methods, lenses and vocabularies' (Lin 2016, 2). In other words, air is *territory*.

Refiguring the air as territory rather than an indistinct host to the vectors of verticality requires an intimate knowledge of, and a method of rule in, the properties, undulations, and fluxes of this unwieldy realm (Adey 2014). Indeed, it is by strategically manipulating these dynamic qualities that "air" becomes amenable to control and spatialisation as territory. A related corpus of work delineating the materialities of atmospheres captures this complex relationship between air as an elemental state and as a volume with vertical and horizontal resonances. While Mark Whitehead (2009) argues that state-led meteorological projects to gauge the presence of contaminants were responsible for generating a stratified notion of air pollution over Britain, Martin Mahony (2014) and Tim Winter (2013) both show how, at scales ranging from room to region, atmospheric science has been responsible for generating different normative discourses about "ideal" climates, and about what constitutes profligacy, comfort, degeneration, or progress. Put succinctly, these studies draw attention to the fact that *air* is a contrived concept tied to various scientific, managerial, and geo-discursive interventions that render its properties imaginable and spatially manipulable. As Steven Connor (2010) avers, it is because of these cultural knowledges – gained through observation, measurement, experimentation, and speculation – that the air becomes suitable for appropriation and, by extension, territorialisation.

Drawing on and extending these ideas, the remainder of this chapter teases out the power-laden ways in which state actors have likewise striven to create – or get others to buy into – particular territorial knowledges about the air in civil aviation. Specifically, this analysis is achieved by expounding on various highly-specialised laws governing air navigation in terms of air sovereignty, air traffic management, and air traffic services oversight. In tracing how the elemental forces, idiosyncrasies, and recalcitrant natures of air interfere with and inform each of these endeavours in territory-making, I explain why and how the air is ultimately ordered as the unequally accessible realm that it is today. At the same time, I articulate the interstate (geo)politics that is wrapped up around air in these spatialising acts, and extend understandings of traditional territorial contests to these atmospheric power grabs.

SPACING THE ATMOSPHERE

Since the dawn of aviation the air has ceased to be an ethereal space, over and above us. Rather, it is a transect and interface that shares deep resonances with imperatives on the ground, and that is tamed to fulfil earthly desires for moving, not least by aeroplane. It has been alchemised into a realm of physical substance replete with spatial meaning and methods of organisation. Through flight, the air is inscribed with specific Cartesian techniques geared to harness what is above for trade and market access on the ground (Kasarda and Lindsay 2011). As Peter Adey (2010, 2) asserts, both 'the ground and the air reside together in vertical reciprocity'; or, in stronger geographical parlance, space 'in its vertical and horizontal planes, is connected' (Adey 2010, 5). Exploring the organisation of airspace thus requires more than just explaining air travel in the twenty-first century (Cwerner 2009). More critically, it involves apprehending how another space, another zone, another *territory* has been measured out for economic and political ends.

Notwithstanding this imperative, academic writings have not always been very precise in articulating airspace as such a politicised form of territory. Much early work – not least that dominated by engineering, law, and the sciences – has tended to treat airspace as a utilitarian aeromobile medium to be improved or managed in more productive ways. While, for engineers, airspace is plainly an operational medium to be equipped with the most advanced air traffic management technologies for the conduct of air traffic (Bianco et al. 1997; Field 1985), it is, for legal experts and planners, a zone whose use needs to be agreed upon and systematised among states as a matter of fact (Diederiks-Verschoor 1983; Underdown 1995). For transport geographers, airspace is construed as a canvas on which the world's aerial networks splay out. Composed of lines that connect nodes of global and regional importance in agglomerating patterns, these networks tell a story of airlines' hubbing activities and the urban hierarchies that result from them (Derudder and Witlox 2008; Graham 1995; O'Kelly 1998). Yet, though perceptive of air travel trends and infrastructural needs, none of these interpretations sufficiently addresses the logics by which airspace came into being as a particular kind of territory. By taking as a starting point the notion that airspace is a self-evident medium for air travel, these renderings evacuate the air of any spatial genesis, cultural assumptions, and politics, and focus instead on developing cogent reasons for smoothing aeromobility for those already benefitting from it.

Since the late 2000s, a second body of work has emerged to chart the *social and cultural* geographies of airspace (Adey et al. 2007), swinging the pendulum to its opposite end. Concerned with the aesthetics, aspirations, affects, and social asymmetries of flight, many writers approach airspace as a shorthand for the "softer" aspects of aeromobility, departing from earlier preoccupations with infrastructural organisation and optimisation. Partly inspired by literary theorist David Pascoe's (2001) reflections on terminal design, aerial views, and the ethos of air wars and air disasters, these interpretations adopt a more figurative sense of the word airspace, and attend to a variety of sociocultural phenomena found within, and/or arising from the art of staging, aeromobility. But, once again, they continue to leave unanswered questions about the formation of *navigational* airspaces that enable aeromobility in the first place. Additionally, in directing the focus away from the literal realm of the air they, too, have sidelined the spatial techniques and elemental logics that airspace's producers employ to turn hazy atmospheres into orderly territories to traverse. Hence, while demonstrating a more reflexive stance towards the emergence of airspaces, such a perspective equally obfuscates important geographical questions relating to the organisation of the air.

In this context, rather than tackling aviation spaces of all sorts that have lately come to be subsumed under the ambit of "airspace", and to chart out these lesser known and territorialising processes intrinsic to the air, this chapter returns to a more conventional and literal set of aerial concerns to do with air sovereignty, air traffic management, and air traffic services oversight. Such an orientation should not be mistaken for an attempt to revive utilitarian thinking to improve the socio-technical medium through which flying takes place; rather, it should be read as an effort to enjoin airspace with critical studies on territory to unearth the rationales, strategies, and spatialising techniques guiding the organisation of an amorphous sky. Moreover, by uncovering the connections between air, airspace, and their corresponding spatial forms, the chapter exposes and critiques the effects, implications, and tacit injustices immanent within seemingly innocuous legal and technical activities in managing and controlling vertical spaces (Elden 2009). Attending to such territorial logics with respect to the air allows transport scholars to better grasp the conduits by which select cities and states are able monopolistically to expand their airline networks at the expense of others – a pattern that is identified but not explained in transport geography (Lin 2017a). This attention also encourages scholars to reflect on states' choices in organising airspace amid air's elemental agencies, while providing an opportunity to judge the ethics of these expansionary tactics. In the process, air travel can be better appreciated for its alliances with territorial logics that sustain aviation's growth, and also perpetuate the privilege of particular mobile populations.

AIR SOVEREIGNTY:
TERRITORIALISING TO (DENY) ACCESS

A fundamental concern in the territorialisation of the air, or any space, pertains to the right of inhabitation. This question may appear as an age-old geopolitical conundrum over spatial access but, when transposed to the air, it takes an especially complex formulation. Extending the technocratic organisation of land into 'a completely occupied and fully charted' international mobility order (Ó Tuathail 1996, 15), and of oceans into a calculated politico-economic interface with land-space (Steinberg 2001), the air, too, has been transformed into a strategic territory. That territory is then further entangled with the atmosphere's unique elemental properties such as its unboundedness, invisibility, verticality, and lightness. With the introduction of flying technologies, this previously unregulated realm suddenly took on awesome responsibilities, at once holding great mobility potential by dint of its transcendence of surface barriers (Cosgrove 2001) and affording those who control it the power to engage in punitive aerial warfare (Williams 2013). It is no wonder that the air became a target of spatial organisation soon after flying machines first occupied it. In other words, it had to be subject to territorialising practices.

Military uses of the air had a strong influence on the laws and logics governing this territorialisation. Despite popular portrayals of the wonder and romance of flight, the first decades of the air's occupation were in fact marked by a time of intense interstate rivalry, such that even "innocent" aircraft were built with warfare and easy convertibility for military use in mind (Higham 1965). In a perverse twist of Leonardo da Vinci's assertion that 'once you have tasted flight you will walk the earth with your eyes turned skywards', this "longing" to return to the sky was one born out of a desire to master a new frontier for geopolitical power, whether, in Britain's case, to extend its then-unsurpassed land possessions and naval supremacy, or for rivalling states, to contest it. Germany, with its advanced Zeppelin technology, was a strong contender in this respect, prompting the United Kingdom to propose in 1910 that all countries observe each other's national sovereignty in the air. This projection of delimited land territories upwards, though non-binding, for a time kept the open air above Britain out-of-bounds to German Zeppelins (Butler 2001).

Yet this idea soon proved unenforceable when two German airships infiltrated the sky above during the First World War to engage in the world's first aerial bombardment in Norfolk in 1915 (Wyatt 1990). With further German attacks throughout the course of the war, when hostilities ended, the Anglo-French-led 1919 Versailles Convention on aerial navigation instituted stricter rules on the use of the air (Butler 2001). Allied Powers excluded Germany from participation in all international use of airspace thereafter (Woodhouse 1920). Every other state, on the other hand, would have complete and exclusive rights to only the air above their jurisdictions, solidifying the first notions of an international airspace organised by territorial rights.

The air's segmentation in ways that mirrored the ground gained further currency during the postcolonial period but was also elaborated on as part of the burgeoning global nation-state system. Notably, rapid decolonisation and new state formation in Asia and Africa meant that more political entities were able to exercise territorial rights in the air, fragmenting airspace into a patch-work of jurisdictions. However, whereas the ability to transit through the air made the idea of an ill-defined, uncontrolled atmosphere unacceptable in times of war, the beginning of *Pax Americana* and notions of a world founded more and more on trade and mobility in peacetime rendered contradictory overly-restrictive boundaries carved out of an element that by nature is amor-phous and unobstructed. In the 1940s, resolving these countervailing visions was thus a priority among states. As the only nation with the financial where-withal to launch air services worldwide following the Second World War, the United States proposed open access to all airspaces – including former imperial ones – without prejudice. Europeans insisted on the continuation of territorial exclusivity in the use of the air: this time in an effort to protect not populations from bombardment but national air travel markets from foreign profiteering (Oum 1998). A middle ground was struck when states agreed to institute pacts known as air services agreements to govern the air's use. Under this system, states would reciprocally negotiate for rights to enter each other's national airspace by treaties, of which the 1946 US–UK Bermuda I and the 1977 Bermuda II bilateral agreements[1] were prototypes (Toh 1998). While the right to free commercial overflight was secured in the 1945 International Air Services Transit Agreement, passenger- and goods-carrying landings and take-offs were to be individually bartered in a horse-trading game and inter-national exchange of access rights.

Constituting a set of self-imposed rules that ration blocks of airspace according to whether or not, at what frequency, and at what capacity (for example, number of seats) a country's airlines may launch air services in another's jurisdiction, this system upholds the air's territorialisation as selectively permeable only to some countries' aircraft and at certain rates of flow – not unlike, and in fact adding a further constraint to, national borders' exclusionary stance towards certain nationalities and passport holders. On the one hand, the system maintains the norm that every state has an exclusive say on air navigation in its national airspace; but, on the other, it reimagines the air as penetrable and amenable to foreign use on a case-by-case, mutually agreeable basis (Hinkelman 2008). Such an arrangement is tantamount to regulating 'the supply of international air transport services through govern-mental control' such that 'the non-existence of routes does not imply the lack of demand' but indicates the current configuration of a state's extension of its airspace to others (Raguraman 1986, 66). Less restrictive "Open Skies"[2] agreements started making their appearance in 1982 and remain in place even today, their basic principle being to require states to seek advance consent on routing, frequency, and capacity before mounting air services (Button and Taylor 2000, 211).

This protectionist stance is seldom equally meted out but tends to set in motion an uneven distribution of airspace rights, and hence uneven aeromo-bile geography, that often benefits influential air powers – that is, those with large, affluent air travel markets. Consider, for instance, British carriers' long-standing links with (former) colonies. On the back of the country's and, especially, London's metropolitan position, the United Kingdom has histori-cally enjoyed an upper hand in negotiating for air rights for British carriers to fly to dependent states, without having to reciprocate by giving the latter access to British airspace. Consider also how airlines based in the United States today are lobbying for the withdrawal of air rights from competitors such as the Middle East Three (ME3 carriers; Emirates, Etihad, Qatar); this contemporary case again demonstrates influential states' ability to change the rules of airspace's use without fear of retribution from less powerful ones (Campbell 2017). By virtue of their stronger bargaining power (Raguraman 1986), the United Kingdom and United States have been able to shape global air territorial access in pace with the growth of their airlines, generating par-ticular rhythms in the opening and closing of air travel markets according to their own interests. Air's advantage as a formless, transcendental medium that circumvents land and sea may thus promise unprecedented freedom in movement, but it is a freedom that is the preserve of only some. Through the technology of territory, the air is at once accessible and blockaded, depending on which side of power a nation-state is found.

AIR TRAFFIC MANAGEMENT: TERRITORIALISING TO MAKE SAFE (AND MAKE MOVE)

Availing and denying airspaces to foreign states are acts that represent only the tip of the iceberg in the wider quest to territorialise the air for aviation.

With the introduction of jet technologies in the post-war period, organising and regulating flight has involved much more than simply deciding who is permitted to access certain blocks of airspace. Indeed, flying is a peculiar form of spatial occupation that requires specific technical know-how in how air works. For starters, to get a modern jet off the ground and to have it cruise for thousands of miles across the globe requires a science that accounts for air's lifting capabilities, the effects of its differential pressures, its dynamic qualities, and the susceptibility of its occupiers to its turbulences. As if this knowledge was not marvellous enough, engineers also have to account for the temperamental nature of air, which has divergent responses according to where it is found – whether in the cool climate of the temperate belt or in the hot and humid conditions of the tropics (Caprotti 2011). Even contaminants such as volcanic ash can affect aircraft, as these intruders can cause airspace to cease to afford a pristine environment for planes to operate in (Adey et al. 2011; Budd et al. 2011). In short, and despite the seemingly unbridled way air envelops the Earth, it has internal fluxes and sensitivities that also render it a fragile element to fly in. In this fragility lurks another form of territorialisation that deserves scrutiny.

One way in which this cautionary need for territorialisation manifests is via the parameters put in place in air traffic management to make aviation safe. Of these, what stands out for its spatial implications is the airspace planning logic of aircraft separation – a redundancy measure to space out aircraft to guard against unwanted drifts.[3] Aircraft separation is defined by the International Civil Aviation Organisation (ICAO 1998, 3) as 'action on the part of air traffic services to keep aircraft operating in the same area at such distances from each other that the risk of collision is maintained below an acceptable safe level'. As a set of rules and procedures, it works to reorganise the air into a three-dimensional space defined by appropriate buffers and gaps between its constituents. In an age when the skies are increasingly saturated with aircraft, these buffers re-rationalise airspace as an orderly geometric body with vertical, lateral, and longitudinal error thresholds calculated in terms of the minimum distance required between aircraft on top of each other, between aircraft to the side, and between successive aircraft, respectively. Such a rendering appears, at first, to mirror Stuart Elden's (2013, 35) understanding of territory as a volume with 'calculable resonances'. But, on closer look, this aspect of the aircraft safety regime expresses those dimensions – as measured in required spacing between moving objects – in the negative, figuring them not as products of active observation, but compensations for what airspace planners *cannot* know. Because of the unpredictability of air, and the dangers of having to travel at high speeds through a featureless medium, airspace is "spaced out" so that it is bulwarked against accidental collisions. In the process, it gets transmuted again from "medium" to another kind of territory, this time associated less with the delimitation of access than with the spacing that adjacent aircraft need to adhere to.

The Mach number technique is one such calculative logic used to derive (a type of) aircraft separation, and thereby slice the air into multiple "safe" zones for navigation. This computation takes into account the confidence limits of flight technologies, and also enrols the atmospheric and aerodynamic science of airspace in its (e)valuations. Central to its arithmetic reasoning is the behaviour of aircraft's forward motion in air. Assuming that flights within a given area 'are normally subject to approximately the same wind and temperature conditions', its objective is to ensure 'that successive aircraft . . . along the same track' maintain a fixed longitudinal time interval from each other by keeping to a uniform Mach speed (ICAO 1984, II-2-2-1). Based on experience gained from test trials in the North Atlantic airspace, the Mach number technique effectively substitutes the dearth of absolute positional knowledge of moving/drifting objects in air with confidence-correlated time lag allowances between aircraft ranging from five minutes (with support from radar or other forms of surveillance) to fifteen minutes (corresponding to about 120 nautical miles for areas under air traffic surveillance). By rationalising an aircraft's behaviour in air and its risks, the technique mathematically builds in delays and redundancies in airspace against unwanted gusts or slowdowns. Notably, the technique works by dynamically territorialising the air, not just as static lines or sectors on a map, but as moving conveyors of territories that aircraft enter into and vacate at strict temporal rhythms. Accordingly, each aircraft occupies and travels along a designated airspace slot that is always relational to others, producing linear territories through their mobility.

Two other models for determining aircraft separation are the Minimum Navigation Performance Specifications (MNPS) and related Required Navigation Performance (RNP) techniques. Again, in both cases, air traffic management is approached as an exercise in pre-empting drift tendencies, and in spatialising them into permissible distance thresholds for safety. This time, however, to determine how separations are to be calculated in that airspace, airspace planners capitalise on the highest navigational capabilities present among the majority of aircraft in a flight region. First introduced in the 1970s, with the North Atlantic as again the test case, MNPS describe 'a level of navigation performance' whereby aircraft operating in a region must be able to 'follow its intended or assigned flight path within defined tolerances' both vertically and horizontally with the aid of satellite waypoints (ICAO 1984, II-2-4-1). With the adoption of the United States' global positioning system in the 1990s, updated operating procedures under RNP rules tightened these specifications by defining them in terms of an aircraft team's ability to monitor its own track on-board, and generate alerts during times of excessive drifts. The latter rules would become one important determinant of separation standards, first in the North Atlantic and then elsewhere (ICAO 2008). These self-alerting applications can help increase confidence in the auto detection of deviations and enable the *reduction* of aircraft separation to a more space-efficient thirty to fifty miles (forty-eight to eighty kilometres) horizontally and 1,000 feet (from 2,000 feet) vertically (around 304 to 609 metres) – if an airspace environment could support such a conversion (ICAO 1998). These technologies may not have eradicated all uncertainties in aerial movements. Yet, they have been instrumental in promoting new ways of (re)territorialising airspace for more efficient and productive occupation by relegating aircraft – as with passengers *within* aircraft cabins – to smaller and smaller units of operating space.

These rules have certainly contributed to the orderliness of global air travel, but they have also differentiated airspaces by prescribing certain normative technological ideals and separation minima standards for each region. They represent an international regulatory system to formalise the use of an increasingly crowded airspace, but such regulation compels each state to adhere to a normalised vision of how airspace ought to be appropriately parcelled out into "safely" buffered zones to fly in. Notably, within this schema the North Atlantic repeatedly surfaces as the arbiter of such standards, making that region a *de facto* testbed for the most advanced solutions to the air's lingering uncertainties, and a leader in airspace capacity augmentation because of the separation reductions it sanctions. In this respect, the North Atlantic serves as a model from which other comparable regional airspaces should take their cues. It also acts as a paradigmatic space that is perennially ahead of the curve in aeromobile intensification and economic development, because its governments and aeronautical industries are able to claim a leading edge in relation to safety authority and technological innovations (Lin 2016). Clearly, despite the safety intentions of air traffic management, the air is not just innocently or uniformly carved out for use; rather, to achieve both the outcome of collective mobility and uneven rates of movement, it is strategically organised, measured out, and *territorialised* – partly in response to air's temperaments and partly according to the perceptions of flight capabilities in a region.

AIR TRAFFIC SERVICES OVERSIGHT:
TERRITORIALISING TO (DIS)POSSESS

The simultaneous need to respect individual states' sovereign rights and to ensure safety in flight leads to a third form of territorialisation that further reveals the malleability of air and the multifaceted nature of airspace's territorial politics. While states continue to hold on to the ideal of having absolute control over national airspaces, especially on matters regarding the military, they concomitantly covet the safe and efficient traversal of the air for commercial use. As seen earlier, the latter partly requires the establishment of clear safety parameters, such as aircraft separation, in an airspace according to each region's technological capabilities. On a day-to-day, real-time basis, however, it more immediately requires the tactical provision of air traffic services – control oversight to regulate and assist aircraft. The larger the area over which a state can influence the provision of such services – whether by direct control or synchronisation with other states – the more it is able to influence air traffic management rules, shape aerial activities, and intensify traffic. This derivation of practical benefits through airspace control coincides with Kevin Lynch's (1962, 118) idea about the circulatory role embedded in space, in that without 'the ability to enter, to leave, and move, within it, to receive and transmit information or goods, space is of no value'. Even so, the ability to control this circulation is of high priority among states. Another overlapping form of territorialisation is at hand, to secure and possess that right to master live aeromobilities.

This imperative translates into a concurrent division of the world's atmosphere into, on the one hand, the familiar suite of national versus international airspaces and, on the other, a separate system of air traffic control zones known as flight information regions (FIRs). As forms of spatial organisation to guide live traffic, FIRs are not the same as – and can even contradict – national airspaces, and they comprise another schema whereby some states are assigned mutually exclusive roles to provide air traffic services for an extended region. FIR control is usually delegated to the state directly underlying the airspace in question (ICAO 1974). Yet, the process of determining air traffic services responsibilities in myriad airspaces that can span international high seas, areas of uncertain sovereignty, and territories deemed too close to each other[4] intimates that FIRs do not always map neatly onto national airspaces. The airspace enveloping the North Pacific (Oakland), for instance, is nearly entirely under American control, as an oceanic FIR above the high seas. Some states, in contrast, possess oversight authority over airspaces directly encroaching on others' sovereign territories – such as Indonesia over parts of Australia, Singapore over parts of Indonesia, Belgium over Luxembourg, and Switzerland over Liechtenstein, making FIRs a matter of extraterritorial oversight on occasions (Hakim 2016). Because of such potential for sovereign disjuncture, the control of FIRs is often a privilege that states fight over. It is a sticking point whereby states seek to return safety oversight to (yet more) territorial segmentation, despite their professed intentions to harmonise the air for seamless travel.

Such contests for the responsibility to provide air traffic services – an expensive affair given the equipment and personnel involved – may seem counter-intuitive, but there are significant political and economic gains to be made by having such territorial control. Indeed, FIRs confer designee states with power that sometimes overshadows rulings on airspace sovereignty. On the military front, a state doubling as a foreign traffic administrator, while unable to scramble its military jets into that airspace, has the authority to police the controlled nation's air exercises in the name of safety. As Chappy Hakim (2016, n.p.), a former Indonesian air force chief, reveals in protesting Singapore's rei(g)n over his country's aerial activities in the Riau Islands, all aircraft operating in the area, including those of a military nature, 'must have obtained permission even at the time when its engines are ignited. In other words, [the Indonesians] still have to seek permission from Singapore for all flight operations . . . even though the area is still within [Indonesian] homeland'.

Such disputes can be scaled up to involve superpower rivalry too. A case in point is China's unilateral declaration of an Air Defence Identification Zone over the East China Sea in 2013, in defiance of a military space normally controlled by US allies. Acting on the offensive, China demanded that all passing aircraft identify themselves to Chinese air traffic controllers, upend-ing established rulings on air traffic services designation in that region, and side-stepping Japan's existing FIR authority (Nicolaysen 2013). Executing this manoeuvre, China was effectively enacting a re-territorialisation of the control space over the East China Sea and obtaining information on aerial activities to which it had not been privy.

On the commercial front, there are further gains to be made by the FIR designee. Not least, the provider of air traffic services has the prerogative to levy navigation charges on all aircraft users of the airspace. Such charges can amount to significant sums and potentially benefit states controlling extensive swaths of these quasi-territories. The United States proposes to raise charges between 2017 and 2019 from US\$58.45 to US\$61.75 per 100 nautical miles for flights along popular 'en route' corridors in its control zones, including the vast Oakland FIR (Federal Aviation Administration/FAA 2017). At the same time, Russia collected over US\$331 million in trans-Siberian overflight fees from just EU carriers in 2006 alone (Lin 2013). This price-setting power does not yet account for the other indirect geo-economic advantages that designee states can derive, especially when their FIRs overlap with interna-tional and foreign airspaces. Specifically, such states can direct equipment change in foreign air territories according to their growth needs, implement new separation reduction regimes for the region by mandating technological upgrades among all users of those FIRs and even arbitrate how the air's finite traffic-carrying capacity is to be apportioned among competing states. Osten-sibly, these regulatory powers deepen the politics of previous rounds of oper-ations-related territory-making in air traffic management, by empowering

FIR designee states to make calls on the rules of aeromobility that may not be amenable to the rest of the region. Vested with such authority, the control of FIRs potentially trounces even the territorial logic of sovereignty, having immense and practical implications on which states truly hold the keys to the air's circulations.

Seen in this light, the prospect of controlling an FIR is tantamount to a state possessing the reins to the *mechanics* of movement in that territory. Plots to secure the management rights to the world's finite FIRs thus often occupy the minds of state strategists, both to possess that power and to dispossess others of it. Banking on the necessity of air traffic services provision when travelling through a featureless medium, states frequently use the safety implications of these control zones as a prime reason, if not a smokescreen, for the reorganisation of airspace for navigation. Consider Russia's 2014 annexation of a strategic trans-Europe corridor in the Simferopol FIR over Crimea in the name of "aviation safety" (Rosaviatsia 2016). Consider also the FIR dispute between Fiji and New Zealand in 2001 over "equipment compatibility", which was really about the fair distribution of the A$2.6 million (US$1.35 million in 2001 dollars) in overflight charges collected for Samoa and Tonga, but not released, by Fiji (ABC Radio Australia 2001). Even Indonesia's spirited demand to reunite Riau Islands airspace under the nation's air traffic safety rule is an intent to undermine Singapore's hub position and, in the word of a former Indonesian Air Force Chief, leave the city 'destroyed' (Desker 2015, n.p.). All these efforts to redraw air traffic services maps do not in fact purely represent the safety interests of the flying public as they should. Instead, and disturbingly, they are more often territorial pawns that states deploy to derive ever-increasing political and economic gains for themselves, preferably at the expense of others.

CONCLUSION

This chapter has examined a range of political and economic imperatives by which states organise the air as territory for aviation. The work presented here supplements research by which scholars have come to appreciate airspace for its aesthetics, aspirations, affects, social asymmetries, and air power (Adey et al. 2007; Budd 2009; Engelmann 2015; Powell 2007; Williams 2013). I have sought here to shift some of the attention away from the preponderant focus on the air's impacts on social lives (Adey 2010) and towards the particular methods, techniques, and logics by which society practices and parses air as space for strategic uses. As a space both to transit through and to arrive by, the air is structured to grant *and* deny access to foreign states using diverse territorial rights and treaties that determine the possibility of overflight and/or revenue traffic among external parties (Button and Taylor 2000). In addition, to ensure safety the air is further dissected into separate(d) slots for navigation under the planning rubrics of air traffic management, as well as designated control zones over which (some) states have exclusive air traffic services responsibilities. These overlapping systems of organisation are all symptomatic of the extension – but also the adaptation – of territorial logics to the sky. In the process, air is no longer an indistinct host to aerial vectors but has become an airspace known for its spatial rules.

These territorialising logics reflect at the same time the elemental qualities of air. As Adey (2014) underscores, the ethereality of air – the invisible and nearly ungraspable nature of this element – has made it especially liable to cultural imagination, management, and manipulation (see also Connor 2010). In aviation's context, the unbounded way in which air hovers over the Earth's surface – which at once makes it promising for mobility and portentous of foreign interference and intrusion – is what drives states to want to hem in airspace along the lines of sovereignty and conditional access for others (Butler 2001). Intersecting with this Westphalian order, the formless and turbulent nature of air and the need to generate lift at high speeds have further contributed to an aerial regime characterised by spatial parameters of safety, the obligation of air traffic services and the appointment of certain states to serve as providers of those services – all of which lead to more territorialisation (Lin 2016). These peculiarities signal a need to intertwine territory studies more closely with the agencies of the vibrant matter that make up (air)space (Bennett 2010). Devising territory is indeed often executed not despite, but alongside, the dictates of its elements.

While such material influences can lead to divergent outcomes, some traits of territory-making remain steadfast. One of these relates to the geopolitical struggles and calculations that persist even in the creation of forms like airspace. From the outset, claiming airspace for use and occupation by states evidently does not lessen but advances existing logics of territory-making to attain power. While airspace may not contain traditionally usable resources such as those that land and sea do, thereby triggering the territorial demarcation of resource use rights (Steinberg 2001), its affordance as a space for transit and transcendence has already made this realm, itself, invaluable and contentious as a resource for mobility, war, and trade. Not surprisingly, as the chapter's three expositions demonstrate, states do not create these air territories simply to regulate or even exclude. Rather, state policies often harbour complicated plots to benefit from, usurp, and dispossess others using tactics such as unequally distributed air rights, unevenly planned airspaces, and disproportionate levels of circulatory control. These more sinister undercurrents in the production of airspaces ought to spur more conversations on the ethics and morality of aerial territorialisations, in aviation and other contexts – from air pollution governance (Whitehead 2009) to wireless signals transmission (Ash 2013). In a world where frontiers are increasingly opened up, but in which more fences are being erected, these are important questions that warrant urgent tackling. Without answering them, we risk being oblivious to the subtle power of territories.

NOTES

1. The 1946 Bermuda Agreement and, later, the renegotiated 1977 Bermuda II Agreement were bilateral air transport agreements signed in Bermuda between the United States and the United Kingdom to regulate civil aviation services between the two countries. Intended to ensure equal division of air services, the agreements were designed to prevent domination or excessive profiteering by either country. They set a precedent for at least 3,000 similar bilateral treaties between nations seeking to protect their air travel markets.

2. Open Skies is an international air transport policy that calls for the complete liberalisation of, or removal of restrictions in, civil aviation between signatory states. While first pursued by the United States soon after the Second World War, Open Skies agreements only gained traction in the 1980s, beginning with the United States and a few small countries.

3. High altitude winds and turbulences routinely cause aircraft to deviate from their planned flight tracks, not unlike how winds and currents may cause ships to change course.

4. FIRs do not correspond to national territories in such cases as fine aerial divisions would increase pilots' workload and compromise safety as they switch from one air traffic services provider to the next.

Chapter 4

WATER

Order and the Offshore: The Territories of Deep-Water Oil Production

Jon Phillips

How might territory in the deep oceans be practiced differently from more familiar terrestrial environments? In this chapter, I consider the reterritorialisation of space that enables offshore oil production and countervailing processes of deterritorialisation that have complicated the practice of territory. Oil companies are concerned with discovering and extracting materials that are territorially bound in geological deposits, whereas the ocean environments that they encounter are, by their nature, in flux, and constantly moving independent of efforts to calculate and to control territory. In contrast to deterritorialised industries and globalised flows of capital, the oil industry remains closely tied to place yet operates in environments where place is continually reformed by the movement of water and all that moves with it and through it. This temporal-spatial disjuncture between the ocean and the subterranean world is associated with distinct practices of territorial control both enabled and constrained by the material conditions under which the offshore oil industry operates.

In what follows, I analyse the social life of the offshore territories of oil. The practice of territory in the offshore oil industry demonstrates the broad ways in which territory is socially and materially produced in environments not defined by the fixed and stable points on the surface of land. I describe processes of territorialisation in three distinct but related spaces united in one offshore oil field: the subterranean territories of oil exploration; the (sub)marine spaces of offshore oil production; and the atmospheric spaces of carbon commodification and trade. By focusing on one extractive site of the global oil industry in Ghana, I demonstrate how space is produced in three different domains with material characteristics very different to one another. The materiality of the subsurface, the oceans, and the atmosphere are critical in facilitating, undermining, and reworking the practice of territory.

Geographical debates have been animated in recent years by different ways to account for materiality. Specifically, some scholars have utilised actor network theory or concepts of assemblage to draw attention to the agency of non-human actors in ways that are said to be poorly captured by historical materialist ontologies (Bennett 2010; Castree 2002; Deleuze and Guattari 2004; Whatmore 2006). "Nonhuman actors" in the oceans could refer to fish, an anchor, water, nutrients or ocean currents, for example. The term can also refer to less tangible entities and forces that, under some readings, can be considered as "actants" (Lambert et al. 2006; Latour 2005). Examples might include narratives such as the tragedy of the commons (Gordon 1954), or liberal management norms on how to manage oil production appropriately (EITI 2013). Such narratives and norms come together with human action to co-produce ocean environments (Anderson 2012b; Bear 2013).

Similar post-structural ideas have shaped recent debates over the conceptualisation of space. For Joe Painter (2010), Bruno Latour's (2005) actor network theory provides the conceptual framework with which to understand 'territory-as-effect . . . necessarily porous, historical, mutable, uneven and perishable. It is a laborious work in progress, prone to failure and permeated by tension and contradiction'. As an *effect* of networked socio-technical practices territory is not an *a priori* foundation of state power (see also Mitchell 1991). Nor is it incommensurable with networked forms of spatial organisation. Rather, territory and networks are instead understood as interconnected. Meanwhile, topological forms of power offer something distinct to the analysis of how power is expressed over space. Topology refers to networked forms of political ordering and relationships that are not directly related through their proximity to one another (Allen 2009). In contrast to networks of relations that are organised across a topographical landscape, topological space is folded and twisted, such that relations are made between human and non-human actors that would otherwise be separated by distance (Martin and Secor 2013).

Here, I seek an epistemological middle ground that employs complementary lenses from post-structural thought, while maintaining a dialectical understanding of the power relations and historical processes through which things – human and non-human entities and forces – come together (Bumpus 2011; Sneddon 2007). I adopt the same relational understanding of how space can be organised, in which territory is produced as the effect of socio-material relations between the human and non-human world, while the same space can simultaneously be folded in ways described by topological sensibilities (Allen 2009). Through this lens, I examine the spatial and socio-material conditions under which the Ghanaian state and international oil companies have sought to organise *territory beyond terra* – in the subterranean, marine, and atmospheric spaces of offshore oil.

The chapter proceeds as follows. First, I describe the creation of new sub-terranean territories of fossil fuel exploration through which resource discoveries are made and the value of oil is created and captured. Next, I discuss the reterritorialisation of the marine environment to protect the infrastructural assets of the oil industry from other users of ocean space. Last, I describe how air has been territorialised to produce carbon as commodity, enabling the global trade of carbon emissions generated by the consumption oil. The analysis draws on a selection of sixty interviews conducted in Ghana between February and October 2014 with policymakers, regulators, oil company officials, activists, and industry analysts.

VOLUMETRIC TERRITORIES OF
OFFSHORE OIL PRODUCTION

In recent years, the spatial form of extractive industries has come under renewed scrutiny. For many authors, and in contrast to the universalising grid of the modernist state (Scott 1999), this work has meant accounting for extractive "enclaves" as operating through a spatially distinctive political-economic logic (Ferguson 2005). Territorialisation is critical to contemporary extractive industries but in ways that do not necessarily align with the borders and boundaries of the nation-state. These spaces are captured well in James Ferguson's (2005, 378–79) description of the offshore oil industry as an archetypal enclave industry, where investment does not flow so much as 'skips and hops' across Africa, 'concentrated in secured enclaves, often with little or no economic benefit to the wider society'. Where foreign capital is primarily concerned with securing access to particular "holes" into the sub-surface, a highly selective territorialisation is performed to enable extraction (Bridge 2009).

However, although extractive enclaves might be sited in remote locations, by no means are they politically isolated. In particular, the imaginary of the securitised, privatised enclave discounts the important role of the state and processes of territorialisation in securing enclave space for extractive capital. Even the most remote extractive sites are connected to the world around them in multiple ways, not least by the territorialising practices of different state agents (Appel 2012; Hönke 2010; Mohan 2013). Spatial control can be extended by resource discoveries, shaped by the limits and demands that states and capital place upon one another (Chalfin 2015; Emel et al. 2011); the technological capacity of international oil companies is sought by state actors who, in turn, serve as gatekeepers to extractive territories. In a globalised world of flows, oil production nonetheless depends on particular extractive territories and processes of territorialisation.

Here, I consider these spaces of extraction anew by considering their expression in three-dimensional space. Often, the oceans have been analysed as flat, two-dimensional spaces to be traversed and divided into territories in a horizontal plane (see Steinberg and Peters 2015). Recently, verticality has gained greater attention in geographical analysis as an important axis through which power can be expressed over territory – below, through, and above ground, water, air, and various states between (Braun 2000; Scott 2012). Influenced by the development of extractive industries, Africa is "re-spaced" (Engel and Nugent 2010) through dialectical processes of deterritorialisation and reterritorialisation – in the horizontal plane, and in three dimensions. Yet, as Stuart Elden (2013b, 45) has argued, there is more to this exercise than merely adding a vertical axis to the analysis of area: to comprehend volume requires attention to 'instability, force, resistance, depth, and matter alongside the simply vertical'. In short, analysis of volume implies consideration of relationships between space and matter.

VOLUMETRIC TERRITORIES
OF OFFSHORE OIL IN GHANA

The discovery of oil in Ghana's territorial waters in 2007 has led to some familiar and some less familiar processes of territorialisation. For example, international borders are being contested and redrawn, both in the horizontal plane and in the vertical plane. Contesting the horizontal, the government of Côte d'Ivoire has made a challenge at the International Tribunal on the Law of the Sea (ITLOS) over the position of the maritime border with Ghana (ITLOS 2015). The two national governments dispute the position of the line that bisects their territories, drawn during the colonial period as originating from an administrative outpost and now given heightened importance with the discovery of the Tweneboa, Enyenra, and Ntomme (TEN) oil fields beneath. The Tribunal is asked to mediate over a familiar dispute for which there is a precedent: planar expressions of sovereignty over the ocean surface that confer control of the resources beneath, in which territorial control is divided between states.

Recent efforts to extend the scope of state territories in the ocean have involved new expressions of sovereignty over depth. In the vertical plane, the Ghanaian government has successfully applied to the UN Commission on the Limits of the Continental Shelf (CLCS) to extend the state's ownership of seabed resources out to the edge of the continental shelf (Government of Ghana 2009). Precise scientific calculations of Ghana's underwater topography (bathymetry) are required to delimit which parts of the seabed comprise the 'natural prolongation of its land territory', while the water above remains international waters (UNCLOS 1982 Article 76; see also Sammler 2015). To define the limits of the continental shelf is to recodify a relationship between sovereignty and vertical and volumetric spaces. These new frontiers of resource exploration involve processes of reterritorialisation that reconstitute the relationship between sovereignty and space in three dimensions.

Subterranean Territories

Oil exploration and production in the deep oceans is associated with processes of reterritorialisation that, in addition, are not so closely tied to national borders. Before oil production comes oil exploration and, with it, the territorialisation of three-dimensional subterranean spaces. Maps of oil concessions divide the water's surface into large, angular, two-dimensional blocks of territory that remain the property of the state, but over which – for their ability to identify resource-rich subterranean territories – oil companies are granted temporary exclusive extraction rights over state property. During the costly process of exploration, oil companies maintain a shallow connection to place that enables the mobility of an industry in which resource exploration yields more failures than successes and where the ability to cease exploration in an unprofitable concession is integral to the business model. Yet, in contrast to the abstraction of two-dimensional concession maps, oil exploration depends on rendering subterranean space legible using distinctly three-dimensional technologies. Two-dimensional seismic surveys can produce vertical planes of information on the geological composition of the subsurface, but the deployment of three-dimensional seismic surveys gives much greater certainty over the commercial viability of a site before expensive exploration wells are drilled. Modern oil exploration in itself is a process concerned with the calculation of volumetric space (Bridge 2013).

The legibility of subterranean space is thus a significant factor in the creation and distribution of value and the governance of resources. When the National Democratic Congress (NDC) came to power in Ghana in 2008, it contested the fiscal terms of the petroleum agreement that had been signed with Texan oil firm Kosmos Energy by the previous government (Phillips et al. 2016). That the terms granted to Kosmos Energy were generous was not in dispute. Yet, whether they represented a fair deal reflecting the risk of investment, or a corrupt deal reflecting graft or privileged corporate access, is a judgement that rests, in large part, on how different parties judged the value-addition of three-dimensional seismic surveys that were shot by Kosmos prior to the discovery of the Jubilee oil field. Moreover, calculations and categorisations of volumetric space remain important throughout the lifespan of an oil field, and similar dynamics were at play two years later in 2010 when Kosmos Energy sought to sell its stake to ExxonMobil against the express wishes of the Ghanaian government. Determining the value of the equity stake depended on specifying a level of certainty over the proportion of reserves that could be categorised as either proved (1P), probable (2P) or possible (3P). Hence, the legibility of these inaccessible spaces remains a matter of determining probabilities of their material properties. During both exploration and production, the subterranean spaces of oil are visualised, calculated, and rendered legible as volumetric spaces – a process that is both a technical challenge and a political act shaping the distribution of risk, reward, and resources.

Marine Territories

Territorialisation

The creation of new territories in the ocean has also been practiced over volumetric space, but through a medium with very different material properties to those of the underground, beneath the water. The Jubilee oil field is Ghana's first major oil field development, seventy-five kilometres (forty-six miles) offshore (figure 4.1).

The depiction of the exclusion zone is typical of cartographic representations of the ocean in that it displays a static and stable bounded area on the surface of an indefinite fluid environment. Here oil and gas are extracted and collected by a floating production storage and offloading (FPSO) vessel, which serves a purpose similar to that performed by an oil platform, but which is better suited to deep-water and ultra-deep-water environments. FPSO vessels float on the surface, moored by sets of chains that hold them in position against ocean currents and weather systems. Flexible risers transport oil through the water column to the vessels and are also designed to accommodate ocean currents. Contrary to the common imaginary of a singular vertical pipe sunk into the seabed like a drinking straw, offshore oil fields typically draw from seabed installations that are many kilometres apart, connected across a mountainous bathymetry. The great depths that these installations occupy generate technical challenges to their safe operation, but it is at the surface that other human users of the ocean are encountered, generating requirements for more exclusionary territorial spaces. With necessarily high safety standards, all offshore oil installations are thus subject to exclusion zones.

The exclusion zone that surrounds the Jubilee field FPSO vessel exists as part of a globally standardised practice under international law, taking its size and spatial form from terrestrial installations and environmental conditions (UNCLOS 1982). Safety zones for oil installation were first codified in international law to isolate the risk of the spread of fire (UN Convention on the Continental Shelf 1958). Five hundred metres (1,640 feet) was considered an

The FPSO, *Kwame Nkrumah MV21*, with mooring

– – – – Boundary of the Area to be Avoided

Figure 4.1 The extended safety zone of Ghana's Jubilee oil field ("Area to be Avoided").
Note: The Floating Production, Storage and Offloading (FPSO) vessel *Kwame Nkrumah MV21* ('Jubilee Terminal') is moored sixty kilometres (thirty-seven miles) from the Ghanaian coast. The "Area to be Avoided " covers an area of radius five nautical miles centred on subsea oil wells. The larger concentric circle displayed is the area covered by radio transmissions that are broadcast from the FPSO to warn off intruders. *Source:* Admiralty Standard Nautical Chart 1383: Lagune Abey to Tema, United Kingdom Hydrographic Office (UKHO)/Service Hydrographique et Océanographique de la Marine (SHOM). Reproduced with permission from the United Kingdom Hydrographic Office (UKHO).

appropriate distance to isolate an installation from neighbouring infrastructure and populations. As technology advanced to enable production offshore, these onshore safety zones were reproduced in ocean environments. They were later reviewed, and a case was made to increase the size of the zones to reflect the indeterminacies of ocean environments (UNCLOS 1982, Article 60). But they remained restricted to a 500-metre radius, this time reflecting the interests of several UN member states for which the protection of offshore installations conflicted with the principle of freedom of navigation for shipping. Oil installations are considered sufficiently hazardous that no other vessels should come within 500 metres of the FPSO vessel at any time, while in Ghana the state has successfully extended this specification to cover a radius of five nautical miles, centred on the subsea infrastructure of wells and pipes over 1,000 metres below (see figure 4.1; also Ghana Shipping [Protection of Offshore Operations and Assets] Regulations 2012).

The creation of safety zones is a process of *reterritorialisation*. The original enclosure was created by the 1982 UN Convention on the Law of the Sea (UNCLOS), which incrementally extended state control over oceanic resources to 200 nautical miles from shore. Hence, the Jubilee oil field and the ocean spaces above it were the property of the state long before the exclusion zone was gazetted, along with all resources 'in, under or above' Ghana's land and waters (Ghana Constitution, Article 257[6], 1992). But the safety zone extends elements of state territorial control in important ways, establishing the FPSO vessel as a new artificial island that enables an extension of Ghanaian sovereignty over space in the Exclusive Economic Zone – a jurisdiction where only partial sovereignty would otherwise be held (UNCLOS 1982). Within the exclusion zone, a broader range of economic activities can be directed, regulated and governed by the state (Chalfin 2015; Ghana Maritime Authority 2011). Historically, the intersecting paths of ships played an important role in creating the uneven territories of imperialism in Africa, producing corridors of control that contrast with the imaginary of colonial territorial rule over entire nation-states (Benton 2010). As a fixed (but temporary) installation on the ocean surface, the FPSO is subject to modalities of territorial control different from those of colonial ships, yet it produces a similarly partial and layered picture of sovereignty.

Enforcing the zone is not a trivial task. The water is too deep to mark the border of the zone on the surface with buoys, without which some fishers have contested any sanctions levelled against them for incursion, particularly since fishing boats and nets drift with the current. In the absence of physical markers on the ocean surface, radio signals are broadcast over the airwaves to inform mariners that they are in the vicinity of an exclusion zone (see figure 4.1). These signals can be received by shipping companies or industrial and semi-industrial fishing vessels but are not of use in communicating with canoe fishers who typically do not travel with radio receivers nor navigate with the maps that specify the location of the zones. Rather, the zone is guarded from canoe fishermen by the navy – the classic spatial expression of sovereignty at sea. Navy forces periodically patrol the zone on board a boat funded by the oil companies for purposes of both deterrent and enforcement of a new territorial zone.

Deterritorialisation

The territorial zones created to bring order to extractive marine spaces are typical of cartographic representations in their delimitation of static and stable zones. Yet the material environments in which these zones exist are distinct from land and generate different forms of control and exclusion. Notably, the conceived space of the exclusion zone contrasts with the lived space of the fishers whom it excludes (see Lefebvre 1991). It also contrasts with the spatial and temporal movements of the fish that fishers seek and of multiple other non-human actors that occupy the space on a temporary basis. Critically, the movements of fish and fishers operate on a notably deterritorialised basis with respect to the exclusion zone. Fishers follow fish to different parts of the ocean at different times of year and, in turn, fish populations migrate in accordance with their lifecycles and seasonally in pursuit of nutrients driven by global ocean currents. The upwelling of nutrients on the coast of West Africa makes the fishery particularly productive and has provided the basis of local livelihoods and export economies for decades (Alder and Sumaila 2004). The temporal-spatiality of fishing reflects how depth becomes surface and surface becomes depth over relatively short time frames.

Importantly, oil installations in the ocean are not neutral additions to these marine ecosystems. For example, the legs of oil platforms can create a solid substrate upon which corals can grow. Under some conditions this process can form the basis of an artificial reef that attracts small fish and, in turn, larger predators (Claisse et al. 2014). In the Gulf of Mexico, targeted "rig-to-reef" interventions have been designed to create these new socio-environments by sinking oil platforms to the seabed when they have reached the end of their serviceable life (Jørgensen 2009). Likewise, the FPSO vessel is not a neutral addition to the waterscape; attracted by light, fish are observed to assemble around the vessel at night when Ghanaian fishermen take to the water. The effect is similar to the use of lights as fish-aggregating devices – a common (illegal) fishing method that reduces fishing effort. The important difference is that fish are aggregated in a territory around the FPSO from which fishers are explicitly excluded.

As such, the territorialisation of the FPSO exclusion zone became one of the most contentious issues in the early years of the Ghanaian oil industry.

Fishers report that they experience the costs of oil production without the wealth and benefits it generates. While there are lively public debates over the allocation of oil revenues, the efficacy of Corporate Social Responsibility (CSR) programmes, the rising cost of living in cities that serve the oil industry, objections to the exclusion zone are the complaints most closely associated with a claim of livelihood impacts. The fish aggregation effect ensures that the significance of such zones is greater than the relatively small area set aside. Managers of fishery certification schemes face similar inadequacies in drawing lines on a map in their efforts to delimit a sustainable fishery (Bear and Eden 2008). Whether the subject of management is the extraction of (mobile) fish or (non-mobile) fossil fuels, efforts to construct territory in the deep ocean that build upon terrestrial ontological assumptions have been confounded by the movement of water and the human and non-human actors that move with it and through it.

Reterritorialisation

Although the borders of the exclusion zones contrast with the rapid flows of the oceans, they are not as static as they may first appear. They have to be made and remade continually, and they take on meanings that their inscription on maps does not capture. Exclusion zones have to be created and maintained through territorial practice, and the circulation of the oceans has generated calls from various actors for reterritorialisation, reaffirming the physical borders of the exclusion zone. The way that the territorial exclusion zone operates in practice is an effect of socio-natural relations.

Information has been an important means through which to remake the territorial zones in light of the effects of FPSO vessels on fish aggregation. Critical to this assessment has been the question of whether oil installations can be demonstrated to increase fish productivity *in situ* or simply attract fish populations from further afield. Artificial reefs have been shown to increase fish populations in some circumstances (Claisse et al. 2014); FPSO vessels have not been shown to have the same effect. Either way, the accuracy of these assessments is of secondary importance to the argument here. More relevant is the question of how the assessment of environmental impacts has been used to redraw territorial lines on the ocean and among the actors that use it. This process has been something that three sets of actors have all engaged with to different ends, but on similar territorial terms: state actors, oil companies, and fishers.

As the guarantors of enclosure, Ghanaian government agencies have had to answer to fishers with respect to the latter's exclusion from ocean space. The Environmental Protection Agency maintains that the safety zone is necessary for the safe operation of the oil field, but a second set of ideas emerges as a supporting justification for exclusion, and that is summarised by a manager in the Environmental Protection Agency: 'Incidentally, this area is serving as a refuge for fish . . . in the long term we can project that it will rather help to improve the already degraded fisheries'. The suggestion is that the zones act as *de facto* marine reserves, sheltering vulnerable juvenile fish populations from over-harvesting; this is a familiar terrestrial narrative of fortress conservation translated to the marine environment. Yet, that observation is at odds with the relevant environmental impact assessment, which suggests that the size of the zones is too small – and the time that fish spend within them too short – to have any conservation effect. The narrative also expresses the same territorial logic as that which created the zone and is used to support the exclusion of fishermen on the grounds of sustainability.

For staff of the operator of the Jubilee oil field, Tullow Oil, becoming embroiled in fisheries governance conflicts with a business model emphasising strategic disengagement with national territories beyond the extractive site itself. The company's response to the complaints of fishers has been to stress the conclusions reached in environmental impact assessments – that fish stocks will be unaffected, because fish will not *remain* within the zones; they will "spill-over". According to staff working on Tullow Oil's CSR programmes, the company's interventions reflect their assessment that the company owes to fishers no compensation or *alternative* livelihood:

> For the fishermen we are saying it's livelihood support, unlike alternative livelihoods, which was the norm in the past. We can't take them off the sea and provide them with something else. Some of them have been fishermen since aged twelve or eleven, up to forty years. It is difficult to give them new skills to take them off the sea and weave baskets and sell them. So let them continue with their fishing activities . . . (Interview with Communications staff, Tullow Oil Plc, August 2014)

Hence, support is provided for *existing* fishing livelihoods, with fishers given ice boxes or assistance to improve fish-smoking ovens. Livelihood support is presented as neutral with respect to responsibility, but nevertheless is helpful to the company as it seeks to secure from local residents an informal social license to operate. In contrast, when people are defined as members of the affected communities of oil production (and therefore the subjects of CSR programmes), boundaries around them are drawn partly on the basis of modelling of coastal areas that would suffer from a potential oil spill – something for which oil companies would in principle accept responsibility.

Given these provisions, it is noteworthy that fishers themselves typically do not claim that safety zones have *caused* a decline in fish stock, since their experience of the fisheries crisis pre-dates the advent of oil production in 2010. Rather, fishers have objected to their exclusion from territories where fish aggregate by using territorial logics of their own. Frustrations are articulated by professional representatives of Ghanaian fishermen in statements directed at state agencies for redress: 'They should know that national security will be at stake if [fishers] are not employed. Just look at Nigeria'. This reference is to one of the longest-standing complaints of artisanal fishers – the failure of state authorities to exclude foreign industrial fishing vessels from the inshore waters reserved for Ghanaian canoes. The dispossessed fishers of the Niger Delta are mobilised by Ghanaians to suggest a threat may be posed to the state by surplus labour, and to spur supportive state intervention motivated by enlightened self-interest (see Duffield 2007).

The positions of all three sets of actors illustrate the social life of borders in ocean space and highlight the discursive and material power of those who create, experience, and maintain them. One distinction from terrestrial environments underpinning all three are the links among resource, territory, and depth. The relative location of fish in oceans is different from that of bauxite in land or cocoa on land, and representations of the spatiality and temporality of fish movements have been used by all three sets of actors to argue for particular rules of resource management. Two notable proposals for alternatives to the exclusion zone have been raised by fishers during consultation exercises. The first proposal is to "desaturate" the zone, allowing occasional temporary access to fishers. But a second proposal mobilises a different logic: to exclude fish from the zone by sinking an impenetrable perimeter fence to the ocean floor. This solution may be practically unfeasible in deep water but shows that access to the territory is a means to catch fish. Likewise, some Ghanaian NGOs have called for coordinated processes of marine spatial planning that would seek to balance the interests of different users of marine space more equitably than do the exclusion zones; this would be guided by participatory principles, mimicking the territorial logics of Marine Protected Areas observable elsewhere in the world (Bear and Eden 2008; Pieraccini 2015). Processes of territorialisation pervade modern fisheries, and so it is perhaps unsurprising that the flows of the oceans have generated from a range of actors these calls to reassert boundaries in various forms. The spatiality and temporality of fish movements are up for definition and contestation for particular ends.

Atmospheric Territories

The marine territories described above represent relatively new locations for old territorial logics, in which ocean space is reterritorialised to accommodate the material flows of the ocean under a new extractive imperative. However, the volumetric spaces of offshore oil are not only subterranean and sub-marine; they are also atmospheric. The atmosphere is globally mixed on relatively short time frames such that it can be considered deterritorialised – uncontained by national or regional borders – but the FPSO vessel is one of many new sites for the territorialisation of air. In addition to oil, the Jubilee field produces natural gas, which has to be either transported to land where it can be used productively or flared at sea. By investing in the infrastructure to pipe gas onshore, the developers of the project can claim to have reduced greenhouse gas emissions that would otherwise have been emitted by gas flaring. Such effort allows them to earn carbon credits under a UN scheme to offset emissions in the North using low carbon development projects in the South (UNFCCC 2012). Sixty kilometres (thirty-seven miles) offshore, sub-terranean carbon is extracted as crude oil and, on that same site, atmospheric carbon is produced as a commodified waste product for global trade.

The creation and trade of a unit of carbon makes both territorial and topological space. In contrast to the production of marine territories in geometric space, the spaces of global carbon trade are produced through the relationship between the distant sites of fossil fuel production and consumption rather than their proximity, yet they also depend on accounting for atmospheric space within national boundaries. The UN system of carbon emission reductions is based on a deterritorialised, globally mixed atmosphere such that a reduction in carbon emissions in country A is considered equivalent to the same reduction in country B. But the system also reframes climate change in territorial terms in order to make a North-South trade in units of carbon (a "carbon offset") possible: carbon can be traded globally once measured, reported, and constrained within the statist frame (Lövbrand and Stripple 2006). The process thus brings distant sites of carbon consumption such as a German steel plant into relation with the Ghanaian oil field. The carbon trade creates new, national atmospheric territories in the global atmosphere, while simultaneously bringing distant sites of carbon consumption and reduction into relation through the twisting and folding of space.

Again, information is central to this process. The creation of carbon as a commodity and its virtual trade depends on a number of spatially expansive "technological zones": spaces where 'the differences between technical practices, procedures or forms have been reduced, or common standards have been established' (Barry 2006, 239). These zones allow a common spatially, socially, and historically abstracted unit of carbon to be created in sites as diverse as a Thai forest or a Ghanaian oil field. Standardisation is required such that a definable, measurable, verifiable unit of carbon can be made legible, tradable, and ultimately governable (MacKenzie 2009). The borders of these zones are not those associated with the nation-state but rather are those that 'constrain the movement of certain categories of persons, objects and information' (Barry 2006, 239). Simultaneous processes of territorialisation and deterritorialisation enable a trade that generates a flow of climate finance from the North to the temporary locations of the transnational oil industry in the South. To create new territories in the atmosphere, the geometric space over which oil tankers transport petroleum from Ghana to markets in Europe or North America is folded and twisted to enable a new virtual trade in carbon credits over topological space.

Moreover, these norms of carbon accounting that enable this trade present only one instance of how technological zones have shaped the physical spaces described in this chapter. Zones of qualification might also describe UN conventions that create the safety zone around the FPSO and delimit the continental shelf (Convention on the Continental Shelf 1958; UNCLOS 1982), the voluntary codes of oil company CSR programmes (Tullow Oil 2013), the *Voluntary Principles on Security and Human Rights* that are used to train Ghanaian naval officers to police the FPSO exclusion zone, the environmental impact statements for the Jubilee field (ERM 2014), or the political and commercial risk assessments of the petroleum industry. All embody or employ highly standardised sets of transnational practices developed outside of the confines of the territorial nation-state; yet each has been instrumental in shaping the contested processes of territorialisation. The spaces described are neither territorially bound spaces demarcated by state borders nor globally abstracted, deterritorialised spaces of global capitalism (Amin 2000; Ong and Collier 2005).

CONCLUSION

In this chapter, I have examined how volumetric offshore spaces have been territorialised, deterritorialised, and reterritorialised to enable offshore oil production. Territoriality remains a governmental technology of great importance to the oil and gas industry (Bebbington and Bury 2013; Bridge 2011). The bounded physical spaces of extraction are, of course, intimately linked with the globalised flows of capital associated with West African oil production. Yet, although globalisation evokes images of power expressed beyond territory, and although the term "offshore" is often used to imply deregulated spaces in a globalised world (Urry 2014), states and capital continue to depend on territorialisation to reproduce the spaces of petro-capitalism.

Petroleum resources are "landed" with respect to their fixed locations and embeddedness in the territorial structures of the nation-state, ensuring that authority over physical space will continue to be critical to the politics of oil and gas (Bridge 2009). Yet, the multiplication of territories such as zones, hubs, and corridors of investment has created a more complex picture of the practice of territory (Easterling 2014). The spaces of offshore oil are connected to the world around them by transnational governance systems, community engagement programmes, and transnational circulations of capital, standards, norms of governance, knowledge, and information connected both across networked topographical space and in topological space. A detailed study of Ghana's Jubilee oil field demonstrates how topographical and topological spaces coexist and can be produced as an effect of the mutual dependence, cooperation, and tension between state and capital (see Duffield 2007). This relational account of sovereignty (Emel et al. 2013) and territory (Painter 2010) highlights again the inadequacies of understanding territory-making as a state-led project alone. More importantly, the account moves the debate beyond a simple binary of state and capital that presupposes that state and corporate powers are necessarily in opposition in the production of territory at different scales.

These spaces of offshore extraction produce physical zones over which broader socio-material relations are contested. Where capital 'skips and hops' between securitised zones (Ferguson 2005, 378), enclaves of extraction are nonetheless produced through relations between multiple human and non-human actors. In this account, I have highlighted the socially and materially constructed spaces of the subterranean, sub-marine, and atmospheric domains, where territories are expressed as socio-material volumes. Offshore infrastructures encounter a historically contingent set of political relations that are shaped by the materiality of resources and the environments in which territory is produced: human activity, non-human life, and the biophysical characteristics of the oceans, subsoil, and atmosphere all complicate the exercise of control over space. Efforts to construct territories in water that mimic the determinate boundaries and surfaces of land have been both confounded and partially enabled by the material environments that offshore oil production encounters. Territorial practices that are largely unproblematic when anchored to fixed points on stable land are partially reworked and adapted in the fluid, deep oceans to enable successful oil exploration and profitable oil production. Nevertheless, infrastructure in the oceans continues to be organised as territory by different human actors for different ends. Oil companies, state agents, and fishing associations have all proposed and implemented territorial solutions to the disruptive flows of the oceans. Meanwhile a vast array of geophysicists, engineers, accountants, auditors, and managerial staff are required to visualise, calculate, and realise the subterranean spaces of oil and the commodity form of atmospheric carbon. In many ways, the agency of non-human actors has been built into these new territorial systems of governance as the effect of human–non-human relations. What is governed in these spaces is not water, hydrocarbons, fish, rock, or air *per se*, but the relations between materials and actors.

In these inherently relational environments, time has been an equally important factor shaping the practice of territory over space. The offshore oil industry operates in both a geo-social, subterranean world and a hydro-social, marine world (Peters 2012; Whatmore 2006). More recently, the climate-forcing impacts of oil production and consumption have also opened sites of resource commodification in the atmosphere. New territories have been cre-ated in all three spaces through different modalities. In this respect, the sea floor and ocean surface provide liminal planes between spaces that conform to different spatial-temporal dynamics. Above the seabed, the oceans are mixed on short timescales such that place is continually reproduced. Global ocean currents carry nutrients to the surface that create the biannual fishing seasons in Ghana's coastal waters, conflicting with the spatial form of oil's exclusive zones. Here, the spatial power of the zone is expressed as a tempo-ral force, while the movements of the oceans and those that move with it pro-duce opposing spatial-temporalities that remake territory. Below the seabed, oil production is similarly expressed as a temporal force, penetrating through layers of carboniferous deposits laid down over millennia to access the fuels that underpin modern life (Clark 2016). Oil production creates 'a transfer of geological space and time that has underpinned the compression of time and space in modernity' (Bridge 2009, 47). Moreover, as the current and future climatic impacts of fossil fuel consumption have become apparent, novel schemes have arisen to commodify carbon as a waste product at the other end of the carbon commodity chain (Bridge 2011).

The spatial form of territory for the offshore oil industry reflects this disjuncture between subterranean and sub-marine worlds. For Nigel Clark (2012, 1), 'there are no territories without exposed strata, no exposed strata without multiple layers of subtending strata, no subtending strata without deep, temporal dynamics'. The Earth's geological strata that have produced subterranean oil deposits and that, in the future, will bear signatures of the Anthropocene can be captured by these geographies of verticality. Yet the process of visualising the underground in extractive industries relies on political technologies that visualise and calculate the earth's strata in three dimensions to enable accumulation. Moreover, the different spatial-temporal dynamics of the oceans provide the basis of a contrasting volumetric account of rapid flows of oceans and those human and non-human actors that move in, on, and through them (Steinberg and Peters 2015). Meanwhile, the carbon trade is built on calculations of the future, in which projections of counterfac-tual scenarios are required to estimate the volume of carbon emissions that will have been hypothetically avoided by any low carbon investment in ten or twenty years' time. In short, territory in three dimensions is subject not only to multiple spatialities but also to multiple temporalities that can only be understood in relation to space in an analytically whole category (Massey 1992). These temporal-spatialities are constitutive of the governance of whom or what is able to control space, and whom or what is not. In this respect, analysis of the practice of territory at sea shares conceptual ground with long-standing principles of terrestrial resource studies: that understanding relationships between enclosure, commodification, and struggle is central to understanding the transformation of landscapes (Bebbington and Bury 2013).

There is a long history to representations of the oceans as empty spaces, devoid of human activity and relations (Anderson and Peters 2014; Steinberg 2001). More recently, the language of ocean grabbing has gained prominence, mobilising territorial metaphors similar to the terrestrial equivalent of land grabbing. The UN Special Rapporteur on Food warned in 2012 that 'shady access agreements that harm small-scale fishers, unreported catch, incursions into protected waters, and the diversion of resources away from local populations – can be as serious a threat as "land-grabbing"' (De Schutter 2012, 1). Feelings about the justice and injustice of certain circumstances are different for different people in different contexts (Sikor 2013). What is important, in this light, is the question of how particular notions of justice gain traction in public discourse and in some cases become hegemonic. A socio-material reading of territorial practices illuminates important processes in which territory and space are made through relations between state and capital, and between human and non-human worlds. The links between the territories of the underground, the (sub)marine, and the atmosphere and the various resources therein are complex and changing, such that the exclusionary and inclusionary effects of enclosure cannot be assumed. They can, however, be accounted for by attending to the historical production of *territory beyond terra* in and across three-dimensional spaces continually re-created through social practices.

Chapter 5

FIRE

Pyropolitics for a Planet of Fire

Nigel Clark

The World Wide Fund for Nature tagged it "the Year the World Caught Fire". In 1997–1998, the coupled ocean-atmosphere system, the El Niño Southern Oscillation, went through an especially intense version of one of its periodic changes in direction. Drought came to characteristically humid regions, desiccating tropical rainforests, while heavy rain fell on normally arid zones: both, environmental historian Stephen Pyne (2001) explains, plumped up fuel loads in their respective ecosystems. Where there is fuel there will be fire, whether the spark comes from natural sources like lightning or from human ignition. Soon tens of thousands of blazes were raging across Australia and Amazonia, and from Siberia to Sumatra.

As Pyne (2001, 172) wryly observes, the 'fires were telegenic, they were timely'. Television, itself a pulsing and flickering of light, has an affinity with fire. Tracking the blazes around the Pacific Rim and across the Americas, global media knew they were onto a winning topic. This was a time of ascending anxiety about human-induced global warming, but neither figures of rising atmospheric carbon concentration nor global circulation models offered much in the way of visceral sensory charge. What the mass-mediated spectacle of the world's forests ablaze provided was the graphic interface that global warming had been lacking: here was an infernal iconography fitting for an era of runaway planetary heating (Pyne 2001).

If the 1980s and 1990s were decades when capital seemed to be roving the globe with unprecedented license, so too they were a moment when environmentalists were increasingly developing transborder tactics and alliances, as were climatologists and environmental scientists (Tsing 2005). While 1997–1998 was neither the first nor the last year of widespread wildfire, the tropical rainforests that burnt in those seasons were a focus for the political problematisation of transboundary environmental threats. But fire, in this sense, may be more than just one more ascendant object of political concern. It is the propensity of fire to sear its way across the Earth's surface and to transform the air in which we see, move, and breathe that makes it the kind of event that troubles the relationship between politics and the stuff of the world. Pyne (1997a, 5) points to an emergent understanding that localised fire is inseparable from the Earth's atmosphere, adding up to what he describes as a 'new mythological metamorphosis' in which air 'joins fire anywhere with fire everywhere'. Analogously, for philosopher Michael Marder (2015, 4), a planetary convergence of combustive processes and their atmospheric impacts is recomposing politics at the most elemental level: 'Our situation today', he declares, 'is that of *neither land nor sea*; updated for the twenty-first century, the central political elements are the dyad of air and fire'.

This chapter explores the idea of fire as a shifting and changeable elemental process that poses challenges to all who set out to manage parcels of the Earth's surface. At the same time, skilled operators can use fire to enrich and help secure a land or place of dwelling. There is no inhabited region of the Earth where fire is not to some degree integral to the carving out and sustaining of territories, and fire is also increasingly experienced as a transboundary force that can unsettle received understandings of territory as stable and enduring. As we will see, it is this combination of being at once local and global, grounded and circulatory, site-specific yet planetary in its connections and consequences that makes fire such a provocation for rethinking territorial imaginaries.

I take my bearings from "The Year the World Caught Fire", which soon opens out into a succession of fiery years, and I focus on the islands of Indonesia – described as one of planet's pre-eminent frontiers of fire (Pyne 2001). Along with the Amazon, Indonesia – and particularly Kalimantan, the Indonesian bulk of the island of Borneo – has been the site of extensive forest burning to make way for plantation agroecosystems. Harmful enough in themselves, many such fires have escaped control. Encompassing severe impacts on forest habitats and on traditional ways of life, Indonesian fire is a major source of the air pollution that plagues much of Southeast Asia. As well as addressing the causes of Indonesia's fire problem, I consider the collaborative efforts of the Association of Southeast Asian Nations (ASEAN) to deal with fire-induced "haze".

This account, however, will be far from a simple one about a new transboundary problem engendering novel transnational responses. Despite the efforts of ASEAN members – and non-governmental actors – this story is yet without a happy ending. What is more, the question of what a transboundary political issue is or might yet be can draw us beyond even the most concerted efforts of contemporary transnational environmental governance. If we imagine that the only boundaries that really matter are those inscribed by human actors around the parcels of the Earth's surface we call nation-states, then we may already be setting our sights too low – or perhaps not low enough. For in a world in which the operating state of the Earth system is a matter pressing concern, the thresholds that matter politically are no longer simply those that define nation-states, but those that distinguish one state of the Earth system or one geological epoch from another.

Given the well-established role of fossil fuel combustion as a driver of change, fire and its entanglement with Earth's atmosphere is a central concern when it comes to trying to protect crucial boundaries in the Earth system. Here too, Indonesia is a key player, for the archipelagic nation is a major exporter of coal. In this chapter, then, I ask how these two different kinds of combustion – fire that burns phytomass on the Earth's surface and fire that consumes fossilised biomass from the subsurface – are converging. I consider how they are fusing and being confused. For the very idea that all fire is bad fire, that the flaming forests are necessarily in collusion with combusting fossil fuels in destabilising the Earth system, is something we need to question. What makes riveting television in an environmental age may not be the best foundation for a fire-centred rethinking of territory through and beyond *terra*.

As both Pyne and Marder suggest, fire may well have been a formidable and constitutive force in politics for much longer than most of us imagine (see also Dalby 2017). Moreover, when we start to think in a searching way about the great subterranean beds of fossilised hydrocarbons now causing so much climatic and earth system strife, their existence raises questions about how stable and immutable the ground beneath our feet has been. For just as the fire that drifts across the boundary between one nation-state and another can perturb our sense of what constitutes a given political territory, so too can the fires that blaze across the boundary between one geological epoch and another unsettle our sense of the givenness of the Earth itself.

TERRITORIALISING FIRE

During the extreme El Niño episodes of 1982–1983 and 1997–1998, even evergreens in the normally lush tropical forest of Sumatra and Kalimantan shed their leaves, providing the dry biomass conducive to wildfire outbreak (Pyne 2001). But "normal" needs qualifying. As fire scientist Johann Gold-ammer (2007, 14) points out: 'Fire has been present in the Southeast Asian biota since the Pleistocene. Long-term climate variability (glacial *versus* non-glacial climate) and short-term climate oscillations caused by the El Niño – Southern Oscillation event have repeatedly created conditions that make even rainforest susceptible to wildfires'.

While I will not be exonerating the political or economic actors behind the latest outbreaks of intentional fire, it is vital to look at the broader socio-material context in which Indonesia burns. Alongside the syncopated inter-annual rhythms of El Niño, it is the alternating annual wet-dry cycles of the Asian monsoon that make fire as crucial an element of the biogeography of the Indonesian archipelago as rainfall or moisture (Pyne 1997b). And for perhaps 800,000 years, fire-wielding hominids have been part of this ecology. The East Indies, in Pyne's (1997b, 418) words, is 'one of the great hearths of anthropogenic fire'. For thousands of years shifting cultivators have followed fire-fallow regimes – what is often described as "swidden" or, in more discerning indigenous vocabulary, *jhum*, *kaingin*, or *lading*. The distribution of teak and other hardwoods, spices, and many tropical fruits is believed to be in large measure an expression of this fire-catalysed gardening (Pyne 1997b).

It is important to recognise that Indonesian fire is not the same as European fire. This distinction matters because, in the context of colonisation, emissaries from Europe took it upon themselves to manage land across much of the rest of the Earth's surface, including the East Indies. What Europeans so often failed to understand was that in many parts of the world – especially the tropics – fire is a necessary preparatory phase of agriculture (Pyne 2001, 88). As Pyne (1997b, 420) writes of the European colonial encounter with Indonesia: 'Europe didn't trust roving villages, didn't believe shifting cultivation was sustainable, didn't ascribe value to "minor forest products" that foraging natives did, and didn't like fire'.

The roots of this European distrust of fire and of fire-fallow people's farming are deep and complex. North-west and central Europe, Pyne explains, is unusual for its perennial dampness – for the absence of wet and dry rhythms that lend the Indonesian archipelago and much of the rest of the world a distinctive fire season. European soils, churned and revitalised by geologically recent glaciation, are exceptionally tolerant of the ongoing ecological disturbance that is agriculture (Pyne 1997b, 2001). This characteristic enabled Europe to become an anomalous patch of the Earth so intensely cultivated that fire can be almost totally domesticated – extinguished in the wild and reduced to little more than a farming implement (Clark and Yusoff 2014; Pyne 2001).

Even so, the periodic firing of forest and the regular burning of fallow remained the cornerstone of European agroecosystems for millennia, as it was in Indonesia and most other places where agriculture was practiced. But then in early modernity, fire suppression in Europe took a further turn, without parallel anywhere else in the world. "Enlightened" agronomists, newly converted to the idea of endless spirals of economic accumulation, became convinced that surplus organic matter needed to be cycled back into soil or forest rather than "squandered" in flame (Pyne 1997b). At the same time, metropolitan authorities, anxious about the incendiary inclinations of the urban masses, were ever more disposed to see open fire as an expression of social breakdown and disorder. As Michel Foucault (1991) so influentially depicted, modernising states during this period were increasingly concerned with the *qualities* of their territory – taking upon themselves the responsibility to optimise the wealth and vitality of the spaces and populations under their jurisdiction.

As Europe's burgeoning urban masses were being induced to channel and augment their bodily energies, so too were its peasant farmers being compelled to quench their fires and desist from torching fallow – in the interests of tightening the energetic circuits of agricultural production. It is no coincidence that the institution of curfew to constrain the spatio-temporal movements of urban bodies is derived from *couvre feu* – the covering or quelling of fire (Clark 2011; Pyne 2001). Such insights suggest that the definitive modalities, tactics, and practices of governing territory that crystallised in a modernising Europe had at their heart a certain orientation to fire. But it was a disposition so utterly intent on fire's exorcism that European thinkers have rarely dwelled on the fiery underbelly of political modernity. Or as I put it elsewhere:

> it is perhaps only in Europe that we could imagine a "biopolitics" that was not first and foremost a "pyropolitics" – centred on the regulation, manipulation and enhancement of fire. Or is what we have come to call biopolitics, already, covertly, a set of practices concerning the governance of what can be burned, how, where and by whom? (Clark 2011, 164–65).

If, in the course of their drive for global expansion, Europeans were willing to displace their repressed desire to burn onto distant lands, as the imperative to govern in "productive" and "optimising" ways was extended to colonial territories such as the East Indies, so, too, were sanctions against open fire. What began as a provincial mutation, a geographically and culturally specific renunciation of fire, was gradually assembled into a global norm: a set of prohibitions that cultivators, pastoralists, and forest dwellers the world over were expected to abide by. As Pyne (1997b, 495) admonishes: 'the principles of fire conservancy became a dogma of British – indeed, of European – environmental policy. In what is surely one of the most paradoxical outcomes of European expansion, some of the most pyrophobic peoples on the planet assumed control over some of the Earth's most pyrophilic biotas'.

The East Indies caught the full force of this attempt to excise fire from constitutively fire-prone ecosystems. Europeans were certainly not immune to learning from novel environments or from harsh experience. Indeed, as environmental historian Richard Grove (1995) notes, much of the early imperative towards early forms of conversation came from observations that deforesting tropical lands – especially islands – could lead to desiccation, erosion, and even total biotic collapse. For authorities tasked with enhancing the "natural" productivity of the larger islands of the East Indies, it seemed as though fire reduction was the key to keeping landscapes well watered and fertile.

While the Dutch colonists of the late eighteenth century had earlier grasped that intentional use of fire was deeply entrenched and of customary significance, later colonial administrators – justifiably concerned over the impacts of commercial logging operations – turned to fire control as the pathway to watershed protection (Pyne 1997b). But undiscerning fire proscription quickly came up against the fire-inducing wet-dry pulsing of both the Asian monsoon and El Niño; more than this, injunctions against burning met with vigorous resistance by indigenous peoples. 'The more the Dutch objected to fire', observes Pyne (1997b, 423), 'the more often the natives were inclined to use it'. In the process, colonial foresters' intent on harvesting teak missed the point that the deciduous, semi-tropical hardwood tree flourished where it was exposed to regular fire.

We can view this as a collision between competing ways of territorialising fire. Europe became a site in which the suppression of fire's mobile, mutable aspects played a key part in the fixing and bounding of territory at scales ranging from the farm to the nation. Indeed, pyropolitics – collective decision-making over fire – may well have played a much greater role in the characteristic grounding or stabilisation of territory in the "Old World" much greater than most political theorists have acknowledged. The rural people of the East Indies had their own pyropolitics: their own ways of setting fire to work to shape, manage, and render productive specific pockets of land. But like the element of fire itself, these territories tended to shift and transform in response to environmental variability.

Over the latter nineteenth and early twentieth centuries, official policy in the East Indies was a variant of the European territorialising of fire. Fire suppression combined with irrigation was at the core of colonial strategies to substitute new export commodities such as coffee and sugar for fire-catalysed shifting cultivation across the inner islands of Indonesia (Pyne 1997b). Fire, needless to say, persisted. With independence came a relaxation of fire prohibition, but this change was hardly in the interest of traditional fire-fallow farming or the ecosystems it promoted. By the 1980s, concern over expanding populations and the belief that accelerating economic growth was the answer to political instability led to state-supported expansion to the "outer islands", especially Sumatra and Kalimantan (Tsing 2005). This time around, logging and plantation agriculture were to reach deep into the inland tropical rainforests, into an interior that had proven resistant to even the most avid colonial improvers. And fire was the most economical and convenient means of clearing the land.

FIRE AS A TRANSBOUNDARY PROBLEM

As Pyne (1997a, 2001) insists, ideas about fire are both cultural and geographically specific – although, like flames, they tend to migrate and insinuate themselves in new environments. Neither inherently good nor bad, wildland fire is a manifestation of the different elements – oxygen, fuel-loads, ignition source, topography, weather conditions – that it brings together in what is always a unique event (Pyne 2014). But some blazes are exceptional. Since the early 1980s, fires that have been searing through the Indonesian interior have turned periodic combustive events into conflagrations too wide-ranging and incessant to allow for recovery and regrowth – which is often the point.

Until the 1970s, the tropical rainforests of Kalimantan and Sumatra had escaped large-scale logging, their very biodiversity presenting too much heterogeneity to suit the industrial harvester. From then on, a state-sponsored "New Order" offering concessions to overseas corporations opened the way to a regime of mechanised extraction, quickly elevating Indonesia to the world's leading exporter of tropical timber (Tsing 2005). Regeneration was not a priority. Once commercially valuable wood was removed, the remaining vegetation was frequently burnt off to clear the ground and fertilise the soil for plantation crops. Prising open the canopy resulted in drier microclimates, increasing the susceptibility of surrounding forest to further fire (Herawati and Santoso 2011). By the early 1980s, fire-driven rainforest conversion was generating an annual pall of airborne aerosol pollution – euphemistically termed haze – blanketing Indonesia and neighbouring nations.

The El Niño–compounded fire season of 1997–1998 burned over eight million hectares across Kalimantan and Sumatra, creating acrid haze that affected the health of some seventy-five million people in the region, and exacting serious socio-economic impacts across six Southeast Asian nations. The smoke reduced rainfall, exacerbating the El Niño effect and increasing forest flammability. As well as having serious impacts on regional agriculture and biological diversity, the atmospheric effects of the fires helped elevate Indonesia to one of the world's highest carbon dioxide emitters (Mayer 2006).

In the early years of the transboundary haze problem, traditional fire-fallow cultivators and migrant farmers were frequently held to blame. By the early 2000s, satellite imaging cross-referenced with concession maps linked plantation companies to eighty per cent of the fires (Varkkey 2013), with land clearance for the burgeoning palm oil industry regarded as the leading incentive for burning (Jones 2004). While using fire to clear land is technically illegal under Indonesian law, liability is hard to establish. In the messy ground-level reality of rainforest 'development', smaller fires accidently grow into larger fires or can be encouraged to become so. Fire can be deliberately used to degrade 'pristine' rainforest so it can be legally reclassified as convertible to plantation farming. Palm oil and rubber companies and other big operators devolve 'land preparation' to a host of unregulated and ephemerally operating subcontractors, some of whom reputedly set fires on villagers' lands and allow it to spread to where it is required (Varkkey 2013).

Indeed, it is fire's propensity to overflow lines and markers inscribed on the surface of the Earth that helps make it such a recalcitrant object of regulation, a challenge no less complicated in relation to the transboundary effects of smoke. When it came to engaging with the increasingly intolerable effects of air pollution, it was fortuitous that the affected populations/governments were already members of Association of Southeast Asian Nations (ASEAN), the political and economic organisation founded in 1967 by Indonesian, Malaysian, and Singaporean governments – and subsequently expanded to include Brunei, Thailand, the Philippines, Cambodia, Vietnam, Laos, and Myanmar/Burma. ASEAN's response to the haze problem has been widely praised, with the United Nations Environment Programme, among others, commending the Association's collaborative air pollution mitigation efforts as a potential global model for addressing transboundary issues (see Varkkey 2012).

Despite political regime changes, Indonesia's own leadership has remained steadfastly committed to export-led economic growth and has tended to tolerate haze and carbon emission problems as regrettable side effects of the drive for prosperity. 'Environmental protection is weighed against economic concerns', political scientist Christopher Atkinson (2014, 254) observes, and it has been rare for the former to tip the balance. But Indonesia's lack of concern with the wider impacts of its "frontier of fire" has not necessarily been out of keeping with international law and policy. Even the 1992 United Nations Conference on the Human Environment affirms each state's 'sovereign right to utilize, manage and develop their forests' – with no explicit reference to international cooperation over forest fire prevention (cited Robinson 2001, 463). This oversight seems to stem from the assumption that all nations would properly attend to their own forest fires rather than implying any reconciliation with forest fire *per se*.

Held between 1992 and 1996, ASEAN's workshops on transboundary haze and the resultant Cooperation Plan on Transboundary Pollution certainly showed promise (Jones 2004; Robinson 2001); as did the more demanding Agreement on Transboundary Haze Pollution, signed by six member states in November 2002. The latter initiative – effectively an international treaty – stresses prevention and monitoring of transboundary haze, including interstate cooperation in developing early warning systems, fire-fighting capability, and preventive measures such as education, awareness-building, and community participation (ASEAN 2016). But while the Agreement is legally binding on signatory states, critical commentators note that ASEAN's foundational principles of non-interference in each other's domestic affairs compromises the Agreement's effectiveness (Jones 2004). This limitation was compounded by Indonesia's delay in ratifying the agreement until 2014 – making it the last of the signatories to fully commit.

A certain softening of the ASEAN hard line on respecting sovereign space is suggested by joint ventures such as Malaysia, Singapore, and Indonesia's collaboration in cloud-seeding operations to extinguish fires in East Sumatra and West Kalimantan in 2005 – which was significant because it involved sharing national airspace and the possibility of redirecting rainfall across international borders (Mayer 2006). Critics note, however, that the root causes of forest burning are inadequately addressed by the technical focus of such actions or by the Haze Agreement's central provisions more broadly (Mayer 2006). Much comes down to the Indonesian government's inability or unwillingness to enforce its environmental laws, a failure attributed to entrenched patronage relationships between the state and powerful corporate actors (Jones 2004; Varkkey 2012). Such complicity between political and economic elites characterises ASEAN member states more generally, as does the prioritisation of economic development over environmental protection (Robinson 2001).

It is important to recall that Indonesia is not the only ASEAN nation in which fire is used to clear forest (Jones 2004), and to note that Malaysian and Singaporean companies contribute significantly to Indonesian forest burning (Mayer 2006). In brief, plantation agriculture is big business across much of the region, and maximising growth and profitability in this sector is viewed as a keystone of economic and political stability (Jones 2004). As Helena Varkkey (2012, 83) pointedly concludes: 'ASEAN initiatives on haze have resulted in outcomes that protect national economic interests, preserve state sovereignty, and deflect responsibility on the haze issue, instead of actually reducing or eradicating haze'.

Increasing pressure from environmental NGOs in Indonesia and across the region, a concerted ASEAN response to the severe fire season of 2013, and Indonesia's belated ratification of the Transboundary Haze Agreement suggest that the governance of forest burning in Southeast Asia is an unfinished story. As the haze problem drives home, the quality of daily life in the streets of Kuala Lumpur or Singapore is intimately linked to what happens deep in the forests of Kalimantan and Sumatra. Just as fire sears its way across ground-level administrative borderlines and demarcations, so too do its airborne effects drift across national boundaries and enmesh themselves in the global atmosphere. In this way, the fearsome dyad of air and fire continues to test interstate capacities, provoking national, regional, and international actors to forge new alliances and agreements.

At the same time, however, there is much in the regional haze problem that is resoundingly familiar: the recalcitrance of territorial sovereignty, nation-based preoccupations with economic performance, and the unfaltering ease with which capital crosses borders relative to those agencies that would constrain or limit its actions.

COMBUSTION AND THE POLITICS OF STRATA

As environmental lawyer Nicholas Robinson (2001, 504) intones on the Indonesian predicament: 'Forest fires are a clear and present danger, not merely to territory within a nation, but globally and transnationally'. Reviewing the use of fire in Indonesia by powerful plantation and logging interests for forest conversion – and its biospheric and atmospheric repercussions – one could hardly disagree. But not all the implications and complications of combustion are quite so *clear and present*. And *territory* – usually taken to mean the exclusive parcelling out of the Earth's surface between more or less sovereign states – is not necessarily the first or last word in political probity, even when these bounded spaces are overflowed by unruly and transgressive forces.

Thus far, for all our attending to irruptions, driftings, circulations – we have still been focused on or over the Earth's surface – on events that play out on a globe whose curvature and contours are laid out before us. But the fires we have been tracking also draw us downward, into an underworld that is both part of the planet's deep past and implicated in its possible futures (Clark 2016; Dalby 2017). For the combustion that is now taking place in Indonesia, I want to suggest, is enmeshed not only with the sociopolitical formations of polities such as Indonesia, Malaysia, or Singapore, but imbricated with the geological formations of the Eocene, the Miocene, and the Pliocene – and whatever epochs are yet to come. And this traversing of the Earth's strata raises challenges to territorial imaginations every bit as profound as flows that move across the planet's surface.

ASEAN's Agreement on Transboundary Haze Pollution was followed by the Peatland Management Strategy (ASEAN 2006). Indonesia contains some fifty-three per cent of the world's tropical peatlands, and much of this area was burnt in the 1982–1983 and 1997–1998 fire seasons. Peat swamps contain considerable biodiversity and are vital components of the global carbon cycle. It is estimated that in 1997 these peat fires generated the equivalent of forty per cent of the world's fossil fuel carbon emissions (Chokkalingam, Kurniawan and Ruchiat 2005). While the draining and firing of Indonesia's peat swamps is a well-publicised environmental threat, less attention has been given to the ignition of coal seams by forest fires. The areas of Sumatra and Kalimantan where forest burning has been most extensive are also the sites of ninety per cent of Indonesia's coal reserves. Here, forest fires frequently ignite exposed coal seams. Whereas forest and peat fires burn out or are extinguished by rainfall, coal fires can smoulder for decades. Researchers estimate that there are up to 3,000 coal fires burning in East Kalimantan, any one of which can ignite new forest fires (Whitehouse and Mulyana 2004). Added to these accidental ignitions is the massive intentional exhuming and burning of fossil fuel deposits. Indonesia – the world's largest exporter of thermal coal – is a significant contributor (Belkin 2009, 261). Going against global trends for downsizing coal reserves, Indonesia is one of few nations for which known reserves have being growing, with deposits estimated at fifty-seven trillion tons in the early 2000s (Fatah 2008). Concentrated in East and South Kalimantan and South Sumatra provinces, annual coal production has risen from 118 million tons (metric tons) in 2005 to a 2014 total of 458 million tons (BP 2015; Fatah 2008).

Coal – like petroleum – is effectively sunshine structured into biomass, compressed, transmuted and sequestered beneath the Earth's surface. Despite the evidence linking the burning of fossil fuels with global environmental change, mobilising nation-states into effective action to mitigate these changes has proved to be a formidable political challenge. Although critical scientific witnesses insist that the outcome of the 2015 United Nations Climate Change Conference in Paris is nowhere near sufficient to prevent dangerous climate change (Anderson 2015), it is noteworthy that for the first time delegates agreed in principle that a significant proportion of known fossil fuel reserves must remain in the ground.

ASEAN officials, convening on the sidelines of the Paris Conference, set the region the task of controlling its forest fires and becoming largely "haze free" by 2020. As put by Faizal Parish, director of the Malaysian-based Global Environment Centre: 'Without stopping peatland fires and degradation, ASEAN will continue to be a major emitter of greenhouse gases' (cited in Wangkiat 2015, n.p.). Indonesia's ratification of the Transboundary Haze Pollution Agreement is obviously crucial. Currently the world's sixth-largest emitter of greenhouse gases, Indonesia's ranking is raised by the exceptionally high proportion of its emissions arising from deforestation and land-use change; this also contributes to the excessive level of the carbon intensity of the Indonesian economy. At just under 1,000 tons of greenhouse gas emitted per million dollars of Gross Domestic Product (the global average is 372 tonnes), Indonesia's emissions intensity is by far the highest in the world (Ge et al. 2014).

But what such a hefty deforestation component in the national carbon tally means in practice is that Indonesia and a number of its ASEAN fellow members can propose more-or-less acceptable targets for overall emission reduction *without* significantly cutting fossil fuel consumption (Witoelar in Rappler.com 2015). As Malaysia's undersecretary of climate change makes plain, immediate reductions in the region's reliance on coal are unlikely

(Theseira in Wangkiat 2015). That may be an understatement. The Indonesian government plans to construct 119 new coal-fired power plants, aiming to have twenty gigawatts of coal-fired capacity in place by 2020 (Energy and Climate Intelligence Unit 2016, 20–21). Much of this coal will be supplied from opencast mining and mountain top removal (Fatah 2008). However, there are signs that local resistance over air pollution concerns, especially on the populous island of Java, may be slowing progress (Energy and Climate Intelligence Unit 2016, 20–21).

These matters bring us to a 'deeper' point. Some sixty to seventy million years ago, when the present Indonesian islands were part of the Sundaland subcontinent, rifting tectonic plates in the region produced shallow basins that were infilled by fluvial deposits. Here, peat swamps flourished. Peat development – which eventually produced Indonesia's relatively young coal beds – took place during warm, wet climatic phases strung out over the next forty million years, including the early and mid-Eocene, the late Oligocene, and the early Miocene, tailing off during a glacial episode in global climate, then resuming around five million years ago in the early Pliocene (Belkin 2009; Davis et al. 2007). In short, the events that produced the fossilised hydrocarbons that Indonesia is now adding to the global carbon budget are the product of a tectonically active zone on what is an exceptionally tectonically active and climatically changeable planet. Indeed, as geologist Jan Zalasiewicz (2008, 14–15) reminds us, there is no astronomical body in the solar system whose tectonic plates are so mobile and whose geological strata are so rich and varied as those of the Earth.

From the surface layers of biological life through the shallow stratum of recently deposited peat, and into the multiple strata of coal and its companion lithic layers, the issues of combustion in Indonesia draw us "vertically" into the deep, geological time-space of the Earth (see Clark 2016; Elden 2013b). This is immediately politically troublesome terrain. When it comes to Kalimantan's problem of forest fires that ignite coal seams, or coal seams that set forests alight, it is by no means clear which government departments ought to be responding:

> the Ministry of Energy and Mineral Resources . . . was certain coal fires were not their responsibility. MEMR's position was that while some coal fires occur within the areas of active mines where they have jurisdiction, they most often occur in forests, parklands and rural neighborhoods where they have no jurisdiction. (Whitehouse and Mulyana 2004, 93)

But the problem is bigger than this, for what the issue of extracting and combusting fossil fuels raises is the challenge of how to manage our transactions with the substrata of the Earth. To put it another way, where the haze problem is transboundary in the international sense, the question of whether or not to exhume and burn fossilised hydrocarbons concerns the possible transgressing of *geologic* boundaries. More than a matter of a collection of sovereign states trying to balance their interests, the challenge of "managing" global climate or attempting to "govern" Earth systems requires economic agents to renegotiate their relationships with geologic body of the Earth (see Rockström et al. 2009). Climate change and Earth system change raise the possibility of a dynamic Earth lurching into a new operating state – or even a novel geological epoch, as the Anthropocene thesis proposes. The triggers of these transformations are anthropogenic processes of exhuming and setting to work the productions of past geological periods, and also involve the inherent changeability of the Earth system. And this means that the collective responses called forth are at once a politics of *territory* and *flow* and a politics of *strata* (Clark 2014, 2017).

It is worth recalling that the Earth's atmosphere is also stratified, although these layers flow and recompose themselves much faster than the rocky material of the Earth's crust. Smoke from Indonesia's burning biomass enters turbulent and circulating currents of the troposphere – the lowest, most mobile stratum of the atmosphere – through which it is transported over neighbouring regions. And it is here, in the troposphere, that the two different kinds of "transboundary" combustion we have been talking about come together – burning phytomass on the Earth's surface and burning fossilised hydrocarbons from the subsurface. For especially above dense urban centres such as Singapore or Bangkok, smoke from forest fires forms a toxic admixture with emissions that come from motor vehicles, industry, and other forms of combusting fossil fuel (Aiken 2004).

As a political issue that involves both the stratification of the Earth's lithic crust and the atmosphere, governing fossil fuel combustion would seem to fit well within recent research that explores how the project of making and maintaining territory is now being extended vertically or volumetrically (Elden 2013b). However, little of this work has yet seriously considered the *dynamic* nature of the processes that generate the Earth's rocky or atmospheric strata. For as Earth scientists insist, strata-forming processes are incessantly active, and the uppermost layers of the Earth's crust are in constant interaction with the swirling mobility of air, water, and life at the planet's surface (Zalasiewicz et al. 2017). As a reaction that integrates air, water, life, and rock, fire is a vital part of this dynamic interchange. But if inherited political architectures struggle to come to terms with socio-material processes that overflow bounded constructions of territory, arguably we are even more stymied by the challenge of elemental forces that well up from the geological depths of the Earth. In short, it is not only that modern territorial imaginaries have tended to focus overwhelmingly on land rather than the relatively mobile elements of sea, air, ice, or life; it is that *terra* itself – viewed in the long term – is a much more shifting and mutable entity than most political thinkers or practitioners have assumed. In the concluding section, I tease out some of these themes in the context of the fraught politics of Indonesia's multiple layers of combustion. Here, too, I return to the idea that all politics is, sooner or later, pyropolitical, and consider the urgency and complexity of today's pyropolitics.

CONCLUSION:
PYROPOLITICS FOR A DYNAMIC PLANET

Fire does have a "positive" role in the iconography of European politics and culture. An inextinguishable flame symbolises belonging to family, community, and nation. As Martin Heidegger muses, 'the hearth, the homestead of the homely, is Being itself in whose light and radiance, glow and warmth, all beings already have gathered' (cited in Capobianco 2010, 62). This hearth around which the community gathers – the ontological ground of the polis – is emphatically an enclosed and domesticated fire. In the Western tradition, going back to the Greeks, the hearth is literally fixed to the ground, and in this way it is 'identified with the earth, immobile and stable' (Beistegui 1997, 139). Contained fire, in short, is the symbolic counterpart of territorial boundedness and anchoring in an enduring Earth. However, for all Heidegger's commitment to Earth-rooted community, even he recognised that there was something *unheimlich* – uncanny, unsettling – in the way that flame and smoke left the terrestrial abode and wafted up into the heavens (Beistegui 1997, 139).

Leave perennially soggy Europe and venture into the wet-dry pulsing of the tropics and fire becomes "unhomely" in ways Heidegger never dreamed of. But these are latitudes in which there are peoples at home with open fire, cultures for whom selectively burning vegetated land has long been the fulcrum of their sustenance and relations with a living world. Fire for them is a means of carving out and shaping territory – but territory that tends to be porously bounded and inclined to move in sync with environmental rhythms and flows. In the "environmental era", however, European bias against burning biomass still commands authority. 'A world war fought on its own soil and the postwar loss of empire did little to diminish Europe's influence on global fire', laments Pyne (1997a, 532). Shades of lingering European fire aversion might be discerned in the 2008 UN Initiative on Reducing Emissions from Deforestation and Forest Degradation (REDD), launched in 2008, which is currently rolling out financial incentives across the developing world to promote the shift from swiddening to more commercial agroecosystems. Indonesia, a prime recipient, hosts forty-four projects.

As Alan Ziegler and his colleagues (2012, 3095) observe: 'Indonesia's REDD+ strategy proposes agricultural intensification (permanent cropland) and planting of oil palm and trees for pulp and timber (plantations) as alternatives to unsustainable forest harvest and slash-and-burn agriculture'. Contra REDD directives, their study of rural Indonesia demonstrates the superiority of long fallow swidden systems over monoculture and agroforestry for long-term carbon capture. Ziegler et al. (2012, 3096) encourage further research that delves beneath the cycling of carbon through living phytomass, calling for 'particular focus on below-ground carbon, which can sway decisions regarding optimal land use'. This conclusion resonates with earlier work by atmospheric chemist and Anthropocene theorist Paul Crutzen, who questioned the validity of studies derogating tropical swidden agriculture and suggested that some forms of burning biomass were 'possible net sinks for atmospheric CO_2' (Seiler and Crutzen 1980, 241). As Johann Goldammer and Paul Crutzen (1993, 11) later conclude in work that sets out to integrate the fields of wildland fire science and atmospheric chemistry, 'the preservation and study of fire will assist humanity in its larger stewardship of the Earth'.

The connection, via Crutzen, to the Anthropocene thesis is significant, for it reminds us that fire is intimately linked to the different states through which the Earth system has passed and to processes of geological transition. As Pyne (2014, n.p.) puts it, 'the fires of the Carboniferous period differ from those of the Permian. Miocene fires rippling over grasslands differed from Eocene fires that had no grasses to burn'. Just as fire flourishes at junctures in the planet's mobile crust – the volcano-strewn East African Rift Valley, the Pacific Ring of Fire – so too does it proliferate at transitional points in the Earth system. Fire, observes Pyne (1994, 890), 'appears more profusely during times of rapid and extreme climatic change'. And this is one reason why fire-wielding hominids need to be ready, need to know what they are doing with fire, need the full range of burning practices at their disposal.

For *Homo sapiens* across most of the world, fire has been the pre-eminent means of dealing with climatic irregularity. Skilled application of fire is a way to massage the Earth's sustaining capacities, to care for land, to forestall larger, fiercer conflagrations: in other words, a way to forge and hold territory that befits a dynamic planet. This is why peoples who find their customary burning practices prohibited or have alien fires introduced into their world tend to respond with the ploy they know best. They set fire.

Michael Marder's (2015) searching ruminations on the "pyropolitical" capture the insurrectionary connotations of fire. But as with most Eurocentric accounts of fire these reflections lean towards the metaphorical rather than the pragmatic – although he is surely right to insist 'that pyropolitics is co-extensive with the concept *and* the event of the political' (p. 10). Whereas Marder's collective actors tend to play variations on the theme of fire's

insurgent associations, other analysts of political fire emphasise the inseparability of flame as symbolic and material force. As an expression of agrarian
discontent, rural incendiarism belongs 'to that shadowy realm between crime
and protest where it is often no easy matter to tell the two apart' (Rude cited
in Kuhlken 1999, 344–45). Christian Kull (2002, 949) adds that what may
first appear to be acts of politically motivated arson may well turn out to be
'straightforward livelihood practice': that is, traditional land management
techniques rendered clandestine and revitalised under cover of social unrest.

Indonesian fire is all this and more. Researchers on Java in the 1960s noted
that fire was used for clearing land, 'for hunting, for pleasure, for pestering
neighbors or neighboring villages' (van Steenis in Kuhlken 1999, 357). In
Kalimantan and Sumatra, clashing land developers and small farmers each
use fire to assert their rights: 'Companies used it to stake claims to locally
held land, and rural dwellers, embittered by several decades of marginal-
ization and widespread appropriation of their natural resources, used it to
destroy estate crops and timber plantations' (Aiken 2004, 74). As complex in
motivation as they are in physical-material composition, such fires tend to be
extremely difficult to extinguish.

It is crucial to remember that fires which burn live or recently living
phytomass are part of the Earth's constant solar income, whereas fires that
consume fossilised biomass dig into a kind of geological solar capital. While
they both release the energy locked in carbon bonds, these fires have very
different implications for the Earth system. Pyne (1997a, 2001) insists that
one of Western modernity's greatest mistakes is to imagine that the contained
fire of combusting fossil fuels can replace the open fire of burning vegetation. Across much of the Earth's surface – he is not writing about permanent
conversion of forested land here – there is far too much fossil-fuelled flame
but not nearly enough blazing phytomass. And both the superfluity and the
shortage are profoundly politically challenging.

Among ASEAN members, the ongoing tussle with the transboundary haze
problem is a reminder of how contentious it is to deal with fire within the
borders of another nation. At the same time, the unresolved issue of global
climate change demonstrates the diabolical difficulty of trying to manage
how nation-states and non-state actors interchange with the Earth's substrata.
For there are two different but enmeshed transboundary problems here: the
challenge of navigating the boundaries between sociopolitical formations and
the challenge of negotiating the boundaries between geological formations.
The pyropolitics of *territory* and the pyropolitics of *strata* are not yet "talking" to each other nearly as much as they need to be.

Mounting scientific evidence suggests that the relatively stable climate
the Earth has enjoyed over the past 10,500 years may be ending, and that we
should expect more instability in the Earth system. Fire is one of our species'

time-honoured means of dealing with environmental variability, but a changing Earth system will inevitably bring new and strange fires. Fire can never simply be a political act, but is always also to some degree an experiment: a symbolic gesture as well as a medium of material intervention, learning, trial and error (Clark 2008, 2015). In the Indonesian archipelago, pyropolitics poses difficult questions about who gets to experiment, where, and when. At the same time, it raises the question of how to deal with experiments that fall short or go awry – as they surely will, sooner or later. For on planet that is itself in constant transformation, working with fire comes with no assurance or guarantee.

Part II

ENVIRONMENTS

Preface

Philip Steinberg

If one were to produce a twenty-first-century update to Raymond Williams's classic *Keywords* (1976/1983), a new entry would be needed for the word "environment". Over the forty years since Williams first published his book, few words have so completely reflected (and precipitated) a transformation in the ways in which scholars, politicians, authors, artists, and people going about their everyday lives understand and attempt to shape the world.

In that time, we have become acutely aware of the complexities and inter-dependencies of earth-ocean-atmosphere ecologies (Steffen et al. 2004), the vulnerabilities of these ecologies and their potential to endanger as well as sustain human life (Carson 1962) and the realisation that humans are trans-forming linked biogeophysical systems at an unprecedented rate (Crutzen 2002). As a result, it has become *de rigeur* for any proposal for the sustain-able development of economies or societies to proclaim an attentiveness to "environmental" concerns. To train the next generation of experts with the appropriate environmental sensitivities, universities have developed an exten-sive repertoire of degree programmes dedicated to environmental studies, science, planning, management, or humanities. In turn, these programmes' graduates are employed by a plethora of government agencies and non-government organisations dedicated to the environment's protection. Plan-ning can no longer occur without consideration of a project's environmental impacts, and plans must contain proposals for remediating those impacts.

But what precisely is this "environment", and how can a consideration of its many meanings enhance our understanding of territory? A starting point might be to think of environment as *nature*, which *does* appear in Williams's listing. Williams (1983, 219) identifies nature as 'perhaps the most complex word in the [English] language' as it refers simultaneously to essence, inher-ent force, and underlying matter. However, there are significant differences between the two terms. Nature, whether referenced as essence, force, or matter (or a combination of the three), suggests the ideal of a (meta)physical universe that ontologically and chronologically precedes society and that serves as an underlying condition or resource base for human existence. An environment, by contrast, is inherently interactive. While natures are *used*, environments are *lived*.

Another similar term is "ecology", which was one of the twenty-one keywords added in Williams's 1983 revised edition. Again, although there are overlaps with the concept of "environment", the two are hardly synonymous. Ecology implies a degree of order, complementarity, and underlying logic (and hence constraints) amid the intersection of elements and processes. An environment, by contrast, is indeterminate. It is made and continually remade through ongoing interactions between human communities and the surrounding biogeophysical world, with few limiting factors. As such, an environment is not simply an ecology but a *space*, an ever-imminent arena of embodiment and interaction (Massey 2005).

Environments are also *atmospheres*, structures of understanding that exist prior to human encounter but that also are transformed by that encounter (Anderson 2009). Atmospheres neither exist purely in the material nor in the immaterial, neither purely as an external object nor as that object's subjective experience. Existing between the subject and the object, atmospheric properties structure actions, but they also structure what one thinks is possible.

In short, an environment is simultaneously nature, space, and atmosphere. As such, an environment can be arena, object, or force of social organisation and contestation. In many cases, these contestations are mobilised by efforts to define the environment's boundaries, and these include both its spatial boundaries and its conceptual boundaries. Thus, in the next chapter of this volume, Clayton Whitt profiles conflicts in Bolivia over not just *where* mud is but *what* mud is, as land or water, surface or volume. In the chapter after that, on flood control infrastructure in Canada, Stephanie Kane asks not just *where* a flood plain is but *what* it is, a hazard or resource, a norm or an exception. Following that, Ross Exo Adams explores the historic conceptualisation of the urban as a marine environment, a history that challenges accepted notions of both urban and maritime natures and spaces. In the part's final chapter, on Arctic ice islands, Johanne Bruun and Philip Steinberg chronicle scientists, politicians, and jurists debating not just *where* ice islands are and who controls them but *what* an ice island foundationally is vis-à-vis other environments, geophysically (with reference to glaciers, ice floes, oceans, islands, molecules, and ships), geopolitically (with reference to territories, extra-territories, and non-territories), and scientifically (whether as objects for facilitating science or as objects of science).

By exploring various attempts to write order to space by defining the conceptual and spatial parameters of earthly environments, the contributors to this part all explore environments as *territories*. Indeed, it is in the territorial aspect of their investigations that the complexity of the environment, as a lived, indeterminate arena, most clearly contrasts with the discrete resources of nature that are idealised by those who would will its social control. While "nature" may be broken into resources, an environment is always an assemblage. Indeed, none of the environments considered in the following chapters ever exists in a pure state. Mud alternately hardens and becomes land-like and then becomes water-logged and viscous. It eventually disintegrates into its constitutive parts, flowing water and deposited silt, but these then recombine in an ongoing cycle that perpetually transforms both landscapes and lifescapes, and which itself is continually interrupted and manipulated by human intervention. Similarly, engineering infrastructures fail and are rebuilt, cities are defined with varying relations to the ocean, ice melts and freezes. Attempts to calculate and order space (that is, to implement territory) that are based on models that assume flat, solid, and stable environments quickly run aground when one extends beyond the flat, two-dimensional conceptualisation of *terra*. Environments are neither singular nor stable.

Situated between the "element" and the "edge", conceptually as well as in the structure of this book, the "environment" is neither essence nor limn. Rather, a focus on environments highlights the complexities that emerge as politics is enacted across a range of landscapes and seascapes. In mud, flood plains, cities, and ice, environments challenge us to consider the ways in which territory both relies upon and exceeds its underpinning materiality.

Chapter 6

MUDFLATS

Fluid Terrain: Climate Contestations in the Mudflats of the Bolivian Highlands

Clayton Whitt

Anthropogenic climate change transcends territory. Once greenhouse gases such as carbon dioxide are expelled from industrial smokestacks, burning forests, or the tail pipes of the Earth's 1.2 billion cars, they mix into the atmosphere and circulate, disregarding the lines of the map and insinuating themselves into the most far-flung reaches of the planet. Nowhere is spared a changed atmosphere. Even so, the effects of climate change are not uniform from place to place. Rather, a disparate geography of fragmented effects arises in the intersections between things and beings.

To the body, all climate change is local, even though bodies are placed in terrains and may be located within territorial boundaries. It is at the intersection of terrain, territory, and bodies that I seek to shed light on how climate change can unsettle notions of territory through material transformations. I focus on how practices of territory are situated among different material bodies, reflecting on the argument that territory is an historically-situated political technology that 'is itself a process, made and remade, shaped and shaping, active and reactive' (Elden 2013a, 17). I examine a dispute witnessed in 2014 during a year of field research in El Choro, a rural municipality in highland western Bolivia. For two days of that year, I joined local residents as they blockaded a bridge on the main road to El Choro with vehicles, rocks, burning tyres, and their bodies. Their aim was to prevent a construction company from removing gravel for a highway building project. Over the course of the blockade, I spoke with participants and leaders, and listened to negotiations with representatives from the construction company and the national highway agency. I came to realise that the dispute took place precisely at the intersection of fluid terrain and territory. Blockaders took action, they said, to assert control over their collective indigenous territory and demand compensation from the construction company for damaging their road and removing gravel from their region. In return, the highway builders asserted the state's imperative to integrate national territory through road building and El Choro's responsibility to contribute to the effort.

Amid the confluence of materialities enlisted in this conflict, one liminal substance – part liquid and part solid – emerged as central to the ways in which entities were contesting the territorialisation of space: *mud*. I wondered if perhaps the mud upon which we were standing was both the sticky backdrop for the blockade and central to the dispute. Connecting mud to the intensified midsummer rains associated with anthropogenic climate change in the Bolivian Andes, I started to think about its fluid materiality as an intersection between the Earth's modified atmosphere and the complex politics of territory. From such musing and by reference to this specific dispute, in this chapter I seek to trace the emergent localised politics of climate change in the mud under people's feet and in the ways that they invoked the fluidity of terrain alongside different conceptions of territory. As I will show, the very materiality of what territory encircles acts on and is refracted through bodies that act in political ways, and it is among the ways that territory is made and remade, and is active and reactive.

Diverse literatures document the experiences of the body in mud and the emotional effects of the association between mud and conditions such as immobility and uncleanliness; this is particularly so in relation to soldiers' bodies in warfare (Das 2005; Gregory 2015; Ugolini 2014; Wood 2006) and natural disasters (Forth 2009). I see mud as a mundane entity with a subtly transformative capacity related to changes in climate. So when mud manifests, how does it influence politics? How could mud's "intensification" – in volume, flow, viscosity, even in its sheer presence – intersect with practices of territory? In addressing these questions, I offer up to the broader literature on climate change and its relationship to politics and spatiality a small-scale and grounded consideration of the body's experience under environmental transformations.[1] By focusing on experiences such as a body slogging through mud, or a dumper truck's tyres chewing up a muddy road, I want to ask how climate change influences day-to-day politics in a place such as the study village in El Choro municipality. Such consideration, however, must avoid what Mike Hulme (2011) has called climate reductionism: the tendency to envision humanity's future as solely shaped by climate and climate change, erasing agency and ingenuity as well as diverse influences such as politics and ecology (see also Dalby 2013). One way to avoid this reductionism is to focus on people's affective relationships with their surrounding environments. Such a focus creates space for webs of intermingling influences rather than mechanical linkages; such matters are central here.

As this chapter proceeds, then, I first introduce the field site, El Choro, and consider how the current effects of climate change are inscribed into the terrain through heavy rains and thick mud. I then reflect on bodies and mud and the ways in which to conceptualise their relationships with each other in space, asking how such relationships emerge in politics. Finally, I move to my case and show how body/mud politics interweaves in and shapes a territorial dispute. I argue that one way the materiality encircled by territory emerges in the production of that territory is by refraction through bodies, illustrating entanglements between bodies, terrain, and territory in their unsettling and unsettledness.

CLIMATE CHANGE IN THE MUDFLATS

In 2013 and 2014, I carried out fieldwork among the Quechua-speaking people of the rural municipality of El Choro, located in the Altiplano region of western Bolivia. The Altiplano is a treeless intermontane plain 3,750 metres (12,303 feet) above sea level and ringed by the peaks of the central Andes. The municipal territory of El Choro begins close to the edge of the city of Oruro, capital of Oruro Department, one of Bolivia's nine departments, the primary subnational division of territory. It stretches sixty kilometres (thirty-seven miles) south from Lake Uru Uru along the Desaguadero River until it reaches the north-western shores of the central Altiplano's principal body of water, the brackish and polluted Lake Poopó. This region is a floodplain, a former lakebed of soft, sandy soil, devoid of trees. The main vegetation types are sharp, straw-like plants known locally as *paja* and small woody shrubs that people call *leña*, the Spanish word for "firewood", reflecting its primary use. The chief economic activities in El Choro are raising sheep and cows for meat and milk and growing quinoa, formerly a subsistence crop but now mostly for export. Livestock production is undergirded by introduced forage crops such as alfalfa and barley, as well as by endemics such as *kawchi* that take on the high salt content of the soil and are credited by shepherds with producing local sheep meat's salty flavour.

On many occasions I heard farmers proclaim that El Choro's sustenance depended on the municipality's extensive irrigation system, which some people referred to as El Choro's "backbone". The irrigation system consists of a web of canals that deliver water from the Desaguadero River to hundreds of farmsteads spread throughout the municipality. These canals, many hand-dug and over fifty years old, are managed by local canal zones, organisations comprising dues-paying members who elect their leadership, manage maintenance projects, organise irrigation turns, and coordinate development and agricultural improvement projects. Farmers use the canals to fill watering holes for livestock during the dry season and to irrigate fields of food crops and forage, especially at the margins of the growing season when rainfall is unreliable. While the canals are critically important sources of water during dry periods and smooth out the vagaries of annual climate variability, water quality is under intense pressure from pollution linked to upstream discharges of untreated mine waste into the Desaguadero watershed (Garcia et al. 2008; Quintanilla et al. 1995; Ramos Ramos et al. 2012). Repeated cycles of irrigation on land with poor drainage leave a white crust of salt and pollutants on the soil, which many farmers told me could eventually take the land out of production.

Even as the irrigation system becomes less dependable, anthropogenic climate change is reducing the reliability of rainfall. Current climate change literature for the Altiplano region shows that the hydrological cycle is changing. Rainfall is decreasing in the early rainy season, which comes in the late spring and early summer months between October and December, but so far there is no net decrease in annual rainfall (Valdivia et al. 2010, 2013). This pattern suggests the rainy season is being contained in a shorter period of time, which many farmers described to me during my fieldwork; as a young farmer named Eligio reported, 'four months of rain now fall in two months'. Farmers told me that they have to delay planting because of low rainfall early in summer. When the rain does come in January and February, lands may be subject to flooding. By the end of the growing season, farmers stare down fall frosts while crops are at the final stages of maturation. Many farmers described such changes by comparing them with memories of a more predictable climate. They said that everything was 'mixed up' (*mezclado*) now – the weather increasingly perceived to be occurring 'out of season' (*fuera de su estación* or *fuera de su temporada*), or that weather was 'no longer seasonal at all' (*el tiempo ya no es estacional*). 'This weather isn't what our grandparents saw', a local leader named Fabián told me.

Predictably, when rain mixes with the old lakebed, it creates a muddy mess that ebbs and flows, and during some years such conditions can last for many months in the middle of the growing season. Mud is not new with climate change, but for rural Altiplano residents one of the tangible and unavoidable effects from multiple days of intense rainfall is the transformation of the surface of the earth into fluid terrain. Mud is an immediate, daily experience for bodies mutually bound with the terrain during the climate change–altered rainy season. It is also political.

TERRAIN AND AFFECTIVE POLITICS

Stuart Elden (2013b, 49) has asked, 'How would our thinking of geo-power, geo-politics and geo-metrics work if we took the earth; the air and the subsoil; questions of land, terrain, territory; earth processes and understandings of the

world as the central terms at stake, rather than a looser sense of the "global"?'
Philip Steinberg and Kimberly Peters (2015) take up this question in developing a range of ideas about "wet ontologies", wherein they use the oceans to
conceptualise space in terms of fluidity, churning, and chaos, bringing materiality into considerations of volume and territory. They argue that thinking
about space and territory using the ocean unearths 'a material perspective that
acknowledges the volumes within which territory is practiced: a world of fluidities where place is forever in formation and where power is simultaneously
projected on, through, in, and about space' (p. 261). They draw attention to a
post-humanist politics generated in fluid materialisation, and by reference to
surfing, swimming, and kayaking consider how fluid materiality is embodied
by the human actor.

Exploring the role of mud in a territorial dispute, I seek to build upon
the question of how fluid materiality and churning can be embodied experiences that have important political and territorial dimensions. I argue that an
important part of terrain's emergence in territorial disputes is through bodily
relationships that develop with the terrain itself and that are then refracted into
political action. First, however, it is important to note that mud has distinct
qualities as an intermediate state that is not-quite-land and not-quite-water;
one with some capacities of both. Depending on elements such as moisture
content, soil type, and topography, as well as one's mode of movement, mud
can be solid enough to traverse with minor inconvenience or impassably
viscous or flowing. Over time, mud fluctuates widely while still holding a
state recognisable *as mud*. Mud is the materialisation of weather into the
earth; rainstorms pass by but their effects shift into a new timescale as the
earth remains persistently sticky long after clouds have cleared. Even when
mud dries, it leaves enduring marks – solidified undulations, ridges, pits, and
crinkles – that call to mind the muddy past and the potentially muddy future
and point toward land's constant capacity to make fluid shifts. Mud reveals
how, as Tim Ingold (2011, 130) writes, 'The ground is not the surface of
materiality itself, but a textured composite of diverse materials that are grown,
deposited and woven together through a dynamic interplay across the permeable interface between the medium and the substances with which it comes
into contact'. Land is not as solid as it appears; it is, as Ingold also observes,
'the more or less ephemeral congelate of a generative movement' (p. 24).

The ephemeral solidity of land, underlined by mud, highlights how terrain –
which is defined by Gastón Gordillo (2014) as the tangible space of the
world – is unruly and ever-changing. Gordillo (2015, 23) highlights what he
calls terrain's 'pure multiplicity' and argues that it is 'an unassailable con-
stellation of very diverse materialities, objects, and vectors of force *affecting each other* through physical contact, collisions, and friction' (original
emphasis). This is what Ingold (2011, 71) calls the domain of entanglement,

where everything in the world meets and intertwines, including organisms. This entanglement encompasses the relationships between terrain and other physical bodies of the planet, including bodies of water and air that affect, shape, and mix boundlessly with each other. As earth, atmosphere, and water intermix their differing forces, materialities, and porosities, they transform one another. Thus on the Bolivian Altiplano, the sun-baked earth yields when spring rains halt the long, dry winter. Under wind, water, and gravity, fresh mud finds new mobilities and motions in what had just seemed as solid earth.

What binds terrain and bodies together can be analysed using what Gordillo (2015) calls an affective geometry, a concept he draws from Spinoza, and which speaks to how bodies relate to each other in space. According to Spinoza (1677), bodies are not closed and bounded systems but rather are open and exist relationally with other bodies; they are capable of affecting each other, or increasing and decreasing the capacity of other bodies to act. For Spinoza, according to Deleuze, a 'body can be anything; it can be an animal, a body of sounds, a mind or an idea; it can be a linguistic corpus, a social body, a collectivity' (Deleuze 1988, 127); it is the capacity to affect another body that 'defines a body in its individuality' (p. 123). Such diverse bodies affect each other in ways that are inherently unpredictable, open and open-ended – for the full range of capabilities and capacities of the body are unknown (Spinoza 1677, III, ii). In turn, the unique 'lived past' of each body shapes its capacities to affect and be affected (Massumi 2015, 49). Gordillo's appeal to a Spinozan affective geometry points to the nondeterministic spatial arrangements of human and non-human bodies, and focuses on the more-than-discursive ways in which bodies relate in their openness to each other. The terrain meets with and influences air and water, and human bodies, increasing and decreasing their capacities to act.

These relationships between bodies have political dimensions that, as I will argue, translate into the making and unmaking of territory. Affective politics is, as Massumi (2015, 56) describes, 'an art of emitting the interruptive signs, triggering the cues, that attune bodies while activating their capacities differentially'; due to affect's openness, such attunements have uncertain results. Massumi (2015, 55–56) suggests that even if they are 'cued in concert' bodies do not all act the same because each carries a different set of 'tendencies and capacities'. Other authors argue that affective attunement is not only part of politics, but it is predominant. For instance, Jon Beasley-Murray (2010, 132) writes that history 'is no more or less than the recomposition or movement of bodies, a series of modulations in and through affect. Anything else is mere tableau'. Whether or not one wants to go that far, accounting for affective politics invites consideration of how physical and spatial transformations such as climate change can influence the politics of territory in more-than-discursive ways. By their open, undetermined nature, such affective capacities are difficult to pinpoint and put into words, but this does not make them any less consequential. To paraphrase Jane Bennett (2010, 4), the physical world issues a call, even if we do not understand what it is saying. When people respond to the call of mud, bodies are attuned, and the result is messy political negotiations of people with each other and between people and mud. One result from these messy negotiations is that the unruliness of ever-fluctuating terrain is refracted into the process of territory via the relationships that emerge between terrain and bodies.

THE CONTESTED ROAD

As the condor flies, the village of El Choro, capital of the eponymous municipality, is forty-five kilometres (twenty-eight miles) south of the city of Oruro, separated from it only by the flat terrain of the Altiplano and the marshlands of Lake Uru Uru. Oruro is close enough to light up the northern horizon at night, and an observer in the village can see the brightly illuminated Virgin Mary statue that stands forty-five metres (147 feet) on a hilltop above the city. Despite such proximity, the journey from village to city can take an hour at best or longer. A road platform was built crossing the flood-prone plain a few decades ago, supplanting the improvised dry season truck tracks that in turn had replaced the donkey trains of earlier years. Yet the gravel surface of the road receives scant maintenance and is deeply pitted; during the rainy season parts of the road are chewed into muddy bogs.

In 2013, the road became the site of conflict. Shortly after my arrival in the village late that year, I noticed that many dumper trucks entered and exited the main municipal road every day, hauling material out of a site near a community about halfway between the village of El Choro and Oruro. I soon learned that the dumper truck drivers were working on a road project about forty kilometres (twenty-five miles) to the northwest. The government of Oruro Department had contracted a private company called Congar to pave one of the final stretches of the international highway connecting the city of Oruro to the town of Pisiga, on the Chilean border, a project started in the late 1990s but still unfinished.[2] Congar was granted the contract in 2013 after the government rescinded it from the previous contractor for advancing too slowly. With a mandate to finish in fourteen months, Congar rushed to establish local material sources. In July 2013, it reached an agreement with members of a settlement called Cruce Belén in the municipality of El Choro to provide construction aggregate for a fourteen-kilometre (nine-mile) stretch of the highway. At the time, local media reported that people in Cruce Belén agreed to stop obstructing the removal of material from a nearby hill in exchange for benefits such as guaranteed maintenance of the main road and enrolment in a rural settlement electrification program. Regional leaders and the media portrayed the highway as critical for international trade related to a broader three-nation project, the *corredor transoceánico*, to connect the Pacific and Atlantic coasts of South America through the heart of the continent; the project was a key plank of Oruro Department's efforts to be at the centre of Bolivia's economic integration. This portrayal was also evident in a 2012 editorial on Oruro's road building efforts in the local newspaper *La Patria* that stated, perhaps with some hyperbole, that 'Oruro turns out to be the heart of the country where the veins transporting progress arrive and from where they radiate out to the four cardinal points of our nation' (*La Patria* 2012).[3] Along with other projects of integration, such as Oruro's new international airport, the Pisiga highway was a bid for Oruro Department to be at the centre of improvements in Bolivia's arterial flow. It is likewise reminiscent of other great road building projects of the twentieth century, which were also depicted using anatomical analogies (Merriman 2007).

In a broad sense, road building in western Bolivia has public support, and expanding the road network has been a centrepiece of the national government's economic development goals under the leadership of President Evo Morales and the left-wing political party Movement Toward Socialism (Movimiento al Socialismo, or MAS).[4] But these projects met with friction when they encountered the sticky bindings of bodies and earth. In the case of the Oruro-Pisiga highway, in order to haul the material out from Cruce Belén to the worksite, Congar's heavy dumper trucks drove dozens of times a day up and down a seventeen-kilometre (eleven-mile) stretch of El Choro's unpaved main road. Five months after people in the community of Cruce Belén agreed to allow Congar to remove aggregate, residents of the municipality of El Choro blocked trucks from entering the removal site for the second time, demanding improvements to the road.[5] A committee spearheaded by the governor of Oruro led negotiations. As reported in *La Patria*, a member of Oruro Department's legislative assembly visited the community and implored people to lift the blockade so that this project could proceed on the basis that it 'is fundamental for the development of Oruro and desired by the whole population'.[6] Eventually residents agreed to lift the blockade in exchange for the construction of a 600-metre (1,968-feet) stretch of road connecting the community to the nearby cantonal capital of Crucero Belén.

A few months later, however, I heard rumbles that Congar's work was again to be blockaded. The action materialised in late March 2014. On the morning of the blockade I listened to a radio programme out of Oruro as local indigenous leader Mama Ruperta[7] made a case for action against Congar that focused on the instability of the muddy earth. She explained that the decision had come from the indigenous authorities in the *ayllu*[8] of Crucero Belén, who had traditional jurisdiction over settling territorial disputes in the territory where the aggregate production site was located. She used a phrase that I was to hear time and time again that day, referring to what happens when Congar's dumper trucks intersect with the fluidity of the terrain: she said that the main road had been worn down 'all the way to the earth' (*hasta la tierra*) and that in the midst of a heavy rainy season it was just mud and barely passable in places. Mama Ruperta's evocative phrase, 'all the way down to the earth', pointed to the feelings of insecurity that resulted from the road's ephemeral solidity; her comment emphasised that while the earth was soft and unreliable for transit, without proper care interventions to overcome this softness also yielded over time to moisture, mud, and dumper truck tyres. The blockade, she explained, was to demand that Congar carry out its obligation to maintain the road and put pressure on the government to follow through on a planned paving project. The official call to blockade, signed by local indigenous authorities and later read on-air by the radio announcer, also reflected this feeling of insecurity in relation to the road's soft surface: 'Brothers and sisters, we're supporting the construction of the highway to Pisiga, but our road is deteriorating, and there are places where it is worn down to the earth'. The call to blockade the project reflected how mobility is differentiated and relational, reinforcing or challenging power relations depending on context (Adey 2006; Cresswell 1996). For people in El Choro, expanded mobility for Bolivia at large meant that they faced diminished mobility at home through the wearing down of the muddy road. So to contest this possibility, they planned a collective immobilisation of their own, targeting Congar's trucks and the highway project by closing access to and through their territory.

Later that morning, I arrived at the blockade on my bicycle. The site was seventeen kilometres (eleven miles) north of the village of El Choro, at the intersection of the main road with the connector leading out to the village of Crucero Belén and onward to the small community where Congar had set up its machinery. Immediately north of the intersection on the main road was a bridge over a canal that Herminio, a bus driver and local official, had blocked with his bus. Congar's dumper trucks stacked up on the connector; before long, eight or so were parked in a line, their drivers milling about, performing maintenance on their trucks, and chatting with the blockade participants, who continued to arrive by bicycle, motorcycle and minivan. Blockaders stood on the leeward side of Herminio's bus, sheltering from the smoke of two burning tyres that served as a sort of beacon at the north end of the canal bridge.

Soon the first participant meeting of the day was called, one of a series first to set the terms of the blockade and later to negotiate with visiting representatives from Congar, the government of Oruro Department, and the national highway agency (ABC, or *Administradora Boliviana de Carreteras*). Over the course of those meetings, I noted how participants situated the debate in terms of territory and terrain. Many speakers' appeals echoed Mama

Ruperta's phrase from the radio that morning and invoked continuing insecurity and fear of immobility: the road had been worn down to the earth by the combination of rains and the passage of heavy dumper trucks. It was muddy and difficult to traverse after storms. The mud persisted and in dry times left a legacy of wear and potholes. With their access to El Choro threatened, participants demanded that Congar fix the road with a new gravel layer on the entire seventeen-kilometre stretch that their dumper trucks regularly utilised. If not, blockaders were prepared indefinitely to prevent Congar from having further access to their territory, an action that threatened the national government's efforts to further integrate some of its remote territories in western Oruro Department as well as to improve international territorial connections through the new highway.

The concerns about mud and mobility that I heard at the blockade were not unique to this dispute. Throughout my field experience, I found that mud related to much anxiety and stress during the rainy season, a time so muddy that some people referred to it as the mud season (*época del barro*). Mud inhibited many aspects of daily life through its viscosity, depth, and immensity. After thick rains, getting ever worse under climate change, farmers had difficulty travelling between their fields, which could be far outside the village, many kilometres apart from each other, and interspersed with muddy expanses. Those fields were mostly accessible by bare tracks or bike paths worn into the surface of the Altiplano over the years, and were impassable on bicycles or motorcycles after the churn of a heavy rain, since their tyres either sank into the depths of the muck or dredged up so much sticky material that they became caked and immobilised. It was also difficult for livestock to graze in deep mud. As a herder named Eduardo told me when I encountered him on a particularly muddy day, 'Imagine the cows, they're 400 kilos [880 pounds], walking around in the mud. They just sink in'. He told me the cows crushed alfalfa plants into the muck, making it necessary to herd them to firmer fields, a slow and difficult journey in such conditions. And the pervasiveness of mud – its persistent ubiquity in the old lakebed after heavy rainfall – made the search for less muddy ground a fruitless effort at times. The intensifying rains of climate change made full access to the territory of El Choro more and more difficult during certain times of year.

The heavy mud also made ploughing nearly impossible because tractors churned into the fluid terrain and became stuck, causing operators to cancel or postpone many days of work or even to abandon machines and tools in muddy fields until conditions improved. Such delays in ploughing meant late planting, and that could prove costly if frosts arrived early. I found that people talked about the mud much as they talked about the weather: which mud followed and materialised in the terrain but then shifted into its own time scale, making the effects of *days* of rain last for *weeks* in the landscape. In conversation people predicted mud intensity, expressed concern that a coming rain storm would make it worse, assessed mud conditions before heading out for work, and even opened passing conversations on the road with quips such as 'a lot of mud today' or 'too much mud!' Typical was a brief conversation I had with an acquaintance named Salvador when I met him walking on a muddy road near the village late in January 2014. After greetings, he pointed at my tall, mud-caked boots, and commented that he liked them. 'Yes', I said, 'well, I need these because it is very muddy, isn't it?' This observation seemed to open the floodgates for Salvador. 'Yes', he said, raising and quickening his speech, 'it rained all night, there is a lot of mud, just too much mud! It has rained harder than normal, there is so much mud, you cannot use a bicycle or a motorcycle but rather have to walk everywhere. That's why I'm walking'. He looked up toward the half-clouded sky and exclaimed, 'Let there be sun today! It needs to dry out a bit'.

Salvador's comments show how mud is an experience that forces the body into intimacy with it since two-wheeled vehicles cannot pass and one is forced to walk through mud's depth and stickiness. Mud brought on bodily-affective discomfort through such encounters and through their anticipation as one stared out at approaching rain clouds or, as we shall see, the rutted road worn down to the earth. Salvador's comments also reflect Peter Merriman's contention (2012, 9) that 'There is no mobility *in*, *across* or *through* space and time, only movements *with*, which are marked by emerging rhythms, forces, spatialities, affects, gellings, temporalities and much more' (original emphasis). Salvador does not merely move through space; the viscosity of the mud does not allow this. Rather, to move Salvador must continually negotiate *with* the mud and its rhythms, forces, temporalities, and affects. Mud is the vehicle translating between Salvador's body and the ground, sticking him to the earth, binding bodies through mutual porosity, and entangling climate change with daily practices. It is inescapable.

At the blockade, I heard similar concerns about mud's affective stickiness and its rhythms and forces of viscosity and fluidity. The road was supposed to provide year-round access to and through the municipality's territory, but negotiations with the fluid earth were impossible to avoid, and blockaders spoke of the earth churning into an impassable and disquieting mire under the mix of rain and the weight of heavy trucks, or in the words of El Choro's mayor, 'The earth is, sadly, made into mud'. In the words of Salomón, an elderly bus driver, 'We're facing danger on the road. Holes are opening up'. The constant potential for such transformations was reflected at the morning blockade meeting in a comment by an indigenous leader from Crucero Belén, Tata Régulo. He stated that his people would not allow Congar to remove any more material and added, 'Imagine if it rained today, with the road worn down to the earth in some spots, it could interrupt traffic'. It was not raining, but that could change; future mud, like present mud, had affective potential.

Herminio also complained that, with the velocity of the passing dumper trucks, the material of the road achieved new velocities even as it slowed down future vehicular movements: he said that truck tyres frequently kicked up flying rocks that could break other vehicles' windshields. But mud, holes, and flying rocks were not the only fluid transformations at the heart of the dispute. In dry times, blockade participants observed that the material of the road blew away as trucks passed, showering residents, animals, and crops with dust. Tata Régulo said that dust also coated forage crops, with livestock either refusing to eat the dusty plants or suffering ill effects when they did, while schoolchildren breathed in the dust every day as the trucks passed their school.

Pascuala, a woman living close to the road, spoke angrily at the meeting about the dust of the trucks: 'Every day they scrape and scrape the road. There is so much smoke from the dumper trucks that they look like a train. You can't wash or even eat. Whenever I try to complain, they say, "Who are you?" When my house falls down I'm going to live in the town hall. The road looks like a camel's back now. Let these trucks go by in peace or go by no more!' Like other blockaders, Pascuala demanded changes in the trucks' daily negotiations with the earth – that they 'go by in peace' instead of whipping the road into mud and dust that affected local bodies – and if not then she suggested that the municipality's territory should be closed off to Congar, their trucks immobilised for good.

The fluidity of terrain was also cited in blockaders' appeals to protect the territorial integrity of their lands from its material removability. Blockaders saw the material underlying their territory being carted out in the back of dumper trucks with no compensation, and they wanted to put a stop to it. In response to this demand, the highway agency and the departmental government appealed to the importance of national territorial integration through the road project, argued that it was in the national interest and asserted that all Bolivians would benefit; this was why, project representatives said, neither the people of Cruce Belén nor those in El Choro more broadly could be paid for the material that Congar removed. As a Congar executive said on the first day of negotiations, explaining why there was no monetary compensation, 'Supposedly these materials should be provided to the project because the highway is in the national interest, to the benefit of all Bolivians'.

This idea of supporting the broader development aims of the state was also wrapped up in the notion to support the MAS-controlled national government, which was popular in the region. For instance, on the second day of blockade negotiations, an official from Cruce Belén who had consented to the removal of material in the first place, defended his decision to do so. Referring to another community in the same province the official, Quirino, said 'Why has President Evo Morales complained about that community? Because they wanted to sell their gravel! But here in my community, we don't sell it. We're giving a hand to Evo Morales and the process of change. But some people here are against the process of change'.[9] The message was that the municipality of El Choro should freely contribute to the highway project, for to do otherwise was to stand in the way of national progress and therefore the construction of a national territory.

Other members of the community, however, argued that such contributions of material could not be made without broader consultation and consent across the municipality. They sought traction for their argument in the fact that the municipality's territory was contiguous with a registered *Tierra Comunitaria de Origen* (TCO), a category of land ownership recognising indigenous collective land rights established in 1994 constitutional reforms under the first administration of President Gonzalo (Goni) Sánchez de Lozada (Bottazzi and Rist 2012). It was difficult to see how El Choro's TCO played out in daily life, for people there still held individual property titles and worked their parcels individually.[10] Still, while Congar's culpability for damaging the road was the central plank in their case, many blockaders also made this appeal to the legal underpinnings of the TCO in order to accuse Congar of the additional crime of removing collectively owned material without collective consent. Some blockaders may have seen this charge as having a stronger legal basis against Congar than diminished mobility because the TCO had legally recognised collective sovereignty over the material in its territory, while Congar shared culpability for the damage to the road with a range of causes, from weather to climate change to local vehicles. While they focused on collective harms to mobility and the TCO, many blockaders downplayed the role of protecting private property in the dispute. Indeed, when the owner of the hill itself where Congar was removing aggregate, a bespectacled man in a dusty sport coat named Baldomero, stood up during the negotiations to insist that Congar had damaged his property and that he was willing to defend his land 'to the death', the rest of the blockaders expressed little sympathy for him and responded by emphasising how Congar's harms were experienced collectively. Several pointed out that the material removed for the road was irreplaceable. One indigenous leader, Tata Vidal, observed that El Choro had only a handful of hills, and each one had its own history: 'Our grandparents could tell us stories about them. Not one bucket more should be taken out!' Abilio, a community member, said that the hill was the patrimony of El Choro and argued for collective, rather than private, ownership, adding, 'No one can own stones!' He said that seeing half the hill taken apart, and the destruction of several small waterfalls, 'sometimes was very painful'. Both Vidal and Abilio's comments suggest that the material itself had an affective capacity felt keenly as a collective sense of loss when it was removed. But the representative from Congar remained unmoved by these appeals to the laws and emotional attachments of territory, retorting that during initial negotiations over access to the material the authorities of the TCO were 'missing' and that sometimes a TCO is 'just a banner'. To him it seemed that this territorial configuration had only recently emerged with any force.

In the end, the appeal to the TCO was ultimately inconsequential in the settlement of the blockade; Congar did not agree to any compensation for removed material. Rather, it was the argument for improved mobility that won out. After two days of negotiations, participants agreed to lift the blockade in exchange for promises that local authorities would form a commission to monitor the condition of the road and that Congar would carry out regular maintenance until its work was finished. Over the following months, local leaders complained that Congar's road maintenance was inadequate, but in late fall as the rainy season faded away and the Altiplano entered a long, dry winter, concern faded too, and there were no more blockades. The road was rutted and worn but dry and passable. Many people placed their hopes in the government's promise to pave the road within the next two years, a project that may have been accelerated by the March blockade. In mid-winter surveyors were seen making measurements for the project although its conclusion would be, at best, several years away.

CONCLUSION

The March 2014 road conflict in El Choro demonstrates that the apparent fixity of both terrain and territory is provisional and ultimately illusory, and highlights the point that the surface of the earth is never still. In this case, it mixed with the heavy rains of the Altiplano summer, intensified as they were by climate change. The result was mud, a sticky interface where bodies are bound to the earth, moving through and with its viscous materiality. This mud affected bodies: during the rainy season, and in its ubiquity, depth, and viscosity, mud was disquieting for people who spent many of their waking hours dealing with the limited mobility that it imposed on them and their livestock. They worried about further loss of movement and hoped for the return of the sun to dry the earthbound remnants of recent rainstorms.

This sticky surface had territorial implications when it was churned by Congar's dumper trucks. Faced by the unease of diminished mobility, the removal of one of El Choro's few hills and little compensation, local indigenous leaders charged with settling disputes over territory mounted a defence by leading a collective immobilisation of Congar's dumper trucks. The territories that the people of El Choro identified as their own – the municipality, the *Tierra Comunitaria de Origen* – were closed to Congar and roadwork on Bolivia's international highway was interrupted. Thus a small territorial action carried out in the name of mud was capable of disrupting a larger act of territorial integration.

In the final analysis, then, this blockade highlights how territorial and terrestrial unsettlements emerge alongside each other in how they act on and through bodies. Bodies affected by mud make political decisions – in this case to protect their territory from the threat of further mud and to guard their mobility by implementing immobility for Congar. These political decisions are reflected in the broader making of territory but, like mud, these territorial decisions make marks that fade and transform over time. After a few days Congar employees returned to work in the shadow of the blockade, inscribed in the territory like tyre tracks in dried mud.

NOTES

1. Much of this literature focuses on examinations of conflict and international security and gives less consideration to the political ramifications of bodily experiences under climate change (see Barnett and Adger 2007; Dalby 2009, 2013; Dumaine and Mintzer 2015; Hendrix and Salehyan 2012; Hsiang and Burke 2014; Selby and Hoffmann 2014; Swyngedouw 2010).

2. Details for the background of this project are mostly from the local Oruro newspaper *La Patria*. See *La Patria* (2013a, 2013b, 2013c, 2013d, 2013e).

3. See comments by a departmental assembly member on regional integration (Campos Velasco 2010).

4. See *La Patria* (2015), and contrast with the controversies over the infamous TIPNIS case (see Calla 2011; Fabricant and Postero 2015; Lorenzo 2011; McNeish 2013; Rossell Arce 2011).

5. This event occurred days after I arrived for my 2013–2014 field work, and I was unable to attend this blockade, which received limited media coverage; see *La Patria* (2013f).

6. From *La Patria* (2013f). The original quote, which is a paraphrase by the newspaper article's unsigned author, is: *Por su parte, el asambleísta Froilán Fulguera pidió a los comunarios no perjudicar el avance de este tramo que es fundamental para el desarrollo de Oruro y es anhelado por toda la población.*

7. "Mama" is the proper form of address for a woman elected as an Indigenous authority, or *jilacata*. Mama Ruperta, like most Indigenous authorities in the highlands, was elected as part of a husband/wife pair who serve a year together and are addressed, respectively, by the Quechua terms for father and mother, *tata* and *mama*.

8. A pre-colonial territorial designation.

9. The phrase Quirino used to indicate the process of change, "*proceso de cambio*", was a political slogan that President Morales and the MAS-IPSP party used to brand their government's agenda and, as such, by using this phrase Quirino was evoking the broad reach of this agenda.

10. As explained to me by the anthropologist Marcelo Lara of the Centre for Ecology and Andean Peoples in Oruro (*Centro de Ecología y Pueblos Andinos*, or CEPA), collective ownership in the Andean highlands had been systematically dismantled by the state after independence, land reform in 1953 cementing the notion that highland farmers held title to their lands.

ACKNOWLEDGEMENTS

I am grateful to the Wenner-Gren Foundation for Anthropological Research, the Liu Institute for Global Issues at the University of British Columbia, and the UBC Faculty of Arts for supporting my field research. Special appreciation goes to the Vanier Canada Graduate Scholarships for supporting my graduate work at UBC and the Centro de Ecología y Pueblos Andinos in Oruro, Bolivia, for invaluable assistance. I am grateful to my research supervisor Gastón Gordillo and my colleagues Kamal Arora and Mascha Gugganig for helpful comments on drafts of this chapter.

Chapter 7

FLOODPLAINS

Where Sheets of Water Intersect:
Infrastructural Culture – From Flooding
to Hydropower in Winnipeg, Manitoba

Stephanie C. Kane

Globally, urban water infrastructure represents a significant aspect of how state power, realised through federal, provincial, and city entities, furthers humanity's dominion over nature.[1] In contrast to a state's strategic use of violence to attain legitimate power over territory, a state can establish (or lose) legitimate power over territory by building (or failing to build) earthworks that control water flow. Thus, even as flood waters confound attempts at constructing territory, their forces, and the forces deployed to control them, can themselves be enlisted as territorial technologies.

In writing about the construction of a seventeenth-century inter-oceanic canal through France, Mukerji (2009) identifies the emergence of an alternate form of state empowerment based on the combination of logistical efforts to organise things, including elements of nature, with the strategic efforts to organise human relations. Mukerji shows how different kinds of knowledge and logics of action – brought together in infrastructural logistics – alter 'the political significance of nature, [by] using the sturdiness of stone, the buoyant qualities of water, the binding properties of cement mixtures, and the flexibility of timber' (p. 215). Moving emphasis away from a purely anthropocentric politics, Mukerji argues that enrolling 'nature in politics was not the same as the struggles among interest groups or elites seeking advantages, but the material transformation of places could nonetheless change the playing field on which political contests took place' (p. 215).

Focusing on the active reshaping of volumetric earth forms to establish dominion over national territory, Mukerji's work resonates with, even as it complicates, the idea of territory as 'a *political technology* that joins ideas of land (property that can be controlled) with terrain (surface over which power can be organized and projected)' (Elden 2010, 811). Using an historical analysis to consider social interactions, cartography, surveying, folk engineering, and hybrid forms of sheer inventiveness that were involved in a series of failures and triumphs, Mukerji compels the consideration of the complex challenges entailed in converting any life-supporting spatial materiality into a political technology.

To explore the phenomena that these questions and observations raise both culturally and politically, I sketch the infrastructural logistics for controlling water movement through Manitoba's flood bowl at provincial and neighbourhood scales, enlisting the concept of the technozone (Barry 2006) to show how flood control and hydropower infrastructural systems extend their spheres of influence across large but distinct swaths of provincial space and political discourse. Each system strives systematically to secure the city and the province at the macro-scale, but sometimes to the detriment of constituent neighbourhoods within the city and the province, and not without public controversy.

Scalar mismatches are a given in any large infrastructural system; operations and their effects may be misaligned causing disruptions, inefficiencies, breakdowns.[2] But only some problems caused by scalar mismatches become explicitly political. Others remain unremarked, part of the mundane give and take of workaday river cities – in places such as Winnipeg, Manitoba, featured here, and in other places elsewhere. Which kinds of unavoidable systemic contradictions are ignored while other kinds of predicaments manifest as dramas that take and hold the political stage? If territory is a political technology, as Stuart Elden (2010, 2013a) suggests, is some of that politics only implicit, immanent, or repressed because it would be too complex, too entangled in everyday life, to negotiate, much less resolve? And how do such questions implicate urban water infrastructure and its ethnographies?[3]

WATER'S POWER

Melting and rising, freezing and falling, variations of the Red and the Assiniboine Rivers manifest the pulse of seasons. Meeting in historic downtown Winnipeg, at the confluence that inhabitants call The Forks, the Red River flows northward across the Canada–USA border from the Dakotas, while the Assiniboine River flows eastward into the city, its source in the distant Canadian Rockies. Sometimes the rivers rise beyond all engineered restraints, assuming gargantuan shapes that swallow families, pets, homes, businesses, streets, farms, and livestock. Although the city has been securitised with modern infrastructure since the mid-twentieth century, devastating floods nevertheless always represent a threat (Warkentin 1961).

While the city is kept safe, perennial re-enactments of water's power manifesting as engulfing sheets of water are never unexpected. Extreme flood events blur conceptual and material boundaries between urban insides and outsides, natures and cultures, waters and lands. While the Red and Assiniboine rivers are the two major waterways running through the heart of the city, and the most direct sources of devastation for Winnipeggers, the city must also be appreciated as a small but critical spot in a provincial terrain composed of prairie, tundra, and boreal forests interlaced by a penetrating meshwork of rivers, lakes, ponds, and marshes. The human tragedies caused by extreme flood events assume classical form in historical representations that are communicated across generations of the Manitoban public. In family photo albums, newspapers, books, museums, archives, and their digitised counterparts, Winnipeggers archive documentary visions of the uncanny scarcity of land. In this photographic flood world, pedestrian and automobile pathways through the city and its environs can be read by the tops of telephone poles and the strands of tracks held down on raised embankments by intentionally abandoned railroad cars.

From my perspective, the apocalyptic images of intersecting sheets of water bring the collective creation of cities into the perspective of geological time. Juxtaposing historical and geoscientific visualisations of a melting Laurentian Ice Sheet transposes the ethnographer's sense of ground as she and her neighbours walk daily along the riverside. Floods re-enact the demise of the glacial lobes that slid, scraped, and eventually combined to cover North America until their dramatic retreat back to the poles at the end of the last Ice Age, 12,000 years ago. Their repetition suggests that the geological power of water is both ancient and present, and invokes the awesome elemental nature of "vibrant matter" (Bennett 2010).

Extreme floods provide a compelling rationale for the build-up and maintenance of the state's logistical power. They may also threaten to disrupt established forms of urbanisation on the wet prairie. The failure of infrastructure to protect the citizenry may thus undercut the legitimacy and authority of provincial territoriality, which are at least partially based on maintenance of stable dry-land surfaces susceptible to survey, ownership, and the making of home. Facing this existential threat and supported by their fellow citizens and government organisations, Manitoban engineers have the know-how and resources to confront and substantially subdue water's power. They manage the rivers by using measurement, diversion, and capture by redistributing and appropriating them. While the active presence of a geological timescale is not foremost in most inhabitants' minds, it is present in the everyday practices of engineers whose adjustments of the river-city relationship depend on a spatiotemporal depth of material perception modulated by constant vigilance.

Geological time aside, what everyone in Winnipeg does know is that the city's future depends on keeping the crucial lands near the riverbanks dry; that is, it depends on planning, designing, building, and maintaining them to ensure their stability as *terra*, as stable dry land, to prevent them from reverting to their naturally ambiguous state – wetland prairie floodplains. The transformation of this low point in a vast flood bowl into securitised patterns of separate wetlands and drylands demands that the economic, legal, and technical expertise and resources of the city and province are bent to, or at least kept as compatible as possible with, prioritising the control of rivers that might flow out of their banks and morph across the flat landscape.

The next section of the chapter moves to consider two residential neighbourhoods on opposite banks of the Red River to show how inhabitants' sense of security is shaped by problems in infrastructural logistics at the land-water interface. Well within the interstices of the flood control technozone, the river reach shows how the macro-scale priorities of the flood control system can have negative consequences at the meso-scale; that is, in the interlinked landscapes that compose the protected heart of the city. Indeed, although varying in kind and effect, geophysical problems caused by provincial flood control may be commonplace features of macro-scale infrastructural systems more generally. They hover in the background; neighbourhood scale riverbank problems generally do not appear in the foreground of urban politics and culture. In this sense, they are mundane, apolitical, or neglected aspects of material life in the meso-scale. Nevertheless, it is in the meso-scale of interlinked riverine neighbourhoods that the precedents for territorial disasters build, and where the state must attempt to enact disaster prevention.

Like the patterns formed by the combined paths of inhabitants as they enact their daily routines, the rarely-considered arrangement of shape-shifting inhabited river edges may also be considered a part of what de Certeau (1984, 93) has identified as an urban "text". As an urban text, the shifting land/water edges in neighbourhoods enter analysis and the city from 'down below' the thresholds at which visibility begins (ibid.). Each riverside neighbourhood offers a different urban text or analytic entryway for conceptualising territory as a political technology in Manitoba. In particular, the contrasting effects of public and private ownership practices suggest how infrastructural culture – as a category of analysis – can illuminate urban efforts to "secure the volume" (after Elden 2013b).

SECURING THE VOLUME #1: TECHNOZONES IN THE PROVINCIAL FLOOD BOWL

The entrenched consensus supporting the commitment to flood control began with European colonisation. Early settlers impressed their mode of relating to the Earth's surface on the riverine spaces surrounding the Red-Assiniboine confluence by merging the conquest and colonisation of indigenous peoples with that of landscape. Earliest documented settlements of First Nations, then later, of French, Métis, and Anglo settlers, show that proximity to the riverbanks around The Forks was valued cross-culturally (Warkentin 1961). Everyone used the rivers to get around. The Forks was a transport node that linked settlements to regional hunting, fishing, trade, and exploration routes through east-west and north-south waterways and that also provided fertile lands for growing food. Early settlers had a fierce need to hold on to their claimed positions on the banks: they escaped the direst floods with their animals only in the last possible instance. As settlers succeeded in dominating the continent's interior terrain, they extended the practice of living beside the river across all seasons, establishing sedentary habitation as a valued condition linked to privatisation of riverbank plots. In the process, the settlers dispossessed First Nation peoples whose seasonal migration pattern – moving camps close in when the rivers were low and moving outward when the rivers flooded – was blocked by settlers who claimed land ownership with force and who institutionalised claims with "legal" text and maps.

The settler impulse to stabilise riverbanks intensified with each extreme flood event and each new wave of immigration that punctuated Winnipeg's history, eventually becoming the infrastructure-rich built environment of contemporary southern Manitoba. In this process, also repeated in fits and starts throughout the world, the Anglo-European cultural model of concentrated, sedentary settlements dependent on sophisticated flood control infrastructure displaced the indigenous cultural model that relied on moving with, rather than controlling, the rivers. Out of the subsequent intergenerational efforts to predict, prevent, and control the aquatic flows that sustained and threatened them, a strong cultural disposition to centralise the importance of water management emerged in the contemporary city of Winnipeg, the provincial capital and the largest city. The infrastructural practices that generations of Manitobans have reproduced within their pieces of territory are regional-specific versions of humanity's dominion over natural earth forms and processes more generally – a nature simultaneously more vulnerable and more unconquerable than humans generally like to believe.

From the city of Winnipeg it is an easy drive to Lake Winnipeg and Lake Manitoba, two long and shallow freshwater lakes that are among the largest in the world. As active remnants of glacial Lake Agassiz, Lakes Winnipeg and Manitoba receive waters from a network of rivers that stretch across the continental interior. In the geographic centre of North America, gravitational pull draws water down into a vast flood bowl and channels it through Winnipeg towards Hudson Bay and the North Pole. Created over a million years ago, their lacustrine beds and surface waters have been made into terrains for organising, preserving, and projecting power – a political-technological enactment of human agency that converts *terra* into territory in geographically, historically, and culturally specific ways (see Elden 2010, 811). The lakes, with their bounteous fish populations, functioned as transport nodes in the vast intra-continental fluvial network that linked the continental interior to the northern oceans and to the eastern seaboard, supporting many generations of first peoples. Before settler collectives reorganised the watery, difficult-to-traverse prairie wetlands that would become Manitoba, Canada, the lakes oriented and provided pathways for colonisation. Over time, they became integrated into flood control and hydroelectricity production (described in more detail below), as well as agriculture, fishing, recreation, and tourism. The lakes are also central to the cultural identity of those who live along the southern edge of the province (see, for example, Russell 2004).

Inhabiting the edge of some of the planet's coldest wildlands, Winnipeggers must contend with the confounding power of ice for much of the year.[4] Frigid temperatures make energy for home heating as central to survival as flood control. Without the infrastructural culture that emerged from settler culture and flourished with the help of modern engineering, there would be no way for the diverse population of over 700,000 to take everyday life for granted either in deep winter or in spring flood. Two major institutions of water management have emerged in response to the double existential demand for dry land and warm houses: the Ministry of Infrastructure and Transport (MIT) manages flooding at a considerable provincial expense; Manitoba Hydro generates enough electrical power to supply Winnipeg with ample energy and still sell enough to refill provincial coffers.

These tandem institutions, MIT and Manitoba Hydro, have established dominions over provincial flood bowl space. Both agencies provide essential services and headquarter in Winnipeg, but their public profiles are quite distinct. Except in the midst of flooding crisis, MIT tends to stay in the background and is generally thought of as a helping institution dependent on public funding and support. Its offices are tucked away inside a downtown office building and in a complex well outside of the centre. In contrast, Manitoba Hydro Place is an environmentally sustainable architectural icon prominently located on Portage Avenue. The architecture celebrates the economic and engineering prowess associated with hydroelectric production. Its interior offices include designated spaces for representatives of First Nations communities working with Manitoba Hydro, and the public plaza outside provides a space for protests by First Nations peoples harmed by dam operations up north and other farmers and landowners angry about the licensing and construction of high power voltage lines across the province.[5]

The agencies rely on the two lakes to function as mediating infrastructure sustaining the panorama of public and private property in and around Winnipeg: Lake Manitoba in flood control and Lake Winnipeg in electricity production.[6] In basic design and operational procedures, engineers have enrolled the qualities and shapes of their natural forms (large holding basins) and relationships (with each other, with rivers, and with rain, snow, and ice). Provincial law specifies the exact level within which each lake can be manipulated by engineers for optimum system function in each season. Nevertheless, in flood conditions, the intended effects of the engineers' manipulations can be dramatically confounded by the speed and intensity with which natural forces combine: for example, strong winds in concert with flooding in the midst of spring storms. (Wind has a disproportionate impact on shallow lakes, creating waves akin to those that occur on an ocean coastline.) Some of the lakes' effects on people and property within their direct path are predictable, enabling the provincial government to regulate allowable maxima and minima.

In an interview with me at Manitoba Hydro, a natural resource manager emphasised the point that while the lakes can be regulated, they cannot be controlled.[7] This distinction inevitability opens up engineering to politics. The manager said that ordinary people *mistakenly* believe that the corporation intentionally keeps Winnipeg Lake high in order to produce more electricity. But property owners I talked to along the lake believe in the manifold and manipulative powers of Manitoba Hydro. Grounded in their experience and interpretation of historical change along the lakefront, they do not consider themselves mistaken. They suspect Manitoba Hydro can and should lower lake levels, especially in the spring, to mitigate shoreline erosion.[8] Similarly, levels of water in Lake Manitoba are legally stipulated and regulated by MIT. The extent and duration that the lake is made to function as a holding tank for the Assiniboine is a contested matter argued about in the press and in legal and scholarly arenas.[9]

Working with both law and nature, engineers make two basic technical decisions with regard to lake levels: (1) how high to raise or lower a lake level and (2) how long the level should artificially stay raised or lowered. The regulation of lake levels allows engineers to even out water flows in the larger flood control or hydroelectric system. Raising lake levels has unintended but unavoidable consequences which are unequally distributed among landscapes and inhabitants. So although based on technical analyses, lake level decisions are scrutinised by policymakers, politicians, and ordinary people. The impulse to scrutinise is tied to specific cultural and historical differences in the ways that powerful decision-makers have calculated infrastructural benefits and sacrifices. Most importantly, legacies of conquest and colonialism persist in infrastructural culture. The rights of rural First Nation communities have been routinely sacrificed in the name of water management: both freshwater provision and flood control for Winnipeg have caused long-term flood destruction. Resulting instances of destabilisation and dispossession are not unrelated to poverty and to high suicide and disappearance rates among First Nation youths, especially girls and young women. Since the flood of

2011, whole communities such as Lake St Martin First Nation have been permanently displaced from ancestral homes.[10] Patterns of inequality can also be discerned in contemporary settler culture. For example, some believe the relatively higher class position and influence of Lake Winnipeg cottagers – compared to those along Lake Manitoba – predispose lake level decisions that protect the former. And, too, shoreline communities are put at risk when Assiniboine River water is diverted into Lake Manitoba in order to protect the tourism activities downstream at The Forks.[11]

Technical decisions are another focal point organising debate in the media, the streets, and the courts. They transcend their own technicality as they penetrate sociality. The idea that lake levels matter proliferates in the landscape and is manifest, for example, in the form of ribbons tied around telephone poles indicating the height to which one must rebuild one's house – a legally defined minimum height based on the lake level in recent large floods. Remember, the lakes are enrolled in technozones as mediators: the lakes help protect or energise the city's residents – and this sometimes requires that those who live, play, and work along the lakeshores are put at significant risk. Ribbons on trees visually code legal construction requirements and carry the emotion and memory of sacrifice for affected infrastructural minorities, such as those whose homes have been destroyed by natural flooding and artificial flood control.[12] In other words, the focus on lake levels exemplifies how a technical matter can also function as a key cognitive category that organises relationships and conflicts.[13] Lake levels simultaneously act as material water formation, data, law, and infrastructure, and as cognitive, emotive, and discursive focal points. As abstractions with various material manifestations, lake levels are the building blocks of cultural repertoires in negotiations about how unintended or unavoidable harms might be prevented or made right. Abstraction is not the only point at issue, but it is representative of the kind of technical-cultural slippage characteristic of the taken-for-granted dynamics of infrastructural culture.

In this context, I find Barry's (2006, 239) technozones as a type or use of space doubly helpful for comparing and contrasting the technology-based infrastructural systems in which the lakes are enrolled. Barry's definition of technozone works well in two ways for the purpose of this analysis: first, not unlike Elden's and Mukerji's works, the technozone leaves the question of culture open. Second, so defined, the technozone suggests that a bridge can be crafted between science and technology studies (STS) and the ethnography of infrastructure. For Barry, then, a technozone assumes dominion over a spatial expanse by establishing common standards (legal lake levels, for instance), technical practices, procedures, and operational forms that distinguish what happens there from what happens elsewhere.

Ethnographically and thus for my purposes, the technozone pertains to a spatial expanse subject to a shared culture that is informed by science-based technical norms, decision-making processes, modes of authority, and truth-value. Because their motives and means are married to rivers, these technozones are as much about nature as they are about technology. Following Pritchard's (2011, 20) work about the twentieth-century development of hydroelectric and nuclear industries along the Rhône in France, the technozones produced by MIT and Manitoba Hydro may also be described as 'envirotechnical systems [that] . . . may coexist or compete within, or throughout, scales and societies'. State power extends, transforming *terra* into territory, by means of these water-based envirotechnical systems or technozones.

MIT and Manitoba Hydro

One of my first tasks in the field was to understand how – with entirely different functions pertaining to river flow – MIT and Manitoba Hydro did not get in each other's way. By mapping and drafting the connections between the monumental infrastructural components of each system I could discern the redefined land/water spaces within each outline. I could then see that although flood control and hydroelectric systems both benefitted the city, and its southern environs above all, their operations and public works, with the exception of intersections in Winnipeg, occupied distinct parts of the greater provincial terrain – a key shape juridically bounded in the south by the international border with the United States, north by Hudson Bay and Nunavut, west by Saskatchewan, and east by Ontario.

My infrastructural mapping exercise showed the extent to which an organisation's geophysical footprint may be relatively small even when its provincial responsibility and authority is relatively great. Together MIT and Manitoba Hydro produce the partial fiction that the cartographic wet-dry spaces within its boundaries constitute, or merge with, the political entity that is the province. Territorialisation, in other words, just needs enough *terra* to sustain the operational effectiveness of provincial organisations responsible for water management. According to this city-based territorial logic, most of the hinterland can remain wet, and even be flooded, as have First Nation settlements been flooded by hydroelectricity infrastructure across the north. And in flood emergencies, for example such as that in 2011, MIT can sacrifice small communities such as Hoop and Holler when, in consultation with provincial politicians, senior agency engineers decide that a tactical *controlled* breach of an Assiniboine bend dike must be engineered to allay the threat of an *uncontrollable* one.[14]

MIT's decision-making process is fully under the power of the provincial government as it fulfils its responsibilities for the distribution of freshwater in flood and drought. In the current prolonged wet cycle, MIT's main function is to produce and maintain *terra* – the stable, dry land – without which large-scale urbanisation and industrial farming in the province's south would be impossible. MIT has established a technozone in provincial terrain that stretches out from the city of Winnipeg west across the demographic and agricultural heartland. The technozone grows out from the Y shape of The Forks. Most prominently, on the south-to-north axis, the monumental Red River Floodway – an engineering feat built in the wake of the great Flood of 1950 – stops floodwaters moving north before they enter the southern edge of the city, shunting it around through a forty-seven-kilometre (twenty-nine-mile) channel and then dumping it back in the river upstream near Selkirk. The floodway substantively addresses the problem of the Red River; it successfully contained the Great Flood of 1997 (although barely; additional public works ensued in subsequent years). On the west-to-east axis, three infrastructures are central to MIT's mission to control flooding along the Assiniboine River. First, the Shellmouth dam and reservoir on the border with Saskatchewan regulates the Assiniboine as it flows east into Manitoba and closer to the city. Second, the Portage Diversion sends excess water to Manitoba Lake. Third, that excess water then rushes the rest of the way down to Winnipeg. More or less viable dikes or embankments – some public and some private – weave between these large-scale infrastructures throughout the province to protect homes, farms, and transport routes.

Manitoba Hydro, a Crown corporation, has semi-autonomous decision-making powers over an immense provincial terrain. The corporation has dramatically restructured the flow of waters from Ontario in the southeast through the Winnipeg River into Lake Winnipeg. Then, after mixing, the water continues flowing northward out of the lake across a series of step dams through the Nelson River system – into which the Churchill River system was diverted – before flowing out into Hudson Bay. The primary function of this reterritorialisation of provincial and First Nation aquatic spaces is to generate electricity to heat and light Winnipeg and its environs. Flood control is a secondary function, a product of operational, political, and legal necessity to regulate Lake Winnipeg. Flooding complicates decision-making in Manitoba Hydro, mostly because it entails political debate about the corporation's negative effects on northern communities and because the law requires it to send excess water out the spillways during major floods – water then lost to electricity production.

Thus the two aquatic technozones protecting from floodwater and extracting energy from steady water flow establish their dominion over distinct spatial expanses. Each has common standards, technical practices, procedures, and operational forms that distinguish one from the other and from the spaces outside their purviews. Yet both MIT and Manitoba Hydro contract out much of their construction, maintenance, and operations needs to private engineering firms. Both rely on real-time digitised satellite data streams from a network of collection points located along rivers and confluences throughout the province and managed by Manitoba Water Stewardship. By these combined means, in Barry's terms MIT and Manitoba Hydro qualify as the bureaucratic arms of technozones that accelerate and intensify in particular directions the agency of people and water – the impulse and effect of action and relationship. These instrumentalities and their effects also exemplify Barry's supposition that technozones have unpredictable effects and that, insofar as they have limits, those limits are contested, unstable, and uncertain – characteristics that apply here.

Consideration of the relationship between technozone and territory – as concepts and geophysical spaces – highlights the pragmatic uncertainties central to both. To recapitulate, both MIT and Manitoba Hydro signify the *whole* of provincial territory, even though they only have jurisdiction over *parts*. Their engineering practices only *partially and temporarily* succeed in dominating the power of water and ice to propel flux. And yet, using the language and logistics of measurement, calculation, and infrastructural operation, those with key capacity to influence cultural discourses spin the abstract political ideal of provincial territory into a wettish but viable social and material fact. The extent to which this fact – or facticity itself – is taken for granted literally depends on where and how one is situated in this variegated terrain. To understand the transformation of the wetland prairies of southern Manitoba into *terra* and territory, it is important to see a fuller spread of the envirotechnical in relation to the place-based specificities of the social and cultural. Here, rather than the social interactional scale of technozone operations, I focus on the territorial mundane in the meso-scale, on water-land infrastructural situations that escape the kind of dramas that are most recognisable as explicitly political or cultural. The following exploration of infrastructural culture focuses on a river reach within MIT's technozone that so far has escaped politicisation. One riverbank, publicly owned, has been the object of geotechnical fortification; the other side, divided into privately owned lots, has not. My aim is to explore the ways in which culture intertwines with the technical, legal, economic, and strategic dimensions of human efforts to maintain enough *terra* in the territory. The case holds politics neutral, for now.

SECURING THE VOLUME #2: RIVERBANK
RESTORATION AND ITS LIMITS

The Norwood-Saint Boniface Neighbourhood
on the East Bank of the Red

During the fieldwork component of this project, I lived a few steps from the east bank of the Red River in Norwood-Saint Boniface, a neighbourhood that occupies the curved expanse inside the first big bend south of The Forks. The curved green wedge of land at the tip of the bend, not a good place to build, is now a popular public park. In the Great Flood of 1950, when Winnipeg evacuated 100,000 people, the parkland sat underwater. Now, as a neighbour showed me what his father showed him, if one looks closely at the colour of tree bark one can see a subtle difference in shade between the lower trunks that sat under water and the upper that did not. Looking at one particular grove, moving the eye from tree to tree, one can trace a connecting line that indexes the height of the flood waters in 1950. Nature encodes a material fact in the landscape, conveying knowledge passed across generations and to newcomers to keep alive the memory of the last devastating flood. Such embodied and narrated memories are crucial because younger generations are born and raised within the infrastructural zone of protection. Without the kind of knowledge that can be conveyed, for example, by arboreal signs, evidence of the extreme dangers an unprepared citizenry would have to confront might fade from consciousness. In disaster-prone urban environments, infrastructural investment and the ability to survive when infrastructure fails depend on a cultural disposition that values detailed knowledge of historical disasters (Kane 2016).

Keeping alive the memories of historic floods is not the only stimulus sustaining infrastructural culture. Current conditions can still shock. Even within protected zones, floodwaters can and do dramatically change the landscape, impressing inhabitants with water's power. Indeed, pieces of the riverbank adjacent to Lyndale Drive are still prone to collapse. (Lyndale Drive, which borders the riverbank, is part of the city's primary diking system and, as such, it provides a formidable barrier to the Red. The Lyndale Drive dike is the highest part of the neighbourhood landscape, forming a crucial dividing line between houses on the inside and the river park on the outside.) In any case, the flood of 1950 convinced Manitobans to build the modern flood control system in operation today. The investment proved worthwhile for the first time in the Red River flood of 1997, which would have devastated the city again had the flood control system not functioned sufficiently.

On my daily walks, the push of the wind-ruffled silvery grey water moving through the channel is a source of pleasure, puzzlement, and study. Looking carefully at the pattern of rocks, earth, plant life, timber, cement, metal, and asphalt, it is clear that there has been much tending of the interface between water and land. As visually unobtrusive as the material culture of the riverbank is, if one looks for mute evidence of the mundane micro-actions that reinforce today's sedentary settlements, there is much that meets the eye. One day, I am happy to see a group of people planting trees in a cleared slope along the reach of the Red.[15] It turns out that they are employees of the city government's Naturalist Service Office working on one of the final stages of the Lyndale Restoration Project. They are planting clumps of riparian trees (such as Basswood and American elm), bushes that will reseed, and seedlings held down by hydro-mulching for moisture retention and erosion control. As the plants grow, they will help secure the engineering project that has restructured the bank below ground. If I am to learn more about that effect, the botany squad tells me I will have to talk to the geotechnical engineer in charge of the project, Kendall Thiessen.[16]

When I meet Thiessen at the site, I learn that he has recently acquired a PhD in geotechnical engineering from the University of Manitoba, his dissertation based on the Lyndale Restoration Project. It is 10th October and already cold out by the river. The lower bank has failed historically at this stretch where river comes out of the bend into the channel wall. In the 1970s, the city government built a wall of logs to try to hold back the clay, which has a tendency to slide off into the channel. Its engineering workforce also dug clay out from the wall to make a flatter, more stable slope. Our conversation takes us underground and into the geological past. As Thiessen explains things to me, he draws pictures of the glacial formations upon which we stand. Basically, a clay layer covers the whole region and where it interfaces with the river, forming the channel walls, the force of the current erodes it; large curves of clay slip down or, in the more vertical parts of the bank, fall off in big hunks. For his project, Thiessen (2010) studied the underground structure of the bank then constructed three rows of columns, each 2.1 metres (6.8 feet) in diameter and filled them with crushed limestone. The columns anchor the clay in the glacial till formation below.

The Lyndale Project restores a bank that continues to confront forces both natural and technological. It is in part the result of MIT's macro-scale system-wide decision-making processes that cause bank failure on the Red as it passes through – even in the protected zone of the inner city. To explain: the strength of the bank is affected by how much water infiltrates into the ground from rain, snow melt, surface run-off, and flooding. Higher water pressure decreases soil strength and contributes to the instability of the riverbank. But bank failure tends to happen only *after* the flood. During a flood, the higher water pressure in the channel pushes back against the bank. But thereafter, the river level drops, and sometimes it drops more precipitously than ordinarily it would due to MIT's operations. When a sudden drop occurs in the pressure and height of river water pressing into the bank from the channel, and does so at the same period as water pressure and water levels inside the bank continue to press outward, the possibility of bank failure increases.

But MIT has responsibility for flood control in the *province*. To achieve success, the operational tempo is keyed to the seasons.[17] Most relevant here are the adjustments of the water level in Shellmouth Reservoir, which regulates the volume of water coming into the system through the Assiniboine

River – and ultimately at The Forks – into the Red River. In winter, MIT adjusts the water level in the system to keep it as low as possible. There are two reasons for this: first, the lower the water in the channel, the more room the channel has to accommodate spring floodwaters without overtopping the dikes; second, the lower the water levels on the Red and the Assiniboine, the less ice forms in the channel. Because spring hits the Dakotas in the south before it arrives in Manitoba in the north, the spring meltwater can rush into Winnipeg when the river there is still frozen. Ice can block the meltwaters rushing in on the Red; in specific spots, it can force those meltwaters out of the channel and onto the flat floodplain. The lower the river level coming into winter, the less ice, and the lesser the chance of having to break up and clear an ice jam. In short, to avoid ice problems, the river is kept low.

When MIT lowers the Assiniboine in the autumn, it also lowers the Red along Lyndale Drive, which can trigger bank failure. (Although the Assiniboine flows into the Red and primarily keeps flowing north, there is a considerable backflow effect south of the confluence.) So, here is a case of scalar mismatch where operational decisions at the provincial scale adversely affect a particular river bank that is part of the city's primary dike system. Many homes on the interior side of Lyndale Drive are actually set below the roadway-dike and are vulnerable to flooding should the dike system fail. Yet people seem confident in their city and province, as well they should be, given the vigilance of the city's geotechnical engineers and naturalists.

Geofluvial forces have always weakened the Red's banks; this is the nature of river dynamics. And, too, because land beside the bank has always been subject to flooding, people have set their dwellings well back from the edge. Eventually, the floodplain became public lands under the jurisdiction of the City of Winnipeg. And since the advent of the floodway, the neighbourhood has not been vulnerable to extreme flooding. Yet, operating the system that protects them from floods – lowering winter river levels in preparation for spring – exacerbates risk of bank collapse in the autumn. In other words, at the provincial scale water management techniques contradict geophysical reality at the neighbourhood scale. Responsibility for correcting the negative consequences of system operation falls on city engineers such as Thiessen, who – with a combination of public and private funds – tested and installed the set of rockfill columns that stabilise the bank. This case shows that the territorialisation of *terra* is an uneven and complicated achievement sustained by fixing problems that arise within technozones. Neighbourhood vulnerability can be characterised as a patchwork of good and bad. Because the flood control engineering is good overall, and because the unintentionally bad occurs on public land that is accessible and fixable, this whole arrangement is a rather mundane affair. In this case, territory is a political technology (Elden 2010, 2013a) insofar as it constructs the continuity of existing spatial arrangements. That its politicality is visible at all is only due to the exchange between engineer and ethnographer.

The Riverview Neighbourhood on the West Bank of the Red

On the opposite side of the river is another side to the story. As the outside bend of the Red flows towards The Forks, it erodes the forested shoreline of Riverview. But the city government does not have the authority to manage the bank failure problems that may be exacerbated by MIT's system-wide adjustment of river levels; it cannot restore the bank nor try to prevent more serious bank failure because it does not own the riverbank.

Thiessen meets me on that bank to explain the predicament.[18,19] It is already mid-November, and I realise I did not know what cold was back in October. Thiessen shows me a section with a steep slope and little wedge failures that may be one, two, or several years old. We observe eroded sections where the bank has fallen and aggraded sections where the alluvium is piled high enough to strangle trees. The visual pattern indicates deep instabilities in the clay. When it does go, Thiessen predicts that the bank will 'fail big'.

Recall that bank failure has happened recently along Lyndale Drive in Norwood-Saint Boniface, but there the bank was part of a park set aside to be used as public green space in recognition of its geophysical vulnerability. In Riverview, privately owned buildings and yards extend into the forested shore. The foundation of an adjacent apartment building has a crack going up the corner, while the cement platform serving as its parking lot had the soil eroded from under it. These signs indicate that the building has already been affected by the shifting riverbank.

The dynamic geophysical processes that lead to a river's changing shape are natural, preceding all development. The law separates natural and artificial causes, attributing blame to public agencies only when the causes are artificial. So neither the city nor the provincial governments can be blamed for causing or failing to prevent bank failures because of, for example, the unintended consequences of provincial flood control operations. Lack of liability does not obviate the possibility of negative consequences. Yet, the geotechnical engineers cannot set about restoration: they can only watch and warn.

Private ownership of the riverbank thus complicates three technical problems. First, risk: in the Lyndale Restoration Project, Thiessen knew that drilling into the rock to install the columns increased the risk of bank failure. He could nevertheless assume the calculated risk entailed in building-in long-term stability because the privately owned neighbourhood homes were some way distant on the other side of the dike. On the Riverview side, it would be difficult to ensure that restoration work would not have negative effects on the buildings. Second, complexity: because the Riverview shoreline was built up by private property owners who did not coordinate activities, the shoreline fragmentation created a level of complexity that makes stabilisation efforts more difficult. For the city government, working on the Riverview shoreline is high risk but low priority; there are more suitable places to focus restoration efforts. Third, socio-economic considerations: bank failures do not coincide with property lines; they are much bigger. So, for example, if a problem section extends 150 to 200 metres (492 to 656 feet) along the shore and property owners each owns twenty-five to fifty metres (82 to 164 feet) of riverbank, the four to eight owners of properties at risk would have to cooperate in restoration efforts. Such cooperation is rare.

Consider that the cost of a major work would account for a large proportion of a property's value, especially in larger, more desirable lots (about CA$10,000 [US$7,300 or GB£5,700] per lineal metre). Property owners are not prepared for, and do not necessarily understand, the risks entailed in owning shoreline. When the city government tried a pilot grant program to help such owners pay for restoration, applicants were few and those who needed such support the most did not apply. Imagine, for example, an eighty-five-year-old pensioner disinterested in investing her remaining life savings to fix the portion of bank failure running through her back garden. The way urban riverbank space is socially organised may lead decision-makers to opt for passivity instead of engineering. The socio-techno-natural contradictions are intractable; they are probably not uncommon. Certainly, Thiessen does not see this problem being solved in his lifetime.

In Riverside, the shoreline has been divided up into private lots. Architects, developers, and residents have built houses and apartment buildings too close to the riverbank. While the provincial flood control system protects them from extreme floods, geofluvial dynamics – in concert with system-wide lowering of winter river levels – create the same problems of bank instability that threaten Lyndale Drive. In Riverside, however, no strip of public land separates the built environment from the river. The social and economic organisation of infrastructural decision-making does not support adequate shoreline management, even when the city created a grant program to overcome the neighbourhood lack. On this side of the river, the balance of good and bad shifts towards the latter. Flood control engineering may be good overall, but because the unintentionally bad is occurring on private land that is inaccessible to city engineers, the bad cannot be corrected. Yet, the situation is also mundane, ignored even by residents with cracking foundations. The Riverside case shows that territory is a political technology (Elden 2010, 2013a) insofar as it sets up conditions for collapse. Rather than the infrastructure-enabled sense of continuity observed on Lyndale Drive, the politicality of Riverside's spatial arrangement shifts to the near future, when a disaster conditioned on impending collapse might topple a series of privately owned buildings.

Comparison of the two neighbourhoods dramatises the fact that infrastructural culture is public culture. Collective action for the public good can be supported, as in Lyndale Drive, or inhibited or overwhelmed, as in Riverside. The resulting strengths and weaknesses can be read in the socio-topography and earthworks that characterise water-land juxtapositions in river cities.

CONCLUSION

This comparison of two riverside neighbourhoods offers contrasting cultural orientations. One draws on historical experience and geophysical knowledge to engineer the public good resulting in more stable *terra*; the other relies on more personal or commercial interests that effectively cede power to the river. The neighbourhoods occupy a single reach of the Red, a tiny but central niche in two tandem technozones that together provide a *terra* kept warm and dry by virtue of the very river they are kept separate from. This mode of territorialisation is perhaps peculiar to the far north but nevertheless is suggestive of the kinds of infrastructural culture that climate change must provoke as the world's cities learn to remake their water-land boundaries.

This chapter is a part of a larger ethnographic project on the infrastructure of contemporary social life in Canada. Together, the design and management of earthworks and accompanying data streams manage water flows across provincial space, funding and protecting city and provincial governments and constituencies. But by its nature infrastructure always requires sacrifices, even while benefitting as much terrain and as many neighbourhoods as possible. Territorialising is never uniform and, although often mundane, is always political. Even in a democracy, infrastructural minorities are sacrificed. Infrastructural logistics impose contradictory consequences on territory. Protecting the whole city may require public works to mitigate hazards within neighbourhoods. But among river neighbourhoods divided into privately owned lots, for example, some may opt out of engineered safeguards. And in far reaches of the province effective public works may be endlessly deferred causing havoc in the lives of minorities to protect urban majorities. Such contradictions call for technical and symbolic fixes in order to sustain their legitimacy in infrastructural culture and provincial politics. Scholars and the media tend to focus on the most dramatic contradictions and injustices that arise when governments act to secure territory through infrastructure. I cannot help but wonder, however, how much of territorialising is more a combination of organised efforts and *ad hoc* muddling than the citizenry would like to think.

As an anthropologist, I look for cultural matrices and outcrops in all of this territorialising, the taken-for-granted, and the publicly ritualised. My aim here is to understand Winnipeg's confrontation with its flooded terrain as a cultural problem that assumes unique configurations for people who live in flood-prone cities. For it takes language, negotiation, and a certain degree of collective faith in engineering to mobilise infrastructural logistics, which requires resources that could be allocated otherwise and which, although designed to protect the majority, cannot protect everyone equally and inevitably does harm to some. And so, to Stuart Elden's (2013b, 49) call to experiment with thinking about geo-power, geo-politics, and geo-metrics in ways that make earth processes and understandings of the world central, I add culture to the mix – a culture whose elements include material and aesthetic forms of measurements, maps, regulatory codes, and the very engineering techniques that connect humans to their shape-shifting province. I resist my initial impulse to set culture off as its own category of analysis. Rather than thinking of culture as a fifth register to add to Elden's (2010, 2013a) four – economic, strategic, legal, and technical – I consider these registers here as already cultural. Furthermore, I aim to stretch the cultural stuff – the bonds and boundaries, milieux and genres that organise and orient the 'political and historical specificities [of water flowing through] territories' (Elden 2013b, 49) – into a deeper sense of geological space and time than is usual for ethnography.

River cities such as Winnipeg must contend with the volatile and powerful force of water by planning, designing, building, maintaining, and operating infrastructure. Although the territorial vision and legal bases of Manitoba's flood control system are as vast as the province, the actual material footprint of the infrastructural system is scaled down to encompass only the most populous southern swath of terrain. And even within the technozones (or enviro-technical systems) enabled by flood control infrastructure in the southern swath, the protective powers of the state are distributed unevenly. Geofluvial dynamics, the socio-legal organisation of decision-making, and the situated cultural identities of inhabitants combine to complicate ongoing technical problems and management solutions. These dimensions, in dynamic tension, shape the techno-politics of territoriality. In effect, the investigation of the two Winnipeg neighbourhoods on the Red River and their relationship with Lakes Manitoba and Winnipeg taught me that infrastructure is the partially calculated encounter between culture and matter. To understand territoriality in the wet prairielands and elsewhere, one must pay close attention to both.

NOTES

1. Recent interdisciplinary scholarly literature on urban water infrastructure and the state is growing. See, for example, Bennett and Joyce (2010), Graham (2010), Heynen, Kaika, and Swyngedouw (2006), Kante (2012a), Rademacher (2011), and Soll (2013).

2. For definition of scalar mismatches see Cumming et al. (2006, 16); for mismatches between ecological experience and political/infrastructural power see Kane (2012b).

3. The chapter draws from four months of ethnographic fieldwork with Winnipeg's engineers, forecasters, and ordinary inhabitants in Autumn 2014. The analysis considers expert knowledge production and the institutional arrangements of water management in the context of infrastructural culture more broadly. The conceptual framework has also been developed through a series of additional short fieldwork projects (2013–2015) on flash flooding in Singapore, on the 2007 tsunami in Peru, and on an engineered flood zone/nature park in Croatia.

4. Wildlands is a term used in the anthropogenic biome or "anthrome" classification system (Ellis and Ramankutty 2008).

5. "Manitoba Hydro Place" at http://www.archdaily.com/44596/manitoba-hydro-kpmb-architects/. For protests staged at headquarters in 2014 see, for example, "First Nation brings hydro protest to headquarters" at http://www.winnipegfreepress.com/local/first-nation-brings-hydro-protest-to-hq-280281572.html. See also "Bipole-iii anger boils over at Manitoba Hydro protest", http://www.cbc.ca/news/canada/manitoba/bipole-iii-anger-boils-over-at-manitoba-hydro-protest-1.2584318. All sites accessed 13 May 2016.

6. On how technology-based water infrastructures mediate human-natural interactions see Pritchard (2011) and White (1995).

7. Based on conversations and interviews that took place during site visits in Lake Manitoba in 2014 (St Laurent and Woodland, 13 August); Lake Winnipeg (Victoria Beach Grand Beach, 20 and 27 August); Delta Beach and Gimli (27 and 28 August); Dunnattor (21 October, 19 November); and Winnipeg Beach (19 November).

8. Interview, DH, 17 September 2014, Bk #1, p. 137.

9. Interviews and site visit with Scott Forbes in 2014 (13 August, 24 September, and 28 October). He is professor of zoology, ecology, evolutionary biology, University of Winnipeg, cottager in the St Laurent community on Lake Manitoba, and writer of many newspaper articles debating the routine use of the Portage Diversion. See, for example, "Nightmare on Lake Manitoba Continues". Accessed 10 July 2014. http://www.winnipegfreepress.com/opinion/analysis/nightmare-on-lake-manitoba-continues-278335361.html?cx_navSource=d-tiles-1.

10. Ballard, M., Klatt, R., and Thompson, S., 2012. "Flooding Hope: The Lake St Martin First Nation Story [Video]". Accessed 13 May 2016. http://www.youtube.com/watch?v=SQStePF5jeg.

11. See Forbes, note 9.

12. See Forbes, note 9, and Ballard et al., note 10.

13. For geotechnical and cultural analysis of a lake in Bahia Brazil, see Kane 2012a, 23–40.

14. See, for example, "Manitoba Flood 2011 Breach of the Hoop and Holler Bend Dike". Accessed 13 May 2016. https://www.youtube.com/watch?v=RmQRRs9WsUs.

15. Lyndale Drive, which borders the riverbank, is part of the city's primary diking system and, as such, provides a formidable barrier to the Red. The Lyndale Drive dike is the highest part of the neighbourhood landscape, forming a crucial dividing line between houses on the inside and the river park on the outside.

16. Site visit, 15 September 2014, Field notes Bk#1 pp. 110–12.

17. Kendall Thiessen. Interview and site visit 10 October 2014, Field notes Bk#2, pp. 94–108. See also Thiessen (2010).

18. ST and CP. Interview at MIT, 2 October 2014, Field notes Bk#2, pp. 20–31.

19. Kendall Thiessen. Interview and site visit 13 November 2014, Field notes Bk#3, pp. 73–179.

ACKNOWLEDGEMENTS

I would like to thank my friends and interlocutors in Winnipeg for generously sharing deep knowledge of the riverine landscape. Special thanks to Danny Blair and Pauline Greenhill of the University of Winnipeg, for being inspiring hosts and colleagues. Fieldwork was sponsored by the Council for the International Exchange of Scholars (CIES), Fulbright, and Indiana University's College of Arts and Sciences and the Office of the Vice Provost for Research of Indiana University.

Chapter 8

CITIES

Mare Magnum: Urbanisation of Land and Sea

Ross Exo Adams

To speak or write of urbanising the sea may invite familiar images of empty mansions dotting palm-shaped islands in Dubai or the spectacular architectural expansion of Monaco's real estate into the Ligurian Sea. Likewise, it may remind us of the pretensions of Nigeria's new "Eko Atlantic" project, dredging into existence a new swath of land to create an extraterritorial zone of private development and trade. It may also recall far more expansive cartographies of resource extraction, maps of concessions, global pipelines, and fibre-optic cables of intercontinental communication. An example such as Singapore reveals both phenomena in its simultaneous construction of firm land and its broader territorialising of ocean-space into operational seascapes and vast oceanic hinterland – all in response to the pressures urban space makes to extend supply lines to wherever resources (and "land") may be found (Topolovic 2014). We are increasingly drawn to an imaginary of the spaces beyond the city, thanks in part to planetary examinations of "extended urbanisation" by Neil Brenner and Christian Schmid (2011) (see also Brenner 2013), in which maps trace an image of the urban through networks of circulation of oil, commodities, and data that run across seabeds and over the sea surface, encircling the planet's oceans with threads of infrastructural fluidity.

This smooth perception of urbanised ocean-space may recall yet another way in which urbanising the sea has taken form: in the architecture of the floating city. In the 1960s a certain landless utopian spirit took hold of the architectural imaginary; in the sea, architecture could escape the dross of post-war urban space by imagining cities as great interconnected web-like arks whose edgeless structures could colonise a particularly placid ocean. Today, just as we are confronted with new dystopian realities of the violence of climate change and a rising ocean inundating urban (and other) spaces worldwide, we see a return of the floating city, this time as a project of neo-liberal entrepreneurialism and techno-futurist philanthropy (Steinberg et al. 2012).

I would like to move beyond the immediacy of such realities, considering instead what it could mean to speak of the "urbanisation of the sea" as a problem of the present that accompanies the ontological and epistemological formation of the urban itself. That is to say, I would like to see how such issues shed light on the historical relation between the urban and ocean-space. What could it mean to speak of the ontologies produced in the early modern experiences of ocean-space that, in turn, lends to the task various ideas relevant to the practical *re*imagination of terrestrial spaces? If today we know the spaces that the territorialisation of the ocean has produced (Steinberg 2001), what kinds of spaces may have resulted from a "maritimisation of the land"?

This work explores a speculative history of a maritimisation of the land in which the modern notion of territory as a political technology (Elden 2013a) was augmented by a spatiality that developed not on land but over the course of three centuries of maritime activities that followed Columbus's crossing of the Atlantic. Across this period, a consistent ontological resonance can be traced between representations of ocean-space and constructions of territory on land (Steinberg 2009), yet by the nineteenth century a fundamentally new representation of terrestrial space appeared that effectively collapsed the two spatialities into one. Examining the writings of the Saint-Simonian engineer and statesman Michel Chevalier (1806–1879), we will see how he adopts the concept of network (*réseau*) from medical and hydrological sciences to propose a radically new counter-state, counter-territorial geographical imaginary – a powerfully seductive space that would be free of the political oppression and divisions that territory had inscribed onto the land. Here, territory could be conceptually overcome *and* tacitly resurrected as a benign, social technology made to animate a globe of fluid, controlled circulation whose order would be built around a hierarchy of nested scales of private, economic traffic. A post-revolutionary idealisation of a world to come, this counter-state imaginary profoundly influenced the development of international trade, capitalism, and the liberal nation-state, and would generate the political and economic will to begin constructing the first planetary infrastructures necessary for this transformation shortly thereafter.

Curiously, this new planetary spatial order would inadvertently find its conceptual foundation less in the scientific, mathematical roots of *réseau* than in the epistemologies of early modern ocean-space; its hydrological origin reappears in later attemtps to directly apply the mathematics of hydrology to "scientifically" control all forms of human movement (Picon 2002). Indeed, privileging a logic of circulation over enclosure, Chevalier's world organised by networks resulted less in the disappearance of territory than in its adaptation to a new set of demands, allowing it to be reimagined as a technology useful for organising a borderless space, the idealised extents of which would be the globe itself. Shifting the emphasis of territory from the border to the corridor, Chevalier's geography enabled the simultaneous measurement and control of space across multiple scales, opening up a space that could be ordered according to a single logic applied to all scales at once. And it is precisely for this reason that the shift to a corridor-based, maritime geography inspired by the idea of the network would lay the foundations for a wholly new spatiality to appear whose intricate geographies we are still only beginning to grasp: *urbanisation* (Adams in press).

At the heart of this story is a history of circulation, a quiet, yet historically consistent accomplice in and common denominator between the various spatial distinctions and political orders that have structured and restructured the Western world since the sixteenth century. From enclosed territories to colonial spaces, across land and sea, from global empires to an urbanised planet, it is circulation that opens up a historical geography of power less interested in the essentialised qualities of land or sea, but rather in the abstract logics of modern power that cut across both.

URBANIZACIÓN

It is hardly coincidential that the first theorist of urbanisation, the Spanish engineer Ildefonso Cerdá (1815–1876), would base his entire theory on the notion of network. Nor is it by chance that the space he imagined under the name *urbanización* – a term he coined in 1861 – would be one thoroughly endowed with maritime ontologies. For Cerdá, *urbanización* represented nothing less than a natural desire prehistorically inscribed in the human condition. Urbanisation was, for him, the realisation of a human-technological project suppressed by centuries of political excess: it was at once humanity's distant past and its irresistible destiny. In 1867, pushing well beyond any of his peers at the time, Cerdá published his opus, *Teoría general de urbanización* (*General Theory of Urbanization*), a 1,500-page work in which he laid out a proposal for a comprehensive spatio-governmental apparatus that promised not to reform existing cities, but to replace them entirely with a radically new systematic spatiality he called the *urbe*. Much more than a city, Cerdá's *urbe* was to be a universal, technologically-mediated, domestic spatial order – a generic grid of human habitation predicated on and enabling limitless circulation (a principle he called *vialidad*) and its perpetual self-expansion (*urbanización*).

Cerdá's project of urbanisation had deep political aspirations. It aimed to rid the modern world of the inadequacies of the city, and make redundant altogether the state and the political. Like many other liberals of his time, Cerdá placed endless faith in the development of technology, which he believed could in itself overcome outdated political divisions, while joining humanity in the shared interest in infrastructures of international exchange. For Cerdá, the *urbe* was to be endowed with the historical force that permitted it systematically to transgress all historical, sociopolitical boundaries, and distinctions, subsuming them under a singular, statistically-modulated spatial order. From blurring boundaries between public and private to erasing distinctions between itself and the countryside, the *urbe* would project its calculated grid in all directions, absorbing towns, villages, cities, hamlets, and open landscapes, transcribing them all as a smooth, regularised order distinguished only by spaces of rest and movement; the biological and the economic; fixed capital and labour. Even its inherent, notional opposition to the rural was subsumed under what Cerdá came to refer to as "ruralised urbanisation". Mountainous regions, deserts, even the sea itself, were to be sites of unlimited urbanisation, where nature, civilisation, technology, and economy would be distributed according to an abstract mathematics. In this space, city blocks would become regulated biological machines of human reproduction, and the network of streets, drained of any representational capcity, would instead cohere as a coordinated economic machine, complete with a clock at each intersection to synchronise the circulation of traffic with the rhythms of a burgeoning international capitalism. Embodying the expansive energies of an ascendant bourgeois society, this new domestic-economic template was to stretch across the entire Earth, uniting classes and civilisations in a single, undifferentiated *urbe*, transforming the world itself into an apolitical spatial union of private property and peaceful circulation. The zeal of Cerdá's project may be best captured in the injunction that appears on the frontispiece of his *Teoría*: 'Ruralise the urban: urbanise the rural: . . . *Replete terram* [fill the Earth]' (Cerdá 1867).

'MARE MAGNUM'

What is fascinating in Cerdá's work is how he repeatedly draws on metaphors of the ocean to describe the unbounded forces that drive *urbanización*. Ocean-space seems to endow the urban with a boundless vitality: from his early narrations of this space – romanticised as a 'vast swirling *mare-magnum* of people, of things, of interests of every sort' (1867, 29) – to his utopian historicisation of it, where 'Urbanisation . . . has always marched forward along the path of its perfection, on which the Almighty chose not to set limits as he had done for the waves of the Ocean' (49–50). That the ocean for Cerdá

could be urbanised was not simply a rhetorical extreme of his spatial imaginary: it was the very expression of the fluid space of the urban constituted by
perpetual, rhythmic motion and expansion in all directions. And this thinking
went beyond metaphors: for Cerdá, the mutual exchange of services between
any two vessels at sea constituted a fundamental *urbe*, leading him to theorise
a distinction between what he called *urbes acuáticas* and *urbes terrestres*
(Cerdá 1867). From this thinking, the *via* ("way"), rooted in his neologism
vialidad, can refer either to a street or to its older meaning of a ship's wake.
Yet most powerfully, the idea of "filling the Earth" conjures a liquid geography of biblical proportions that would flood the land, urbanisation wiping
out any barrier or obstacle produced to that point, washing the Earth of all
traces of the political.

One could argue that imagining an order capable of overcoming spatial and
political barriers is commensurate with the logic of industrial capitalism. Yet
as much as he embraced capitalism, Cerdá was a socialist reformer: for him,
capital's promise was in its ability to distribute wealth equally. Indeed, his
writings on urbanisation speak to a far greater drive of his – not simply to create a capitalist order, but to construct a process that would reclaim the space of
the state. More than a space of capitalist flows, his was a project to depoliticise
state space by reconstituting it as a technology of pure human circulation, the
expression of nineteenth-century liberal idealism. Indeed, in a letter penned
shortly before his death, Cerdá (1875) reflected on the idea of *urbanización*,
realising it was another word for the *colonisation* of the state in the name of
"society". Urbanisation, for Cerdá, first and foremost was an apparatus that
could seize territory, draining it of its political history and reconstituting it
instead as an *economic technology* to be put to use for bourgeois society. It
was *land* to be appropriated, distributed, and produced by organising it as a
legally administered, private economic continuum made fluid by an expansive
web of roads, rails, and canals – a limitless grid of infrastructure and private
property. The urban – both a space *and* a process – was an order created to
totalise the universality of the state by incrementally *urbanising* its territory.

As we will see, the urbanisation of territory is both a concrete process of
filling out the space of the state (territory as a bounded spatial entity) and a
conceptual process of fundamentally transforming its capacity to measure
and control space (territory as a political technology) – two processes that
are inseparable from one another. This ceaseless expansion was an attribute
necessary to produce a spatial order fit for an apolitical world: Cerdá's *urbanización* itself was to be a perpetual, bloodless revolution in which technology
would overthrow politics. Yet precisely for this reason, the attempt to do
away with territory would only serve to expand its range of intervention as a
political technology and deepen its capillary purchase on society.

RÉSEAU

Cerdá was not the first to reimagine territory as an apolitical technology. Just thirty-five years prior to the publication of the *Teoría*, a text entitled *La Système de la Méditerranée* (*The Mediterranean System*) was published in *Le Globe* by the Saint-Simonian Michel Chevalier (1832). In this landmark publication, Chevalier proposed a "universal association" between the peoples of Europe and "the Orient", an achievement made possible by extending a coordinated system of banks, rails, rivers, and canals throughout Europe and across the Levant.

What makes the text remarkable is that Chevalier founded this spatial system on the concept of *réseau* (network), a concept long used in medical and hydrological sciences, which he interpreted as a general, spatial concept for the first time. Chevalier held that nations organised around networks could achieve a state of perpetual peace through the natural interstate interdependencies that would arise with the unlimited circulation of goods and finance that a network space would enable. More importantly for Chevalier, such networks would inherently undermine the absolution of territorial geographies wherein political excesses had prevented this international, free trade-based peace, dividing the world into warring civilisations. He imagined a new, unified Mediterranean region seen not as an aggregate of competing, politically determined territories fronting a sea, but as 'a series of great gulfs, each of which is the entrance to a vast country on the sea' (Chevalier 1832, 39). It was a spatiality that emerged with a forceful indifference to the "artificial" logic of territorial division and closure, and that was based instead on hierarchies of fluid movement, extending from the scale of architecture to that of the planet (Picon 2002). No longer burdened by the failed "balance" of territorial powers, the spatial order that Chevalier gave life to would be partially fulfilled over the nineteenth century in other writings, plans, negotiations, and works by the vast group of bankers, engineers, financiers, politicians, and urbanists who subscribed to the Saint-Simonian movement, of which Chevalier was a key proponent (Taylor 1975). Threading throughout this body of work is an ideal spatiality constructed according to a single terrestrial polity (a "vast country on the sea"), one that imagines a world ordered by a globally extensive hierarchy of nested scales of networks of circulation.

By all accounts, the spatiality that Chevalier proposed appeared to be everything that modern territory was not. A borderless globe of industrially driven, mobile societies suggests a utopian space in mirror-like opposition to eighteenth-century European statehood and which, by the early nineteenth century, the Saint-Simonians so openly (if not belatedly) rejected. For nearly two centuries prior to Chevalier's intervention, the European world had been reshaped by a political geography in which the primary order of measure and control over space was *territory* – a political technology that helped to universalise the modern state as a new polity constituted within and responsible for a European balance of powers. Territory provided a set of tools through which modern sovereignty could measure its power over land and control what happens within its bounded space.

Stuart Elden (2013a) has written in great depth on this history, tracing an archaeology of territory through its discursive appearance, inflections, and developments. Here, I build upon that reading by examining the discursive and non-discursive maturation of this category, considering the spatial and epistemological role that circulation played in the construction of the space, knowledge, and rationality of modern territory. Modern territory was developed in the epistemological frame of *raison d'État* – a form of knowledge in which state power would be discovered to reside increasingly in the measurement and movement of wealth. As such, its calculations, measurements, and structures of control elevated the status of traffic and the infrastructures, techniques, and technologies that would enable it. More broadly, the concept of circulation offered a scientific means by which the interior spaces of territory could be understood, quantified, and spatially disciplined, thus producing a mechanism by which to achieve absolute control, calculation, and measurement.

In the face of this history, Chevalier's proposal for a counter-territorial spatial imaginary appears to confront only a partial notion of territory, reduced to its mere spatial manifestation as a politically-bounded swath of land. His attempt to use a network ontology to transgress territorial boundaries and invert the antagonistic relationship between states to one of interdependence, clever as it may be, ignored the complexity of the myriad technologies that constantly upheld boundaries, managed circulations, measured state power, and strategised expansions, invasions, defensive measures, and colonial occupations. Indeed, by tracing the role that circulation played in the historical construction of terrirory, we will see that the Saint-Simonian response to it was not only a utopian *reinterpretation* of territory (and *not*, as it may have appeared, a counter-geography to it), but one whose reforming principles drew inadvertently from an inherent relation that territory shared with maritime ontologies since its modern emergence.

SECULARISING THE CIRCLE

Just as spatial networks of all sorts existed before their emergence in Saint-Simonian thought, the history of circulation did not begin in the sixteenth century with its discovery as a concept – *circulatio*.[1] Rather, it has its roots in ancient notions of circularity, circumference, and concentricity that preceded its emergence as such – notions that drew upon new interpretations from a centuries-old "metaphor of the circle" (Nicolson 1960). The circle is a crucial epistemological referent: a central marker of divine order confirming the inherent relations between the godly and the fleshy, the eternal and the ephemeral. Because of this, Western history is rife with references to circularity and cyclical motion seen as signs of divine Providence, and metaphors for luck and fate that preside over the corporeal microcosms of earthly affairs. Indeed, by the twelfth century, at its height, the divine status of the circle was articulated in a maxim that would spread throughout Europe: *Deus est sphaera infinita, cuius centrum est ubique, circumferentia nusquam* – God is a circle whose centre is everywhere and whose circumference is nowhere (Small 1983, 90).

Yet from the fifteenth century, the infinite gap that had separated macrocosm from microcosm would, over three centuries, slowly collapse in on itself. In *Learned Ignorance*, written in 1440, Nicolas of Cusa introduced a bizarre reading of God as a circle. Because only God was able to master perfect geometry, the world should instead be understood as an infinity of "apparent" centres embodied by every individual: 'In consequence, there will be a *machina mundi* whose center, so to speak, is everywhere, whose circumference is nowhere' (quoted in Small 1983, 95). For Nicolas, the world and God were made identical, a notion carried forward a century and a half later by Giordano Bruno (1584) in *Della causa, principio e uno* (*Cause, Principle and Unity*), which described not the world but the universe as that which has its centre everywhere and its circumference nowhere. This kind of thinking would soon be punctuated by Pascal's more expansive use of the maxim in his *Pensées*, replacing the universe with "Nature" itself understood as the infinite object of human reason (Pagel 1951, 96–97).

What is effectively a secularisation of God thus consists in the gradual collapse of the distance between macrocosm and microcosm, progressively folding one circle in on the other. The result of this shift is the validation of a new kind of relativism of individual, human centrality, where the centre that, in God, was everywhere now coincides with the infinity of knowledge (Lowry 1974). In this new horizon, reason is used to fill the infinite space that had consistently been the domain of God's solitary centrality in the cosmos: each individual now acts as an equivalent centre, an identical source of natural reason, displacing a singular source of meaning with a plurality of subjects (Small 1983). As Nietzsche (2001 [1882], 239) would later lament, the pursuit of rational knowledge of the *finiteness of things* would invoke 'scientific' and 'mechanistic' interpretations of the world in which all appreciation and comprehension of it would rest solely on its being 'counted, calculated and expressed in formulas'. This perception would open up a world whose wholeness could be given over to an infinitely grand and abstract space accounted for as a *thing* whose properties present themselves to the rational subject as quantities available to calculation and measurement.

From this vantage point, circularity would no longer stand as the confirmation of a divine continuum between God and the cyclical systems that order the universe. Instead, the circle would now offer itself as an abstract geometrical model through which the human world could, in turn, project order *onto* the world (Galli 2010). This is why the discovery of the circulation of blood made in 1628 could offer something well beyond anatomical knowledge: it presented itself simultaneously as an abstract, measurable concept *and* principle for the organisation of human affairs. As the distinction between microcosm and macrocosm grew vague, so too did that between the labours of humanity and the works of God. And just as the systems of circularity observable in nature had long provided evidence of a divine order, the edifice of the modern Western world would be constructed by evermore sophisticated systems of objects, thoughts, materials, and bodies bound up in perpetual circulation, only to be retroactively portrayed as the work of a divine, invisible hand. The ancient role that the circle had played as the signature of divine truth would not be overturned by this transformation. Rather, the rootedness of circulation in an ancient metaphorical trope reveals why, as a concept, it could emerge as an immediately self-justifying phenomenon – a manifestation of early modern political vitality *in itself*. Indeed, as we will see in the following sections, once circulation became visible as a rational concept, it would acquire the status of both a principle of political order and a fundamental diagram for an emergent economic knowledge. Both of them would inscribe new, yet divergent geometries of movement onto land and across oceans.

CIRCULATION AND TERRITORY

By the late sixteenth century, a modern conception of circulation had begun to find its place in theories of the nascent modern state. One of the earliest to identify an emergent configuration of power with circulation was Giovanni Botero, who wrote two texts of note: *Delle causa della grandezza delle città* (*A Treatise Concerning the Causes and the Magnificence and Greatness of Cities*) in 1588, and *Della ragion di stato* (*Reason of State*) in 1589. Disclosing a kind of proto-Malthusian conception, in *Reason of State* Botero shows that the city's population (expressed as the number of citizens or inhabitants) is a central factor through which all others proportionately relate or are determined. Noting that a city's population (and thus its inferred greatness) must be nourished by a constant intake of food and made wealthy by exchange, Botero looks to establish all the relations between resources, wealth, physical geography, trade, and circulation (*commoditie*) that may influence increases or decreases in the number of inhabitants of a city, and thus in its magnificence. For Botero, if the historical origin of the city is based on the government of exchange, it requires the effective administration of its infrastructures.

Following William Harvey's discovery of blood's circulation, in 1651 Thomas Hobbes developed a similar principle regarding the administration of the Commonwealth that he incorporated into the *Leviathan*. In contrast to Botero's work, Hobbes's ideas could make direct (if flawed) reference to the model provided by Harvey:

> And in this also, the Artificiall Man maintains his resemblance with the Naturall; whose Veins receiving the Bloud from the severall Parts of the Body, carry it to the Heart; where being made Vitall, the Heart by the Arteries sends it out again, to enliven, and enable for motion all the Members of the same. (Hobbes 1986 [1651], 301)

For Hobbes, circulation was a *de facto* component in the mechanics of his *Leviathan* – a system among others. Like Botero, Hobbes's Commonwealth established the object of such circulation as maintaining vitality in its subjects: 'For naturall Bloud is in like manner made of the fruits of the Earth; and circulating, nourisheth by the way, every Member of the Body of Man' (Hobbes 1986 [1651], 300). By endowing circulation with both power and political vitality in the nascent modern European state, Hobbes had identified a central concern on which to base political calculations. The result would be a "mechanical" explanation of both how "man" behaves and a means by which he could be made to form a Body Politique. *Leviathan* thus proposed a geometrical order between sovereignty and subjectivity based on obedience. Turning to geometry, Hobbes sketched the mechanics of the new form of state and described a logic of spatiality in relation to this "Body Politique" that would unfold across continental Europe over three centuries, marking a period in which the relationship between circulation and sovereign power became both integral and necessary.[2]

While it is impossible to chart the extent of Hobbes's influence on European thought, it is clear that his writings resonate with many subsequent developments in the relation between spatial order and political power. Consider, for example, the work of Jean-Baptiste Colbert, whose administration over France in the latter half of the seventeenth century saw vast construction projects and the standardisation of roadways, canals, tunnels, and bridges – this at the same time that the city walls surrounding Paris were ordered to be demolished. Accompanied by the extraordinarily rapid fortification of France's borders, Colbert mobilised new cartographic techniques to know, measure, and strategise in great detail the territorial interior of the realm – a space conceived as an apparatus of managed traffic. At the centre of these works was the military engineer, Sébastien Le Prestre de Vauban, a figure whose office of engineers overseeing city fortification would give way over the course of the eighteenth century to the establishment of both the Corps des Ponts et Chaussées in 1716 and the École des Ponts et Chaussées in 1747 – the corps and school of civil engineering. The inauguration of both institutions marked a period in which engineers formally rejected their traditional proximity to architects, identifying their practice instead with a completely new form of knowledge that treated the entire landscape of France as their medium of transformation (Picon 1992). Over the course of the eighteenth century, the École des Ponts et Chaussées succeeded in translating landscape into an inventory of resources and an abstract space open for the first time to its "perfection" (an early version of planning). The techniques of perfecting this space involved almost exclusively patterns of movement: *boulevards, carrefours, étoiles*, and *rond-points* (avenues, cross-roads, stars, and round-abouts) would carve the landscape into baroque geometries and corridors of movement – abstract infrastructures that would discipline the lands into quantifiable spaces of production and connect it with measurable, controlled lines of circulation. Over the course of the eighteenth century, the engineers of the Ponts et Chaussées stood as a crucial technological arm of the state in its construction of territory as both a form of knowledge and a coordinated interior space of circulation.

The epistemological horizon against which such projects were formulated also gave ground to new theoretical work. Treatises such as *La metropolitée, ou, De l'êtablissement des villes capitales* (*The Metropolis, or, Of the establishment of capital cities*) by Alexandre Le Maître (1682) theorised the state as a space in which cities, towns, and villages were to be concentrically organised around the capital city and coordinated by a system of infrastructure, depicting the state as a space for the efficient circulation of wealth. For Le Maître circulation stands as a self-evident and virtuous process that assists in making functional and whole its territorial interior. That Le Maître's text lacks any formal framework for its analysis speaks not so much to an undeveloped form of knowledge but to the fact that circulation *in itself* had become a kind of modern political truth within an emergent territorial epistemology. Le Maître's treatise offers an idealistic socio-spatial template that would be filled out with a more rigorous analytical thinking by the Physiocrats in the following century – a group whose work directly inspired the practices of the École des Ponts et Chaussées (Picon 1992). For example, like Le Maître, Richard Cantillon and François Quesnay would both see society as consisting of three classes or estates. Cantillon (1959) devised a spatialised economic sociology organising the three estates into a generalised distribution where class, dwelling, and function coincided in a new disciplinary territorial order. Arguing that both wealth and the power of the state spring from the land, Cantillon was the first to construct an economic model that traced the circulation and transformation of wealth cultivated by farmers in villages to its exchange in towns and cities, ultimately returning to the farmers who begin the cycle again.

The increasing centrality that circulation played in both the thought and practices of this period is hard to overstate. From the end of the sixteenth century until well into the eighteenth century, circulation, implicit in modernising ideas of sovereignty and territory, would unfold over the terrestrial spaces of Europe, constructing a geography of modern power inscribed in the landscape as geometries of traffic. Indeed, one could argue that the modern formation of territory would not have been possible without having coincided with the emergence and widespread uptake of circulation as a concept.

CIRCULATION AND OCEAN-SPACE

However, it was not only on land that circulation would play a fundamental role. During the same period in which rigid, geometrical corridors of movement were imprinted onto the landscapes of Europe's territorial states, circulation would also assist in the formation of ocean-space, stretching a new order of rationalised movement across the surface of the Earth. Indeed, for Carl Schmitt (2006), the foundation of the first truly global order would rest on this very tension between the spatial order of firm land and that of the free sea – a distinction that appeared increasingly dominant following Columbus's "discovery" of the Americas. It is no small coincidence that *Leviathan* was published in the same year that Oliver Cromwell's Navigation Acts were passed. Nor is it incidental that Hobbes used a traditionally understood sea animal as the symbol for his terrestrial Commonwealth. For him, Leviathan represented a great artificial man drawing from mythical associations with a "great whale": both representations underscored the capacity of the Commonwealth to maintain peace (Schmitt 2008, 21).

Yet this distinction was not absolute, and, from a different perspective, the two spaces may be seen as joined in a process of co-production (Steinberg 2009). Indeed, it may be that, precisely because of its prolific discursive uptake following Harvey's discovery, circulation could become one of the few ideas to bridge over the epistemological gulf between land and sea, and that the early modern world, one might suggest, was shaped by a *nomos* of movement. However, unlike on land, circulation in ocean-space, interpreted by the technologies, policies, and practices of maritime powers, would give rise to a very different experience and knowledge of space that we may ret-rospectively understand as a network.

Only five years before Harvey would publish *De motu cordis* (*On the Motion of the Heart*) in 1628, Edward Misselden (1969 [1623], n.p.) had writ-ten his *Circle of Commerce*, in which he expounded upon a nascent principle of circulation that he believed underpinned commercial trade: 'all rivers of Trade spring out of this source and empty themselves again into this Ocean. All that waight of Trade falles to this center, & comes within the circuit of this Circle'. Just fifteen years later, Lewes Roberts would dedicate his 1638 *Merchants Map of Commerce* to Harvey and his five brothers (all of whom were involved in trade) – a fact that demonstrates the significance that the concept of circulation would play in early modern maritime affairs. In con-trast to the spatiality of the continental states, an *empty* space owned at once by no one and everyone was opened up by English sea-farers and it would become a space dominated by England's non-state fleets of merchant traders. Empire, as it reemerged in the sixteenth century, would be a regime predicted on travel, transportation, and *traffic*.

If land appropriation lay at the basis of the territorial power of the state, sea appropriation would take the form of commercial trade routes and colonial shipping lanes. Its space was one of movement, a realm of free, reciprocat-ing traffic. For this reason, while trade remained a measure of the territorial state's power, for England, it was a source of its new global, imperial power. Space understood from an English perspective could be said to be state space turned inside out which, for that reason, could encompass the entire globe. What remained common to both conceptions of space, and would span the entirety of the modern world, was the dependency of each on the category of *traffic*. If the roads and highways that criss-crossed the territory of a state were a measure of both the space and power of the Body Politique, on the open sea the movement itself of trade vessels was the direct experience of a universal freedom made possible by England's "open" oceanic dominion (Schmitt 2006). In this space, measurable only against an astrological datum, what matters is movement itself: destinations, waypoints, passages, and cor-ridors. It is a space that, because impossible to mark physically, would be given to the virtuality of a logic of circulation itself – a logic that we can approximate by the notion *network*: 'Authentic traffic can only come about with a network that makes a given zone accessible, whether as *terra cognita* or *mare cognitum*, for routine crossings' (Sloterdijk 2013, 34). As suggested in the next section, the distinction between the two spatialities slowly begins to collapse once the concept of network is wrested from its medical/hydro-logical use and expanded into a general spatial framework fit for a world of circulation.

MARITIMISATION OF LAND

By shifting attention to the corridors of movement in both territorial and sea-based imperial orders, we can witness elements of one replicated in the other at different scales and by different means; this is particularly true with regard to security. While territorial circulation had become both a source of state power and the result of its heavily securitised enclosure in England, an analogous notion of security would circumscribe not its territory, but the various circulatory routes of trade that composed England's world empire outside of it: 'The English world began to think in terms of bases and lines of communication' (Schmitt 1997, 51; see also Schmitt 2011). On land and in France, this same demand would be answered by Colbert when he instituted the police as a force to provide maintenance for the circulation of goods in and out of the city. The effect of the police was integral to the administration and political power of the state as a territorial whole, an institution inseparable from its politics of commercial competition within Europe (Foucault 2009). Furthermore, the sense of infinity perceived in the experiences of maritime trade and colonial exploration found its aesthetic correlate in the garden design that André Le Nôtre popularised across Europe in the late seventeenth century. Emerging out of paradigmatic projects such as the construction of Versailles, Le Nôtre's work was a crucial reference for the engineers of the Ponts et Chaussées, who would transform the baroque garden into 'a grammar of planning' (Picon 1992, 220) that could in turn rationalise the space of the territory as a geometric space of measured traffic.

In a sense, the conditions for the maritimisation of the land that Chevalier and his followers imagined were already in place nearly two centuries prior under the broader construction of what Schmitt (2006) called the *nomos* of the Earth. Yet Chevalier's reference to the sea makes this explicit: if modern territory had produced a spatial interior of circulation, composed of baroque geometries, radiating *carrefours*, and *étoiles*, one which disciplined its landscape into striated *tableaux* of resources, then Chevalier's spatiality seemed to draw instead from an ontology befitting the maritime empires that had, since the sixteenth century, carved through the world's oceans with global lines of traffic. For Chevalier, the network literally imprinted on land what had conceptually developed in the space and experience of modern power at sea. Indeed, Chevalier, Saint-Simon, and all their followers embraced an *imperial* order – an 'empire of man over things' in the words of Francis Bacon (2000 [1620], 100) – the missionary duty of which was to extend an enlightened order of circulation and industry to the farthest corners of the earth (Taylor 1975). Without the boundaries of territory that defined its absolute interior, land could become – at least in ideal projections – a sea-like space in which unbounded, private trade could be conducted in regulated channels of traffic stretching across continents. As with Cerdá, the task of erasing boundaries was a first step to instituting a new, apolitical order on the basis that territorial boundaries were, for both men, the most overt manifestation of a politics whose moment in history had come to a close. The brilliance of the *réseau* was its ability to turn the *technologies* of territory against the *space* of territory, unleashing a fluid and limitless space of technologically-administered industrial peace (figure 8.1).

One of the consequences of this utopian spatiality would be an implicit indifference between land and sea. In a world imagined as an empire of "man over things", one abstraction replaces another: political boundaries begin to recede behind endless corridors of traffic, and power begins to measure itself almost exclusively against the global flows of commodities, resources, and people. Joseph Minard captured this new geography of planetary circulation perhaps most clearly in his famous cartographic technique of representing space in fluid webs of quantified movement across oceans, over continents,

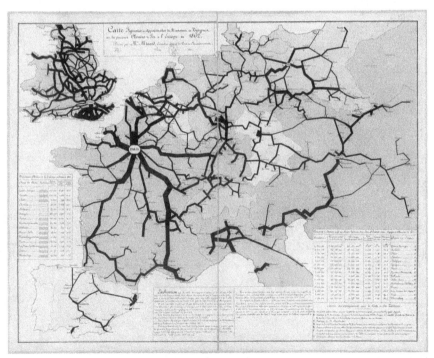

Figure 8.1 Charles Joseph Minard, *Carte figurative et approximative du mouvemens des voyageurs sur les principaux chemins de fer de l'Europe en 1862 (Figurative and approximate map of the movements of travellers on the main railroads of Europe in 1862). Source:* Régnier et Dourdet, Paris, 1865. Reproduced with permission from la Bibliothèque nationale de France.

and within cities alike, capturing acutely the growing indifference about the physical variation of the world. Such perspectives reflect a changing ontology of ocean-space as much as they point to a changing ontology of territory. If ocean-space since the sixteenth century had been represented as a contested space of traffic, by the nineteenth century the technological efforts to smooth it into a machinic space of capitalist circulation would share a clear affinity with Chevalier's imaginary. Naming this space "network" (*réseau*) was perhaps not any discovery of a new spatial perception, but rather marked the fulfilment of what Sloterdijk (2013, 37) has called 'location-spatial thought' that had been forming since the sixteenth century (figure 8.2).

It was precisely this abstract quality of such an order that revealed a kind of *scalelessness* inherent in the idea of the *réseau*. Chevalier's preoccupation with the *réseau* had the effect of liberating circulation from its rigid relations to both landscape and maritime traffic, giving birth to a spatial imaginary that could account for both. The *réseau* offered a single system of circulation that could coordinate multiple scalar registers simultaneously, from buildings to

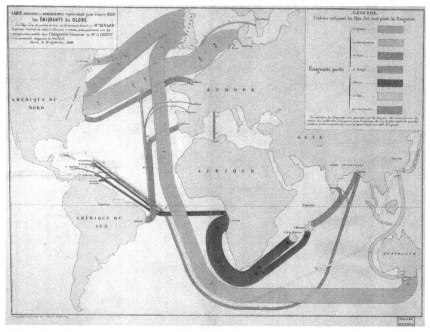

Figure 8.2 Charles Joseph Minard, *Carte figurative et approximative représantant pour l'année 1858 les émigrants du globe (Map – Figurative and approximate representative for the year 1858 for the emigrants of the globe)*. *Source:* Régnier et Dourdet, Paris, 1865. Reproduced with permission from la Bibliothèque nationale de France.

cities to networks that would wrap traffic around the entire planet. By integrating both medical metaphors and hydrological mathematics, the *réseau* could justify implicitly the "insignificance" of state borders by reference to the way that networks of blood and nervous tissue unify the functions of the whole organism precisely by coordinating *across* individually bounded organs; the direct application of hydrological mathematics, in turn, would provide the technological means by which to constitute order in a world of boundless, regulated circulation (Picon 2002). From the transcontinental to the architectural in scale, the idea of a single network – *a single spatial logic* – provided a powerful tool for the construction of modern space.

A conceptual apparatus built out of the territorial technologies of the seventeenth century and abstracted through the utopian universalism of the early nineteenth century, the *réseau* helped to redefine the ontological status of the territory. No longer the definitive political spatiality of the modern world, territory could be imagined as emptied of its political force, reduced to but one of several administrative octaves of an apolitical space of unlimited circulation. Yet far from rendering the *réseau* politically innocuous, its abstract scalelessness helped to emancipate territory as a political technology, allowing its logic to escape its historically bound spatial confines. Once put into practice, the *réseau* allowed territorial technologies to embed themselves in all scales and dimensions of space at once. In this process, security was no longer a matter of enclosing a single political space but could instead be abstracted through a hydrological calculus in the perpetual regulation of circulation itself. While playing up to maritime ontologies of freedom, openness, and mobility, the *réseau* unwittingly unleashed on land what had always accompanied imperial ocean-space: a logic of security, regulation, and control.

CONCLUSION: CIRCULATION UNBOUND

Although the core group of Saint-Simonians restricted their imaginaries to writings, their legacy was prolific – one perhaps most clearly exhibited in the work of Baron Georges-Eugene Haussmann. Haussmann's entire project for the reconstruction of Paris over the middle decades of the 1800s was one of the most consistent products of Saint-Simonian thought: from his selection of engineers to the financial structure of the banking system created by the Periere brothers to the political leverage of Napoleon III. His famous *trois réseaux* gave body to the first form of urban design conceived consciously around the notion of network. As if fulfilling Chevalier's *Système de la Méditerranée*, Paris was both a network composed of smaller networks and conceived as a node within a much greater network of rails that Haussmann advocated, connecting Paris to the whole of Europe and the Levant.

But perhaps truer to Chevalier's project was the work of Haussmann's contemporary, Cerdá. Despite the grandeur of Haussmann's work, it nevertheless remained a one-off project, confined to the historical particularities of the Second Empire. Cerdá, like all Saint-Simonians, was after a much more universal transformation of space. Weaving a patchwork of historical, colonial, administrative, and maritime diagrams onto the broader conceptual framework of Chevalier's network, Cerdá had finally made explicit the true trajectory of urbanisation as a single spatio-governmental logic operating at multiple scales to rationally and apolitically reorder territory. In his constant overturning of spatial oppositions, he would reinterpret the difference between rural and urban not as two distinct spheres, but rather as a single, unified process composed of two simultaneous processes – urbanisation and ruralisation – each occurring within the other: inasmuch as the rural was to be urbanised, the urban too was to be "ruralised" by incorporating measured parcels of "rural" land (primarily gardens) within the structure of each *intervia*, or city block. At once network and grid, urban and rural, interior and exterior, respite and movement, biopolitical and territorial, a new spatial order had been realised in the political spaces opened up in the contingencies and chaos of nineteenth-century Europe. The means by which to constitute this space, as it turns out, was through a directed project of "colonisation" of the spaces of the state with the same territorial technologies cultivated over three centuries in both Europe and the New World, washed over with the domestic moralism of liberal society.

While conditioning nearly all spatial dimensions of the *urbe*, the use of the network and the conceptual centrality that circulation (*vialidad*) occupied both stand as more than simply principles of design. Rather, they must be seen together as the signature of the reorganisation of political power in space: by building itself as an extendable network, rather than a finite spatial entity (a "city") what results is a hybrid spatiality; the urban emerges as *both* territory *and* city while being neither at the same time – a space in excess of both ontologies. As the urban today spills across both land and sea, this excess more clearly reveals itself as the unboundedness of ocean-space that has silently conditioned it since the nineteenth century – a remainder that has allowed it to transform both city and territory through its endless expansion across *all* spaces.

"Replete Terram"

Cerdá did not "invent" urbanisation. Rather, he is perhaps its first accidental biographer, someone whose self-aggrandised polemics inadvertently lend a degree of clarity to the political mechanics of an entirely new spatial order that had in fact been emerging all around him – a space that, today, still lacks thorough historical-theoretical reflection.

While ocean-space may remain a conceptual excess in the urban – a kind of historical catalyst in its epistemological formation – what appears here is rather the excess of *territory:* the technologies and knowledge that helped give rise to the urban some two centuries ago. If territory is a political technology, today it is at least partially operative in the circulations and infrastructures that distribute themselves across the many scales, spaces, processes, and machinic surfaces of the urban. By engaging a history of ocean-space, as a way to locate the emergence of the urban, we encounter another history in the co-production of territory and network – two categories whose interrelations have been the subject of much critical debate in the social sciences. Just as the Saint-Simonians had presumed the two to be oppositional concepts, Manuel Castells built his own analogous opposition between the "space of flows" and the "space of places". For Castells, the predominance that network configurations of society came to occupy by the late twentieth century drove subsequent socio-spatial, technological, political transformations of the state; processes of urbanisation that an informational society brings into existence are thus driven by networking dynamics (Castells 2000, 2010). Network, territory, and urbanisation, while historically mapped onto a broad Marxian framework, nevertheless seem propelled by a quasi-theological essentialism of technological advancement that tends to defy historical time. In contrast, works by Joe Painter (2010, 2011) and John Agnew (2005) problematise the absolution of any putatively oppositional relationship between network and territory by revealing not only their complex interrelations, but also by suggesting their theoretical identity. Largely in agreement with such arguments, my efforts here have been directed at organising the relationality of territory and network around a history of circulation. In this sense, network, territory, and the urban are all historically-grounded political technologies that have in common a quiet yet consistent epistemological core in the unquestioned truth that circulation has provided the Western world for centuries. Indeed, circulation affords a more lateral understanding of Western forms of power by examining a notion central to its logic, rather than constitutive of the effects, spaces, and technologies it produces. If we are to destabilise any essentialised correlation between territory and *terra*, just as much as we are to interrogate the seeming indifference of urbanisation over both land and sea today, it may be in constructing new historical geographies of power that we can best grasp the political spaces and technologies of our world in the present.

NOTES

1. The term "circulation" had been in use prior to this date, as early as 1535, but its appearances as such were still anchored to the metaphorical understanding of circular movement; in this sense, it would take on a properly conceptual valence with Andrea Cesalpino's (1569) use.

2. While we may be able to debate the importance of the role Hobbes occupies in the history of modern territory (Elden 2013a), his invocation of geometry in recentring a new epistemology and its corollary of political space resonated with much of the historical development that would take place across Europe following the publication of *Leviathan*.

Chapter 9

ICE

Placing Territory on Ice: Militarisation, Measurement and Murder in the High Arctic

Johanne Bruun and Philip Steinberg

In August 1946 the crew of a routine flight of the 46th Strategic Reconnaissance Squadron of the United States Air Force (USAF) spotted an enormous mass of floating ice, visibly thicker than the pack ice and more than 200 square miles (518 square kilometres) in area (Koenig et al. 1952, 68). While pondering the potential use value of this discovery, air force personnel continued to monitor the ice mass, code-named Target X. What struck air force personnel most about this mass was its ability to retain shape over time, unlike common ice floes, which continually break and change under the influence of environmental stresses (Crary 1958). These characteristics of Target X led officials to hypothesise that it was an ice *island* – a detached block of glacial ice – rather than a sea ice *floe*.

Inspired by Project Habakkuk, an initiative promoted by Winston Churchill to combat German submarines by constructing an unsinkable aircraft carrier partially from ice, the US military began to speculate as to the military-strategic potential of the ice island and consider its potential for occupation (Wise 1978). Hence, the existence of Target X (later renamed T-1) was initially classified as a military secret. In the years following the discovery of T-1, two other ice islands, T-2 and T-3, were detected. Realising their potential as valuable spaces of science, a group of scientists led by Lieutenant Colonel Joseph Fletcher of the USAF successfully landed an aircraft on T-3 in the spring of 1952 (Crary and Cotell 1952). This event marked the beginning of a more-or-less permanent occupation of the ice island by US military personnel, who used T-3 as a research station as it drifted across the Arctic Ocean, until abandoning it in 1978. During the intervening quarter-century, the island became part of a wider US techno-political network of knowledge production that spanned across the Arctic and beyond (Oldenziel 2011).

During the Cold War, Arctic environments had become exceptionally important. Sea ice in the narrow transpolar gap between the two antagonists was perceived by the United States as a first line of defence against Soviet attacks and also as a source of danger that the enemy might use to conceal its submarines within the ocean's icy depths (Farish 2006). As such, military forces on both sides of the Cold War put a premium on Arctic geophysical research in order to secure their northern frontiers (Doel et al. 2014; Flint 1953). In this context, T-3 offered US military scientists unprecedented access to Arctic geographies (Crary 1960). Constructing T-3 as both a "floating laboratory" and a "floating aircraft carrier" greatly expanded the areal scope that could be covered by military scientists (Koenig et al. 1952), much as ships had done for earlier generations of natural and physical scientists (Lambert et al. 2006; Livingstone 2003). In short, the US military's occupation of T-3 enabled a comprehensive scientific programme that went well beyond studies of the ice island itself. Rather, research on T-3 aimed to promote a sense of territorial cohesion as scientists sought an understanding of the Arctic environment in its totality through a multifaceted study of relationships within and between atmospheric and oceanic forces. The science undertaken on T-3 thus facilitated both an *intensification* of territory through acquisition of knowledge of the ice island itself and an *extensification* of territory as T-3 came to be enrolled as infrastructure for extending knowledge about the broader Arctic environment.

As Braun (2000) notes, research into a place's physical geography is inherently territorialising. The science undertaken on T-3 was part of a large network of practices directed at rendering Arctic environments legible for the purpose of political intervention and control in order to incorporate the Arctic within a vast US military apparatus. At the same time, however, the occupation of T-3 and the research conducted there posed challenges to assumed notions of territory founded on distinctions between territorial land, non-territorial sea, and extraterritorial floating objects. After Latour's (1993) *modern settlement*, we call this the *territorial settlement* – a foundational, idealised division continually reasserted and crossed. The US military's activities on T-3 established a basis for extending the construction of territory beyond both the spatial and material bounds of what is normally considered sovereign space. However, we will argue here that in undertaking these territorialising activities the military simultaneously challenged formative assumptions about territory's underlying materiality.

To explore how the military's activities on T-3 simultaneously extended and challenged foundational (land-based) notions of territory, this chapter tells two very different stories of territory construction. First, we discuss how the scientific research programme on T-3 functioned as a technology of territory, bringing an entire environment within the reach of the American state by extending territorial logics of control far beyond the confines of official state boundaries. The work of scientists on T-3 made it possible to skeletonise an endlessly complex physical world, its elements, and reciprocities between them – tying them together to form a coherent whole. Territorial power was not simply projected onto T-3 and the spaces it crossed; territory was *constructed* there, albeit not through the public performances that have typically accompanied sovereign claims to Arctic territory (Dodds 2010). Scientific practices on T-3 effectively recast matter and motion in terms of instruments of action; prosthetic technologies of territory that allowed the United States to harness the latent power of a fluid environment by operationalising and attuning to the ice island's drift. In short, scientists on T-3 harnessed a notion of territory to a space that, in addition to being located far beyond the sovereign borders of the United States, existed in an environment whose physical properties – in terms of mobilities, depths, volumes, and dynamisms – challenged commonplace understandings of terrain. As such, research on T-3 suggested new possibilities for establishing territory beyond the limits of the United States and the limits of *terra* itself.

After developing this story, however, we turn to a counter-narrative. Even as the US military's scientific efforts sought to extend territorial power to new frontiers, the US government became concerned about the impact that this extension might have on the territorial settlement as well as, more specifically, US interests as global hegemon. The persistence of this counter-narrative reveals a tension between, on the one hand, the will to use science to extend territory and, on the other hand, the fear that this extension will challenge fundamental norms. This tension came to a head on 16 July 1970 when the itinerant community of scientists and technicians on the ice island suffered its first casualty, when the station chief was shot dead. The ensuing legal debate over jurisdiction and procedure, although seemingly playing out in a register entirely different from that characterising the scientific research programme, ultimately resonated with the same question that the military had been implicitly trying to answer in practice: How could an environment of shifting mobile solid water that could be "occupied" but not "possessed" be assimilated into a system of spatial organisation that assumes divisions between solid and liquid, between land and water, and between "inside" (territory) and "outside" (non-territory)? How, in other words, could the territorial settlement be placed on ice?

ACCESSING AN ENVIRONMENT OF ICE

The Arctic Ocean is an environment informed by ice in its multiple manifestations, from the vastness of its winter icecap to the tiny crystals known as "diamond dust" flickering in the air. As ice perforates every aspect of this complex and dynamic ecosystem, it complicates land-water binaries, and not just at the surface. Blowing snow and ice vapours connect the air above to land and water in both its solid and fluid states. Indeed, under the right conditions air, land, and water blur into an indivisible frozen whiteness. Ice thus bridges all elements of the polar region, making it a key strategic component of such an environment. Limited knowledge of the materiality of ice and the elemental reciprocities of the Arctic Ocean environment made this bridge a critical barrier to Cold War US defence operations (Flint 1953). Ice-laden waters presented a distinct danger to seafaring vessels at the surface and below, while Arctic cyclones and the much-feared white-out phenomenon made polar aviation a perilous feat (Cronin 2010; Leary 1999).

For the United States, the Arctic Ocean was a potential battleground: a terrain that foremost served as a space of mobility to be negotiated by aircraft, ships, and submarines. Successful navigation of this space was predicated on establishing a coherent network of knowledge of the material components of the polar environment and their interrelationships. As Lieutenant Colonel Fletcher noted in defence of his proposed research programme:

> Mother Nature is a factor that cannot be ignored. . . . She is a partner in every operation. Ignorance and fear of natural elements constitute the greatest barrier to effective operations. Ignorance and fear are banished by objective investigation, experience, and training. By gaining understanding of natural conditions throughout the areas in which we replace speculation with fact, [we] make nature an ally and increase the effectiveness and safety of Air Force operations. (quoted in Wise 1978, 49)

In the years immediately after the Second World War, US military scientists began to explore whether ice could be made one such "ally" by using ice floes as floating research stations (Althoff 2007). However, experimentation revealed a series of severe shortcomings with such plans. Ice floes consist of frozen seawater and therefore have a lower melting point than freshwater ice, making them highly susceptible to deformation (Pyne 1987). At an experimental US drift station in the early 1950s, it was discovered that equipment left on the ice overnight melted straight through the floe. In similar fashion, the smallest drop of oil from an exhaust pipe quickly perforated the ice mass (Wise 1978). Although the ice floe was thought to have a life expectancy of four years (Crary 1960), it took as little as two weeks before a dangerous crack cut the ice floe in half, forcing the evacuation of the drift station (Wise 1978).

T-3, however, was different. Based on a visual evaluation of its distinctive surface morphology, scientists gauged that T-3 had most likely calved from the Canadian ice shelf (Koenig et al. 1952; Smith 1960). This putative origin implied that the structural cryology of T-3 differed substantially from that of a sea ice floe, rendering it more durable. As such, T-3 promised a much more favourable means of extending the US political sphere into the Arctic Ocean (Fletcher 1997).

KNOWING THE ICE ISLAND

At the initiative of Lieutenant Colonel Fletcher, a scientific programme with two distinct purposes was devised for T-3. First, the structural cryology of the ice island would be subjected to intense scrutiny to determine its infrastructural value. Second, T-3 would serve as a platform from which the Arctic Ocean environment could be studied to gain new insights into its oceanography, subsea geology, and meteorology (Crary 1958).

To gain structural insights into the geophysical composition of T-3, scientists conducted seismic soundings to determine the thickness and elasticity of the material that constituted the ice island (Crary 1954). A number of ice cores were extracted from sites throughout the island to directly examine the internal properties of T-3 in terms of its density, temperature profile, and structural deformation, shedding light on its past movements as well as its history as part of the Canadian ice shelf (Crary 1958). As a floating mass of glacial ice, T-3 had existed for a period of circa twenty years, a blink in geological time but a lifespan that already had outlasted the sturdiest sea ice floe (Polunin 1958). Studies of its deep structures revealed that the oldest part of T-3 had most likely accumulated and compressed over a period of no fewer than 3,000 years. Indeed, despite the ephemeral nature of ice and the relatively short livelihood of T-3 as a detached structure, T-3 had formed over millennia, making it older than some landmasses.

Just as T-3 integrated a range of temporalities, it also integrated a range of materialities. Although juridically a component of the (liquid) ocean and under the continual influence of the ocean's mobilities, T-3 was valued by the military because the encounter with it resembled encounters with solid ground. Furthermore, the ice island offered a set of unique possibilities for studying the intersectionality between ice, ocean, and atmosphere. Hence, the materiality of T-3 allowed it to be mobilised as a bridging agent, bringing the United States directly in touch with the processes of the Arctic marine environment.

Amid these dynamic intersections of temporalities and materialities, the intrinsic stability of T-3, which was so highly valued by the military, was as much a representational construct as a material fact. The scientists had carefully mapped the substructures of T-3, dividing it vertically as well as horizontally in terms of the strata of its upper layers of iced firn, the harder blue ice below and intruding bodies of frozen lake ice. Each stratum was ascribed its own discrete identity and positioned firmly in both space and time. Evidence of internal flow and deformation was associated with the island's landlocked past (Crary 1958). The multiple histories of T-3 were condensed so that T-3 came to be seen as a fragment of a history effectively frozen solid. The deep material "vibrancy" of T-3 (Bennett 2010) was subsumed beneath the material properties associated with the experience of stability. In short, the *political* territorialisation of the island brought about by military occupation was accompanied by an *epistemological* territorialisation led by scientists who reduced the ephemeral, floating ice island to a seemingly solid piece of infrastructure.

T-3 AS INFRASTRUCTURE

Although T-3 had been framed as internally stable, its surface features showed signs of continual change. Since one of the long-term aspirations for T-3 was to establish an unsinkable "aircraft carrier" (Wise 1978), the military deemed it essential to have an in-depth understanding of T-3's surface morphology in terms of its development patterns and engineering properties. Despite its predominantly monomineralic constitution, the T-3 icescape was richly textured and diverse. Its surface and internal structures were defined by multiple types of freshwater ice, each with its own characteristic lithology, structure, ablation pattern, and surface expression (Crary 1958; Smith 1960).

Because the albedo of ice is governed by its structural lithology (that is, the grain orientation and morphology of the individual crystals of the ice mosaic), the effects of the summer thaw were uneven across the ice island's surface. During the ablation season, the most resistant ice features weathered into topographical prominence, posing hazards to vehicles and aircrafts. Hence, in order to render the surface navigable, the dominant ice structures of T-3 were divided into distinct categories in accordance with their material structure and formation history (Smith 1960). To establish a link between lithology and ablation, core samples of different kinds of ice were placed in the sun so that scientists could observe their ablation patterns, while thin sections cut from each body of ice were meticulously studied under microscopes to determine the orientation, size, type, and shape of the ice crystals (Well and Slover 1962). Comprehensive maps drew hard boundaries between bodies of ice, distinguishing them from their surroundings. Cross sections delineated where hidden bodies of durable lake ice might surface in the years to come. Mapping such subglacial structures yielded information about the forces that had acted upon T-3 in the past, but also, more importantly, these vertical representations of T-3's cryology served as windows into possible futures (Koenig et al. 1952; Smith 1960).

T-3 had its own unique micro-climate, its own distinct seasonality, and the effects of annual cycles of frost and thaw were inconsistent because of T-3's non-linear drift across latitudes, a drift that was constituted within a web of drifting mobilities (Peters 2015). Landing an aircraft was not simply a question of where and how, but when. During summer months, the surface was defined by many fast-flowing streams and zones of low-viscosity slush ice, accentuating the island's regular patterns of broad, parallel ridges separated by narrow, water-filled troughs. To ensure an effective militarisation of T-3, these dynamic properties were mapped alongside the topographic expression of durable bodies of ice (Smith 1960).

Even with this detailed knowledge, landing aircraft on T-3's uneven and changing surface represented a series of unique engineering challenges due to its complicated surface morphology (Well and Slover 1962). Past landings on the island had been rough, sometimes resulting in irreparable damage to equipment (Fletcher 1997). Hence, hopes of conducting routine landings on T-3 rested on enhancing "natural" infrastructures, using the only directly available building material: ice.

The basic concept behind the ice runway was to construct areas of controlled flooding, creating uniform platforms elevated above the surrounding ice masses so that winds would keep them free of snow. Before putting up the plastic diking that would serve as a mould for the runway structure, it was necessary to even out the surface and clear away masses of snow (Well and Slover 1962). By covering surface areas with thin layers of coal dust to lower its albedo, solar radiation energy was retained and mobilised to remove unwanted snow at minimal cost.

Although the feasibility of ice runways was demonstrated in principle, their construction was costly and required constant maintenance work. The ice persistently asserted itself, seeping into the cracks of the apparatus put in place to manage and control it, blocking suction and discharge hoses, and rendering equipment inoperable. Establishing a ready source of water also proved challenging. Sea water was plentiful, but its higher melting point led to uneven ablation patterns and the development of potholes (Well and Slover 1962). The project to turn T-3 into a floating aircraft carrier was never fully realised, and the surface morphology of T-3 countered narratives of its solidity and quality as effective *terra firma*. However, these barriers did not prevent T-3 from being enrolled as a critical piece of infrastructure.

MAPPING AN ENVIRONMENT, ORDERING CHAOS

As noted, US territorialisation on T-3 had two modalities: the application of territorial power/knowledge to T-3 as "land" and its utilisation as infrastructure for constructing a *terrain* within and across which power could be mobilised. Terrain, as Gordillo (2013) notes, is pure multiplicity. Construed as terrain, the Arctic Ocean ecosystem comprised vast stretches of perennial cap ice, ice-laden ocean plane, freezing water beneath it, and harsh atmosphere above. In the Arctic Ocean, the conceptual *terra* of terrain and territory comprised a complex of overlapping and entangled materialities as well as exchanges between them. Mapping and ordering this chaotic multiplicity was the primary objective of the scientific programmes on T-3 (Crary et al. 1952).

The apparent permanence of the ice island made it an ideal site for meteorological research. Weather data gathered on T-3 vastly improved the US's ability to monitor and predict the course of potentially destructive Arctic cyclones and significantly increased the quality of synoptic weather maps covering the entire Arctic region (Crary et al. 1952). T-3 served as a platform from which to study Arctic Ocean pack ice, both in relation to its immediate surface qualities and the ice canopy underneath. By observing the ice island's drift in terms of speed and rotation, scientists were able to generate valuable information about ocean currents and ocean depth in the areas along T-3's path (Crary and Cotell 1952). The oceanic soundscape was mapped by installing permanent hydrophones both within the structure and beneath the island (Buck 1965).

To forge a coherent whole from the chaotic multiplicity of the Arctic Ocean, these different knowledges were mapped onto each other to identify correlations between elements and forces. In this manner, territory was constructed out of chaos through the application of classificatory schemes that accorded with human goals and desires. Following Grosz (2008, 20), 'territory is established only once qualities/properties come to have their own resonance, their own forms of repetition and reconstruction; territory is the spatiotemporal configuration of [Earth's] rhythms and forces'. From their ice island platform, the scientists of T-3 effectively rendered the rhythmic forcefulness of the ocean, the atmosphere, and the cryosphere expressive in novel ways. Each element was bound, framed, and identified as a distinct physical entity, a coherent assemblage of individual molecules acting as a whole that was both more and less than the sum of its parts. An imperceptible quality was extracted from the Arctic Ocean ecosystem – a quality that emerged only subsequent to the practices that first brought it into being as terrain: its territorialisation.

HARNESSING DRIFT

The scientific programmes on T-3 projected a degree of ontological stability onto an environment defined by layer upon layer of movement. The scientists meticulously accounted for both the external displacement and internal flows of the ice island, tracing its crudely elliptical orbit across the ocean and its slow clockwise rotations (Crary 1958; Smith 1960). The erratic drift of T-3 was caught up in a multiplicity of motion, spanning from the molecular vibrancy of matter to the planetary movement of the earth and the gravitational pull of the moon (Hessler 1966; Leschack 1964). Following Peters (2015), T-3's drifting constituted a particular typology of mobility, comprising its own distinct politics of movement. The territorial politics of T-3 was inextricably linked to its drift; the mobility of knowledge depended on the mobility of the island (Wise 1978).

For the T-3 scientists, mobility translated into access and knowledge and, as such, it became a political resource in its own right. Beyond a simple question of movement, the politics of T-3's drift was rooted in the practices through which mobility was rehearsed and rendered meaningful (Cresswell 2010; Peters 2015). To capitalise on the drift of T-3, scientists mapped its erratic and largely unpredictable movements and shifting orientation. Disrupting the ideal of mobility as smooth, linear motion, T-3's journey was characterised by friction and ruptures. Concurrently, though, the patterns of drift were smoothed over, stabilised, and captured on maps and graphs, revealing a largely cyclical pattern of motion at a near-constant daily pace of 1.2 miles (1.9 kilometres) (Koenig et al. 1952). In other words, by reconceptualising drift as "motion", the ice island was constructed as territory.

The drift of T-3 was uncontrolled and uncontrollable. It was neither planned nor purposeful. Nonetheless, drift was the very source of territorial power, and it is telling that when T-3 stopped drifting – when it was temporarily grounded in shallow waters off the coast of Alaska – it was abandoned, only to be reoccupied when it began drifting again. The scientists experimented with novel ways to operationalise the drift of T-3, modelling its movements within a drift ecology constituted by other, complementary elements that were also characterised by drift, including ocean currents and atmospheric systems. In this sense, the purpose of the scientific programmes on T-3 was not merely to ensure the strict ontological stability of an environment in flux or to "freeze" movement through cartopolitical logics of stasis (Strandsbjerg 2010). Rather, power and control were linked to the possibility of using science to attune the US military apparatus to the rhythmic pulsations of the environment and, as such, extract power by drawing on and over the forces of the Earth (Grosz 2008; Peters 2015). By striating movement, slowing it down, and rendering it intelligible and predictable, researchers sought to enlist it as a formative part of a coherent territorial whole (Grosz 2005).

As Steinberg and Peters (2015, 248) note, territorialising environments defined by continual change involves 'account[ing] for the chaotic but *rhythmic* turbulence of the material world, in which, even amidst unique events of coming together, there is a persistent, underlying churn – a dynamic pattern

of repetition that provides stability and texture in an environment of underlying instability'. In significant ways, the scientific programme on T-3 was
directed towards dissecting movement and mapping interwoven mobilities
and patterns. Movement was divided into a series of discrete spatio-temporal
moments, captured in the strata of the ice mass (a material manifestation of
time), by discrete locational markers on maps and meteorological data points.
These moments represented points in space and time when material elements
were brought together and temporarily stabilised. From a string of moments,
a trend was extrapolated. In this sense, a territorial order was loosely assembled from a series of foregone moments from which a mappable trajectory
of movement was induced (Grosz 2005). The resulting territorial formation
was one of emergence, but by threading these moments together, emergence
became essence in its own right.

T-3 AS PROSTHESIS

To summarise our argument thus far, T-3 had brought the US military apparatus in touch with the Arctic Ocean environment by facilitating a series of
direct material encounters. T-3 served as a point of connection and sustained
connectivity far beyond the confines of the ice island itself. By effectively
skeletonising a chaotic, harsh, complex, and seemingly unpredictable environment, the US scientists multiplied accessibilities and possible actions
within the targeted geographies. Airplanes could navigate with greater
certainty thanks to more reliable weather data. Submariners had more information about the contours of the ice canopy, the directionality and force of
ocean currents, and the influence of ambient noise on their communication
devices. Framing, dividing, and cataloguing the Arctic Ocean, the scientific
programme that T-3 made possible did more than simply project territorial
power onto an unruly environment. It recast the Arctic Ocean as a source of
military-strategic power: not just *terra* but *terrain*.

In constructing T-3 as military-scientific infrastructure, T-3 (and its icy
matter) was enlisted not merely as an "ally", as Lieutenant Colonel Fletcher
had proposed, but as a "prosthesis" (Grosz 2005, 139), an agent that at various times served as meteorological archive, research station, potential aircraft
carrier, and instrument of science. As a prosthetic technology of territory,
T-3 served as an elemental nodal point, pulling together a complex territorial
assemblage of matter and meaning. T-3 thus enabled the US to capitalise on
the elemental forcefulness of the Arctic Ocean by facilitating direct, physical
access to the environment, which allowed matter and movement to be pas-
sively consumed and actively enacted and engaged. To produce a coherent
territory, a meaningful terrain, the Arctic environment was separated into

discrete, bounded elements that were dissected, deconstructed, analysed, and subsequently reassembled in the form of a new, meaningful whole. The Arctic Ocean was framed as an ordered and coherent geography through which power could be extended in all thinkable directions, through all thinkable elements, at all thinkable scales.

And yet, even as T-3 was constructed as a coherent thinkable territory, a space of control and definition, it was also a space that defied definition, a space of *un*thinkability. While the concept of territory establishes limits by delimiting space through boundaries, it also works within preconceived geophysical limits, including those implied by the territorial settlement that restricts territory to the finite extent of land-space. By suggesting the potential for extending territory to new environments, the research on T-3 exposed the tensions that lay within such an extension. While these tensions were present in the everyday actions of the scientists (for example, when engineering the surface of T-3 so that it could host a viable runway), they reached a head when T-3 was placed within a domain particularly prone to reify fixed categorisations: law.

A PLATFORM *OF* TERRITORY /
A PLATFORM *FOR* TERRITORY

Since the twentieth century, the United States has maintained that the territorial settlement requires no modification in the Arctic, a position affirmed by international law. From this perspective, it makes no difference whether or not a marine environment is liquid or solid: water in any state is the political antithesis to land and, as such, is not amenable to construction as territory. However, other states, and Canada in particular, have had different interpretations (Steinberg et al. 2015; Steinberg and Kristoffersen 2017).[1] Canadian history is littered with accounts of high-ranking officials making semi-official declarations that Canadian sovereignty applies to land *and* (frozen) water in the ocean to its north, in a sectoral wedge extending from the easternmost and westernmost points of Canadian land territory up to the North Pole. In 1945, Ambassador Lester Pearson declared that Canada's sovereignty included 'frozen sea . . . extended to the North Pole' (cited in Cruickshank 1971, 185), while in 2007 Minister of Foreign Affairs Peter Mackay asserted that when the Russian flag was planted on the seabed beneath the sea ice at the North Pole it was a violation of 'our property . . . our water' (cited in Steinberg et al. 2015, 21). Canadian officials have alternated these assertions of the "sectoral theory" with contradictory statements declaring that there is nothing special about territory in the Arctic. However, official Canadian maps continue to denote 'international boundaries' that extend along lines that cut through the frozen ocean to the North Pole (for example, Natural Resources Canada 2015). Scholarly works analysing these apparent inconsistencies in Canadian constructions of maritime sovereignty suggest that Canadian attitudes towards the legal status of sea ice resemble the substance's liminal geophysical status. Just as sea ice is geochemically identical to water but phenomenologically suggestive of an altogether different kind of substance, sea ice is legally acknowledged to be "of the sea" but is regularly mobilised to suggest alternative futures outside the territorial settlement inherited from continental-temperate environments (Boyd 1984; Byers 2013; Dufresne 2007; Franckx 1993; Pharand 2009; Rothwell 1996).

Donat Pharand, arguably the leading twentieth-century Canadian authority on Arctic waters, contends that while normal rules of sovereignty and territory apply in the Arctic (for example, ice floes are no different from liquid ocean), ice *islands* may present a special case because they are amenable to occupation for extended periods of time. Pharand asks:

> Being capable of occupation, can these ice islands be considered as floating pieces of territory? Or are they perhaps more of the nature of ships? Or do they possibly constitute a special phenomenon of nature not yet capable of legal qualification? (Pharand 1969, 467)

Pharand concludes that 'ice islands do not have the qualities of permanency and stability which are basic characteristics of any piece of territory' (p. 473) and that they cannot be classified as ships because they cannot be navigated. Nonetheless, he identifies a lacuna in our understanding of territory that, short of applying the sectoral principle that would identify entire swaths of the Arctic as sovereign space, may require a new international convention if human occupation of ice islands increases.

UNITED STATES V. ESCAMILLA

As it turned out, just one year after Pharand published his article on ice islands, an incident occurred that required international jurists to directly consider the territorial status of these formations. Mario Escamilla, an electronics technician working on T-3, learned that another staff member, Donald "Porky" Leavitt, had stolen Escamilla's fifteen-gallon jug of homemade raisin wine. When Escamilla confronted Leavitt, the station chief, Bennie Lightsy, who was drinking with Leavitt at the time, attempted to placate Escamilla. In the struggle that ensued, Escamilla's rifle accidentally discharged, leaving Lightsy dead on the floor of Escamilla's cabin.

When Escamilla was brought back to the United States by military police, he was arraigned before the Eastern District Court of Virginia, with the United States claiming 'special maritime and territorial jurisdiction' (SMTJ), which is reserved for 'any vessel belonging . . . to the United States or any citizen . . . when such vessel is . . . out of the jurisdiction of any particular state' (18 United States Code 7(1)). Escamilla's defence team protested that the SMTJ provision of US Code did not apply because, in this particular instance, there was no vessel.

The United States might have argued that T-3 was effectively a vessel, but this claim would have opened up a new set of questions:

> Had it been argued that T-3 was a "vessel", the United States would have had to face a number of problems which it did not wish to deal with. Was T-3 a public or private ship? Should not criminal statutes be strictly construed? T-3 had already grounded once off Alaska – what would be the responsibilities of the United States if T-3, regarded as a United States vessel, grounded in Canadian territorial seas, or constituted a danger to navigation? (Auburn 1973, 554)

Alternatively, the United States could have argued that T-3 was an island over which it had sovereignty (perhaps of a provisional nature, in the same way that it had claimed sovereignty over "guano islands" in the Pacific in the mid-nineteenth century). However, in addition to the conceptual problems arising from equating T-3 with land noted earlier by Pharand, designating T-3 as an island would have established a precedent for territorialising the sea, in direct opposition to the territorial settlement and contrary to US global maritime interests that prioritised the maintenance of freedom of navigation. Instead, the United States argued that because "vessel-related activities" occurred on T-3 the case met the spirit, if not the letter, of the SMTJ provision in US Code.

For Canada, the United States' decision to treat T-3 as equivalent to (but not actually) a vessel was an ideal resolution to a difficult problem. The shooting occurred shortly after US-Canada tensions had been elevated by the unauthorised transit of the *SS Manhattan* icebreaker through the Northwest Passage. Additionally, preliminary negotiations for the Third United Nations Conference on the Law of the Sea had recently gotten under way. Legal scholars celebrated the opportunity that the *Escamilla* case provided for Canada either to definitively affirm or reject the sectoral theory. Yet political leaders felt that it would be inadvisable to make a precedent-setting declaration in either direction (Auburn 1973; Cruickshank 1971). Instead, in a carefully worded note, Canada informed the United States that '[it] would not object to having the drifting ice formation in question treated as a ship for the purposes of the particular legal proceeding' and that it waved any claim to jurisdiction 'if it is considered necessary for the purposes of the legal proceedings' (cited in Auburn 1973, 554–55).

In short, US jurisdiction over Escamilla was asserted not by claiming that T-3 was a kind of territory (a ship, an island, a military base, or a scientific research station involved in the production/extension of territory) but rather by holding that it was an entirely deterritorialised space, albeit one that had certain ship-like properties. The United States' argument for this position rested on a combination of a very broad interpretation of the SMTJ doctrine and on an appeal to the related concept of "personal jurisdiction" whereby, in the absence of any territorial connection, jurisdiction can be applied to a state's citizens (Pharand 1971). The application of personal jurisdiction was uncontestable in this case, since no state other than the United States could plausibly claim jurisdiction *and* all parties involved (Escamilla, Lightsy, and Leavitt) were US citizens. However, the jurisdiction question could have been much more contentious if one of the parties had been a non-US citizen or if, at the time of the shooting, T-3 had drifted into Canadian waters (Wilkes 1972).

DETERRITORIALISING THE FROZEN SEA

Although we know the argument made by the United States for claiming jurisdiction over Escamilla, we will never know the exact reason why the court granted it. In the District Court case, the judge simply accepted jurisdiction without giving a reason, and Escamilla was found not guilty of second-degree murder but guilty of manslaughter due to gross negligence. Escamilla subsequently appealed on several grounds, including jurisdiction. However, the six-judge appellate panel split 3–3 on the jurisdiction question and thus sidestepped the issue. As a result, no definitive pronouncement on the status of ice islands in US jurisprudence has ever been rendered. One indirect consequence of the jurisdictional issues surrounding the case, however, was the addition of a new line to US Code stating that SMTJ can be applied in 'any place outside the jurisdiction of any nation with respect to an offense by or against a national of the United States' (18 US Code 7(7)), effectively acknowledging that SMTJ does not require the presence of a vessel.

When the case was appealed, a further layer of complexity was added to T-3's designation as a space that lay fundamentally beyond territory. Territory is associated not just with control of borders but with order *within* those borders. Escamilla's conviction was ultimately overturned by the appellate judges because they felt that the district judge had incorrectly instructed the jury to disregard the *disorder* (and hence *lack* of territory) that prevailed on

T-3. In the initial trial, Escamilla's defence team had requested that the jury be instructed to consider the special circumstances of life on T-3, but this request was rejected. Instead, the judge instructed the jury to 'just forget the [T-3] part other than for background'. The appellate panel commented:

> This [jury instruction] we think was [in] error. Gross negligence or even simple negligence is to be determined by all of the facts and circumstances surrounding an act which is asserted to be either. It would seem plan that what is negligent or grossly negligent conduct in the Eastern District of Virginia may not be negligent or grossly negligent on T-3 when it is remembered that T-3 has no governing authority, no police force, is relatively inaccessible from the rest of the world, lacks medical facilities and the dwellings thereon lack locks – in short, that absent self-restraint on the part of those stationed on T-3 and effectiveness of the group leader, T-3 is a place where no recognized means of law enforcement exist and each man must look to himself for the immediate enforcement of his rights. Certainly, all of these factors are ones which should be considered by a jury given the problem of determining whether defendant was grossly negligent. (*United States v. Escamilla* 1972, para. 20)

The question of just how removed T-3 was from civilised norms, and how much that mattered in determining Escamilla's negligence, remained crucial in the retrial that occurred after the appellate decision. Citing a *Washington Post* article, one legal scholar noted that the retrial, which resulted in Escamilla's eventual acquittal, 'was . . . reported to have been "marked by repeated clashes between the judge and [Defence Counsel] McDaniels over how much testimony about living conditions on the Island should be allowed into evidence," the very issue on which this judge had previously been so restrictive' (Wilkes 1973, 704).

In painting a picture of T-3 as a place of extreme disorder – almost a *state of nature* – the appellate panel and Escamilla's attorney were aligning themselves with an image that resonated in the US popular imagination. Partly, this was a gendered image: T-3 was a wild, men's world. The gendered nature of T-3 was briefly challenged shortly after the shooting, when two or three female graduate students were stationed there,[2] but this social experiment was quickly terminated. As one (male) scientist later reflected:

> The UW [University of Washington] had allowed women one year [in 1971 or 1972] and it didn't turn out well. Think Many Men behaving Badly Over a Couple of Women. The only women within thousands of miles. It was the winter, when the camp expanded to about 40 people: 40 men, 2 women, and did I mention guns and alcohol. The UW in their mode of "let's not kill people to make a point" (remember this was back in the early 70s before we let Political Correctness trump Common Sense) decided after that, no more women. (Bost 2014, n.p.)[3]

The exoticisation of T-3 as a wild environment of unruly, non-normative subjects was aided by gratuitous reporting on the racial-ethnic backgrounds of the three key individuals involved in the shooting. A scholarly article in *Polar Record* (Wilkes 1973) made a point that the three protagonists – Escamilla, Lightsy, and Leavitt – were respectively 'Mexican-American', 'Negro', and 'Eskimo', although the article never explained how these characteristics might help one understand the case. Given the significance of sovereignty issues in this case, there potentially could be relevance to Escamilla being a 'Mexican-born American citizen' as *The New York Times* called him (Halloran 1970, 1). However, media reports embellished by also describing Escamilla as 'the pudgy, bespectacled Mexican American from Santa Barbara, California' (Anon 1970, 47) with 'mutton-chop sideburns and a goatee' (Halloran 1970, 18). *Time Magazine* further exoticised the location by opening its story on the trial by equating T-3 with the outer space of science fiction fantasies: 'If the first astronaut on Mars took that one giant step and then brained his partner with a big red rock what court could try him? Who could prosecute the hijacker of a spaceship bound for Alpha Centauri?' (Anon 1970, 47). Scientists had been attempting to enrol T-3 in projects of territorial construction through rational measurement, yet here the ice island was presented as territory's antithesis: a wild space of nature that defied social or spatial order.

CONCLUSION

As the story of T-3 demonstrates, constructing territory in frigid seas is not a straightforward project. Over the course of its twenty-five-year occupation by the United States, T-3 was at various times constructed as prospective territory (when it was being measured and ordered by military scientists); as a vehicle for establishing territorial knowledge in a broader environment (when it served as a base for Arctic operations); as a space that explicitly lacked some of the essential properties of territory (when the United States disavowed territorial sovereignty in the *Escamilla* case); and as a wild antithesis of territory that likely never could be "tamed" (when the media described the society that inhabited the ice island). Intersecting each of these constructions was an acknowledgement or, in some instances, a denial of the ice island's material properties – a geophysical formation that, despite its apparent land-like properties, was perpetually transforming and dissipating in mass as it drifted through space.

Ultimately, it may be impossible to fully assimilate into normative notions of territory ice floes, ice islands, or other frozen formations at sea. The territorial settlement is derived from a specific temperate-zone, continentalist ontological ideal where large bodies of apparently unchanging and timelessly rooted land are separated by hostile and featureless expanses of endlessly fluid water (Lewis and Wigen 1997; Steinberg and Peters 2015). The challenge that frozen ocean poses to this ontology may be so profound that a viable legal regime for the Arctic would require fundamental thinking at a more abstract level, distanced from the foundational material being governed (or territorialised). This is the approach taken by Canadian historian Gordon W. Smith (1966, 249):

> The advent of occupied ice islands must weaken sector claims to regions of floating ice, and especially the claims of extremists to the substance itself. A sector claim, if applied to such a region, must evidently claim what must be termed icespace rather than the ice itself, in the same manner as a state claims the airspace above its soil rather than the air.

[handwritten marginalia: FLOW – / LAND – NO / ICE – NO]

Although specifically addressing the impact that occupied ice islands would have on the viability of the sectoral theory, Smith's proposed solution could potentially be applied to the entire Arctic maritime environment: abandon the territorial settlement by dematerialising ice and reducing it to a spatial abstraction. This was, in a sense, the solution taken in the *Escamilla* case, in which T-3's material solidity and habitability were ignored in favour of a resolution that reified its location within an abstracted, extraterritorial ocean-space.

Another solution, however, might involve rethinking the linear spatial and temporal divisions of the territorial settlement to reengage ice's materiality. As Michael Bravo (2010) suggests, such a re-materialisation of ice-as-territory more closely approximates the porous, textured, and highly temporal territorial formations that emerge as a result of scientific enactments of icy environments, as well as the ways in which ice is actually encountered in the livelihoods of Northern peoples. Bravo proposes that engaging sea ice as a "social object" better reflects the perspectives of *both* scientists and Northern peoples. We suggest here that sea ice and the icy formations that appear in and around frigid seas are not just *social* objects but also *political* objects that are alternately designated as inside or outside, supportive or obstructive of territorial norms. In the vortex of these territorial constructions, the limits of the territorial settlement are exposed, but so too are possibilities for its renegotiation.

NOTES

1. Because the United States and Canada were the two states with the greatest interest in T-3, the discussion here focuses on their perspectives on sea ice and ice islands as territory. Other states proximate to the Arctic (and the Antarctic), however, have other perspectives.

2. The precise number and exact year vary, depending on the account.
3. For female scientists' perspectives, see Lockhart (2014) and Horner (2000).

ACKNOWLEDGEMENTS

Research and writing of this chapter was facilitated by the Leverhulme Trust's support of the ICE LAW Project (Grant IN-2015–033).

Part III

EDGES

Preface

Elaine Stratford

An "edge" can be both noun and verb. Edges may be the sharp meeting points or vertices between planes. Edges can also be lines, boundaries, or borders at which things terminate; brinks or verges; narrow surfaces of thin, flat objects. Edges can refer to sharpness – of appetite, irritation, drive, desire, or voice, for example. They can be fuzzy: their sharpness bled out like lines of ink on blotting paper, their acuity rendered vague, their meaning unsettled or complicated. Enacted, edges are qualities we may give to a project, a pitch, or a campaign; or they may be slow advances towards things – such as ships towards a coastline. Edginess may be ontological. The edges considered in the chapters that follow – bodies, boats, shores, and seabeds – are all of these and more. They highlight territory as a political technology simultaneously reproduced and challenged by individuals as they engage space's dynamic materiality.

In conceptualising the edge, we expand upon David Newman and Anssi Paasi's (1998, 200) work on boundaries, where they prompt geographers to understand how many kinds of boundaries there are: 'from the physical and territorial to the social, personal and symbolic'. They propose that the spatial dimensions of boundaries should be inserted back into scholarly and policy discussions. They also argue that geographers should continue to pay attention to scales – large and small, near and far – and to transboundary dynamics, and they hint at the need to boost capacities to write and speak about the operation and effects of different scales simultaneously at work. They insist on the need for multicultural perspectives – and here they refer not simply to different ethnicities but different cultural milieux. Newman and Paasi also suggest that new ways of thinking should be accommodated in studies of boundaries in nature, especially given its multivalence. However, with the exception of one reference to pollution and its cross-boundary characteristics, their examples to illustrate this multivalence are terrestrial; there is no explicit mention of the multiplicity of elements, surfaces, and volumes – beyond solid surface (*terra*) – that constitute the universe.

As we elaborate in the introduction to this volume, thinking about territory and its borders has moved beyond Newman and Paasi's early intervention, as theorists have sought to understand a world beyond solid surface. Stuart Elden (2013b, 49), in particular, underscores the importance of volume as well as area – of height and of depth. 'How', he asks, 'would our thinking of geo-power, geo-politics and geo-metrics work if we took the earth; the air and the subsoil; questions of land, terrain, territory; earth processes and under-standings of the world as the central terms at stake, rather than a looser sense of the "global"?' How might that question be further extended and reflected upon where horizontal and vertical, and sharp and fuzzy, "edges" of bodies, bodies of water, and watery bodies are implicated?

Each of the chapters in Part III wrestles with such matters. Territory remains central; so, too, water – and the seas and oceans in particular. Ques-tions of asylum dominate. Asylum is from the Greek *a+sulon* (without) (right of seizure), *asulos* (inviolable), and *asulon* (refuge or asylum). Early uses of the term were often in relation to convicts and abject others, a theme that is explored in detail by Elaine Stratford and Thérèse Murray in chapter 10, where they focus on the body of the drowned and the wreck of the *Waterloo* convict ship off the Cape of Good Hope in August 1842. More recent uses have been specific to the period following the advent of the war on terror, a matter on which Kate Coddington provides sustained analysis in chapter 11, on the ways in which Australia attempts to regulate asylum seeker mobility. Coddington explores territory as a functional quality of *fluid* spaces with multiple mobilities and immobilities, and territory is thus employed to both grant and deny asylum. In Leah Gibbs' study of Australia's Shark Meshing (Bather Protection) Program (chapter 12), non-human animals are enlisted in territorialising practices of shore control, and the conceptualised edge between human and shark is transposed into the edge spaces that they both inhabit. Attempts are thus made to draw out edges where humans and sharks achieve asylum from each other. Finally, in chapter 13, Rachael Squire moves to "deep" territories beneath the surface in order to examine the US Navy's Sealab II project, which was one of a series of attempts to live and work on the continental shelf off the eastern seaboard of the United States during the Cold War. Squire illustrates the lengths (or, in fact, depths) to which people go to feel as though elsewhere, offshore, below the seas, there is – or could be – refuge, in this instance, in the face of the cold threat of nuclear war.

Bodies are also a prevailing concern common to the four chapters. Con-sideration is given to the properties of salt and fresh waters as they cross the edges of our cells and precipitate changes that lead to drownings and desiccation. Attention is paid to how drowned bodies dissolve, and settle or move, their real and symbolic purchase as expressions of sovereignty mobilised across stretches of water in ways that have effects and affect different from bodies that survive open ocean crossings and that may or may not be free, citizen, subject. Attention is also paid to the body's surface, its internal and external configurations, exchanges, fluidity, circulation, and situation – in hulks, small tow-back boats, near-shore waters, and constructed sub-marine habitats. The body's uses, responses, conservation, or radicalisation – its edgy anatomo-political and biopolitical capacities – emerge in diverse ways in the pages that follow.

Finally, relatedly, power itself is a fundamental concern among the four chapters. Consideration is given in each to the ways in which bodies, bodies of water, and watery bodies are implicated in real and symbolic acts to etch, erase, exceed, protect, enforce, and claim the edges of territory, as well as their area and their volume. Taken together, the chapters that follow illuminate a range of questions about how the body is implicated in territorial and sovereign power struggles that continue to speak to contemporary conditions and geocorporeal and geopolitical concerns.

Chapter 10

BODIES

The Body of the Drowned: Convicts and Shipwrecks

Elaine Stratford and Thérèse Murray

In this chapter, we draw inspiration from Stuart Elden (2017a, n.p.), who asks how 'can we understand how place-people-power relations were labelled, conceptualised and practiced in different times and places'? What might be gained by placing more emphasis on the 'geocorporeal – the bodies in these spaces', as well as on political, economic, strategic, legal, or technical issues? In what follows, we respond to that question, with a view to pushing forward existing work on settler colonialism; its consequences and affects; and intersections with bodies, sites, regions, territories, and the power relations that co-constitute them.

We begin with a conventional understanding – that sovereignty requires territory, marked by edges and boundaries, and that territory brings economic wealth and power. We also assert that the extraterritorial claims that are essential to practices of territory require labour in the form of slaves, convicts, and the indentured – humans constituted as property[1] and then deemed subhuman, dysfunctional, or diminished. In both real and metaphorical senses, these bodies can be seen as mobilised (manifestations of) territories that are also entangled in the developmental push to keep territory for sovereign ends. Their utility requires a complex juridical system of discipline and punishment, as well as incentives (including those that are deeply perverse). Where the aforementioned extraterritorial claims require transport over water, then rivers, lakes, seas, and oceans are vectors and media through/ on/in which those claims are actualised. In the same way that Indigenous Australians would think of the division between land and sea as a gradient rather than an absolute distinction, other elements of territory are enrolled: islands, island chains, coastal zones, and seabeds (Baker 1999; Jackson 1995; Lehman 2017).

Historically, the advent of these claims and allied commitments to an ideal of common-wealth actually required diverse forms of abjection – slavery, indenture, and convict transportation among them (see, for example, Anderson and Maxwell-Stewart 2013; Mountz et al. 2013). Without these, it would have been impossible to expropriate others' lands (often via sea-based campaigns) and exploit others' resources. In all likelihood, the quest for common-wealth would also have foundered (as would, ironically, the growth of freedoms it was thought to engender *if* attended by a broadly progressive political agenda).

In such light, we explore the enrolment of (incarcerated) bodies in the construction of territory by way of an extended commentary on the shipwreck of the *Waterloo*, a convict transport ship bound for Van Diemen's Land that foundered in waters off Cape Town in South Africa in August 1842. We focus on drowning – the actual as well as metaphorical submersion of a body within territorial waters or extraterritorial spaces. The case of the *Waterloo* furnishes a number of insights about how socio-spatial relations of settler colonialism are broken, rearranged, and remade, complicating and constructing territory on land and sea.

DROWNING NOT WAVING[2]

Water is defined as a sticky universal solvent with high surface tension. Around seventy-five per cent of the body is liquid, which both nourishes us and removes waste from our bodies; the lungs are as much as eighty per cent body-water, but after we are born they are readily affected when water is inhaled – often fatally. That we come from water and are gas, solid, and fluid fascinated Swedish photo-journalist Lennart Nilsson (1965) whose signature image, published on the cover of *Life Magazine*, is a foetus floating in an amniotic sea (see Stratford 2015, ch. 2).[3] Read metonymically, the image invokes John Donne (2001 [1624]): islands we may be, but also archipelagic – solitary and connected at one and the same time.[4]

According to summaries of drowning[5] by David Szpilman et al. (2012) and A. H. Idris et al. (2003), salt water is hypertonic to the ion concentrations in lung cells; thus if one drowns in it, to compensate for the concentration difference that starts to collapse cells body-water from the bloodstream enters the lungs. The blood thickens, putting strain on the circulatory system, which may lead to capillary leak, so we drown both in the salt water and in our own body-water and blood. In fresh water, which is hypotonic to the ion concentrations in lung cells, those cells will swell and burst, as will blood cells, and elevated potassium and depressed sodium levels then affect the heart, leading to ventricular fibrillation and cardiac arrest. The amount of water in the lungs that presents a lethal dose depends on body weight and on whether the water is salt or fresh (Bierens 2006): the amount of *salt* water that is lethal is half that of *fresh* water.

These authors describe how a stage is reached in drowning when, after much water has been swallowed into the stomach, the airway cannot be kept clear and water cannot be spat out, so attempts are made to hold one's breath, which is only ever a momentary response. The *irresistible* urge to breathe in ensures that water is aspirated into the airways, coughing ensues, the larynx may spasm and brain hypoxia – a lack of oxygen in the tissues – follows, alongside the build-up of carbon dioxide in the blood, the acidity of which may also increase.

Those who are rescued from drowning events may suffer long-term effects of 'surfactant dysfunction and washout' (Szpilman et al. 2012, 2104) – their lungs froth and breath bubbles. Massive bleeding and damage to the membrane between alveoli and capillaries can also occur; so too collapsed lungs and breathing difficulties arising from bronchospasms. If a person is rescued after cardiac arrest and then revived, neurological and organ damage may be permanent.

Without rescue, aspiration of water continues, and hypoxemia – abnormally low concentration of oxygen in the blood – quickly leads to loss of consciousness and apnea, where breathing stops. Cardiac rhythms then deteriorate, and the racing heart of tachycardia is followed by the stalling heart of bradycardia. 'The whole drowning process, from submersion or immersion to cardiac arrest, usually occurs in seconds to a few minutes, but in unusual situations, such as hypothermia or drowning in ice water, this process can last for an hour' (Szpilman et al. 2012, 2103). Sometimes, hypothermia provides a 'protective mechanism that allows persons to survive prolonged submersion episodes'; this is because it reduces oxygen consumption in the brain, delaying both oxygen starvation to cells and the depletion of adenosine triphosphate, an organic compound in cells essential for metabolic processes (p. 2104, see also Bierens 2006). Finally, as the vocal cords cease to function, laryngospasms literally rob the drowning person of a voice (Idris et al. 2003). There can then be no call for help at this stage of drowning, only at its fearful inception; drowning is quiet but not peaceful.

Decomposition follows if the body of the drowned person is not recovered. According to William Haglund and Marcella Sorg (2002), this process is not fully understood and depends on several factors – currents, temperature, benthic and littoral conditions, and the presence of varied marine life. In the most general terms, and by reference to drowning in the ocean, Haglund and Sorg note that the body sinks to the sediment surface of the benthic zone: this may happen in stops and starts depending on its weight, proportion of fat, and air content. Then, as decay ensues, gases are generated in the body and it ascends to the surface, which may take days or weeks in colder waters. While submerged, then in various parts of the water column, and again once raised, the body will be scavenged by large and small animals, including insects, as well as algae.

As flesh disappears, and again depending on the body's characteristics and the environment surrounding it, the skeleton begins to disarticulate from the hands and wrists, and feet and ankles, then the head – first mandible, then cranium, and then the rest of the limb structures. The body's drift in currents means that bones may be deposited widely over great distance (Pampín and Rodríguez 2001) or gather in particular areas. Some dissolve, others are colonised and encrusted. As Derek Walcott (2007) has observed of the dead slaves of the Caribbean, 'Bone soldered by coral to bone, | mosaics | mantled by the benediction of the shark's shadow' (see also Rediker 2004).

IN FAVOUR OF FREEDOM

These drowned bodies and their constituent parts, which litter the ocean like small islands, form both an archipelago of arrested life and potential extra-territory, a process echoing the enlistment of the island in the imagination of the continental body politic (Stratford, Baldacchino, et al. 2011). As Philip Steinberg (2005) has suggested, the depiction of the island on the Renaissance era portolan chart, connected by arterial rhumb lines across a feature-less ocean, suggested the possibility that islands could be stepping stones for the territorial claims of increasingly distant sovereigns – what Napoleon is said to have called the confetti of empire. Both insular and continental extra-territorial claims were used to greatly expand economic wealth and political power on the understanding that territory 'doesn't just happen; it has to be worked for' (Painter 2010, 1105), not least in ways by which states exceed their borders (Elden 2009). And such changes cannot be seen simply as based on territory as material. Drawing on Timothy Mitchell's (1991) work on the state, Painter thus suggests that territory 'should be examined . . . as the pow-erful, metaphysical effect of practices that make such spaces appear to exist' (p. 1116). These territorial claims were part of the extraordinary developmen-tal push by states and sovereigns. They were entangled in complex juridical arrangements that enabled certain kinds of persons – slaves, convicts, and the indentured – to be categorised as (degraded) property over which significant forms of punitive power could be exercised, though never without resistance (Scott 1987).

Coterminous with the initiation of the Westphalian system, and particularly from the early 1650s, Thomas Hobbes's ideas on the Commonwealth influ-enced the shape of international geopolitics. Hobbes viewed good and evil as suggestive of appetites and desires either attracted towards or repelled from an object. Hope, for example, he saw as nothing more than an appetite for a certain thing, combined with the opinion that it can be had. Arguably, one such craving was and remains the desire to claim territory, by dint of force if needs be. As outlined in chapter 17 of *Leviathan*, Hobbes's (2016 [1624]) position was that human beings are competitive, envious, hateful, warring, interfering, manipulative, dishonest, and fearful of a violent death. Moreover, Hobbes clearly understood that political community can be oriented around such fear, and he apprehended the efficacy of 'a common power to keep [others] in awe and to direct their actions to the common benefit' (n.p.). John Locke (1823 [1689], 340) later contested such views, writing that humans are naturally in 'a *State of perfect Freedom* to order their Actions . . . as they think fit . . . without asking leave, or depending on the Will of any other Man'. Less than a century later another key founder of liberalism, John Stuart Mill (1963 [1859], 262) was to argue that 'the *a priori* assumption is in favour of freedom'.

Such considerations matter deeply in relation to the body, bodies of water, the drowning bodies of citizens or wards of the state or property, and extra-territorial and imperial claims for land that were enacted away from *terra firma*. In this light, Nikolas Rose's (2007, 131) work on the advent of citizen-ship from the eighteenth century reminds us that this project of nationalism involved such acts as:

> defining those who were entitled to participate in the political affairs of a city or region; imposing a single legal system across a national territory; obliging citizens to speak a single national language; establishing a national system of university compulsory education; designing and planning buildings and public spaces in the hope that they would encourage certain ways of thinking, feeling, and acting; developing social insurance systems to bind national subjects together in the sharing of risks. Such projects for creating citizens were central both to the idea of the national state, and to the practical techniques of the formation of such states.

Rose contends that ideas about citizenship drew on notions about blood relations, patterns of descent, race, and hierarchy that informed political debates about racial deterioration and degeneracy, and the size and fitness of the populations of nation-states, which were pitted against one another in imperial and colonial rivalries. At the time, such ideas clearly shaped the political imagination in colonies and new nations such as Australia (Stratford 1998a, 1998b; Stratford, McMahon, et al. 2011). These sites, of course, were built on extraterritorial geopolitics, as well as the direct use of both prerogative power or diffuse strategies and tactics of governmentality to manage populations (Butler 2006) and of islands and oceans (DeLoughrey 2007; Rediker

2004). As Judith Butler (2006, 55) points out, law 'itself is either suspended, or regarded as an instrument that the state may use in the service of constraining and monitoring a given population'. Like schools, barracks, or hospitals, prisons – *including those on ships* – are meant to act 'with precision upon . . . individual subjects . . . [Yet the] failure of the project was immediate, and was realised virtually from the start . . . Prisons manufactured delinquents, but delinquents turned out to be useful, in the economic domain as much as the political' (Foucault 1980, 39–40).

Inevitably, the generalised utility of slaves and convicts to which Michel Foucault referred was (and is) extracted via sovereign power. Thomas Hansen and Finn Stepputat (2009, 2) consider elements of this kind of value in terms of state-sanctioned 'violence over bodies and populations as well as . . . the simultaneous manufacture of patriotism and use of tactics to ensure it works in support of such violence, most pronouncedly in times of crisis'. In this light, overt demonstrations of 'violence and short term economic exploitation were constitutive of colonial rule' (p. 4). This point holds, notwithstanding other and confounding considerations: that colonies were sites for transformational changes affecting commerce, morality, religion, culture, citizenship, and the struggle for rights – including in relation to property, *habeas corpus*, suffrage, free speech and assembly, and diverse and diffuse social liberties and economic entitlements.

Island penal colonies such as Van Diemen's Land were not immune from these changes either before or after the cessation of transportation. Lauren Benton (2010, 212) refers to these 'island solutions to problems of imperial sovereignty [as part of] . . . dispersed attempts to construct a legally coherent disciplinary order' that, we note, also undergirds sovereignty's extraterritorial claims. Interesting here, however, are not the land-based elements of this project, but the mobile and abject bodies of empire and the moving bodies of oceanic and coastal waters to which so many laid claim, without which no such coherence would be possible (see also Peters and Turner 2015; Turner and Peters 2016).

Of the first category, it is useful to revisit two ideas: that citizenship was a technology of nationalism enacted through bodies – both those deemed citizens and those classified as other; and that bodies were useful in realising sweeping extraterritorial claims to enlarge sovereign power and all that attaches to it. As Anssi Paasi (2012, 2304) reminds us, the 'inseparability of borders and territories [means that] . . . they are dispersed sets of power relations that are mobilized for various purposes'. In turn, Benton (2010, 208) argues that these global dynamics of transportation, incarceration, enslavement, and indenture were structurally linked in state law such that slave 'owners, masters of assigned convicts or servants, governors of penal colonies, and ship captains had authority to administer severe summary punishments'. The sites in which they exercised such authority 'formed different but related parts of a single problem of imperial legal ordering' (p. 208). Like Benton, Evans and Thorpe (1998, 18) underscore the ways in which convictism enabled the discipline of what once had been described as a marginalised mass whose collective bodies could be exploited in similar ways as "slave convicts", underpinned by a 'rationalist masculinity – the denial that people had individual bodies but were rather manifestations of matter'.[6] They refer to work by William Ullathome (1806–1889), a Catholic priest and anti-transportation activist working in the early 1800s. In a submission to the House of Commons Select Committee on Transportation in 1838, Ullathome had described convictism as a form of slavery debasing of the soul and of "right" forms of masculinity that had arisen as part of twenty-three years of struggle between the British and Europeans – mainly French. As Evans and Thorpe expand,

> Arguably, Britain was in its most militaristic mood at this time; with its political rulers and social leaders, like the magistracy, reacting vigorously to any kind of disorder, and especially crimes against property. Australia's foundation as a penal colony was a direct product of these conditions. (p. 21)

The convict transport ship is of immediate concern to us here, for it constitutes sovereign territory beyond terra and, in concert with many colonies, it is a site of martial law, Hobbesian in complexion. In the case of the *Waterloo*, it was also the subject of a mass drowning, a process that, we argued above, is suggestive of the ways in which bodies, water, and land extend state power to extra-territories of extension. In the next section of this chapter, we reflect on the ways in which reports about the demise of the *Waterloo* were framed in 1842, and consider the narratives produced at the parliamentary inquiry in 1843. Here, in anticipation of that reflection, it is worth noting that significant concern was shown for *all* of the drowned "souls", and not just those who were free citizens.[7] For scholars such as Benton (2010), whose own exemplar is a discussion about the Demerara case and an emergent debate about the constitutionality of martial law in British colonies, such matters point to a larger question and underlying anxiety: 'Was there such as thing', she asks, 'as "imperial citizenship" that guaranteed British subjects the same rights everywhere in empire, or could location alter legal status?' (p. 212). If the latter applied, could that lead to the erosion of rights in the metropole in ways decidedly *not* in favour of freedom? In our view, this line of argument should not be taken to imply that those questioning the imposition of martial law in the colonies or the negligent treatment of convicts, wherever located, disputed the "need" for regimes of punishment. Certainly, John Stuart Mill (1806–1873) and others in his circle did not question the sovereign prerogative to punish those who broke the law – although they challenged contemporary methods.

Jeremy Bentham (1748–1832) is perhaps most notable in this respect, and the prison-ship, the prison-island, and Bentham's torus-shaped panopticon prison, reminiscent of an everted island, are parts of an

> imagined legal geography of convict transportation . . . [And on] penal islands themselves . . . martial law was imposed by local commanders who worried that mutineers would run amok . . . the term *mutiny* was not a casual reference but a purposeful transposition of understandings of islands as similar to ships at sea: vulnerabilities to insurrection justified extraordinary measures by commanders to preserve order . . . [which] depended on an understanding of sovereignty that authorized spatial exceptions to institutionalized restraints on the exercise of delegated legal authority . . . [such that] convict transportation multiplied pockets of legal anomaly that challenged emerging visions of imperial order. (Benton 2010, 218–21; original emphasis)[8]

In the case of the British, it was to the antipodes that these so-called undeserving poor were sent, alongside sundry others, not least among them political agitators deemed gravely vexatious from another island to the west, namely Ireland. Many drowned *en route*.

Carl Thompson (2013) notes of shipwrecks that they have been the constant companions of sea travel since ancient times. In his edited collection on long-standing visual and literary representations of shipwrecks, Thompson clarifies the ways in which these events have become significant and sublime tropes of suffering 'often invested with complex layers of existential, religious, and political symbolism, thereby becoming potent metaphors for some supposed larger truth such as the state of the nation, the workings of Providence, or the human condition' (p. 2). Thompson refers to work by the Parliamentary Select Committee on the Causes of Shipwreck in 1836, which established that as many as 5,000 Britons each year lost their lives. In one year, 1881, he notes that 919 ships were wrecked – and that accounts for those just off the British coast. Little wonder, then, that anthologies of shipwrecks were popular in the nineteenth and early twentieth centuries, reflecting the point that the sea

> has often been seen, in western culture at least, as the most profoundly alien and hostile element, with the result that shipwreck is the worst imaginable scenario, evocative of the most extreme fear, horror, and abjection . . . In some contexts, there may also be an ideological agenda here, a need to suggest that perilous sea voyages are worth making and that they may yield great rewards. (p. 6)

At the same time, Thompson describes the ship as emblematic of community and state, a synecdoche of society and a return to the Hobbesian state of nature, or heterotopia in Foucault's (1986) terms – a rupture.

DROWNING NOT WAVING – REPRISE

Consider the loss of the *Waterloo*. Numerous accounts of it published in South African, British, and American newspapers in the third quarter of 1842 drew on a letter dated 29 August that had been carried to London from Cape Town on the *Hyacinth*. Several particulars about the shipwreck are known from the *Hyacinth* letter, as well as from an eye-witness account in the *South African Commercial Advertiser* (Anonymous 1842b), other news reports,[9] and later official accounts to the British Parliament (1843). On 24 August, several ships were anchored at the southeastern beach of Table Bay, approximately two miles from Cape Town near the Salt River mouth. Among them was the *Abercrombie Robinson*, described as a sturdy vessel of 1,500 tons, carrying crew, several passengers, and 501 soldiers and officers of the 91st Regiment. There, too, anchored the *Waterloo*, a convict transport constructed in Bristol, twenty-seven years old, and 414 tons, bound for Van Diemen's Land – now Tasmania. Best estimates suggest there were 330 on board the *Waterloo*: 219 convicts, fifty-one military personnel from the 99th Regiment and some of their families – five wives and thirteen children – as well as sixty ship's crew. Of the ship, the *South African Commercial Advertiser* noted: 'No longer fit to carry logs, she [was] . . . patched up like other whited sepulchres, stuffed with a living cargo by a contractor, and dispatched to the ends of the earth – a voyage of more than twenty thousand miles' (Anonymous 1842b).

On 26 August, a storm began that raged for two more days, at times dropping to a gale – conditions in which much might have been done to alter the course of events. Reports indebted to the *Hyacinth* letter noted how, on the 28th, the storm's high winds and seas grounded the *Abercrombie Robinson* near-shore where, nevertheless, 'she stood upright . . . no lives have been lost. She will probably, or rather certainly, be a total wreck'.[10] Some news reports speculated about the time at which the ship went aground and then hypothesised that, because the *Abercrombie Robinson* was driven ashore at high tide and did not break up, boats could be launched from the shore and the ship reached to rescue those on board.

In stark contrast was the fate of the *Waterloo*. It appears that, on arrival in the bay, the ship's crew had lowered drag anchors at or near the breakers and initially it seemed that they would hold. As the weather deteriorated, however, on neither ship nor shore had obvious preparations been made for the worst outcome, even though there was time to have done so. In particular, 'no life buoys, no coils of ropes lashed to casks, nor any apparatus for establishing a communication with the shore from the Ship' had been organised (Anonymous 1842b). The master had been absent onshore since the ship's arrival, leaving inexperienced junior officers in charge and the *Hyacinth* letter records that late in the storm the ship's surgeon superintendent instructed crew to release the convicts from the prison below-decks, too late to assist in securing and saving the ship, and without plans or means in place to mount an escape from the ship or a rescue from on-shore.

Then, near eleven, the *Waterloo* 'went broadside at nearly low water, and being held by an anchor, she rolled rapidly and heavily against the beach several times' (British Parliament 1843, 13). The sea then broke over the ship again and again (figure 10.1), and it

> took the ground . . . and in fifteen or twenty minutes became a mass of rubbish. And now ensued a most piteous massacre. In about two hours and a half, amidst the crumbling heaps of their perfidious prison . . . men, women and children . . . were crushed, disabled and drowned . . . The scene which now took place I shall remember to the day of my death. The cries of the poor wretches on deck were now heart-breaking. Each sea, as it made a breach over the unfortunate vessel carried a dozen or so into the water . . . There, within a stone's throw, lay 200 or 300 of our fellow-creatures being drowned before our eyes. (Anonymous 1842b)

Figure 10.1 Wreck of the *Waterloo* Convict Ship, Cape of Good Hope, 28th August 1842. *Source:* C. Hutchins, lithographer, from a sketch by Captain Hext, 4th The King's Own regiment. Reproduced with permission from the Allport Library and Museum of Fine Arts, State Library of Tasmania, Hobart, Tasmania.

While initial reports in British newspapers suggested that 250 people died in the wreck of the *Waterloo*, later accounts suggest that it was more likely 190: 143 of the 219 convict males[11] alongside thirty-two of the fifty-one military personnel, including four of the five wives and all thirteen children, and fifteen of the sixty crew. Later, a memorial was erected in a Cape Town cemetery to the men and families of the 99th Regiment who perished on the *Waterloo* (British Genealogy 2009). Publicised there are only the names of the officers who died – the memorial is silent in respect of junior crew, women, and children, and no mention has been found by us of the burial site of the convicts who drowned.

What made the fate of the *Waterloo* different from that of other ships in the storm, and how could the event have been so singularly or selectively destructive of life and property? Conflicting eyewitness statements suggest either that no rescue boats were available or that the *Waterloo*'s situation meant it was impossible to get to. Certainly, in the first major report in the *South African Commercial Advertiser* no mention is made of boat crews trying to get to the *Waterloo* or seeking to rescue those clinging to timbers in the sea.

> On the shore there was no Life Boat, no apparatus for throwing ropes over stranded vessels, nor any thing, in short, to show that the Government or people here had ever before heard of such a thing as a shipwreck. We stood amongst thousands on the beach within a hundred and fifty yards of the dissolving fabric, looking on the agonised faces of our fellow creatures, as they sunk in dozens, battered and bruised and suffocated – useless as children, or idiots, or wild Caffers [*sic*]. As corpse after corpse floated to our feet, and was raised from the brine, there seemed a curse in every dead man's eye on the improvidence, the imbecility, the brutish indifference to human suffering and human life, to which, combined with fiendish avarice, so many miserable souls had been sacrificed. (Anonymous 1842b)

The different fates of the *Abercrombie Robinson* and the *Waterloo* were subject to extensive commentary. The first South African news report was both highly critical and emotional, inferring the case was characterised by negligence and corruption, particularly on the part of those contracted to transport prisoners to the colonies. In that report, a call was made for a parliamentary inquiry and that was reprinted in the *Illustrated London News*, and picked up in the *Caledonian Mercury* (Anonymous 1842d), which also quotes a critical commentary in *The Times*[12] that was apparently couched in terms of a wider debate about the institutional and social indifference shown for the safety of transported convicts.

The next year, the British Parliament (1843, 3) undertook just such an inquiry. Tabled as part of the documentation was a letter from Vice-Admiral Sir E. D. King, commander-in-chief at the Cape of Good Hope Station, addressed to the Honourable Sidney Herbert, secretary of state for the Colonies, and written from King's post at Simon's Bay in Cape Town, on 13 September 1842. Noting the 'sudden and unaccountable' destruction of the *Waterloo*, offended by how 'frightful a sacrifice of human life was occasioned', and alert to the fact that the event 'created great excitement in the public mind', King had instigated a local board of inquiry on the day the *Waterloo* was wrecked. Under direction from Captain Sir John Marshall of Her Majesty's Ship *Isis* the inquiry's purpose was to determine 'whether any and what blame was attributable to the Government agents, the masters, or other persons on board the respective vessels in question'.

Several of King's summative observations are illuminating. He notes, for example, that he had not been apprised of the arrival of the ships in Table Bay and observed that, had he been so informed, he would have insisted on their being removed to the more placid waters of Simon's Bay. In relation to the *Waterloo*, King wrote that the failure of the surgeon-superintendent to notify him of its arrival 'only followed the common and *very reprehensible neglect of duty, in this respect of surgeons superintending convict ships in general*' (British Parliament 1843, 3, emphasis added).

King also reported that he had arranged to convey the surviving convicts to Van Diemen's Land, 'their original destination', and called for 'tenders to supply a suitable vessel for that service'. He closed by referring to the contents of other documents sent to Herbert: a report provided to King by Marshall's board of inquiry; names of the dead and survivors; and 'statements of the stores and provisions already saved from the two vessels, and of articles condemned by survey as too much damaged to be serviceable, and subsequently sold, by my direction, at public auction on the beach for the benefit of the Crown' (p. 3).

Marshall's own report was organised in four sections. The first concerned the state and condition of the *Waterloo*. In company with the port captain, his own master, carpenter, and purser, Marshall inspected the wreckage fragments, which he described as scattered over a third of a mile on the beach and up to a mile to the east of the township. He concluded that the *Waterloo* was unseaworthy when it left England, and that the 'general decay and rottenness of the timbers [appeared] . . . at every step we took' (British Parliament 1843, 4). Iron and copper fastenings were insufficient in number, deficient in placement or, if original to the ship, were 'crumbling to dust with age'. Marshall then enumerated the history of the ship's construction, commissions – some of which were as far as New Zealand, and repairs. He focused on the presence of substandard and aging timber doubling straps, which had been installed some time past to reinforce the *Waterloo*'s hull, and his commentary was supported by several pages of analysis in the form of an appendix produced by his men. Marshall also called into question the accuracy of Lloyd's Register, wherein the *Waterloo* had been described as being in superior condition and 'fit for the safe conveyance of dry and perishable goods to and from all parts of the world' (p. 5). The lack of a third anchor, which Marshall saw as critically important given that people, and not just goods, were being carried, was also emphasised by him. He concluded that the *Waterloo* was 'weak and defective'.

The second part of Marshall's report investigated why the *Waterloo* had anchored at Table Bay. He noted that on 17 August the surgeon-superintendent had given orders to the master to make for Cape Town and Simon's Bay for fresh provisions to counteract scurvy among the prisoners. The master had, nevertheless, hove to at Table Bay and 'allowed the ship to drift to leeward of Cape Point, and . . . he should have put the ship's head to the S.E. in the evening, instead of N.W'. To have done so may have prevented the ship rolling and breaking up.

Marshall's third line of inquiry reveals equally damning findings. The master was away from the ship during the storm, an absence deemed negligent. The care of the ship was entrusted to three mates whose competence was then roundly questioned. Skill in the handling of masts, sails, and anchors was found lacking. The failure to prepare to leave the foundering ship was disastrous (the longboat was on board but filled with heavy spars that might have been cleared when the storm dropped to gales for a period). The chief mate admitted that 'he might have had *any number of convicts* to assist in any requisite work . . . *had they only been directed* by a competent officer, with the assistance of a few seamen' (p. 6; emphasis added). Marshall concluded that these circumstances contributed to an 'appalling catastrophe' that should have been averted (p. 7), even in the absence of the third anchor.

The last of Marshall's considerations most specifically concerned the convicts on board the *Waterloo*. The mates admitted to his board of inquiry that they had no objection to employing the convicts 'in any way for the safety of the ship' (p. 7). Early in the storm event, the prisoners were apparently

> set free, but were afterwards ordered below by the surgeon-superintendent, under an apprehension that they might rush into the boats that should come off to their rescue; he directed them to be bolted down, but it appears that from some inadvertence the corporal of the guard affixed a padlock to the bolt, and locked it without any orders to do so [a matter with which both the surgeon-superintendent and officer of the guard were unacquainted]. (p. 7)

A surviving convict, Edward Alexander, explained that were it not for the presence of a hammer in the prison the loss of all convicts may have resulted. Left there accidentally by a soldier removing leg irons from a prisoner earlier in the storm, the hammer was used to break the padlock when the ship foundered.

In the final analysis, Marshall was excoriating in his assessment of the conduct of the ship's master, and scathing about the master's decision to leave an inexperienced chief mate to care for a ship and so many lives. Under 'these circumstances', and in light of this encounter with the forces of nature, Marshall resolved, 'the preservation of any part of the guard, convicts, and crew may be regarded as a subject of congratulation' (p. 8).

CONCLUSION

If one drowns in national waters (or within cannon shot, as was widely agreed prior to the codification of international laws related to the sea), it seems that one dies within the territory of a nation even if not on *terra firma*. If one is a citizen, people will rise to the rescue, and if they cannot it is tragic and they mourn. But if one is slave or convict, construed as property, and is drowned, is one also spoil to be written off, one's punishment divine providence, one's loss lessened by having status as property and being abject? Perhaps not. All those from the *Waterloo* who perished were known, all were named in official accounts, and collectively they were often referred to in the *Hyacinth* letter and news reports as lost 'souls'. This reference invites consideration of the ways in which Cartesian conceptions of the body have constituted it as the house of the divine, a temple or, in a secular language, of the body as the territory whose sovereign is the mind. As noted earlier, Sara Smith et al. (2016), Mountz et al. (2013), and Paasi (2012) are among those growing numbers of authors who remind us that bodies are central to the constitution of territory and borders. Territory is made through bodies and involves an intimate geopolitics; this is because in water, and in such places as prison hulks and slave ships, bodies 'challenge and subvert state control of territory, become vulnerable to violence due to state bordering practices, and experience and produce smaller-scale forms of territory' (Smith et al. 2016, 258). Bodies actively work to make borders and territories, and the struggles for both play out on the body – on both *terra* and in other spaces of territory beyond the land – and are, in Rose's terms, proxies for the nation in both exalted and abject forms: a necropolitics (Agamben 1998). As Angela Smith (2015, 5) reminds us, the sea is a fundamentally important stage on which play out issues of security, borders, geopolitical contestation, and so forth, and through which living and dead bodies 'test the limits of inclusion and exclusion'. To this we would add other spaces – islands, archipelagos, shorelines, seabeds, and ships wrecked upon them in a 'theatre of coastal catastrophe' (Smith 2015, 65) the modern counterpart of which, graphically geocorporeal as it is, remains all too often in evidence.

NOTES

1. Though see, for a contrary position, Taylor's (2002, n.p.) argument that 'Capitalist economies do not value things that are not property in decision-making processes. The fact that the human body is not property creates an incentive to exploit the resource, degrading it in the eyes of the business sector and the community as a whole. Allowing property rights in fact raises the respect for the human body. The body should be seen as property that is so valuable it cannot be traded. Attributing property rights is a means of providing a framework of legal rights and duties that has been proved effective in protecting individual freedoms and interpersonal responsibilities'.

2. Indebted to the British poet Stevie Smith (1957), and her work 'Not waving but drowning'.

3. See http://100photos.time.com/photos/lennart-nilsson-fetus.

4. John Donne penned Meditation 17 – Devotions upon Emergent Occasions in 1624. The original prose is:

> No man is an iland, intire of it selfe; every man is a peece of the Continent, a part of the maine; if a clod bee washed away by the Sea, Europe is the lesse, as well as if a Promontorie were, as well as if a Mannor of thy friends or of thine owne were; any mans death diminishes me, because I am involved in Mankinde; And therefore never send to know for whom the bell tolls; It tolls for thee.

5. Here, we are using the term "drowning" in two ways. First is the cessation of life in the body as a result of immersion or submersion in water – such as that which might happen when ships overburdened with abject human cargo and their custodians capsize. Second is the risk of submerging our humanity if we use inhumane treatment and the abjection of others to serve our own ends – an abjection that is in itself a kind of a drowning, a submerging of the other's humanity to justify their objectification and our lack of care. And to be clear, our thinking on this topic is motivated by a profound commitment to maintaining faith in our species as *Homo reparans*, the caring species – this despite evidence to the contrary.

6. The reference is to W. Ullathome, *The Horrors of Transportation Briefly Unfolded to the People*, Dublin, 1838, p. 9.

7. Parenthetically, it is noteworthy that the Anglo Saxon and Proto German etymology of "soul" may refer to 'coming from or belonging to the sea', the stopping place of the soul before birth or after death [http://www.etymonline.com/index.php?term=soul].

8. Notwithstanding the merits of Benton's argument, Hamish Maxwell-Stewart (2016, 15) has pointed out that another motivation for the cessation of transportation was this:

> convicts, along with slaves and indentured workers, could be seen as the shock troops of colonialism. While their presence was particularly necessary during the initial stages of colonial development, local opposition to convict transportation was always likely to increase as the expansion of overseas colonies and reductions in shipping costs provided greater opportunities for working-class migration. As a result, colonial labor markets

tended to tighten as colonies developed. As they did so, transportation became increasingly unpopular with free workers because cheap convict labor undercut colonial wage rates.

9. In all, in addition to the report in the South African Commercial Advertiser, twenty-four other accounts were traced in relation to this event (Anonymous 1842a, 1842c, 1842d, 1842e, 1842f, 1842g, 1842h, 1842i, 1842j, 1842k, 1842l, 1842m, 1842n, 1842o, 1842p, 1842q, 1842r, 1842s, 1842t, 1842u, 1842v, 1843a, 1843b).

10. In the *Belfast Newsletter*, it is noted that 'On the same night, the American barque Fairfield, the John Bagshaw, the brigs Reform and Henry Hoyle, the schooner Ghika, and the cutter Albatross, were stranded but no lives were lost' (Anonymous 1842t).

11. The seventy-six surviving convicts were received at the Cape Town Prison on 2 September 1842, and then sent to Van Diemen's Land on board Cape Packet (Bateson 1959).

12. We have been unable to trace or find this particular news item in *The Times*.

Chapter 11

BOATS

Settler Colonial Territorial Imaginaries: Maritime Mobilities and the "Tow-Backs" of Asylum Seekers

Kate Coddington

On 6 February 2014, the Australian Broadcasting Commission (ABC) news service released a silent video. Jerky camera work shows a narrow glimpse of ocean and a military vessel. The camera follows the progress of the vessel for some time before turning the lens on the passengers on a small orange lifeboat being pulled in its wake. The hull of the lifeboat with a white cross is clearly visible through one window; through another, viewers can see an inflatable raft with what appear to be navy personnel on board.

According to the ABC News (2014), the video was received from asylum seekers intercepted somewhere in the Indian Ocean by the Royal Australian Navy, transferred to the orange lifeboat, and towed back towards Indonesian waters. Later in 2014, interviews by reporters with asylum seekers who had experienced similar "tow-backs" more fully described the conditions aboard the orange lifeboats. The asylum seekers' experiences stand in stark contrast to the typical promise of a lifeboat used in rescue operations, which, as Whitlock (2015, 258) writes, 'offers not sanctuary but a visceral experience of suffering, abjection, and expulsion'.

The lifeboats hold fifty-five people but even thirty would feel crowded in their darkened spaces. Only a couple of small, high windows provide light and air. Omar Ali, an Egyptian asylum seeker, recounts his experience: 'No light. Very hot. When the driver opens the door, the water comes inside. We're sick. Everybody sick; there was no air. We have no oxygen. We are very sick. It's like animals. Animals [cannot be treated] like this' (Bachelard 2014, 1). Ali's boat was towed for three hours before being set adrift in the large waves of a bay near the Indonesian village of Kebumen. The asylum seekers aboard the lifeboat were forced to jump into the high surf and swim nearly thirty metres (ninety-eight feet) to shore. As Ali recounted, 'We jumped from the boat. We are at the beach, ocean high. We arrive and drift, arrive and drift. We think we will die. We think we will die. We can't swim' (Bachelard 2014, 1). After making their way to the beach, the asylum seekers climbed a steep slope before being discovered by a local farmer, who called the police.

In this chapter, I consider how experiences such as Ali's underscore the continued role of settler colonial territorial imaginaries in contemporary Australia. The example of the towed-back lifeboats must be situated in the contested Indian Ocean seascape, a maritime space characterised by struggles over asylum seeker mobility and situated within the Australian settler colonial frontier. As a settler colonial frontier space, I argue that the maritime frontier becomes imbued with particular notions of care and responsibility based on exclusion, violence, and the excess of law. I explore how the circulation of bodies, logics, and information within that frontier space takes on the function of constructing, maintaining, and expanding Australian territorial claims-making processes, and perpetuates the particular settler colonial versions of care and responsibility in maritime spaces. The ocean becomes the terrain on which territorial imaginaries become manifest, but its diffuse and uncertain materiality bolsters the ambiguity and fluidity of settler colonial understandings of care and responsibility, which continue to rest on notions of care for some at the expense of others.

CONTESTED WATERS

The sea has always played an outsized role in the articulation of sovereign space in Australia, but the role of the sea has taken on new dimensions in Australia's ongoing reconfiguration of sovereignty, territory, and citizenship since the early 1990s, when the Australian government began its practice of mandatory detention in response to asylum seekers arriving by boat – what the federal government termed unauthorised boat arrivals. Australia is an island nation, and its governments and population have always been heavily invested in conceptions of ocean space. Yet while the Australian national anthem includes the phrase 'for those who've come across the seas, we've boundless plains to share' contemporary attention to the sea as a site of sovereign intervention and contestation dates to the arrival of the Norwegian freighter *M.V. Tampa* in autumn 2001.

In late 2001, a ship carrying 433 asylum seekers departed Indonesian shores. After the ship began to sink, the *M.V. Tampa* rescued them, and its captain attempted to deliver them to Australian offshore territory of Christmas Island, but the Australian government refused to let them ashore for several days. The Howard government 'drew a line in the sea' as Perera (2002, 1) writes, and refused entry to the asylum seekers, threatening the Norwegian captain with people-smuggling charges and ignoring his distress calls. Prime Minister Howard rushed the Border Protection Bill through federal parliament, thus enacting legislation that radically changed the Australian landscape for asylum seekers, including retroactively excising offshore territories for the purposes of migration claims; establishing a dual system of asylum processing for onshore and offshore arrivals; and authorising the interception of asylum seekers arriving by boat by the Australian Defence Force as well as their diversion to Pacific island nations for processing as part of the 'Pacific Solution', continued under the Rudd and Gillard Labor governments, and, in other guises, under the Abbott and Turnbull coalition governments.

Since the *M.V. Tampa* incident, the Australian "seascape" encompassing the Indian Ocean region has become a site of violent sovereign struggle. As the issue of asylum seeker arrivals became highly politicised, successive governments took increasingly harsh measures to reiterate the "line in the sea" by detaining asylum seeker arrivals in onshore and offshore detention centres; and engaging in increased maritime surveillance efforts. In 2013, the Australian government initiated Operation Sovereign Borders (OSB), a military border enforcement programme to reduce the numbers of asylum seekers arriving by boat. Under OSB, the Australian government established a regional deterrence campaign to prevent asylum seekers from leaving Indonesia, which included surveillance, communication campaigns in Indonesia, and funding to "buy back" asylum seeker boats.

Under OSB, Australia's governing Coalition has engaged in tow-backs of intercepted vessels that bring them back to Indonesian waters in ways that parallel Ali's aforementioned experiences (Grewcock 2014). In addition to the lifeboat transfers that I focus on here, other methods to deter people-smuggling by sea include paying smugglers to return vessels to Indonesia (Tang 2015). In 2015, the Australian government purchased a new fleet of ships specifically intended for use in returning asylum seekers interdicted on the ocean (Doherty and Davidson 2015). OSB has been characterised by increasing levels of government secrecy about asylum seeker interdiction and deterrence efforts. OSB and Australia's efforts to curtail the movements of asylum seekers throughout the Indian Ocean region through these extraterritorial strategies have markedly decreased the spaces of asylum available across the Asia-Pacific region (Hyndman and Mountz 2008; Mountz 2010).

Current methods of enforcement echo historical geopolitical tensions in the same seascape related to maritime obligations and responsibilities for refugees. Indeed, the wider Indian Ocean region was the site of the first global debates about the status of asylum seekers who arrived at the borders of other nations by boat. The end of the Vietnam War prompted thousands of Vietnamese refugees to take to the waters. Agreements brokered by the United

Nations High Comissioner for Refugees (UNHCR) in 1978 and again in the 1980s failed to keep up with the rise in numbers of asylum seekers fleeing by boat by the mid-1980s (Newland 2003). While the Australian government faces widespread condemnation from international non-government organ-isations such as the UNHCR for its pushback policies in the Indian Ocean region (*Guardian Staff* 2014), the effectiveness of international agreements in coming to grips with asylum seekers' dangerous maritime journeys is as precarious as it was over thirty years ago. Global attention to debates about responsibilities for asylum seeker boat arrivals has been overshadowed in the region by the increasing geopolitical conflicts over territorial claims and maritime boundaries in the neighbouring South China Sea.

Australia's fixation with curbing asylum seeker arrivals by boat must be situated in an understanding of the Indian Ocean maritime region as part of Australia's settler colonial frontier. I argue throughout this chapter that the settler colonial ontologies that frame this frontier space construct a particular understanding of care and responsibility that takes shape within this space – a notion of care towards and responsibility for upholding settler colonial logics grounded in violence and exclusion as well as the excess of law.

Typically, settler colonialism involves settlers securing permanent control over land by acquiring territory by dispossessing indigenous residents and, crucially, then remaining on that land permanently (Evans 2009). Settler colonisation consists of a long-term and complicated social formation that perpetuates violent and exclusionary logics of elimination over time: 'settler colonialism destroys to replace' (Wolfe 2006, 388). Structural violence, such as practices of representation, contributes to the violent and exclusionary log-ics of settler colonial regimes (Murdocca 2010). For example, Howitt (2001, 234) identifies the Australian spatial imaginaries that treat land and sea as 'quite literally empty' – as part of the violence of settler colonial legal frame-works, even as these frameworks rest uneasily alongside other sovereignties and other territorial ontologies, especially those related to ocean spaces. Tor-res Strait Islander communities along Australia's north coast, for example, understand ownership of country to extend along ridges, water courses, and other water features past the foreshore to hunting traps, reef islands, and other landmarks within the coastal ocean spaces (Mulrennan and Scott 2000). Sea becomes envisioned as part of Aboriginal lands, part of both cosmology and history, an ontology whereby the sea and land are together embodied in the Aboriginal individual (Tuck et al. 2014). For instance, as Torres Strait Meriam Elder George Kaddy explains, 'I am part of the sea and the sea is part of me when I am on it' (in McNiven 2004, 329). With colonial settle-ment, the Australian seascape was reimagined as part of the empty frontier, the layers of Crown sovereignty overlapping with the pre-existing territorial imaginaries of ocean space.

Whereas frontier spaces are often understood to be lawless places where encounter leads inevitably to violence, Evans (2009) argues that frontier spaces are often filled with different, overlapping laws. The imagined emptiness of frontier spaces is only one representation of the violent logics of elimination that underpin settler colonial imaginaries. The frontier also becomes a space of emerging colonial sovereignty, and contested – but still vital – Indigenous sovereignties. However, as Morgensen (2011) contends, settler law violently dominates, becoming part of a regime of global governance that functions, in part, simply to sustain itself. Indigenous rights claims and pushes for sovereignty become slotted into forms of liberal settler law, what Morgensen terms an 'excess of settler colonial governmentality' (p. 64) that allows for further settler intervention into the lives and activities of Indigenous people subject to ongoing forms of colonisation. The use of legal frameworks to maintain settler dominance maps onto contemporary projects of border enforcement in the maritime Australian frontier. For example, Perera (2013, 67) argues that the ocean becomes a type of borderlands where the geopolitics of race, war, and empire are violently circumscribed on the bodies of people such as the contemporary asylum seekers arriving by boat, reinscribing settler colonial struggles on 'a new map of borders and flow geographies' (see also Steinberg and Peters 2015). The lack of law in these ocean spaces is not perhaps their most dangerous characteristic. Indeed, I maintain that it is precisely the settler colonial frontier context that produces an *excess* of law in these maritime frontiers.

Both the excess of law operating in maritime frontier spaces and the violent and exclusionary logics inherent in settler colonialism produce particular colonial versions of care and responsibility for activities taking place within these spaces. The Australian state perpetuates an understanding of *responsibility* for upholding settler colonial logics that presumes settlers' sovereignty and continued rights to claim territory. The territorial imaginaries constructed and maintained through the violent border enforcement mechanisms such as asylum seeker tow-backs are the imaginaries of the settler state reconfigured upon the fluid spaces of the Indian Ocean: *responsibilities* for maintaining settler claims and *care* for the integrity of the settler state. Responsibility and care for asylum seekers, on the other hand, become hidden under layers of legal ambiguity, ultimately endangering them further.

CIRCULATION

The particular version of settler colonial responsibility and care that upholds violent and exclusionary logics is perpetuated through territorial imaginaries that solidify Australia's responsibility and right to maritime frontier spaces.

The territorial imaginaries are themselves claims-making processes, bolstered by the circulation of bodies, logics, and information within and about the maritime frontier. Theories of circulation derived from Foucault are used in geography to understand mobility and logics of sovereign power. For Foucault (2009, 325) circulation involved the 'set of regulations, constraints, and limits, or the facilities and encouragements that will allow the circulation of men and things in the kingdom and possibly beyond its borders'. Moreover, circulation was a question of potential: what became possible through the circulation of such necessary things? Foucault deemed the process of circulation an object of police attention, to reimagine what he termed the 'problem of living and doing a bit better than just living' (p. 326) – the process of life itself becoming an object of governance.

Foucault was not directly concerned with specific forms of mobility, but Salter (2013, 8–9) understands circulation as an important facet of how mobility might be reconceived, and emphasises how circulation 'focuses on the system that makes certain routes and circuits possible, easier, or more difficult'. Such a focus removes attention from the dichotomies and binaries that traditionally have structured discussions of mobility and focuses on the functions through which mobility could be managed. Salter (2013, 12) reframes mobility along a continuum that highlights the 'complexity brought about by the dispersal of what we used to call "sovereign" power'. Staeheli et al. (2016, 378) further develop the connection between mobility and circulation by focusing on citizenship formation as a process that 'is given form, meaning and power through the transactions and circulations that constitute it'. For them, circulation enmeshes proximate and distant spaces, shapes how citizenship politics become entangled within emotional understandings of belonging and identity formation, and helps to define the meaning of citizenship. Circulation makes possible certain understandings of citizenship, and the movement of different kinds of spatial, emotional, and political entanglements help to reify particular forms of governance and control.

Circulation is particularly useful in the case of construction and maintenance of Australia's settler territorial imaginaries because of an emphasis on *functions* rather than *forms*. As Salter (2013) suggests, stressing the system of possible routes and paths through which practices such as mobility take shape focuses on the management of mobility rather than fixed spaces such as the boundaries of the state. The management of mobility becomes a *function* that circulation makes possible, a function of the complex assemblage of sovereign power that includes, but is not limited to, the idea of the state. Exploring the construction of territorial imaginaries through circulation becomes even more useful in the case of the maritime frontier, where the ocean itself becomes foundation or the *terrain* upon which ideas of settler territory becomes grounded. Steinberg and Peters (2015) note, however, that the ocean is anything but stable ground for these imaginaries: the materiality of water – its fluidity, flexibility, and depth serve to challenge stable ontologies of territory, and the understanding of responsibility and care that may accompany it. As suggested by Perera's (2002, 1) phrase describing Prime Minister Howard's actions as '[drawing] a line in the sea', Australia's interdiction of asylum seeker vessels solidifies the imaginaries of where Australian sovereignty can legitimately be performed, and where the mobilities of those deemed 'outside' the Australian national imaginary can be managed. Cementing sovereign claims by managing mobility, Clarsen (2015, 42) argues, is particularly important for settler colonial societies:

> Foundational to settler colonialism are both the actual and the potential capacities of settlers to roam as autonomous sovereign subjects around the world and across the territories they claim as their own – and conversely to circumscribe and control the mobilities of Indigenous peoples.

In contemporary Australian politics, restrictions on and efforts to control the mobilities of those on the margins of Australian national imaginaries include not only Indigenous people, but asylum seekers as well. I argue here that the circulation of certain bodies, logics, and information in practices of maritime interdiction and tow-backs of asylum seeker vessels in Australia gives 'form, meaning and power' to territorial imaginaries, situated within the continuities of settler colonial forms of territorial control that are present there (Staeheli et al. 2016, 378).

BODIES

The bodies of asylum seekers who traverse the waters between Indonesia and Australia represent an obvious form of circulation: from their initial journeys, forced stopping points, and tow-backs to their redirections to offshore detention locations, their mobility becomes the rationale for the Australian government's response. Indeed, the various forms of circulation I describe here are based upon the mobility of asylum seekers both contextualised in relation to global processes of violent upheaval, worldwide trends to tighten migrant management regimes, increasingly limited access to protection *and* situated in Australia's media-saturated, state-driven 'emotionally charged politics of invasion and contagion' (Tazreiter 2015, 100). The asylum seekers' bodies form the central current around which all the other forms of circulation, territorial reimagination, and settler logics of territorial control coalesce. As Perera (2013, 65) writes, a series of

> spatiolegal and spatiotemporal manoeuvres draw and redraw lines in the sea, producing spaces of exception in the form of migration exclusion zones,

offshore holding areas, temporally agile borders and other geographies of shifting sovereignty designed to block transnational subaltern bodies on the move.

Yet the prominence of bodies within the circulations that construct and maintain territorial imaginaries builds also on theories of embodiment that increasingly have been used in political geography and related fields to characterise
concepts such as sovereignty, citizenship, and the state. I argue that embodiment represents a strategic methodological, theoretical, and *geographically
situated* positioning that foregrounds the scale of the body (Coddington et al.
2012). Analysis at the level of the body – such as the vulnerable asylum seekers aboard the towed lifeboat – reveals the violent, material effects of state
practices that analysis at different scales renders invisible (Mountz 2004).

   While many scholars are increasingly drawing connections between mobility and embodiment, a specific focus on the relationship between territory
and embodiment is less common. For Smith et al. (2016, 258, 260), however,
territory is part of an 'intimate geopolitics' in which embodiment is central;
indeed, they argue that 'embodied practices and the materiality of bodies
affect and are inseparable from the production and maintenance of territory'.
The relationship between embodiment and territory can be conceived of in
different ways. Bodies can themselves *be* territory, painfully contested, as
Anzaldúa (1987, 19) envisioned her borderland self as *hieros gamos,* composed by the bringing together of opposites. Viewed differently, experiences
of territory can be manifested through the body, as in the case of female suicide bombers and women in labour at the Palestinian-Israeli border. There,
the 'leakiness of the border' manifests in the women's own dangerously fluid
bodies, as they embody Israeli fears about state territory and the security of
the border (Long 2006, 107). Embodiment and territory are also connected by
the ways in which particular racialised, gendered, and sexed bodies construct
territory. As Pratt (2005, 1062) writes, the gendered and racialised bodies
of murdered sex workers in Vancouver led to their legal abandonment: by
embodying particularly racialised geographies, the sex workers were placed
outside the reach of the law, and the terrain of legal abandonment was constructed through a sex worker's body, concluding that 'she was of the space
where murders happen'.

   In the case of the circulations I depict here, asylum seekers' bodies play
multiple roles. Their bodies *become* contested territory, their forced transit
a response to the Australian categorisation of their bodies as "illegal maritime arrivals", a mobile identity that travels with asylum seekers beyond the
moment of maritime interception, back to the shores of Indonesia (Mountz
et al. 2013. Experiences of territory and processes of territorialisation are
also manifest in the bodies of the asylum seekers, their claustrophobia and
sickness aboard the lifeboat direct, embodied reflections of Australian fears

about their mode of arrival. Their embodied experiences of the material ocean space – the ocean's depths and currents, their fears and anxieties, their resulting sickness and incapacitation – all testify to the particular form of territorial imaginations that can be generated in such as a space. As Steinberg and Peters (2015, 259) argue, embodied encounters with the ocean produce sensations both of churning and of drifting, sensations that differently 'supersede both legal logics and human intentions'. The bodies of asylum seekers represent what Pugliese (2007) terms "geocorpographies" – assemblages of geographically situated bodies marked by geopolitical violence. Australian state notions of responsibility are directed entirely at the preservation of settler colonial logics of territorial control, and care *for* the settler frontier spaces works in violent opposition to care for the bodies of asylum seekers, who are abandoned to the geopolitical threat they represent. Settler processes of territorial claims-making in maritime spaces are driven, too, by the logics of elimination that underpin land conquest. In the case of the lifeboats, asylum seekers' bodies become legible through their embeddedness within processes of territorial claims-making – representing what Pugliese (2007, 12) calls a 'violent enmeshment of the flesh and blood of the body within the geopolitics of war, race and empire'.

LOGICS

Circulating, too, in the tow-backs of asylum seekers in purpose-built lifeboats are different kinds of elements. I argue that what distinguishes the interdictions of asylum seekers and the tow-backs is the creative use of ambiguous, liminal spaces to enforce sovereign law and concurrently, the articulation of sovereign territorial imaginaries. The construction of the spaces of ambiguity in the ocean reflects the construction of other liminal spaces used for migration enforcement, particularly the excision of island – and later mainland – territory from Australia's migration zone, as well as the use of onshore and offshore immigration detention. I argue that the logics that promote the use of such spaces for migration enforcement and articulations of sovereignty circulate to construct territorial imaginaries that promote settler understandings of care and responsibility.

Layers of legal and territorial jurisdictions overlap unevenly to construct such spaces, which become ambiguous through unclear allocation of responsibility and subsequent inability to hold actors accountable within these spaces. Within the layers of jurisdictions are multiple ontologies of territory held by Aboriginal and Torres Strait Islander Australians, yet an excessive and ultimately confounding amount of Western, settler colonial law proliferates in these same spaces as well. Here, in the places where asylum seeker vessels are interdicted, three types of Western legal jurisdictions overlap to produce ambiguous ocean spaces: the *United Nations Convention on the Law of the Sea* (UNCLOS) and related protocols that govern the rights of visiting as well as the treatment of stateless vessels; provisions within UNCLOS that determine search and rescue obligations; and the obligations of signatories to the 1951 and 1967 *Convention and Protocol on the Status of Refugees*. The blurring of jurisdictions and responsibilities under these three laws produces an ambiguous space where the Australian government's responsibilities for the asylum seekers it intercepts are unclear, and recourse for illegal or unethical actions severely limited. The materiality of the maritime space compounds the ambiguity of these multiple legal regimes: as Peters (2014) notes, the mobility, liquidity, scale, and depth of the ocean itself all contribute to the complications of upholding legal regimes in these spaces.

Australia's actions under UNCLOS are determined by where Australian naval vessels encounter asylum seeker vessels in the ocean, and its ability to enforce migration laws correlates to its location. However, Australia has refused to make public both exactly where in the ocean it has interdicted asylum seeker vessels in the past and where the transfers to lifeboats for the tow-backs have occurred. If the interdictions occurred within the twelve-mile territorial sea surrounding Australia's continent's borders, Australia has a right under UNCLOS to exert full sovereignty over territorial waters, and can enforce migration laws, including the interception and detention of asylum seekers seeking protection. If, however, asylum seekers were interdicted in the twenty-four-mile contiguous zone around territorial waters, its obligations become murkier. In the past, Australia has argued that it can act within the contiguous zone to prevent infringement of laws within the territorial waters, and under this premise has removed vessels as far as the edge of the contiguous zone (Klein 2014). However, outside the contiguous zone Australia's right to enforce migration laws becomes even more tenuous. On the high seas, Australia can exert sovereignty only over its own flagged vessels, which presumably would not include asylum seeker vessels. There are exceptions to these guidelines: for instance, Australia is granted the "right of hot pursuit" to chase into international waters vessels that breached Australian law within the territorial sea, and under the "right of visit" Australia is also allowed to approach and board vessels whose captain or crew are suspected of international crimes such as slavery or piracy. In some cases, via bilateral or multilateral treaties the right of visit has been extended to captains or crews accused of terrorism or people smuggling, so there is legal precedent for boarding suspicious vessels in the high seas – *if* a relevant treaty has been signed (Klein 2014); such is not the case in relation to Indonesia, for example.

Yet UNCLOS becomes less clear when it comes to dealing with vessels that have no flagged affiliation whatsoever. Klein (2014) has argued that the jurisdiction of Australia's flagged vessel would authorise a right of visit if confronted with an unflagged vessel on the high seas, but other legal scholars maintain that the nationalities of those aboard the unflagged vessel would give them national status despite being aboard an unflagged vessel, therefore making any right of visit illegal (for example, Churchill and Lowe 1999). Australia would only be able to board such as vessel if, as Klein (2014, 5) writes, they are able to claim that the security of the state is in question, and then 'a valid query may be raised as to whether the arrival of irregular migrants by sea truly threatens the security of a state'. The farther away from Australian territorial waters such interdictions are, the less clear become its rights to interdict asylum seeker vessels as part of national migration law enforcement. Asylum seeker vessels arriving from Indonesian fishing villages are likely flagged to Indonesia or travelling without any flagged affiliation; therefore the legal justifications for boarding these vessels in international waters are slim indeed.

The responsibilities for sovereign activities in ocean territory are extended under UNCLOS to include search and rescue obligations. Signatories to UNCLOS are obliged to rescue vessels in distress and to promote search and rescue operations, as well as coordinate such operations with neighbouring states. Klein (2014) notes that other treaties between Indonesia and Australia reiterate the search and rescue obligations of both parties. The interdiction of asylum seeker vessels could be interpreted as a legal action; therefore, if asylum seeker vessels would be considered to be in distress – this is often, but not always, the case. Furthermore, if Australia interdicts asylum seeker vessels under the provisions of search and rescue obligations, it is required to deliver the people rescued in the high seas to a safe place, and the experiences of the terrified migrants stranded off the Indonesian coastline in the lifeboat indicate that safe delivery is certainly not always a priority in these activities. Simply transferring passengers to another ship is not considered delivering them to a safe destination, according to the terms of UNCLOS (Newland 2003). Furthermore, even without transfer to a lifeboat, the interdiction of asylum seeker vessels *increases* the danger to those on board; for instance, the Kaldor Centre (2015) cites an example of an interdiction where a boat was successfully turned around, only to run aground twelve hours later off the coast of an Indonesian island, resulting in the deaths of three asylum seekers.

Another possible legal justification for interdiction of asylum seeker vessels could be derived from Australia's responsibilities under the 1951 *Convention* and 1967 *Protocol Relating to the Status of Refugees*. The major obligations of signatories to these agreements involve adhering to processes to determine the status of people seeking asylum, and *non-refoulement* – the principle of not returning asylum seekers to places where their lives may be in danger. If Australia were to justify its activities according to the

Convention and *Protocol,* again, the location of the interdiction would be key to determining its legality. It is unclear both from the *Convention* and the *Protocol* where, exactly, the obligation to assess asylum seeker claims begins: at the point of interception, at the edge of territorial waters, or on land itself. In this respect, the US government issued an executive order in 1992 claiming that the refugee assessment and its obligation of *non-refoulement* began at the land boundary, but the practice has been heavily critiqued and was challenged in the *Sale v. Haitian Centers Council Inc* case in 1993. While the executive order was upheld, similar challenges, including the *Haitian Centre for Human Rights v. United States* in 1997 reached the opposite conclusion, so the legal validity of the US practice is in doubt (Klein 2014, 10). It is unclear whether Australia's legal obligations to refugees begin on the high seas, and if so, interdiction without refugee assessment would be illegal. Furthermore, even if interdiction without assessment were to be found legal, as in the Sale case in 1993, under the principle of *non-refoulement* Australia would be obliged to make sure asylum seekers were returned to a safe country. Indonesia's record of human rights protection for refugees and asylum seekers is poor (Nethery et al. 2013), and return to Indonesia would not be necessarily considered return to a safe third country. In ways that are similar to the provisions of UNCLOS, the *Convention* and *Protocol* do not specifically outline a legal method of interdiction, nor do they indicate that such interdictions are entirely illegal. Depending on where on the ocean the interdictions take place, the legality of Australia's actions varies, but nowhere is it distinct.

Together, an ambiguous legal terrain, layered within already-uneasy settler colonial legal claims to ocean spaces, is constructed by the overlapping jurisdictions of the relevant agreements, provisions for sovereign activities or search and rescue obligations under UNCLOS, or the terms of the *Convention* and *Protocol* on refugees. Shades of legality colour the Australian practices on the high seas, and with the uncertainty around legality comes a legal inability to challenge such practices. The spaces of offshore interdictions are characterised by being gradually *less* legal (according to UNCLOS agreements regarding sovereign actions) the farther away from the territorial sea the interdiction occurs, but may be gradually *more* legal – or at least more uncertain – according to the *Convention* and *Protocol* the farther away from the land the interdiction occurs. Such uncertainty leads to lack of recourse, for asylum seekers negotiating interdiction attempts on the water or for legal action in Australia's courts of law.

What circulates here to such devastating effect, I argue, is the *logic* behind the use of such ambiguous legal spaces for migrant enforcement. These ambiguous spaces of the high seas represent the continued use of such logics for migration management, even though scholars have documented the extraordinary legal ambiguity of detention centres, both onshore and offshore (Kaplan 2005; Mountz et al. 2013), and the liminal legal zones produced through repeated processes of excision (Hyndman and Mountz 2008; Perera 2009). The ocean, as Peters (2014) notes, adds another layer of difficulty to determining legal responsibility; its materiality confounds efforts to establish clear legal procedures, even within the space of settler liberal law. The uncertainty of ocean space increases the ambiguity of Australia's legal responsibilities, and Australia takes advantage of these liminal legal spaces to cement settler colonial claims to territory. The excess of applicable law and consequent uncertainty of Australia's legal responsibilities towards asylum seekers allow for the perpetuation of settler logics of violence and exclusion, where care for the settler state and its logics of elimination overshadow the possibilities of care for asylum seekers. Controlling asylum seeker mobilities through the use of such spaces performs a settler colonial form of territorial claims-making. The interdiction of asylum seeker vessels becomes a means of giving 'form, meaning and power' to Australian territorial imaginaries even far from mainland territory (Staeheli et al. 2016, 378). Difficult to understand, nearly impossible to challenge, such ambiguous frontier geographies become the heart of how contemporary Australian sovereign practices and territorial imaginaries are being articulated, and the responsibility for settler logics of control is being upheld.

INFORMATION

The third set of circulations that inform the construction and maintenance of territorial imaginaries in the lifeboat tow-backs of asylum seekers on the high seas are those related to information. Asylum seeker videos of the tow-backs represent one part of the circulations of information that occur, documenting the experiences of secretive and remote border enforcement practices. The circulation of information about border enforcement practices allows for intervention into settler logics of violence and exclusion, challenging state practices of care and responsibility, but not neatly or completely.

Because the Australian government refuses to release information about enforcement practices within OSB, the videos become a testimonial that embodies abstract policy. They were disseminated by the Australian news media, legitimating policies that the Australian government refused to acknowledge, documenting the embodied effects of such policies and contesting official state narratives. As Whitlock (2015, 254) writes, the recording and dissemination of these videos 'challenge the controlled environment of border security discourse . . . and produce a site of microactivism'. Yet the circulation of the videos allowed opinions from all sides of the political spectrum to debate the tow-backs. For example, over seventy per cent of respondents in a 2014 *Sydney Morning Herald* poll supported the government's forced use of tow-backs of asylum seeker vessels after the release of the videos, an indication that that increased information about such practices does not automatically serve to contest them (Flitton 2014).

Indeed, the release of asylum seeker videos of tow-backs occurs within a climate of information circulation about asylum seeker mobility itself. Communication campaigns to deter potential asylum seekers from making the journey to Australia have become an essential element of successive Australian government programmes. In 2013, the Labor government released advertisements across Australia to accompany a campaign of YouTube videos with the tagline: 'If you come here by boat without a visa, you won't be resettled in Australia'. Under OSB, the government has also released similar video and print media declaring 'No way by boat: You will not make Australia home'. Diverse media campaigns in common asylum seeker countries of origin include web advertisements discouraging Iranian asylum seekers as well as a graphic novel directed at potential Afghan asylum seekers that illustrates a traumatic boat journey followed by indefinite detention. Such deterrence campaigns, as Smith (2015, 72) writes, embrace the refugee body itself as a 'scopic spectacle' to be consumed by others, both potential asylum seekers and members of the general public.

Yet despite the hyper-visibility of asylum seekers in the Australian media, the circulation of information is characterised by barriers and secrecy. OSB has become known for the lack of information released about asylum seeker interceptions, movements, and processing arrangements, and indeed videos such as those taken and circulated by asylum seekers become among the few methods to document enforcement practices. In 2014, Michael Pezzullo, the-then chief of the Australian Customs and Border Protection Service, refused to comment on how the Australian government was attempting to 'stop the boats', noting that 'it's actually a maritime security programme' (in Dickson 2015, 445). As such, the Australian government has repeatedly described maritime operations as 'sensitive' or 'tactical', framing border enforcement as a national security threat in order to prevent the disclosure of specific practices such as the tow-backs (Dickson 2015, 445). The dynamic materiality of the maritime frontier (Steinberg and Peters 2015) contributes to the lack of information: the remoteness of interdiction operations and the lack of evidence left behind upon the ocean space challenge attempts to document enforcement practices. Barriers to accessing information about asylum seekers extend to the network of detention facilities, where measures from expensive journalist visas on Nauru (Jabour and Hurst 2014) to the prison sentence for whistle-blowers from within the detention system under the terms of the 2015 Border Force Act allow only for the circulation of particular kinds of information regarding the conditions of asylum seekers within Australia.

Australian government sensitivity about the circulation of information related to asylum seeker enforcement does not always extend to the protection of asylum seekers' confidential information itself. In 2014, the Department of Immigration and Border Protection revealed that it had released personal data relating to nearly 10,000 asylum seekers on its website, jeopardising their claims as well as their personal safety (Tazreiter 2015, 106). When asylum seekers began to file court claims in response to the unauthorised release of their information, some in detention were pressured to sign release forms absolving the government of responsibility for harm caused by the data breach (Laughland and Farrell 2014).

The circulation of information – both to facilitate access to information about enforcement practices and to construct such practices as 'maritime security' secrets – becomes part of what gives 'form, meaning and power' to territorial imaginaries (Staeheli et al. 2016, 378). Here, the key role played by information is to lend legitimacy to who controls the narrative of asylum seeker arrivals: by restricting access to information, and allowing only particular securitised narratives about asylum seeker arrivals as threats to maritime security to circulate, the Australian government attempts to curate and shape the events that take place in the ambiguous spaces on the high seas. Control over information, and especially the imposition of such silences, is essential to strategies to rationalise settler colonial sovereignty. Indeed, 'absence, excision, silences, amnesia and other defensive formations can all be interpreted as discursive necessities of a (settler colonial) need to emphasise the antipolitical impossibility of conflict, class struggle, sectarian divisions, Indigenous survival, ethnic strife' that underscore continued conflict over belonging in places such as Australia (Veracini 2007, 281–82). By controlling the narrative about what occurs in the liminal spaces of border enforcement and forcibly moving the bodies of asylum seekers, the Australian government attempts to make claims to territory and care for the settler state, upholding its *responsibility* to articulate sovereign claims on the high seas.

Yet the embodied presence of asylum seekers who can testify to their own experiences of the lifeboat tow-backs disrupts such settler narratives. Efforts to document border enforcement practices make use of testimonials across different media platforms as well, including the use of Twitter hashtags to document asylum seeker transfers on the island of Nauru and the use of social media sites such as Facebook to document protests and conditions within detention facilities (Coddington and Mountz 2014). Activist networks such as Watch the Med, whose members document the dangers to migrants at the maritime borders of the European Union, are particularly focused on threats posed by the overlapping and ambiguous jurisdictions of maritime spaces, contesting the narratives of sovereign control that border enforcement activities construct. As written on the Watch the Med (2016, 1) site, members' concerns with maritime jurisdictions stem from how these spaces 'represent a form of "unbundled" sovereignty, in which the state's rights and obligations that compose modern state sovereignty on the land are decoupled from each other and applied selectively'. Efforts to expand and reshape the circulations of information contest territorial claims-making that occurs through border enforcement in maritime spaces, articulating demands to care *differently* about territorial claims in ocean spaces by emphasising the vulnerable migrant body as it faces the material dangers of maritime frontier spaces. Such alternative claims to care complicate the territorial imaginaries that information in circulation helps to generate, advocating instead for humanitarian responsibility in ocean spaces.

CONCLUSION

In this chapter, I have argued that the experiences of asylum seekers aboard the towed-back lifeboat represent an articulation of sovereign and territorial claims-making in the contested seascape surrounding Australia. The circulation of bodies, logics, and information helps to construct and maintain territorial imaginaries based upon settler colonial logics that prioritise control over mobility and narratives as key aspects of sovereign power. The ocean becomes the terrain upon which territorial imaginaries are constructed, but its depth and dynamism contribute to the uncertainty and fluidity of the claims to territory that result. The territorial imaginaries constructed upon the maritime frontier bolster settler colonial understandings of responsibility and care that are underpinned by violent, exclusionary strategies that promote the care for some over the care for others.

Contextualising these processes as part of the space of the settler colonial frontier illuminates the ongoing ideologies of settler colonial control that drive Australian territorial imaginaries. As Clarsen (2015) notes, circumscribing the mobilities of those outside the settler colonial national imaginary – both Indigenous people and, I contend, asylum seekers – is a central element in how settler colonial subjects see themselves as belonging to colonised spaces. Both the violent embeddedness of asylum seeker bodies, as well as the logic that drives the use of ambiguous legal spaces in the processes of managing mobility, highlight the extraordinary lengths to which Australia is willing to go to control access to belonging. Furthermore, as Veracini (2007) writes, the control of mobility is not the only circulation that matters in settler colonial sovereignties; so too there is control over the circulation of information. Both what is revealed and what is concealed about the fates of those seeking asylum in Australia become 'discursive necessity[ies]' needed to construct and maintain settler colonial legitimacy in the face of continued conflicts over belonging and identity (Veracini 2007, 281–82). Together, the circulations of bodies, logics, and information crystallise around the experiences aboard the towed-back lifeboat. The vulnerability of asylum seekers interdicted on the high seas and towed towards new forms of danger represents the price of these imaginaries. Caring *for* the settler colonial state occurs in tandem with abandoning responsibility for the asylum seekers in the maritime frontier. Asylum seekers' fates aboard the lifeboats etch deeply the violence of Australia's continued settler colonial preoccupation with controlling the bodies, spaces, and narratives that shape debates over belonging.

Chapter 12

SHORES

Sharks, Nets and More-Than-Human Territory in Eastern Australia

Leah Gibbs

In Australia, for eight months of each year Sydney's most popular beaches are laced with fishing nets. Stretching 150 metres (492 feet) across, and set within 500 metres (1,640 feet) of the shore, the nets are anchored off fifty-one beaches between Newcastle in the north and Wollongong in the south. The aim of the Shark Meshing (Bather Protection) Program NSW is to reduce the risk of dangerous encounters between sharks and people, and specifically to deter sharks from establishing territories (Department of Primary Industries NSW 2009, 2015). Program managers achieve such ends by devising and deploying tools and employing people to catch and kill sharks.

By considering what happens when non-human animals are enlisted in territorialising practices of shore control, this chapter examines and unsettles the interplay between multiple interpretations of territory and the political implications of those interpretations. The work traces the state of New South Wales' Shark Meshing (Bather Protection) Program to understand how territory is claimed, asserted, and confounded at the shore. Grasping the ways in which territory is made and remade at the shore is important conceptually, politically, and practically, as it sheds light on our understanding of territory. More specifically then, this work is also important because these practices have direct implications for the safety and well-being of people, and for the conservation of marine animals, species, and environments. Especially significant in this case is the question of how the Shark Meshing Program plays out for several species of shark that are at once formally recognised as threatened and as potentially threatening to humans.

The shore is our point of departure: the line where the land meets the sea. The broader transitional zone – the coast – includes areas above and below the water line, a zone where terrestrial environments and processes influence marine ones, and vice versa (Woodroffe 2002). This liminal space is neither land nor sea; rather, it is a zone that merges two distinct geo- and biophysical domains. At the shore the land's seeming solidity and stability meet the liquidity and constant motion of water: a marked shift in flux. The coast presents a continually changing land-/sea-scape, as tides advance and retreat, changing water depth and morphology. This place is also one where humans encounter a distinctly non-human world. Permanent human habitation is not possible, yet life thrives. These distinct qualities of the coast are fundamental to its contested use.

By exploring territory beyond land, we also explore territory beyond the human. I argue that asserting, maintaining, and contesting territory are *more-than-human* projects. Non-human animals and materials play vital roles in co-producing territory. In this chapter a series of interrelated accounts of the Shark Meshing (Bather Protection) Program NSW illuminates the more-than-human project of producing territory beyond *terra*. In what follows, I examine four key agents that work outside or alongside governance institutions to make and remake territory at the coast, namely, the coast itself, sharks, bathing human bodies, and nets. But first, an account is needed of territory at the ocean's edge, and contemporary approaches to shark hazard management.

TERRITORY AT THE OCEAN'S EDGE

The shore is where land-based two-dimensional notions of territory as area are augmented by verticality, volume, and the complexity of three-dimensional space (Elden 2013a). But the ocean's edge marks more than a third dimension; and more than volume as metric (Lehman 2013a). Rather, this space is defined by specific material properties, tendencies, and capacities (Dittmer 2014; see also Lehman 2013b). Through these, the ocean and coast (and scholars working in these places) challenge the "grounded" world of Earth's solid surface (Steinberg and Peters 2015), which has so strongly informed political thought and action. In this context, land-based techniques for measuring and controlling space are confounded. The "political technology" of territory – the series of techniques, arts, and practices of government (Elden 2010) – must take an altogether different form.

Geopolitics is significant in our pursuit of understanding territory beyond *terra* – beyond and in addition to the limits of land. Here, *geo*-politics refers not to politics at the global or international scale, but to the materiality of the Earth – its soils, atmosphere, water, and so on (Elden 2013b). 'In a world negotiating geopolitical challenges linked to disease . . . disaster . . . climate change . . . and shifts in the broader biosphere', Dittmer (2014, 396) urges that 'increasingly attention to the biological/environmental/material is a prerequisite for engagement on issues of the day'. If we wish to consider politics with reference to the Earth, that endeavour must include thinking through the planet's oceans. Steinberg and Peters (2015, 260) argue that 'attentiveness to the sea as a space of politics can upend received understandings of political possibilities and limitations'. Attentiveness to the materiality of the ocean 'produces a radically different interpretation of space, and an alternate understanding of who holds power and how they project and reject it'.

Among the materials of the ocean are its animals. Dittmer advocates tracing how animals and other materials influence relations in contingent ways. A posthuman turn in geopolitics, he insists, incorporates animals, nature and other objects into our understandings of geopolitics. Engaging with the posthuman becomes an ethical imperative and lays out a 'line of flight' – a research agenda – for 'making a break with the exclusive hold of humanity on political agency' (Dittmer 2014, 397). Of course, geopolitics is more than material. Attending to animals shines light also on qualities and behaviours, on individuals and groups, on single species and ecosystems, on bodies and affects, on discourses, on how things come together and come apart over and again, and with what effects. To understand the material foundations of political power we must pay close attention to the specific materiality of places and the specific ways in which things interact over time. The conditions of the coast present an opening to reach beyond *terra* and beyond the human as we attempt to understand territory.

In the context of shark hazard management and shore control, territory is made – claimed, asserted, and confounded – via continual engagements between humans, animals, and other materials and processes. The Shark Meshing (Bather Protection) Program NSW is a political institution made by, and with implications for, *more than* humans. Central to the program is its location on the coast: the place where land meets sea, and where humans most frequently encounter the ocean and all that dwells there. The program exists at this distinct contact point between humans and the non-human world. It enlists non-human animals in the making of territory. By exploring the distinct relations at this site, I seek to contribute to our growing knowledge of how human lives, institutions, and politics are enabled, shaped, and limited by non-human life, including animals (Buller 2014), plants (Head et al. 2015), fungi (Tsing 2015), and others. Within this field of multi-species interactions, animals of the sea have been poorly represented, and animals other than mammals especially so (Bear 2013). Thus, I pay particular attention to the ways in which sharks have agency in geopolitics and the making of territory.

MANAGING SHARK HAZARD AND THE SHARK MESHING (BATHER PROTECTION) PROGRAM, NSW

The risk of dangerous shark encounter is extremely low. On average, one person a year is killed by sharks in Australia, and another five or six are injured (measured over the two decades 1990–2010) (West 2011). This rate of incidence compares to at least eighty-seven coastal drownings on average per year (Brighton et al. 2013; West 2011). These low numbers are no comfort to the people affected, but are significant when thinking through shark hazard management. Despite their rarity, shark accidents attract a great deal of media and political attention (Neff 2012), due to both their high drama and the tremendous fear sharks induce in many people. Individual incidents are high profile, and clusters of incidents even more so. Take, for example, the labelling of Western Australia as 'shark attack capital of the world' (Tedmanson 2012), following a spike in shark-related fatalities in the state during the period 2011–2012, and triggering a highly controversial debate. Key moments in the debate included a 'trial' shark cull allowing pre-emptive killing of sharks 'identified in close proximity to beachgoers' (Department of Fisheries 2012); multiple public protests attracting 6,000 people at Perth's Cottesloe Beach, and thousands more around Australia and other parts of the world; a record 12,000 submissions to the Western Australian Environmental Protection Authority against continuing the cull; and the State government's eventual abandonment of the policy (Gibbs and Warren 2014).

Various strategies to reduce the risk of dangerous shark encounter exist around the world; among them, killing is popular. Killing and culling strategies have been adopted in Australia, South Africa, the United States, the French region of Réunion Island, New Zealand, Egypt, Russia, the Seychelles, and Mexico (Gibbs and Warren 2015). On the east coast of Australia, nets are used in New South Wales and Queensland. In addition, since the 1960s Queensland has deployed baited drumlines: large baited hooks tethered to a line and floating drum. The New South Wales netting program has a particular take on hazard reduction. One of its aims is to deter sharks from 'establishing territories' (Department of Primary Industries NSW 2009; Green et al. 2009, 4); the method for achieving such ends is to reduce the number of sharks by entangling and killing them in nets.

The Shark Meshing (Bather Protection) Program NSW was introduced in 1937 as a method of governing ocean spaces adjacent to popular swimming beaches. It was established in response to a number of 'shark accidents' – in the language of the day (Neff 2012) – some of which were fatal. Reid et al. (2011, 676) explain that the 'use of anchored, large mesh gillnets as a preventative measure was pioneered in NSW', following a recommendation by the NSW Shark Menace Committee of 1929 that they may afford a 'cheap and effective way of minimising the shark peril'.

The program began with nets strung out year-round at eighteen of Sydney's most popular beaches. It was gradually expanded and, in 1949, beaches along the Newcastle and Wollongong coasts were added. Today, fifty-one beaches on the New South Wales coastline are netted for eight months each year (Green et al. 2009). The Shark Meshing Program employs 150 metre-long gillnets suspended off shore. Importantly, the nets do not create a barrier between swimmers and the open ocean. There is no "inside" or "outside" a netted zone keeping people and sharks apart. Rather, the nets are anchored approximately 500 metres (1,640 feet) off-shore, with the aim of catching sharks. In this way, the nets do not form territory by creating bounded space. Rather, they function through social power. The Shark Meshing Program produces territory by creating a sense of human control and authority over the entire coastline, and enacting violence against non-human animals.

As noted, lethal methods for managing risks associated with human-shark encounter are common around the world. But in recent years, and particularly following the controversy in Western Australia, kill-based strategies have come under strong criticism (Gibbs and Warren 2014, 2015). In the eight decades since the introduction of the Shark Meshing Program much has changed. Attitudes towards the environment and marine life, including sharks, have shifted dramatically; so too has our knowledge of the ocean. Further, the material conditions of oceans have altered significantly, with reports that marine environments and species have been decimated by over-fishing. Sharks and rays in particular have suffered as a result of human-induced pressures (Dulvy et al. 2014; Worm et al. 2013). A recent study of sharks and their relatives – rays and chimaeras (*chondrichthyan* fishes with cartilaginous skeletons) – found that of 1,041 species worldwide, more than half face elevated risk of extinction. Based on analysis of the International Union for Conservation of Nature's Red List of Threatened Species, at least one quarter of species are threatened and well over one quarter are categorised as near-threatened. The largest sharks and rays are in greatest peril (Dulvy et al. 2014). Among those listed are the great white shark (*Carcharadon carcharius*), tiger shark (*Galeocerdo cuvier*) and bull shark (*Carcharhinus leucas*). These three species are also identified in Australia as the key species that pose a potential threat to humans (Australian Government Department of the Environment n.d.), and therefore provide the focus for shark hazard mitigation strategies.

The Shark Meshing Program has, since December 2003, been listed in New South Wales as a 'Key Threatening Process', because the program 'adversely affects two or more threatened species', and specifically, the vulnerable great white shark and the critically endangered east coast population of grey nurse shark (*Carcharias taurus*). Further, the Scientific Committee established by the Threatened Species Conservation Act found that 'Implementation of shark control programs on ocean beaches results in the bycatch of a wide variety of non-target marine species', including six other threatened species of marine mammals and reptiles (Office of Environment and Heritage NSW 2011).

An old and outdated political technology, the Shark Meshing Program currently faces a new, distinct challenge: to protect beachgoers while upholding legal responsibilities and public expectations to conserve marine life, including species recognised by national and international institutions as being under threat. This obligation marks a shift from the original remit of the program, devised at a time when knowledge of marine environments was comparatively limited, when marine species did not face the extent of peril they do today and when public sentiments about the environment in general – and the possible impacts of human activities in particular – were entirely different.

From 2009, the Shark Meshing Program was to undergo review every five years. In 2014–2015 the nets were in the news. Organised opposition by marine institutions and non-government organisations included a demand that the nets be removed or, at the least, their time in the water be reduced. Opposition is based on two main arguments: that damage to marine life and environments is significant; and that the program's effectiveness in improving human safety remains unproven. Meanwhile, at un-netted beaches on the state's north coast, a vocal minority called for nets to be introduced at local beaches following several shark sightings and bites, including one fatality. For over a year the New South Wales government refused to reduce or extend the reach of shark nets, instead affirming its commitment to trialling non-lethal methods to keep beaches safe. In the face of increased public pressure, the government finally approved nets in the north. Despite the potential of alternate non-lethal strategies, and political will to adopt them, the established political technology for maintaining coastal territory persists.

MAKING TERRITORY THROUGH THE SHARK MESHING PROGRAM

The idea of territory is fundamental to the Shark Meshing Program: one of its explicit aims is to prevent sharks from establishing territories. In this way the program contests the territory of the coast. But within the program the *concept* of territory is also contested. It asserts that sharks establish territories; marine biologists dispute this claim. Through their recreational and professional activities humans use the water, seeking to claim a territory of sorts; yet some people argue that in entering the water we are entering sharks' territory. The New South Wales government claims the coast as human territory and defends it through the most aggressive means possible – killing. In doing so it must negotiate federal and international laws and agreements for protecting marine environments and threatened species, which presents a new challenge in maintaining territory. Inherent in these conflicting ideas and actions is an assumption that humans and sharks cannot use the same area of water and cannot coexist.[1] Yet this assumption is not supported by evidence (see Chapron et al. 2014; Gibbs and Warren 2015).

The specific ways in which these interpretations of territory and territorialising practices play out are determined by the distinct material properties, tendencies and capacities of the coast. In order to better understand how territory is made and remade at the coast, and how non-human animals and materials are enlisted in these processes, the remainder of this chapter examines the materiality of four key agents in the Shark Meshing Program. Specifically, the following sections analyse the roles of the coast, sharks, bathing human bodies, and nets in making and remaking territory.

Coast: Forming Territory

The coast forms the diverse and fluctuating biophysical conditions for territory. Attending to the geopolitics of territory (in the sense discussed above) demands paying close attention to the materiality of the Earth. This work required looking to other fields and specialisms – notably, in this case, coastal geomorphology, marine biology, and ecology. The New South Wales coast that is within the area of the Shark Meshing Program is characterised by a morphology of rocky headlands and sandy embayments. Geological, oceanic, and climate processes come together to form the coast – the transition zone between land and sea (Woodroffe 2002). The coast is both a setting for, and an agent in, the formation of territory. Coastal assemblages of sandy bays, rocky headlands, and estuaries allow and limit human activity, shark behaviour and ecology, and shark hazard mitigation strategies. People, sharks, and hazard mitigation technologies interact in different ways with the material qualities of the coast. The materiality of the Earth affords different opportunities for individual actors and institutions to make or contest territory.

For people, the position of headlands and estuaries, form and profile of beaches, current and wave action, and weather patterns interact to determine swell, surf, and rip current, forming the conditions for swimming and surfing. Rock platforms, waves, and tides come together to make promontories for fishing and places to explore life in rock pools. Beneath the waterline, rocks, reefs, and seabed combine to create habitat for the plant and animal life sought by divers and snorkelers.

For sharks, the coast forms diverse habitat and opportunities for territory. Inshore rocky reefs, islands and caves, and sandy seabeds form habitat for the critically endangered grey nurse shark (Australian Government Department of the Environment 2016), which is loved by divers and harmless to people. The three key potentially dangerous shark species – white, tiger, and bull sharks – also inhabit this coast. White sharks are highly mobile, preferring cool waters (18–20°C/64–69°F). Juveniles display two main behaviour modes: travelling and temporary residency. One of three temporary residency sites on the east coast – Stockton Beach – is on the edge of the netted region, just north of Newcastle. Although adults of this species are without question the most widely feared of sharks, juveniles present little risk, surviving on a diet of *teleosts* (finfish) and *elasmobranchs* (sharks and rays). Temporary residency at Stockton is determined, in part, by abundance of such prey (Bruce and Bradford 2012). In contrast, tiger sharks prefer warm waters. They are widespread and globally distributed in tropical and warm temperate seas, and are most abundant in eastern Australia from December to April when water is at its warmest. They subsist on an exceptionally diverse diet, including carrion (Randall 1992). Bull sharks thrive in estuaries and coastal rivers. They have been recorded in all parts of Sydney Harbour, but only in summer and autumn when water temperatures were above 23°C/73°F (Smoothey et al. 2016). Salinity though is the more important indicator of their presence. They have been observed in salt, brackish, and freshwater, but prefer moderate salinity levels of seven to twenty grams per kilogram (where freshwater is 0–0.5g/kg and average seawater is 35g/kg). Scientists do not fully understand them, but it seems they move in response to changing salinity to conserve energy or due to physiological limitations (Heupel and Simpfendorfer 2008).

The design of shark hazard mitigation strategies is also shaped by the morphology of the coast. Beginning in the final decades of the nineteenth century a series of tidal ocean baths were hewn from the rock platforms around Newcastle, Sydney, and Wollongong. The pools provide swimming places protected from the breaking waves, rips, and variable and sometimes unexpectedly deep water of this stretch of coast. They also serve to keep people and sharks apart: an early effort to create shark and human territory through firm physical demarcation. Today the rock pools are popular with lap swimmers and recreational paddlers, including small children and people under-confident, or unfamiliar, with the sensation of being in the water at a surf beach. At harbour and estuary beaches, much calmer waters afford a different type of swimming area: stretches of beach or coves fully enclosed by nets or steel bars, the explicit purpose of which is to keep people and sharks apart. In contrast, ocean and especially surf beaches are less suited to such structures. To date, strong currents, rough surf, and steeply sloping and variable seabed conditions have prevented construction of swimming enclosures. Now, as in the 1930s, the solution to the problem of people encountering sharks on this stretch of coast is gillnets, which aim to reduce shark accidents by reducing shark numbers.

Sharks: 'Establishing Territories'

At the centre of the Shark Meshing Program are two core assumptions: that sharks establish territories and that this behaviour has negative consequences for people. The media embellish these assumptions, suggesting that sharks aggressively defend territory. Yet the logic is flawed. Scientists describe sharks as displaying diverse movement behaviours, including long-distance seasonal migration, moving over a home range, and periods of temporary residency and travelling (Block et al. 2010; Bruce et al. 2006; Simpfendorfer and Heupel 2012). In the field of ecology, "territory" has specific meaning, signalling an area that an animal consistently defends, usually against members of its own species. There is no evidence of such behaviour from sharks – including, specifically, the "dangerous sharks" targeted by the Shark Meshing Program. Scientists and members of the public object to the misuse of the term territory and its use as a rationale for the program. The range of interpretations of the term territory has led to misinformation, confusion, and poor outcomes from policy- and decision-making. Paying close attention to shark behaviour, rather than to an imagined idea of sharks "establishing territories", is crucial for informing publics and policy. As such, it is worthwhile considering the specific materiality of sharks and the coast amid these debates.

Sharks are surprisingly poorly understood. They are extremely diverse in their biology, ecology, and behaviour. On the east coast of Australia, for example, white sharks are highly mobile, most feared, and listed as both threatening and threatened (Bruce et al. 2006). Populations move the full length of the east coast and southwest to South Australia. Movement is seasonal and highly regular, with animals travelling north during autumn-winter and south in spring and early summer. Individual animals use remarkably similar paths, suggesting reliance on similar cues or a common ability to navigate between destinations. They spend most of their time on the coastal shelf in waters up to 100 metres (328 feet) deep, but at times enter open ocean and cross deep gulfs, including the Tasman Sea. 'Use of environmental cues such as detection of bottom depth, olfactory cues, geomagnetic orientation and orientation to the sun' are likely methods of navigation (Bruce et al. 2006, 171). They may also reside temporarily when food sources are available, moving away quickly when prey disperses. Finfish are especially important, and as white sharks mature – reaching three metres (nearly ten feet) and more in length – they begin to feed on marine mammals. They also show great "plasticity" in their swimming behaviour, including 'prolonged periods at the surface and at depth, oscillatory or "yo-yo" ascents and descents, regular intervals at the surface and at depth, diel periodicity, deep dives at dawn or dusk and periods of highly erratic swimming depth' (Bruce et al. 2006, 170). White sharks, like other species, demonstrate tremendous diversity in their use of ocean spaces, diversity that is not captured by the phrase "establishing territories".

In New South Wales, the governmental review of the Shark Meshing Program during 2014–2015 involved public debate about the premise that sharks establish territories. Here, the *concept* of territory became a factor in public discourse and policymaking. Sharks and the coast came together in policy and public imagination in ways that differ from actual material relations.

The complex and nuanced forms of habitation and mobility, and the diverse behaviours displayed by different species and by animals of different ages described above, are not captured by the overly simplistic, generalised, and inaccurate phrase "establishing territories". Yet that was the imaginary which shaped policy. Paying greater attention to materiality – in this case, shark biology and ecology – can contribute to an alternate geopolitics of the coast by better informing publics and policymakers of the processes, properties, tendencies, and capacities of the Earth. This work may contribute to more effective political technologies and better outcomes for multiple species.[2]

Bathing Bodies: Claiming Territory

Australia has a strong beach culture. Seasons affect who visits the beach and for what purposes, but year-round people are drawn to beaches and rocky headlands of the coast. Ocean, climate, and landscape processes form the swell, surf, rip currents, temperature, weediness, and clarity or cloudiness of water that make the coast. Processes operating across timescales – hourly, daily, seasonal, and longer – constitute the conditions that draw people in, or turn them away to wait another day. But bathing bodies of one kind or another are an everyday feature of the coast, and bodies play a role in claiming territory.

When we enter the water, we seek to establish a place there: to claim a territory of sorts (Anderson 2013; Waitt and Warren 2008). As individuals and as a society we seek power and authority over the coast through our material interactions; we claim territory with our bodies, boards, wetsuits, fins, masks, breathing apparatus, lifeguards, observation towers, jet-skis, beach buggies, and boats. We make use of all these materials and more. But here I want to focus on the human body, which has distinct agency in our efforts to establish territory, and in the specific ways that those efforts are enabled and confounded.

People seek different things when we enter the water: water cools the body and blood; movement in water and waves invigorates and refreshes; surfing and body-boarding provide a surge of endorphins or adrenaline; and snorkelling and diving allow us to see and explore beneath the surface, to observe and interact with some of the living beings that dwell there. People's ability and agility in the water varies tremendously, but some things are common. Most obviously, we need air to breathe, which limits our abilities beneath the surface (breath-hold and SCUBA diving notwithstanding). In the water we are not "in our element", biophysically or figuratively. Irrespective of one's passion for the water, the fact remains that the human body is not biophysically adapted to be on or beneath the water surface for extended periods, and few of us are at our strongest and most alert there. These characteristics confound our efforts to establish territory and shape the political technologies we devise to do so.

Further to our need to breathe air are the material qualities of human sensory perception – in particular, the need to see. Sharks and other fish and marine animals have senses adapted to the material qualities of sea water, including highly sensitive electro-, magnetic, and chemo-reception. In contrast, as a species most humans rely heavily on our sense of sight to make our way around the world. On land we seek cues and devise our living spaces with strong reference to the visual (a fact not lost on people with visual impairment). This key sense is limited in the water. Human eyes are adapted to sight in air. The refractive index of water challenges our ability to focus. Under water we miss much of the world around us. And the limits to our senses remain even with the aid of specially designed underwater technologies. A humble pair of goggles dramatically improves our ability to see, but visibility – including distance and colour perception – remains reduced and distorted.

In two key ways, reduced visibility is relevant in making territory through the Shark Meshing Program. Reduced visibility in water means that we become more vulnerable to potential threats for the simple reason that we may not see them and have no other reliable means for sensing them. We seek to limit those threats by devising political technologies, as the Shark Meshing Program attests. Nets overcome our inability to see beneath the water surface by working independently of our sense of sight. In this way, the political technology we develop to claim territory at the shore helps to overcome our bodies' (in)capacities. But viewed from the land, this realm and our efforts to claim territory in it are largely out of sight. The territory being claimed is not simply an area of water, but a third dimension beneath the water's surface. The strategy we devise to claim territory, and its ecological consequences, is likewise out of sight because this is also a political technology that limits access to information and capacity for public critique.

Nets: Asserting Territory

The New South Wales government asserts power and control over the shore by sanctioning the killing of sharks, exemplifying 'the creation of space through violence, over which violence is then exercised' (Elden 2010, 808). Assertion of territory through the Shark Meshing Program sees sharks and other animals rendered killable.

The program – including the materiality of nets and practices of deployment – is highly regulated. According to Green et al. (2009, 88) the gillnets used in the program work by trapping and entangling animals, which are found when a net is hauled, according to regulation, after being set for no less than twelve hours and no more than ninety-six: 'All reasonable effort' is made to release entrapped marine life. However, many animals are killed in the nets. Depending on species status and other factors, carcasses are dumped outside three miles of the coastline or delivered to the New South Wales Department of Primary Industries. Netting twine, mesh size, hanging coefficient, floatline, leadline, and floats are all specified by work contracts. Method of meshing, vessels and gear, maintenance of equipment, safety of employees, records and reporting, disposal of catch, requirements for trapped marine life, and media communications are also regulated. Nets are 150 metres long, six metres (nearly twenty feet) deep. They are set within 500 metres (1,640 feet) of shore, and are 'bottom set' in water not deeper than twelve metres (nearly forty feet). At some beaches, nets may be 'double set', meaning two nets are strung together to provide a total length of 300 metres (984 feet). Most beaches are significantly longer, meaning that animals and other materials can move to either side and usually above the nets. Mesh size is fifty to sixty centimetres (1.5–1.6 feet), 'measured in accordance with the manner prescribed in Clause 115 of the (General) Regulation 1995 made under the Fisheries Management Act 1994' (Green et al. 2009, 86).

Regulation of the program forces close attention to materials and practices; these aspects of operation are carefully controlled. Yet the technology is blunt. The program attends to its primary aim to 'reduce the risk of shark attack' (Green et al. 2009, 4), but in so doing it has significant consequences for marine life and environments. The nets fail to discriminate. Although their design targets large dangerous sharks and efforts are made to safely release entangled animals, nets regularly catch and kill other fish and marine life. These consequences are not generally publicised. Between January 1950 and July 2008 at least 16,064 animals were caught in the nets. The catch included at least twenty-three species of sharks, fourteen species of finfish, dolphins, turtles, whales, dugongs, seals, and penguins. The animals most commonly caught were species that pose no threat to humans.[3]

To reduce unintended effects, the program is adapted from time to time. Changes have included fitting acoustic devises to nets to deter whales and dolphins, and setting nets on the seabed to reduce interactions with marine mammals, reptiles, and birds (Green et al. 2009). The years 1983 and 1989 saw a two-step removal of nets during the winter months May to August (see also Reid et al. 2011), the period that coincides with reduced numbers of people in the water, and with the bulk of the northerly whale migration. However, efforts to reduce negative consequences have limited effect. In November 2015, a humpback whale calf was entangled in nets off Soldier's Beach on the Central Coast, during the annual southerly migration to Antarctic waters. In this case the animal was eventually released through the combined efforts of several public and private institutions over a five-hour period, to great media attention (Cardozo 2015). Few animals trapped in the nets are as fortunate as this highly charismatic one.

Nets form a material and political technology for managing shark hazard and asserting territory at the shore. They are heavily regulated in their material form and deployment. But despite regulation their negative consequences for non-human life are significant. The Shark Meshing Program manifests a particular politics. It violently asserts territory and, in so doing, renders animals killable. This politics overrides legal obligations to care for threatened species and finds death of individual animals – irrespective of the risk they pose to human safety – an acceptable project outcome. Here, the more-than-human context of the shore highlights the more-than-human consequences of territorialising practices. These consequences demand that we pay greater attention to the full range of effects of our political technologies.

Nets and Knowledge: Maintaining Shore Control

To maintain shore control, the Shark Meshing Program relies on shark nets and on ignorance and misinformation about the technology. Misinformation about nets takes three main forms. First, the nets are out of sight; public awareness of their existence is limited. Second, both what the nets are and where they are located are frequently misunderstood or misrepresented: the nets are not a barrier, but fishing equipment; they are not strung across a bay or beach, but anchored off-shore. In this way, they assert territory not by creating a physical barrier, but by control through violence. Third, precisely how the nets work is rarely described or discussed.

Misinformation about the materiality of the nets works in concert with confusion about the nature of the territory under dispute. The Shark Meshing Program has been based on the idea that sharks establish and defend territories, but scientific knowledge does not support this assumption. Rather, research shows that sharks are highly mobile, usually following prey and inhabiting extensive areas of the sea (Block et al. 2010; Bruce et al. 2006). The program has also been based on an assumption that sharks and people cannot coexist in this disputed territory. When a shark sighting or accident occurs, heated debate ensues in the media and social media about whose territory this is, who has the right to be there and who is responsible for maintaining that right. These questions become points of passionate contention. But the suggestion that sharks and people cannot coexist is contrary to evidence. Research in Western Australia found that people using the ocean reported encountering sharks frequently, without ill effects to people or sharks (Gibbs and Warren 2015).

Misinformation is evident in and exacerbated by the media. At least one tabloid newspaper has reported on the shark net at Sydney's Bondi Beach

(*Daily Telegraph* 2015). An aerial photograph published in the paper showed a squiggly line stretching across the bay, almost reaching both headlands. It created two zones: one on the beach side for people, the other on the ocean side for sharks. This representation suggested that the nets establish territory by creating bounded space. Days later the image was republished, with the text '200m' printed beneath the line representing the net. The headlands at Bondi are approximately 800 metres (2,624 feet) apart. A report from the Department of Primary Industry accurately describes the nets as 150 metres long and illustrates the approximate location of the Bondi net, roughly mid-way between the heads (Green et al. 2009). The image from 2015 reinforced the incorrect view that the program creates safe "netted" areas at the beach that exclude sharks. Confusion about the operation of the Shark Meshing Program is compounded by existence of the "shark nets", described earlier, that form fully enclosed swimming areas at some harbour and estuarine beaches (including Neilson Park, also known as Shark Bay). These strategies for managing shark hazards represent two distinct modes to maintain shore control: asserting territory first through bounded space and second through social power exerted by violence.

The image published in the *Daily Telegraph* misrepresented the extent of the Bondi Beach net in two dimensions, creating an illusion of two distinct realms: territory inside and outside the net. The two-dimensional image further reinforced the common misperception of separated zones by ignoring the third dimension of depth (see Elden 2013b; Steinberg and Peters 2015). Like the other nets used in the Shark Meshing Program, the Bondi net is six metres deep and bottom set. The water here is approximately twelve metres deep (Green et al. 2009). The net can do no more than trap animals and other material moving through the lower part of the water column. The misrepresentation relates both to position and, more significantly, to function. Proliferation of misinformation – about the specific materiality of nets and sharks, and the nature of territory – plays an important part in the acceptance and continuation of the program, and therefore in the maintenance of shore control.

CONCLUSION

This analysis of geopolitics and more-than-human territory at the shore, and of the Shark Meshing (Bather Protection) Program NSW, has sought to examine what happens when non-human animals and materials are enlisted in territorialising processes. In particular, I have argued that territory is made and contested by more-than-human agents. The chapter has illuminated four key agents, of different kinds: the coast itself, sharks, bathing human bodies, and nets. Landscape, non-human animals, humans beyond their capacity to govern, and non-living materials all have agency in making and remaking territory. This analysis has implications for shark hazard management and human safety, and for our thinking about territory beyond *terra*.

Attention to the materiality of the coast has potential to inform strategies to improve the well-being of people and sharks in several ways. First, greater appreciation of the coast could be fostered to improve understanding of shark hazard, and specifically, the influence of coastal morphology on shark habitat and migration. Existing knowledge held by marine and coastal scientists and ocean users could be better integrated into shark hazard mitigation strategies and public information. Second, knowledge of shark biology and ecology should play a greater role in informing hazard mitigation strategies and cultural practice, replacing fantastical ideas about shark behaviour. Efforts are underway in institutions around the world to develop understandings of sharks. Greater effort is needed to incorporate this growing knowledge into policy and practice. Third, paying attention to the bathing human body may lead to more creative approaches for mitigating shark hazards for people, while also protecting other species. The existing strategy examined here – gillnets – overcomes our limited sense of sight beneath the water surface by working independently of it. But nets are indiscriminate. We might learn to draw on other senses to make better use of the specific materiality of water. Several emerging alternative technologies are doing just this, including sonar sensors, artificial kelp forests, and wet-suits that use visual design to play on underwater visibility and sharks' sense of sight. Attention to the human body may spark further innovations. Finally, the nets of the Shark Meshing Program are destructive, yet they are out of sight: the result is that many people are not aware or not fully informed of their existence, their function and their effects. Public critique of this political technology is limited by its invisibility. At a time when environmental concern is high and widespread, information about destructive environmental practices should be more publicly accessible. A more informed citizenry would be better able to support or reject the existing approach and meaningfully contribute to the process of determining alternatives.

The Shark Meshing (Bather Protection) Program NSW also informs our understandings of the concept and practices of territory. Analysis reveals that the program produces diverse interpretations of the term "territory". The New South Wales government asserts that sharks establish territories. The media embellish that assertion, describing sharks as aggressively defending territory when a shark sighting or human-shark encounter occurs. Scientists dispute the use of the term in this context, instead describing sharks' extensive and diverse use of ocean space. People claim territory through bodily engagements with the beach, water, and shore. The nuance of scientific knowledge comes head-to-head with populist understandings of the term territory, just as the space itself is contested. Shore control is claimed and confounded in the interplay between meaning and materials: conflicting interpretations of territory; the specific materiality of the coast; and (mis)understandings of both.

The shore presents a special case for examining territory beyond *terra*. The shore is a liminal space; neither land nor sea, it is a zone in which distinct geophysical, biological, and ecological realms meet. It is a constantly fluctuating environment, challenging thinking and practices of making territory. It is also a place where people meet a distinctly non-human world, which prompts us to pay attention to non-human life and materials, and their roles in politics. Here we find that non-human lifeforms and materials – of very different kinds – are active in asserting, maintaining, and contesting territory. Attending to the roles of non-human lives in the politics of territory obliges us to consider our legal and ethical obligations. Specifically, to notice that our persistent political technology of shore control renders animals – including threatened species – killable. In our encounters with them, animals elicit ethical obligations (Buller 2015; van Dooren 2014). Yet questions of ethics are often overlooked in decisionmaking and practice, as they are here.

More broadly, this case reveals something of our relationships with non-human animals and the non-human world. Making animals killable is a common outcome of human efforts to assert power over space. Such practices are premised on the idea of human exceptionalism. In addition, they assume that territory is disputed; that humans and other potentially threatening species cannot coexist. That assumption is contradicted by the evidence, which shows that they can and do (Chapron et al. 2014; Gibbs and Warren 2015). Popular discourses pertaining to territory in the Shark Meshing Program are consistent with those surrounding conflicts between humans and carnivorous species elsewhere (for example, Collard 2012). This debate is particularly significant in the context of global environmental change, which increasingly sees shifting ecosystems and species under threat. These challenges point to an urgent need to learn how to coexist with non-human others, including those that may pose a threat to us.

If we are to take seriously the agency of non-human lives and materials in shaping the world and genuinely incorporate them into our thinking and practice, we must also consider geopolitics – that is, a politics that pays attention to the material properties, capacities, and tendencies of the Earth (Dittmer 2014; Elden 2013b). The geopolitics of the coast and shore control can be illuminated by attending to the specific materiality of the site. To do so effectively demands looking to and working with other disciplines and fields of expertise. In this way we might better appreciate how the making and remaking of territory beyond *terra*, and of our world, is a more-than-human project.

NOTES

1. In the field of ecology the 'coexistence model' is based upon the idea of 'allowing people and predators together', in contrast to the wilderness or 'separation model' of 'keeping people and predators apart' (Chapron et al. 2014, 1517). Within the humanities and social sciences the concept of coexistence is explored in contrast to present exploitation and extinction of non-human life (for example, see Corbey and Lanjouw 2013).

2. One outcome of this debate was a shift by government away from emphasis on territory. In 2009 the state government's public information 'Primefact' sheet explained that the nets 'are designed to deter sharks from establishing territories, thereby reducing the odds of a shark encounter' (Department of Primary Industries NSW 2009). The 2015 sheet was altered to read that nets 'are designed to reduce the chances of dangerous sharks aggregating near meshed beaches, thereby reducing the chances of a shark interaction' (Department of Primary Industries NSW 2015, n.p.). This new language of aggregation raises new questions about the accuracy of representation of ecological processes. But the shift away from assertion of sharks establishing territories suggests that the public debate influenced policy.

3. The main species caught were hammerhead sharks, rays, whaler sharks, and angel sharks (Green et al. 2009), predominantly species that pose no threat to humans. Bull sharks – listed as potentially threatening – belong to the whaler group (*Carcharhinus spp.*), but are one of at least seven species in the genus present in the catch. The Shark Meshing Program does not identify catch to species level in this group. Meanwhile, white and tiger sharks were caught in low numbers; this may be due to 'low coastal abundance or limited catchability in the gear deployed' (Reid et al. 2011, 690).

Chapter 13

SEABEDS

Sub-Marine Territory: Living and Working on the Seafloor During the Sealab II Experiment

Rachael Squire

During the Cold War, the United States Navy placed great importance on calculating, administering, and speculating on and about the volume of the sea. For military planners and civilian scientists funded by agencies such as the US Office of Naval Research (ONR), the sea was a three-dimensional space in which the enemy could prowl unseen in nuclear-powered submarines cloaked by water and ice, and capable of wreaking havoc on land and from the air. Yet the sea also captured the strategic imagination of those in the US government and military for other reasons, and beyond the water column the seabed itself became the focus of international legal practitioners (Collis and Dodds 2008). One of four conventions negotiated at the first United Nations Conference on the Law of the Sea (UNCLOS I), the 1958 Convention on the Continental Shelf[1] codified the rules of international law. Its architects concluded, as President Truman had done in 1945, that coastal states should have control over the resources in these submerged and subterranean spaces (Truman 1945; UN 1958). Looming large was the prospect of gaining access to great untapped resources, food sources and minerals beneath the sea – this for 'the benefit of all mankind' (O'Neal et al. 1967, i).

It was in this geopolitical context of Cold War uncertainty and precarity that the United States Navy (hereafter US Navy) set about enabling "man"[2] to dwell beneath the sea for prolonged periods of time. From 1964 to 1968, the Sealab I, II, and III experiments were led by Captain George Bond (a diving physiologist and doctor in the US Navy), and resulted in underwater habitats being installed on the seafloor; these were subsequently inhabited by teams of aquanauts for up to forty-five consecutive days.

Sealab II forms the key case study for this chapter. Drawing on written and visual archival accounts of Sealab II from the US Navy and the ONR, the work that follows explores the implications of this Cold War undersea habitat for geographical thinking about territory, the study of which has traditionally remained tied to *terra firma* (see Elden 2010, 2013a). What does it mean, for example, to territorialise the sea and sea floor? How do the human body and infrastructure function in this different, hostile, elemental surround? What are the implications of such questions to our understanding of territory?

To provide some historical context to the Sealab II experiment, the chapter begins by drawing on the work of Matthew Farish (2006, 2013), Ron Doel (2003), and others engaging with the intersections of the Cold War, geopolitics, and science. The second section brings together scholarship on the sea and territory to explore the idea of territory as an immersive and corporeally experienced phenomenon. Moving on to the Sealab endeavour itself, I then consider how frontier imaginaries drove the march to live and work on the seafloor and some of the practicalities of doing so in an ever-changing, shifting, mobile volume. Finally, some of the physiological and psychological implications of being surrounded by a different atmosphere (whether water or artificial air in the habitat) are explored. Far from being an abstract calculation, territory emerges – through this case study at least – as a lived and felt immersive state with its own temporalities, rhythms, and subjectivities. Moreover, as will be reflected upon in the conclusion, Sealab offers opportunities to think through the plurality and complexity of the notion of territory as it exists in one experiment in various forms, volumes within volumes, and territories within territories (sea floor, water column, human body, and habitat). The pressing environment of the sea is, as a result, a useful space through which to think the functions of territory beyond *terra*.

ENVIRONMENTAL MASTERY

The US military was increasingly engaging with extreme environments after the onset of the Cold War. As Paul Nesbitt asserted, when serving as director of the Arctic, Desert, and Tropic Information Centre at Maxwell Air Force Base:

> For our armed forces to operate successfully on a global basis, we must be knowledgeable about the world's different environments in which our forces now operate or are likely to operate in the future as well as about the peculiar operational problems that varied hostile environments present. Major adjustments must be made in areas of climatic extremes – not only physical adjustments but also those involving deep changes in mental and social attitudes prompted by new places'. (Farish 2006, 134; see also 2013)

The Arctic became one such hostile environment: legitimised as such in the name of national and continental defence and for the advancement of economic development and environmental exploitation. In this frontier where geopolitical, military, and scientific practices collided, the high north became a cold and extreme space to test both humans and machines against the antagonist of nature. The body was pitted against the inherently dangerous topography, serving as 'a category, a vessel through which ideas of Arctic geography could be expressed' (Farish 2006, 190). The 'American Cold War on nature' was increasingly configuring the world 'as a patchwork of hostile environments', with any sense of 'geographical comprehension' to be inevitably followed by geographical mastery (Farish 2006, 193).

While the Arctic proved a pivotal testing ground for the US Army and military scientists, it was oceanography and space science that became 'the prime carriers of the American flag' (Doel 2003, 636). Endeavours beneath the sea and in outer space served to symbolise Western, and specifically US, technological achievement against natural conditions that, like an "enemy", were highly dynamic, unpredictable, capable of surprising, and often fully or partly hidden (Farish 2013). According to Jacob Hamblin (2002, 15), the need to 'subdue the ocean environment, to make it a manageable and even an advantageous battle-space' drove the US Navy to increase its knowledge of the oceans during the Cold War. The ONR invested heavily in oceanography to understand more about the environments 'through which men and machines might travel and communicate' (Oreskes 2003, 699) and to 'provide constant operational information for its existing defence systems' (Hamblin 2002, 4). The Sealab initiative took this aspiration one step further: it was an endeavour not to move or communicate in the sea, 'not to play within it, but to live within it, to dwell' (US Navy 1965, n.p.).

Framed as an extension of the efforts of early American pioneers to conquer and tame the Wild West (Jackson Turner 1893) and much like the military's activities in the Arctic, Sealab was described as an assault on the natural unknown (Sullivan 1961). As Miller et al. (1967, 267) stated in one ONR report on Sealab II, 'there are many hostile features [to consider] when living in the ocean'; this was an environment that needed to be 'attacked', where the characteristics of the sea had to be overcome, transformed, and mastered if the navy was to be successful in territorialising the seafloor. The project gained a sense of urgency after the loss of 129 naval personnel and civilians aboard the navy's lead nuclear submarine, the USS *Thresher* after a freak accident on 10 April 1963 that saw the submarine plunge to the sea floor 300 miles off the New England coast. According to Bond (1993, 1), the incident brought about a 'sudden recognition' of the need for deep diving, underwater search and rescue capabilities, and salvage operations at depth.

Thus, after a prolonged period of experimentation in hyperbaric chambers and with a budget of approximately US$150,000[3] the US Navy set about constructing the Sealab I underwater habitat alongside scientists, oceanographers, and engineers. In 1964, Sealab I was pressurised as it was lowered into the water and eventually positioned on the sea floor off the coast of Bermuda to provide a space for four men, or aquanauts as they became known, to live and work for three weeks fifty-eight metres (190 feet) under the sea. The water surrounding Sealab was held at bay by the pressure of the air within the habitat, meaning that the men could move relatively seamlessly from the breathable atmosphere of the habitat to the sea outside without the need for doors or hatches. Much to the disappointment of the aquanauts and personnel on the surface, the project was suspended after eleven days due to an impending hurricane that would have made it difficult for personnel in the support vessel to safely interact with the habitat. In addition, the extreme rise and fall of the waves would have made it a challenge to maintain the necessary pressure inside. Nevertheless, the experiment demonstrated that 'the deep dark sea is a lot more interesting if you can make man a free agent not just for a few minutes but for a few days . . . for a man that endures, a man that simply is, is triumph enough 190ft down' (US Navy 1966, n.p.).

After the success of the first experiment, Sealab II followed a year later in 1965. Rather than utilise the clear and warm conditions of Bermuda's sea, the aquanauts were to face a much more challenging environment on the continental shelf off the US Pacific coast (ONR 1967). The team set about pushing the boundaries set during Sealab I by sending aquanauts to live and work at a depth of sixty-two metres (203 feet), one mile (1.6 kilometres) off Scripps pier at La Jolla, California. Three ten-man aquanaut teams spent fifteen days each living and working at the pressure of the sea floor, while NASA astronaut Scott Carpenter lived below for thirty days in what the ONR (1967, 3) described as 'a pioneer effort to support human life and useful activity in the earth's most hostile environment'.

The stated aims of SEALAB II were multiple and indicative of the 'new role of science as the centrepiece of national security' (Hamblin 2002, 20). In addition to increasing the United States' 'capability to attack many significant oceanographic problems', Sealab II was designed to improve the capacity for military and scientific personnel 'to live and to perform useful work under the sea' including salvage and rescue operations for sunken submarines, downed aircraft, and atomic weapons; to make the sea 'yield some of its secrets' on undersea weather systems, and to expand the capabilities of the military on the continental shelf (ONR 1967, 17). In light of the 1958 Continental Shelf Convention, the US Navy also made numerous references to exploring and exploiting this domain – the sea and sea floor framed as a space of salvation with its wealth of minerals, 'treasure trove of resources', and 'food supply for the proliferating human race' (US Navy 1966, n.p.). 'Knowledge of the oceans is more than a matter of curiosity' stated one document from the US Navy (1966, n.p.): 'our very survival may hinge upon it' and, more importantly, 'knowledge is strength, a step in progress towards the essential strategic goals of the future which will require increasing utilisation of the vast oceanic areas for our security'. Such ambitions were explored and tested through a series of engagements with the undersea environment during the Sealab II experiment and analysis of those engagements stretch and nuance understandings of territory as both concept and practice.

IMMERSIVE TERRITORY

The concept of territory, writes Elden (2010, 1), has been 'under-examined', and this remains the case for understandings of territories, or parts of territories that are immersed in the element of water rather than air. Where the sea is mentioned by Elden (2013a) it is a space through which certain valuable energy sources can be extracted – rather than a space that matters in and of itself. In a certain sense then, territorial scholarship is still rooted at ground level and, as this chapter demonstrates, much could be gained were it to sink down to the seafloor and "hang" in the water column. Redressing this gap represents a significant opportunity given the proven capacity of the sea to raise unsettling questions that have application on *terra firma* and more widely in the discipline of geography (Steinberg and Peters 2015).

   Yet, as with scholarship on volume, writing on the sea has also occasionally lacked the "depth" needed to grapple with the territorialising practices implicit in the Sealab projects. Valuable insight into the sea as a central space in contemporary human geography and geopolitics is offered by studies of ships (Peters 2010), yachts (Spence 2014), surfers, and kayakers (Anderson 2012a, 2014). Nevertheless, these works do not easily accommodate the vast water column that exists beneath the surface on which these objects float and move. Perhaps the volume of the sea lends itself to surficial interventions because the underwater seascape comes into being, in part, through embodied practices (Merchant 2011a). As Steinberg (1999, 369) notes, the sea is 'a space where permanent sedentary habitation is impossible'. Steinberg also highlights the difficulties researchers face in accessing areas 'of the sea which are inhospitable, detached from shore, physically unstable, and immensely deep' (p. 372). It is often remarked that 'the sea is less explored than the moon' but, as Yusoff (2014, 44) speculates, this observation is perhaps unsurprising given that the moon is a visible surface with 'modes of illumination' becoming 'that which we can see' and therefore engage with. The depths of the sea resist our gaze. As such, the sea has remained predominantly as something to move on and rarely under; a substance to look or drift across; a space 'over which man explores and colonises and trades' (Semple in Steinberg

1999, 368). Even the term "under the sea" implies that it is a surface – something to float on rather than be immersed in.

There are valuable exceptions to this surficial analytical tendency within human geography scholarship. For example, Elizabeth Straughan (2012) and Stephanie Merchant (2011a, 2011b, 2014) have established the importance of embodied encounters with undersea space to illustrate that the underwater seascape is, like land, constructed via certain embodied, material, and discursive practices. Through the bodies of divers, the seascape is no longer considered 'an inert background or setting for human action, nor is it understood as solely a pictorial or discursive form of representation' (Merchant 2011a, 216). Such scholarly interventions deal with the body as it immersed in water and consider the social and cultural implications of embodied immersion, yet the geopolitical dimensions of this are absent from geographical discourse. As Kimberley Peters (2012, 1243) notes, questions of power are central to our engagements with the sea: we 'grapple with the power of the sea, harnessing it and manipulating its affects' but, at the same time, are relatively ineffectual at expressing 'power back onto the sea'. This relationship is not reciprocal but it is in these uneven interactions that one can begin to explore the ways in which "man" has sought to exert power over the sea and been subject to its power in return. The lack of attention afforded to these dynamics may be because the sea is a space cemented in imaginaries as 'an uninteresting abyss', as something 'outside of state territory' with attributes that 'deter sedentary habituation' (Steinberg 1999, 369). The experiences of Sealab II offer opportunities to counter these narratives and learn more about the nature of territory as a whole and about the concept of territorial volumes beyond the elemental surrounds of air.

DESTINIES, DIFFICULTIES AND DOMESTICATION

Seafloor Destinies

Prior to positioning the Sealab II habitat on the sea floor, those involved did a great deal of work both practically and imaginatively. Records suggest that, for George Bond, territorialising the sea floor was an almost-spiritual endeavour. The initial animal and early human experiments in sustaining human life at pressure were named 'Project Genesis', with Bond suggesting that man should 'acquire dominion over the seas and the creatures therein' – shifting the biblical emphasis from the 'fish of the sea' to the matter of the sea itself (Hellwarth 2012, 17). Bond's personal chronicles of the Sealab endeavours were littered with biblical terminology suggestive of a predestined, ordained and teleological journey to inhabit the deep. Each member of the team, wrote Bond (1965, 5), must turn 'to his own solitary and necessary road to Damascus'. Once the program had started, the "Sealab prayer" became a mainstay of undersea life and every Sunday Bond would deliver sermons on subjects including "faith" and the long-suffering biblical character, Job. Bond described the Sealab agenda as his "gospel", and those who subscribed to it became "believers". Any tendency for hyperbole in Bond's writing aside, spirituality and faith here are invoked as 'territorial mythologies' (Sage 2014, 14), serving to construct 'seductive geopolitical scripts' that 'explain, naturalise, and reinforce America's exceptional destiny' in frontier spaces (Sage 2008, 29).[4]

In Bond's writing, the sea seemed to offer a stage on which 'America's transcendental mission (could) be realised' (Sage 2014, 34). As with outer space, national identity became inextricably linked to conquering the unknown – to taming the "hostile environment" of the sea. In the process, spatial and temporal frames collapse. While the media compared the success of Sputnik to the discovering of America by Christopher Columbus (Sage 2014), Bond (1965) and the US Navy (1965) also invoked Columbus, Magellan, and Buffalo Bill to continue the territorial myth that "a future without limits" is a distinguishing trait of American national identity. The trope of the "frontier" looms large here with Sealab enfolded into a narrative that framed American expansionism into the West, over the ocean and, in this case, under the sea, as a necessary step in humanity's progression (Sage 2014). Much like America's quest into outer space, this involved freeing "man" from terrestrial limits to access the resources and multiple unknown potentialities lying and suspended beneath the surface of the sea. This imaginative "frontier" projection was a powerful driver for the navy and promoters of ocean exploration in the 1960s (Rozwadowski 2010, 522). The sea proved alluring, and territorial expansion is framed here as something extraordinary and simultaneously inevitable and necessary. Far from being outside of the imaginaries of military personnel, scientists, and engineers the water and floors beneath the surface of the sea were cemented in the minds of some at least, as unclaimed territory ripe for exploration and exploitation. Significantly, this frontier did not merely extend horizontally over land: it brought territorial expansionism into three dimensions, a clear demonstration of American technological and scientific power through and in an unconquered element.

Seafloor Realities

Transcendental agendas aside, Bond and his team first had to reconcile the practicalities of underwater living if their march to the bottom of the sea was to be successful. Before the Sealab II habitat, its extensive equipment and infrastructure, and aquanauts could begin their descent to the continental shelf, the ONR set about establishing the most appropriate site on which their experiment would take place (figure 13.1).

This work involved extensive mapping and modelling of the sea floor on the continental shelf just north of La Jolla off the Californian coastline (ONR 1967). The proximity to Scripps Institute of Oceanography meant that the seafloor was as well charted as any comparable site and, after detailed soundings were completed, it was decided to place the habitat by La Jolla Submarine Canyon. This site would avoid the steep inclinations and great silt deposits identified in preliminary dives to other possible sites, and provide an ideal area for excursion diving to even deeper depths without aquanauts having to swim long, exhausting, and air-demanding distances (ONR 1967, 13).

These mapped lines and visualisations however could not account for what Culpepper et al. (1967, 335) described as an 'extremely uneven and fast changing' seafloor. According to Murray et al. (1967, 371) surveys undertaken prior to Sealab II revealed that approximately '200,000 cubic yards of sand' (152,910 cubic metres) were being lost each year into Scripps canyon while, in the water column itself, 'unusual sediment transport' rendered the visibility at the proposed site next to nothing (Bond 1965, 31). To compound the difficulties, "all black" silt accumulation threatened to obscure what little visibility they had. It seemed 'entirely possible', wrote Bond (1965, 31), 'that the

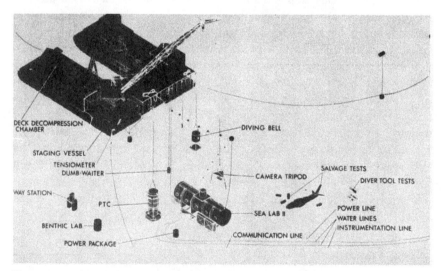

Figure 13.1 An artist's conception of the Sealab II operational configuration. *Note:* The PTC refers to the Personnel Transfer Capsule used to transport the aquanauts at pressure to and from the surface while the Benthic Lab was an unmanned, remotely operated electronics complex. *Source:* Carpenter and Blockwick (1967, 128). Reproduced with permission from the Man in the Sea Museum, Panama City Beach, Florida.

visibility may range from six inches to one foot through the entire operation'. As Merchant (2014) notes, water can be overbearing as it presses in on the diving body, a sense of enclosure that would only have been compounded were the aquanaut rendered effectively blind by suspended sediment. After nearly US$250,000 had been spent on Sealab II's site location, the final siting decision was taken on the basis of the report of a 'single, exceptional underwater human worker'. For Bond (1965, 53) this outcome exemplified the purpose of the program – "man" continues to be the best underwater sensing agent.

From these challenges questions arise about territory as a dynamic construct. It is now widely acknowledged that, as it relates to land, territory is not a static phenomenon. It is mobile, constantly being made and remade and the result of a host of social, political, cultural, environmental, and economic processes (Elden 2010, 2013b). Yet as Steinberg and Peters (2015) highlight, this state of flux is drastically intensified at sea. Acknowledging the sea as a volume 'within which territory is practiced', Steinberg and Peters (2015, 261) point to the constant reformation of territory that is laid bare as the seafloor shifts, moves, and is displaced, becoming part of the water column as it does so. The floor on which Sealab II was to stand and on which the aquanauts were to work was transient and subject to temporalities quite different and distinct from those encountered on *terra firma*.

Since water is 'pre-eminently apt as a means of surrounding' (Ten Bos 2009, 78) and its matter is dynamic (Bremner 2014), the sea will not be the same from one moment to the next because parcels of water are turbulently 'exchanged between one part of the moving fluid and another' (Brown et al. 2004, 40). In addition to raising questions about the temporalities of a territory in motion, this movement creates spatial difficulties. Those on the surface support vessel struggled to maintain their moor over the site. Similarly, once the habitat had been established Bond (1965, 5) noted that:

> Objects of known location on the ocean bottom are not in fact there, but more often eventually found at some considerable distance away, and on a new azimuth . . . it is a solid fact that, though we have been moored over Sealab II, an object nearly the size of a small submarine, for about a month, we still don't know where the habitat lies, nor on what heading.

The mobilities and vectors of the sea were experienced differently by those "topside", disorienting those working on the surface in relation to the habitat beneath. While those in the Sealab habitat later reported being able to 'sense the crest of waves' (Murray et al. 1967, 381), they did not feel that movement in the same way as those on the surface.

Overall then, various geographies generated by the territorialising practices of the Sealab experiments produced a range of temporal and spatial complexities that, both then and now, suggest a need for new understandings and methods of interpreting territory as it exists in volume (Steinberg and Peters 2015). This insight is further illustrated if one considers the capacity of water to suspend and lift sediment and matter from the sea floor into its matter.

DOMESTICATING THE SEAFLOOR

Little by little he transforms the wilderness. (Jackson Turner 1893, 200)

Adey (2015) and Rozwadowski (2010) highlight the potential difficulties in engaging with substances such as air and water because of their sheer scale and omnipresence. For example, Rozwadowski (2010, 521) writes about how the ocean 'seems unimaginably enormous relative to human scale . . . The vastness, in all three dimensions, impedes meaningful scientific knowledge based on direct, personal experience'. Yet, one can begin to explore what it was like to live and work on the seafloor by homing in on how part of this vast volume became an ephemeral locale for the Sealab occupants. It is to some of these localised details that I now turn to explore the lived realities of sea floor life, homesteading practices, and mechanisms to tame the extreme.

As I have highlighted, the environment in which Sealab II's habitat stood was framed as a hostile adversary (ONR 1967). Yet, the choice of language used by both the aquanauts and those topside began to change as the project unfolded. As the first team of aquanauts began their stay in the habitat, Scott Carpenter 'and his boys . . . worked like dogs to complete the cleaning of their front yard' (Bond 1965, 12), and the habitat was continually referred to as 'home' or as the 'house under the sea'. The 'ocean is still a hostile environment' wrote Bond, 'but we are taming some of it, bit by bit' (p. 68). Multiple practices and practicalities were involved in this domestication. In addition to conducting scientific work, oceanographic studies, and excursion dives to the canyon, aquanauts engaged in varied mundane tasks. Housekeeping, for example, was a primary concern. Day-to-day tasks to keep the habitat and their own bodies operational consumed much of the aquanauts' time. In addition to all of the checks on equipment and various new technologies, the men had to cook, clean, and tend to their 'backyard'. They watered seeds to test the feasibility of growing crops in an artificial and alien atmosphere[5] underwater (ONR 1967, 10): while barley proved a success, marigolds produced only one sprout. The US Navy (1965, n.p.) described thirty days passing in a 'methodical and persistent sequence of work inside and outside the habitat, of meals and housekeeping, of human measurement and evaluation under high pressure'. As with Sealab I, 'the interlopers are making themselves at home' (US Navy 1965, n.p.). This sense of routine normalcy was carefully engineered using strict schedules to create a sense of rhythm and impression that the 'normal world' was being brought into 'an abnormal place', that the 'far out' was becoming an 'everyday affair' (1965, n.p.). Achieving this mundanity was more than a technological or logistical feat – it was testament to Bond and the navy's commitment to "taming" what was thought to be the untameable (ONR 1967). Moreover, these small time-consuming practices of cleaning, watering, preparing, checking, and testing were constitutive of wider temporal imaginaries. Making routine the extraordinary was a means of projecting into the future. 'In the murk of the seafloor you see a hint of the future – mining by coring – a miniaturised sample of what might one day be gigantic machines gathering minerals from the bottomland' (US Navy 1965, n.p.). Temporal frames collapse here as everyday practices of territory construction, pioneering, and homesteading were connected to overcome the demands of new frontiers that were meant to extend the boundaries of territory-making. Among them were energy frontiers to mine new resources; security frontiers to secure food or salvage matter; and bodily frontiers to test how well "man" adapted to volumes of deep water. An 'unknown empire that begins before our very eyes on every shore' (US Navy 1965, n.p.) was being imagined in new ways as the ocean was "humbled" (Rozwadowski 2012), and as the routine became synonymous with future geopolitical and geostrategic objectives.

Notwithstanding the significance of the observations above, in his diary Bond expressed concerns that the men might start feeling a little too comfortable in their new immersive surroundings. In a list of his primary concerns, the "breakaway phenomenon" was high among them. With origins in flying and aerospace, the breakaway or break-off phenomenon refers to a sense of estrangement, unreality, or detachment from land (Benson 1973; Tormes and Guedry 1974) or, as Bond (1965, 132) described, a sense of disorientation 'in space, time, and philosophy' where sea, not land, becomes a refuge and home. For the aquanauts, this disorientation manifest in a complacency about their undersea existence, indifference to the chain of command on the surface, an occasional disregard of instructions from those topside, and, sporadically, a lackadaisical approach to safety protocols. One of the psychologists observing the aquanauts from the surface reported on the effects of being 'separated from the world by 200 impenetrable feet (sixty metres) of water' (Helmreich 1967, 37). 'Separated from the world' does not refer merely to physical distance from the surface. Due to the pressure placed on the body by depth, the aquanauts were unable to surface if there was a problem – to do so would mean certain death as the absorbed gas in their cells would be released explosively into their bodies. The only escape mechanism was a small Personnel Transfer Capsule (see figure 13.2), and in the water the aquanauts had to be

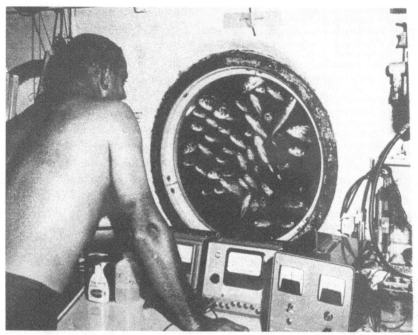

Figure 13.2 An aquanaut and fish exchange glances at a porthole of the Sealab II habitat. *Source:* US Navy Official photography. Reproduced with permission from the Man in the Sea Museum, Panama City Beach, Florida.

weighted down to ensure negative buoyancy. Perhaps as a result of this several aquanauts reported feelings of isolation from the outside world (figure 13.2). Surface personnel were referred to as "earth people" and occasionally held in mock contempt by the sea dwellers. 'On one occasion' Helmreich reported that 'a diver said "I have a message for the earth people. Fuck you!"' (p. 59). Similarly, Helmreich reported that the one aquanaut who communicated most with the 'outside world [was] severely ridiculed by his teammates for his preoccupation with "earth people"' (Helmreich 1967, 59). Until the importance of discipline was reiterated from above, intercom calls went unanswered for 'long minutes'; excursion dives took place on half empty air bottles with no reports on entry and exit times; electrowriter messages were ignored for as much as half an hour; and the daily situation report to be delivered at 20:00 p.m. arrived three hours late on one occasion (Bond 1993, 119).

Clearly, then, psychological aspects of territory-making beneath the sea were important. As Merchant (2014) describes, the sub-surface environment of the sea can be overbearing as it encloses. It is a distinct elemental surround that contributed to the aquanauts' sense of detachment and growing impression that independently they were pioneers breaking "new ground". Perhaps Bond's concerns about this were linked to broader colonial anxieties about Americans "going native", whether in the context of the early pioneers as they sought to claim the West or in the context of Cold War prisoners of war converting to the enemy's way of life. In any sense, the surrounding sea was constitutive of a territorial imaginary that framed "earth dwellers" as somehow distinct from "sea dwellers" and produced an 'emerging relationship with the ocean as part of an (inevitable) evolutionary trajectory' (Rozwadowski 2010, 5).

Of course, physiological adaptations were just as important as psychological considerations. The 'cold, murky, top heavy realm of water' affected the body in multiple ways (US Navy 1965, n.p.). Water robs heat from the body, slows reactions, and reduces the effectiveness of the senses. Inside the habitat itself, the helium-heavy air mixture distorted the human voice and headaches, ear infections, and skin rashes were commonplace. The US Navy (1965, n.p.) mapped and charted physiological changes and bodily adaptation in its bid to understand the 'limits of flesh and blood beneath the waves'. Daily schedules for electrocardiograms, blood and urine samples, motor skills tests, and batteries of physiological tests produced more than 'half a million items of specific information' (Bond 1965, 139). Core samples were taken from their bodies and their enzymes, blood cells, and internal pressures became units of analysis in territorialising practices (Squire 2016b). Analysis of these data would also generate 'guidelines for further extension of man's exploration of the continental shelves or beyond, down the continental slopes – perhaps even to the abyssal plains. Who dares to postulate a barrier?' (Bond 1965, 138). In the process, aquanauts' bodies and minds were folded into the practices of territory and territorial expansion. In a sense, the men were mapped, charted, recorded, and sampled by those topside just as they studied the seafloor and surrounding water column.

In the process, the bodies of the aquanauts were swept up in a much wider territorialising agenda precisely because they were seen to be living successfully in this alien realm. Their bodies 'collectively comprised a medical mystery that if deciphered' might unlock the secret to semi-amphibious man (Farish 2013, 5). The controlled, ordered labs in which this experimentation would take place included the Sealab habitat and the sea, as well as the body itself. The body's molecular matter thus gained a 'visceral agency' with potential application beyond the bodies of the aquanauts to mankind as a whole (Hayes-Conroy and Hayes-Conroy 2010, 1274). This was environmental physiology in practice; the study of human factors 'part of a larger conquest' by the US Navy that would enable adaptation to 'any environment in which he is called to operate' (Farish 2013, 9).

CONCLUSION

According to Paul Nitze, secretary of the US Navy, the success of Sealab II put the United States:

at the threshold of an expanding capability for military operations on the continental shelf where required. Of equal importance to the welfare of the nation, it increased our capabilities in the extraction of chemicals and minerals from the sea, the tending of pipelines, cables and underwater installations, the culture of marine life for food, and of course, the extension of geophysical exploration and general advancement of all earth sciences. (ONR 1967, i)

The sea has long been a vital space among militaries and states and, for 1960s America, it held certain promises related to providing for a burgeoning population and acting pre-emptively in the Cold War. Far from being imagined as an uninhabitable abyss, the sea was space that could be inhabited; its seafloor could be lived on; its water column could be lived in. While similar distinctions could be made between territorialising the Earth's surfaces within the surround of air on land, the water presented fundamentally different challenges. This was a wholly immersive territory, the surface of the seafloor inseparable from water column, and territorialising one necessitated negotiating and managing the other. To conduct work on the seafloor, for example, the aquanauts had to be weighted down to prevent their bodies and air tanks from becoming positively buoyant. On the other hand conducting work in the water column was complicated by a lack of light, by heat diffusing from the bodies of the aquanauts into the surrounding water, and by the matter of the seafloor itself hanging like a three-dimensional curtain limiting their ability to see.

As this chapter has demonstrated, achieving the objective of sub-marine territorialisation involved multiple practices that raise interesting questions for conceptualising territory beyond *terra firma*. As a deep space was translated into 'a relevant place' (Rozwadowski 2010, 251), the construct of territory emerges out of the 'water in unrecognised and unanticipated ways' (Steinberg and Peters 2015, 261). We see, for example, the significance of time and multiple temporal ruptures. First, Sealab was framed as an exploratory extension of historical endeavours by the likes of Columbus and Magellan, and documented as a spiritual endeavour by George Bond to justify and provide impetus for ongoing undersea exploration and exploitation. Simultaneously, time within the habitat was managed to engineer a sense of normalcy, rhythm, and routine, emphasising in the process the potentials and future possibilities of undersea living and working. The body was also brought under this temporal regime with schedules of sampling and monitoring to determine the effects of the environment. Meanwhile, on the surface the shifting conditions on the sea floor and constant movement in the water column presented challenges in both locating and managing the habitat beneath. We might also think about the temporalities of the life surrounding the habitat. George Bond (1965, 85), for example, described how Sealab II was becoming 'part of the seafloor topography, a slate-grey mass surrounded and partially inhabited by swarms of marine life, blending so perfectly into the bottom seascape as to almost escape identification'. Over time, then, the sea has the power to absorb and engulf objects into its terrain and biorhythms. Immersed in water and away from *terra firma*, practicing territory involved a concerted engagement with multiple temporalities. While there has not been room in this chapter to engage with these complexities fully, the significance of "time" in the construction of territory beyond *terra* certainly warrants further attention.

Another theme that resurfaces throughout the chapter is that of embodiment. The volume of water in which the Sealab experiment partly unfurled was experienced as intensively corporeal and haptic: it pressed in on the body. Consequential senses of immersion and enclosure had both psychological and physiological effects as the aquanauts experienced signs of the breakaway phenomenon from 'earth dwellers' and as their bodies experienced myriad physical manifestations of living in the sea. They experienced undersea territory not only through their bodies but in the physiological, minute, environmentally induced changes occurring within them (see Protevi 2009). The body here becomes a prism through which to experience the territory of the sea and to understand how certain voluminous environments affect the inner, intricate, and molecular workings of the body. Beginning with the body in analyses of territory might raise fruitful avenues of enquiry for future geographical research in other extreme spaces such as the Polar Regions (Farish 2013), high altitudes, tunnels, and other immersive spaces where the elements collide with the body's own inner elemental formations (Squire 2016a, 2016b). Territory emerges through this chapter as a construct that not only exists in the world's volumes but as a concept that is constructed by volume as the three dimensional bodies of the environment and the human are brought into conversation with one another. Far from being an abstract calculation, then, territory is a lived and felt immersive state (Adey 2015) with consequences for both body and mind.

Finally, the Sealab experiment(s) demonstrate that territory is both motionful and dynamic and a multifaceted and plural construct. The sea floor and water column, for example, became substances to be mastered and conquered, yet highly differentiated interventions were required to manage their materiality. At the same time, the body's reactions – both physical and psychological – were mapped, charted, and managed, the body itself becoming a voluminous space that interacts with the surrounding environment. It was the volume of the habitat that enabled the sea floor to be inhabited in the first place, and we might think of the air tanks strapped to the aquanauts' backs when in the water column in a similar way. Both are demonstrations of technological, material interventions in which a volume is constructed and filled with a form of life sustaining air to enable the inhabitation of the sea-floor and water column. These overlapping territorialised spaces and volumes that interrelate as various materials, elements, and practices coalesce, demonstrating that while theorisations of space should not exist on a surface (Elden 2013b, 35), nor should they exist in an unproductive dichotomy between 'surface' and 'volume'. Rather, as Sealab demonstrates, there are multiple territorial constructions at play which, at times, may seem contradictory and even messy as substances mix and interact, but which help to account for the multiple overlapping and enfolding territories and volumes that enabled submarine inhabitation.

NOTES

1. The Convention specifically refers to '(a) the seabed and subsoil of the submarine areas adjacent to the coast but outside the area of the territorial sea, to a depth of 200 metres or, beyond that limit, to where the depth of the superjacent waters admits of the exploitation of the natural resources of the said areas; (b) to the seabed and subsoil of similar submarine areas adjacent to the coasts of islands' (UN 1958, Article 1).

2. "Man" is used deliberately throughout the chapter to reflect the highly gendered nature of the projects.

3. The figure is listed as quoted in 1964.

4. Writing about the role of Outer Space in American identity, Sage (2008, 2014) describes how America became a political manifestation of transcendentalism with imperial ambition, puritanism, and spiritual motifs colliding in American imaginaries to shape spatial realities. Within this framework, events unfold through a 'kind of emotionally charged, transcendental resonance' between God, the individual, and 'an indiscernible experience of the vastness and immensity of nature' (Sage 2008, 28).

5. Because nitrogen becomes narcotic and oxygen toxic at depth, the men were living in an atmosphere of eighty-five per cent helium, eleven per cent nitrogen and four per cent oxygen (ONR 1967). Little was therefore known about how plant life (or indeed the human body) would respond.

ACKNOWLEDGEMENTS

Many thanks to Klaus Dodds and Al Pinkerton for their constructive comments on earlier drafts of this chapter. Thanks also to all those at the Man in the Sea Museum for granting me access to its wonderful collections. This research was funded by an ESRC 1+3 scholarship.

References

ABC News Australia (2014) Video appears to show lifeboat being towed by an Australian vessel under Operation Sovereign Borders. Available from https://goo.gl/Jw2W2E. Last accessed on 14 April 2017.

ABC Radio Australia (2001) Fiji loses bid to control Tonga, Samoa air space, *Australia Broadcasting Corporation*, 29 November, Available from https://goo.gl/nm25Fd. Last accessed on 29 March 2017.

Adams, P. C., Craine, J. and Dittmer, J. (2014) *The Ashgate Research Companion to Media Geography*. Farnham: Ashgate.

Adams, R. E. (in press) *Circulation and Urbanization*. London: SAGE Publications Inc.

Adey, P. (2006) If mobility is everything then it is nothing: towards a relational politics of (im)mobilities, *Mobilities* 1(1), 75–94.

———. (2010) *Aerial Life: Spaces, Mobilities, Affects*. Hoboken, NJ: Wiley-Black well Publishing.

———. (2013) Securing the volume/volumen: comments on Stuart Elden's Plenary paper 'Secure the volume', *Political Geography* 34(May), 52–54.

———. (2014) *Air: Nature and Culture*. London: Reaktion Books.

———. (2015) Air's affinities: geopolitics, chemical affect and the force of the elemental, *Dialogues in Human Geography* 5(1), 54–75.

Adey. P., Anderson B. and Guerrero, L. L. (2011) An ash cloud, airspace and environmental threat, *Transactions of the Institute of British Geographers* 36(3), 338–43.

Adey, P., Budd, L. and Hubbard, P. (2007) Flying lessons: exploring the social and cultural geographies of global air travel, *Progress in Human Geography* 31(6), 773–91.

Agamben, G. (1998) *Homo Sacer: Sovereign Power and Bare Life*. Translated by D. Heller-Roazen. Stanford: Stanford University Press.

Agnew, J. (1994) The territorial trap: the geographical assumptions of international relations theory, *Review of International Political Economy* 1(1), 53–80.

———. (2005) Sovereignty regimes: territoriality and state authority in contemporary world politics, *Annals of the Association of American Geographers* 95(2), 437–61.

Aiken, R. (2004) Runaway fires, smoke-haze pollution, and unnatural disasters in Indonesia, *Geographical Review* 94(1), 55–79.

Albert, M. (1998) On boundaries, territory and postmodernity: an international relations perspective, *Geopolitics* 3(1), 53–68.

Alder, J. and Sumaila, R. (2004) Western Africa: a fish basket of Europe past and present, *Journal of Environment and Development* 13(2), 156–78.

Allen, J. (2009) Three spaces of power: territory, networks, plus a topological twist in the tale of domination and authority, *Journal of Power* 2(2), 197–212.

Alleyn, P. (2012) The Chinese Dust Bowl, *The Walrus*. Available from http://thewalrus.ca/the-chinese-dust-bowl/. Last accessed on 20 April 2016.

Althoff, W.F. (2007) *Drift Station: Arctic Outposts of Superpower Science*. Washington, DC: Potomac.

Amato, J.A. (2000) *Dust: A History of the Small and the Invisible*. Berkeley and Los Angeles: University of California Press.

Amin, A. (2000) The European Union as more than a triad market for national economic spaces. In Clark, G., Feldman, M. and Gertler, M. (eds) *The Oxford Handbook of Economic Geography*. Oxford: Oxford University Press, 671–85.

Anderson, B. (2009) Affective atmospheres, *Emotion, Space and Society* 2(2), 77–81.

Anderson, B. and Wylie, J. (2009) On geography and materiality, *Environment and Planning A* 41(2), 318–35.

Anderson, C. and Maxwell-Stewart, H. (2013) Convict labour and the western empires, 1415–1954. In Aldrich, R. and McKenzie, K. (eds) *The Routledge History of Western Empires*. London and New York: Routledge, 102–17.

Anderson, J. (2012a) Exploring the space between words and meaning: understanding the relational sensibility of surf spaces, *Emotion, Space and Society* 10(February), 27–34.

———. (2012b) Relational places: the surfed wave as assemblage and convergence, *Environment and Planning D: Society and Space* 30(4), 570–87.

———. (2013) Cathedrals of the surf zone: regulating access to a space of spirituality, *Social & Cultural Geography* 14(8), 954–72.

———. (2014) What I think about when I think about kayaking. In Anderson, J. and Peters, K. (eds.) *Water Worlds: Human Geographies of the Ocean*. Aldershot: Ashgate, 103–18.

Anderson, J. and Peters, K. (2014a) 'A perfect and absolute blank': human geographies of water worlds. In Anderson, J. and Peters, J. (eds) *Water Worlds: Human Geographies of the Ocean*. Aldershot: Ashgate, 3–23.

———. (eds.) (2014b) *Water Worlds: Human Geographies of the Ocean*. Aldershot: Ashgate.

Anderson, K. (2015) Talks in the City of Light generate more heat, *Nature* 528(7583), 437.

Anonymous (1842a) Issue 1191, Saturday November 19, p. 6. Gale Document Number: R3212004012). Awful shipwrecks. *The Sheffield & Rotherham Independent (Sheffield), British Library Newspapers, Part II: 1800–1900*.

———. (1842b) Cape Town, 31 August 1842. *South African Commercial Advertiser*. https://goo.gl/sniuiq. Last accessed on 17 May 2017.

———. (1842c) Issue 3152, Wednesday November 23, np. Gale Document Number: R3209551420). Disasters at sea. *The Bury and Norwich Post, and East Anglian (Bury Saint Edmunds), British Library Newspapers, Part II: 1800–1900*.

———. (1842d) Issue 19161, Monday November 14, np. Gale Document Number: BB3205442641). Latest news. *Caledonian Mercury (Edinburgh), British Library Newspapers, Part I: 1800–1900.*

———. (1842e) Issue 1009, Saturday November 19, np. Gale Document Number: R3208539861). London. *Hampshire Advertiser & Salisbury Guardian (Southampton) British Library Newspapers, Part II: 1800–1900.*

———. (1842f) Issue 1668, Saturday November 19, np. Gale Document Number: R3213075706). Loss of the convict ship Waterloo. *The Leicester Chronicle: or, Commercial and Agricultural Advertiser (Leicester), British Library Newspapers, Part II: 1800–1900.*

———. (1842g) Tuesday November 22, Issue 800, np. Gale Document Number: BB3200868374). Melancholy loss of the convict ship Waterloo, bound for Sydney. *North Wales Chronicle (Bangor), British Library Newspapers, Part I: 1800–1900.* https://goo.gl/1qjfQR. Last accessed on 17 May 2017.

———. (1842h) Issue 4950, Wednesday, November 23, np. Gale Document Number: BA3205646744). Melancholy loss of the convict ship Waterloo, bound for Sydney. *The Aberdeen Journal (Aberdeen, Scotland), British Library Newspapers, Part I: 1800–1900.*

———. (1842i) Issue 19162, Thursday November 17, np. Gale Document Number: BB3205442651). Melancholy loss of the convict ship Waterloo, bound for Sydney, 250 lives lost out of 330. *Caledonian Mercury (Edinburgh), British Library Newspapers, Part I: 1800–1900.*

———. (1842j) Issue 5405, Saturday November 19, np. Gale Document Number: Y3202555387). Melancholy shipwreck. *The Ipswich Journal (Ipswich, England), British Library Newspapers, Part I: 1800–1900.*

———. (1842k) Issue 458, Thursday, November 17, p. 6. Gale Document Number: R3210334147). Melancholy shipwreck. [?] 250 lives lost. *The Bradford Observer; and Halifax, Huddersfield, and Keighley Reporter (Bradford), British Library Newspapers, Part II: 1800–1900.*

———. (1842l) Issue 5725, Monday November 14, np. Gale Document Number: R3213854716). Melancholy shipwreck. [?] Two hundred and fifty lives lost. *The Standard (London), British Library Newspapers, Part II: 1800–1900.*

———. (1842m) Issue N/A. Wednesday, November 16, np. Gale Document Number: BC3204539400). Melancholy shipwreck. Two hundred and fifty lives lost. *Freeman's Journal and Daily Commercial Advertiser (Dublin, Ireland), British Library Newspapers, Part I: 1800–1900.*

———. (1842n) Issue 1816, Saturday, November 19, np. Gale Document Number: BB3200994219). Melancholy shipwrecks. *The Examiner (London), British Library Newspapers, Part I: 1800–1900.*

———. (1842o) Issue 3660, Saturday November 19, np. Gale Document Number: R3215234728). Melancholy shipwrecks. *The York Herald, and General Advertiser (York), British Library Newspapers, Part II: 1800–1900.*

———. (1842p) Issue 22772, Monday November 14, np. Gale Document Number: BA3207208210). Melancholy shipwrecks of the Abercromby [sic] Robinson and the Waterloo, with great loss of life. *The Morning Chronicle (London, England), British Library Newspapers, Part I: 1800–1900.*

———. (1842q) Issue 19162, Thursday November 17, np. Gale Document Number: BB3205442655). [Multiple news items]. *Caledonian Mercury (Edinburgh), British Library Newspapers, Part I: 1800–1900*.

———. (1842r) Issue 5727, Wednesday November 16, np. Gale Document Number: R3213854772). [Multiple news items]. *The Standard (London), British Library Newspapers, Part II: 1800–1900*.

———. (1842s) Issue 3022, Friday November 18, np. Gale Document Number: BB3205927169). Shipping intelligence. *The Hull Packet (Hull), British Library Newspapers, Part I: 1800–1900*.

———. (1842t) Issue 10995, Tuesday November 22, np. Gale Document Number: Y3202338404). Shipwrecks. *The Belfast News-Letter (Belfast), British Library Newspapers, Part I: 1800–1900*.

———. (1842u) Issue 1646, Friday November 25, np. Gale Document Number: BC3203958274). [Untitled]. *Liverpool Mercury etc (Liverpool), British Library Newspapers, Part I: 1800–1900*.

———. (1842v) Issue 4040, Friday March 24, np. Gale Document Number: R3212744864). [Untitled]. *The Cornwall Royal Gazette, Falmouth Packet and Plymouth Journal (Truro), British Library Newspapers, Part II: 1800–1900*.

———. (1843a) Issue 3169, Wednesday March 22, p. 1. Gale Document Number: R3209551856). Domestic. *The Bury and Norwich Post, and East Anglian (Bury Saint Edmunds), British Library Newspapers, Part II: 1800–1900*.

———. (1843b) Issue 2268, Monday March 27, np. Gale Document Number: BB3206033765). Transport and convict ships. *Hampshire Telegraph and Sussex Chronicle etc (Portsmouth), British Library Newspapers, Part I: 1800–1900*.

———. (1970) Murder in legal limbo, *Time* 28 September, 47.

Anzaldua, G. (1987) *Borderlands/la Frontera: The New Mestiza*. San Francisco: Aunt Lute Books.

Appel, H. (2012) Offshore work: oil, modularity, and the how of capitalism in Equatorial Guinea, *American Ethnologist* 39(4), 692–709.

Ardrey, R. (1966) *The Territorial Imperative: A Personal Inquiry into the Animal Origins of Property and Nations*. New York: Atheneum.

Aristotle (1957) *Physics*, Greek-English edition. Translated by P.H. Wickstead and F.M. Cornford. Cambridge, MA: Harvard University Press, two volumes.

———. (1975) *Metaphysics*, Greek-English edition. Translated by H. Tredennick. Cambridge, MA: Harvard University Press.

Ash, J. (2013) Rethinking affective atmospheres: technology, perturbation and space times of the non-human, *Geoforum* 49(October), 20–28.

Association of Southeast Asian States (2006) *ASEAN Peatland Management Strategy*. Jakarta: ASEAN Secretariat.

———. (2016) ASEAN haze action-online. Available from https://goo.gl/0yMsSu. Last accessed on 20 May 2016.

Atkinson, C. (2014) Deforestation and transboundary haze in Indonesia: path dependence and elite influences, *Environment and Urbanization Asia* 5(2), 253–67.

Auburn, F. M. (1973) International law and sea-ice jurisdiction in the Arctic Ocean (based on U.S. v. Escamilla), *International and Comparative Law Quarterly* 22(3), 552–57.

Australian Government Department of the Environment (2016) *Carcharias taurus* (east coast population). In Species Profile and Threats Database. Available from https://goo.gl/1iODO5. Last accessed on 25 April 2016.

———. (no date) Sharks in Australian waters. Available from https://goo.gl/hbLZvZ. Last accessed on 29 April 2016.

Avery, M. (2003) *The Tea Road: China and Russia Meet Across the Steppe*. Beijing: China Intercontinental Press.

Bachelard, G. (1983 [1942]) *Water and Dreams: An Essay on the Imagination of Matter*. Dallas: Pegasus Foundation.

———. (1984 [1961]) *The Flame of a Candle*. Dallas: The Dallas Institute of Humanities and Culture.

———. (1988 [1943]) *Air and Dreams: An Essay on the Imagination of Movement*. Dallas: The Dallas Institute of Humanities and Culture.

Bachelard, M. (2014) Vomitous and terrifying: the lifeboats used to turn back asylum seekers, *Sydney Morning Herald*, 2 March. https://goo.gl/M3vOpf. Last accessed on 14 April 2017.

Bacon, F. (2000 [1620]) *The New Organum*. Edited by L. Jardine and M. Silverthorne. Cambridge: Cambridge University Press.

Bagnold, R.A. (2005 [1954]) *Physics of Blown Sand and Desert Dune*. New York: Dover Publications Inc.

———. (1990) *Sand, Wind and War: Memoirs of a Desert Explorer*. Tucson, AZ: University of Arizona Press.

Baker, R. (1999) Land is life: a cultural geography of Australian contact history. In Stratford, E. (ed.) *Australian Cultural Geographies*. Melbourne: Oxford University Press, Meridian Series in Geography, Chapter 3.

Ball, P. (2002) *The Elements: A Short Introduction*. Oxford: Oxford University Press.

Barboza, F.R. and Defeo, O. (2015) Global diversity patterns in sandy beach macrofauna: a biogeographic analysis, *Scientific Reports* 5 (14515), 1–9.

Barnett, J. and Adger, W.N. (2007) Climate change, human security and violent conflict. *Political Geography* 26(6), 639–55.

Barry, A. (2006) Technological zones, *European Journal of Social Theory* 9(2), 239–53.

Bateson, C. (1959) *The Convict Ships 1787–1868*. Glasgow: Brown, Son & Ferguson Ltd.

Bear, C. (2013) Assembling the sea: materiality, movement and regulatory practices in the Cardigan Bay scallop fishery, *Cultural Geographies* 20(1), 21–41.

Bear, C. and Eden, S. (2008) Making space for fish: the regional, network and fluid spaces of fisheries certification, *Social & Cultural Geography* 9(5), 487–504.

Beasley-Murray, J. (2010) *Posthegemony: Political Theory and Latin America*. Minneapolis: University of Minnesota Press.

Bebbington, A. and Bury, J. (eds) (2013) *Subterranean Struggles: New Dynamics of Mining, Oil, and Gas in Latin America*. Austin: University of Texas Press.

Beck, J. (2001) Without form and void: the American desert as trope and terrain, *Neplant: Views from the South* 2(1), 63–83.

Beery, J. (2016) Unearthing global natures: outer space and scalar politics. *Political Geography*, 55, 92–101.

References

Beistegui, M. de (1997) *Heidegger and the Political: Dystopias*. London and New York: Routledge.

Belkin, H., Tewalt, S., Hower, J., Stucker, J. and O'Keefe, J. (2009) Geochemistry and petrology of selected coal samples from Sumatra, Kalimantan, Sulawesi, and Papua, Indonesia, *International Journal of Coal Geology* 77(3), 260–68.

Bennett, J. (2004) The force of things: steps toward an ecology of matter, *Political Theory* 32(3), 347–72.

———. (2010) *Vibrant Matter: A Political Ecology of Things*. Durham, NC: Duke University Press.

Bennett, T. and Joyce, P. (eds.) (2010) *Material Powers: Cultural Studies, History and the Material Turn*. London and New York: Routledge.

Benson, A. (1973) Spatial disorientation and the 'break-off' phenomenon, *Aerospace Medicine* 44(8), 944–52.

Benton, L. (2010) *A Search for Sovereignty: Law and Geography in European Empires, 1400–1900*. Cambridge: Cambridge University Press.

Bergmann, L. (2013) Bound by chains of carbon: ecological–economic geographies of globalization, *Annals of the Association of American Geographers*, 103(6), 1348–70.

Bianco, L., Dell'Olmo, P. and Odoni, A. R. (eds.) (1997) *Modelling and Simulation in Air Traffic Management*. New York: Springer-Verlag.

Bierens, J. J. (ed.) (2006) *Handbook on Drowning: Prevention, Rescue, Treatment*. Heidelberg, New York, Dordrecht, London: Springer.

Block. B., Jonsen, I.D., Jorgensen, S.J., Whinship, A.J., et al. (2010) Tracking apex marine predator movements in a dynamic ocean, *Nature* 475(7354), 86–90.

Bond, G (1965) Sealab II Chronicle. US Navy. Archive material accessed at the Man in the Sea Museum, Panama City Beach, Florida.

———. (1993) *Papa Topside: The Sealab Chronicles of Capt. George F. Bond, USN*. Siteri, H. (ed.) Annapolis, MD: Naval Institute Press.

Borges, J. L. (1998) Book of Sand. In Borges, J.L. and Hurley A. (eds.), *Collected Fictions*. London and New York: Viking, 480–83.

Bost, R. (2014) Ice, ice and more ice: my days on ice island T3, Dauntless at Sea [blogpost, 4 July]. Available from https://goo.gl/OccvT1. Last accessed on 13 June 2017.

Botero, G. (1606 [1588]) *A Treatise Concerning the Causes of the Magnificencie and Greatness of Cities*. Translated by R. Peterson. London: T. P. for Richard Ockould.

———. (1956 [1589]) *The Reason of State*. Translated by P. J. and D. P. Waley. New Haven, CT: Yale University Press.

Bottazzi, P. and Rist, S. (2012) Changing land rights means changing society: the sociopolitical effects of agrarian reforms under the government of Evo Morales, *Journal of Agrarian Change* 12(4), 528–51.

Boyd, S. B. (1984) The legal status of Arctic sea ice: a comparative study and a proposal, *Canadian Yearbook of International Law* 22(January), 98–152.

BP. (2015) Statistical Review of World Energy. Available from https://goo.gl/9dUtTb. Last accessed on 20 May 2016.

Braun, B. (2000) Producing vertical territory: geology and governmentality in late Victorian Canada, *Ecumene* 7(1), 7–46.

Bravo, M. (2010) The humanism of sea ice. In Krupnik, I., et al. (eds.) *Siku: Knowing Our Ice*. Berlin: Springer, 445–52.

Bremner, L. (2014) Fluid ontologies in the search for MH370, *Journal of the Indian Ocean Region* 11(1), 1–22.

Brenner, N. (ed.) (2013) *Implosions/Explosions: Towards a Study of Planetary Urbanization*. Berlin: Jovis.

Brenner, N. and Schmid, C. (2011) Planetary urbanization. In Gandy, M. (ed.) *Urban Constellations*. Berlin: Jovis, 10–13.

Bridge, G. (2004) Mapping the bonanza: geographies of mining investment in an era of neoliberal reform, *The Professional Geographer* 56(3), 406–21.

———. (2009) The Hole World: spaces and scales of extraction, *New Geographies* 2(2), 43–48.

———. (2011) Resource geographies I: making carbon economies, old and new, *Progress in Human Geography* 35(6), 820–34.

———. (2013) Territory, now in 3D! *Political Geography* 34(May), 55–57.

Brighton, B., Sherker, S., Brander, R., Thompson, M. and Bradstreet, A. (2013) Rip current related drowning deaths and rescues in Australia 2004–2011, *Natural Hazards Earth System Sciences* 13(4), 1069–75.

British Genealogy (2009) Wreck of the Convict Ship Waterloo 1842. https://goo.gl/6OYlN0. Last accessed on 17 May 2017.

British Parliament (1843) British Parliamentary Papers, House of Commons and Command, Volume 52. Accounts and Papers ~ 32 volumes (23) Trade; Shipping. Session 2 February–24 August. Available from goo.gl/1VnPBZ. Last accessed on 17 May 2017.

Brower, B. C. (2009) *A Desert Named Peace: The Violence of France's Empire in the Algerian Sahara 1804–1902*. Chichester: Columbia University Press.

Brown, E., Colling, A., Park, D., Phillips, J., Rothery, D. and Wright, J. (2004) *Ocean Circulation*. Oxford: Butterworth Heinemann.

Bruce, B. and Bradford, R. (2012) Habitat use and spatial dynamics of juvenile white sharks, *Carcharodon carcharias*, in eastern Australia. In Domeier, M. (ed.) *Global Perspectives on the Biology and Life History of the Great White Shark*. Boca Raton, FL: SRC Press.

Bruce, B., Stevens, J. and Malcom, H. (2006) Movements and swimming behaviour of white sharks (*Carcharodon carcharias*) in Australian waters, *Marine Biology* 150(2), 161–72.

Bruno, G. (1584) *De la Causa, Principio et Uno*. Venice: Venetia.

Buck, B. M. (1965) Ice drilling in Fletcher's Ice Island (T-3) with a portable mechanical drill, *Arctic* 18(1), 51–54.

Budd, L. (2009) The view from the air: the cultural geographies of flight. In Vannini, P. (ed.) *The Cultures of Alternative Mobilities: Routes Less Travelled*. Aldershot: Ashgate, 71–90.

Budd, L., Griggs, S., Howarth, D. and Ison, S. (2011) A fiasco of volcanic proportions? Eyjafjallajökull and the closure of European airspace, *Mobilities* 6(1), 31–40.

Buller, H (2014) Animal geographies I, *Progress in Human Geography* 38(2), 308–18.

———. (2015) Animal geographies III, *Progress in Human Geography* 40(3), 422–30.

Bumpus, A. (2011) The matter of carbon: understanding the materiality of tCO2e in carbon offsets, *Antipode* 43(3), 612–38.

Butler, D. (2001) Technogeopolitics and the struggle for control of world air routes, *Political Geography* 20(5), 635–58.

Butler, J. (2006) *Precarious Life: The Powers of Mourning and Violence*. London and New York: Verso.

Button, K. and Taylor, S. (2000) International air transportation and economic development, *Journal of Air Transport Management* 6(4), 209–22.

Byers, M. (2013) *International Law and the Arctic*. Cambridge: Cambridge University Press.

Calla, R. (2011) TIPNIS y Amazonia: Contradicciones En La Agenda Ecologica de Bolivia, *European Review of Latin American and Caribbean Studies* 91(October), 77–83.

Campbell, M. (2017) Is Emirates Airline running out of sky?, *Bloomberg*, 5 January. Available from https://goo.gl/LWJLba. Last accessed on 6 January 2017.

Campos Velasco, E. (2010) Oruro Y Los Corredores Interoceánicos. *La Patria*, 24 October. p. 3a.

Cane, I. (2014) Community and Company Development Discourses in Mining: The Case of Gender in Mongolia. PhD thesis, School of Social Sciences, University of Queensland.

Cantillon, R. (1959) *Essai sur la nature du commerce en général*. Translated by H. Higgs. London: Frank Cass and Company Ltd.

Capobianco, R. (2010) *Engaging Heidegger*. Toronto: University of Toronto Press.

Caprotti, F. (2011) Visuality, hybridity, and colonialism: imagining Ethiopia through colonial aviation, 1935–1940, *Annals of the Association of American Geographers* 101(2), 380–403.

Cardozo, G. (2015) Whale rescue: humpback calf caught in shark net at Soldiers Beach, *The Australian*, 4 November. Available from https://goo.gl/xCpd6v. Last accessed on 6 April 2016.

Carpenter, E. and Blockwick, T. (1967) The support vessel. In Pauli, D. and Clapper, G. (eds.) *Project Sealab Report: An Experimental 45-Day Undersea Saturation Dive at 205 Feet*. Washington, DC: ONR, 122–31.

Carroll, S. (2015) *An Empire of Air and Water: Uncolonizable Space in the British Imagination 1750–1850*. Philadelphia: University of Pennsylvania Press.

Carson, R. (1962) *Silent Spring*. New York: Houghton Mifflin.

Castells, M (2000) *The Rise of the Network Society*, 2nd edition. Oxford: Blackwell Publishing.

———. (2010) Globalisation, networking, urbanisation: reflections on the spatial dynamics of the information age, *Urban Studies* 47(13), 2737–45.

Castree, N. (2002) False antitheses? Marxism, nature and actor-networks, *Antipode* 34(1), 111–46.

Cerdá, I. (1867) *Teoría general de la urbanización, y aplicación de sus principios y doctrinas a la reforma y ensanche de Barcelona*. Madrid: Imprenta Española.

———. (1875) La carta al Marqués de Corvera. See García-Bellido García de Diego, J., 2000, Ildefonso Cerdà y el nacimiento de la urbanística: la primera propuesta disciplinar de su estructura profunda. *Scripta Nova* No. 61. Available from https://goo.gl/AEhMKI. Last accessed on 4 April 2017.

Certeau, M. de (1984) *The Practice of Everyday Life*. Berkeley: University of California Press.

Cesalpino, A. (1569) *Quaestionum peripateticarum libri V*. Venice: Iantas.

Chalfin, B. (2015) Governing offshore oil: mapping maritime political space in Ghana and the western Gulf of Guinea, *South Atlantic Quarterly* 114(1), 101–18.

Chapron. G., Kaczensky, P., Linnell, J.D.C. et al. (2014) Recovery of large carnivores in Europe's modern human-dominated landscapes, *Science* 346(6216), 1517–19.

Chevalier, M. (1832) *Système de la Méditerranée*. Paris: Aux bureaux du Globe.

China Daily (2013a) Block train service to Russia on fast track. Available from https://goo.gl/oqxAMF. Last accessed on 10 July 2015.

———. (2013b) Green Great Wall to combat sandstorms. Available from https://goo.gl/iZ55qR. Last accessed on 26 April 2016.

———. (2015) China to invest \$900b in Belt and Road Initiative. Available from https://goo.gl/991kso. Last accessed on 10 July 2015.

Chokkalingam, U., Kurniawan, I. and Ruchiat, Y. (2005) Fire, livelihoods, and environmental change in the Middle Mahakam Peatlands, East Kalimantan, *Ecology and Society* 10(1), 26. Available from https://goo.gl/Eg8Z9F. Last accessed on 20 May 2016.

Choy, T. and Zee, J. (2015) Condition – suspension, *Cultural Anthropology* 30(2), 210–23.

Churchill, R.R. and Vaughn Lowe, A. (1999) *The Law of the Sea*. Manchester: Manchester University Press.

Claisse, J., Pondell II, D., Love, M., Zahn, L., Williams, C., Williams, J. and Bull, A. (2014) Oil platforms off California are among the most productive marine fish habitats globally, *Proceedings of the National Academy of Sciences* 111(43): 15462–467.

Clark, N. (2008) Aboriginal cosmopolitanism, *International Journal of Urban and Regional Studies* 32(3), 737–44.

———. (2011) *Inhuman Nature: Sociable Life on a Dynamic Planet*. London: SAGE Publications Inc.

———. (2012) 400ppm: regime change in geo-social formations. *Environment and Planning D*, Forums on 400ppm: Exit Holocene, Enter Anthropocene. Available from http://bit.ly/2swaU79. Last accessed on 14 June 2017.

———. (2014) Geo-politics and the disaster of the Anthropocene, *The Sociological Review* 62(S1), 19–37.

———. (2015) Fiery arts: pyrotechnology and the political aesthetics of the Anthropocene, *GeoHumanities* 1(2), 266–84.

———. (2017) Politics of strata, *Theory, Culture and Society* 34(2–3), 211–31.

———. and Yusoff, K. (2014) Combustion and society: a fire-centred history of energy use, *Theory, Culture & Society* 31(5), 203–26.

Clarsen, G. (2015) Special section on settler-colonial mobilities, *Transfers* 5(3), 41–48.

Coddington, K, Catania, R.T., Loyd, J. Mitchell-Eaton, E. and Mountz, A. (2012) Embodied possibilities, sovereign geographies and island detention: negotiating the 'right to have rights' on Guam, Lampedusa and Christmas Island, *Shima: The International Journal of Research into Islands* 6(2), 27–48.

Coddington, K. and Mountz, A. (2014) Countering isolation with use of technology: how asylum-seeking detainees on islands in the Indian Ocean use social media to transcend their confinement, *Journal of the Indian Ocean Region* 10(1), 97–112.

Cohen, A. (2015) China's 'One Belt – One Road' mega-project will boost Eurasian natural gas opportunities, *Journal of Energy Security*. Available from https://goo.gl/LR8zeI. Last accessed on 10 July 2016.

Cohen, S. (2014) *Transformations of Time and Temporality in Medieval and Renaissance Art*. Leiden: Brill.

Cole, L. (2017) The final frontier. *The Geographical Magazine*. Available from http://geographical.co.uk/geopolitics/geopolitics/item/1907-the-final-frontier. Last accessed on 31 July 2017.

Collard, R. (2012) Cougar-human entanglements and the biopolitical un/making of safe space, *Environment and Planning D: Society and Space* 30(1), 23–42.

Collis, C. and Dodds, K. (2008) Assault on the unknown: the historical and political geographies of the International Geophysical Year (1957–8), *Journal of Historical Geography* 34(4), 555–73.

Connor, S. (2010) *The Matter of Air: Science and the Art of the Ethereal*. London: Reaktion.

Coole, D. and Frost, S. (eds.) (2010) *New Materialisms: Ontology, Agency, and Politics*. Durham, NC: Duke University Press.

Corbey, R. and Lanjouw, A. (eds.) (2013) *The Politics of Species: Reshaping Our Relationships with Other Animals*. Cambridge: Cambridge University Press.

Cosgrove, D. (2001) *Apollo's Eye: A Cartographic Genealogy of the Earth in the Western Imagination*. Baltimore: Johns Hopkins University Press.

Crary, A. P. (1954) Seismic studies on Fletcher's Ice Island, T-3, *Transactions of the American Geophysical Union* 35(2), 293–300.

———. (1958) Arctic ice island and shelf studies: Part I, *Arctic* 11(1), 2–42.

———. (1960) Arctic ice island and shelf studies: Part II, *Arctic* 13(1), 32–50.

Crary, A. P. and Cotell, R. D. (1952) Ice islands in Arctic research, *The Scientific Monthly* 75(5), 298–302.

Crary, A. P., Cotell, R. D. and Sexton, T. F. (1952) Preliminary report on scientific work on 'Fletcher's Ice Island', T3, *Arctic* 5(4), 211–23.

Cresswell, T. (1996) *In Place/Out of Place: Geography, Ideology, and Transgression*. Minneapolis: University of Minnesota Press.

———. (2010) Toward a politics of mobility, *Environment and Planning D: Society & Space* 28(1), 17–31.

Cronin, M. (2010) Polar horizons: images of the Arctic in accounts of Amundsen's polar aviation expeditions, *Scientia Canadensis/Canadian Journal of the History of Science, Technology and Medicine* 33(2), 99–120.

Cruickshank, D. A (1971) Arctic ice and international law: the Escamilla case, *Western Ontario Law Review* 10, 178–94.

Crutzen, P. (2002) Geology of mankind, *Nature* 415(6867), 23.

Crutzen, P. J. and Stoermer, E. F. (2000) Global change newsletter, *The Anthropocene* 41, 17–18.

Culpepper, W., Porter, R., Frost, W. and Deleman, B. (1967) Engineering evaluation of Sealab II. In Pauli, D. and Clapper, G. (eds.) *Project Sealab Report: an experimental 45-day underseasaturation dive at 205 feet*, ONR, 306–48

Cumming, G. S., Cumming, D. H. M. and Redman, C. L. (2006) Scale mismatches in social-ecological systems: causes, consequences, and solutions, *Ecology and Society* 11(1), 14–33.

Cwerner, S. (2009) Introducing aeromobilities. In Cwerner, S., Kesselring, S. and Urry, J. (eds.) *Aeromobilities*. London and New York: Routledge, 1–21.

The Daily Telegraph (2015) Shark nets only offer 'false sense of security' with Bondi Sydney's worst protected beach, 21 January. Available from https://goo.gl/BZ0gIL. Last accessed on 6 April 2016.

Dalby, S. (2009) *Security and Environmental Change*. Cambridge: Polity.

———. (2013) The geopolitics of climate change, *Political Geography* 37(November), 38–47.

———. (2017) Firepower: Geopolitical Cultures in the Anthropocene, *Geopolitics*, doi: 10.1080/14650045.2017.1344835

Das, S. (2005) *Touch and Intimacy in First World War Literature*. Cambridge: Cambridge University Press.

Davis, R., Noon, S. and Harrington, J. (2007) The petroleum potential of tertiary coals from Western Indonesia: relationship to mire type and sequence stratigraphic setting, *International Journal of Coal Geology* 70(1), 35–52.

De Schutter, O. (2012) 'Ocean grabbing' as serious a threat as 'land grabbing' [Press Release]. New York/Geneva: United Nations, 30 October.

Deleuze, G. (1988) *Spinoza: Practical Philosophy*. San Francisco: City Lights Books.

Deleuze, G. and Guattari F. (2004) *A Thousand Plateaus Capitalism and Schizophrenia*. London: Continuum.

DeLoughrey, E. (2007) *Routes and Roots: Navigating Caribbean and Pacific Island Literatures*. Honolulu: University of Hawai'i Press.

Department of Fisheries (2012) Shark mitigation to protect beachgoers, Western Australian Government, 27 September. Available from https://goo.gl/wkB1Ay. Last accessed on 28 April 2016.

Department of Primary Industries (2009) NSW Shark Meshing (Bather Protection) Program Primefact 147, 3rd edition, January. Available from https://goo.gl/0pYtX1. Last accessed on 7 April 2016.

———. (2015) NSW Shark Meshing (Bather Protection) Program Primefact 147, 6th edition, September. Available from https://goo.gl/tv4CaM. Last accessed on 7 April 2016.

Derudder, B. and Witlox, F. (2008) Mapping world city networks through airline flows: context, relevance, and problems, *Journal of Transport Geography* 16(5), 305–12.

Desker, B. (2015) Challenging times in Singapore-Indonesia relations, *The Straits Times* 14 October. Available from https://goo.gl/YHPo4q. Last accessed on 29 March 2017.

Dickson, A. (2015) Distancing asylum seekers from the state: Australia's evolving political geography of immigration and border control, *Australian Geographer* 46(4), 437–54.

Diederiks-Verschoor, I.H. (1983) *An Introduction to Air Law*. Deventer, Netherlands: Kluwer Law and Taxation Publishers.

Dikötter, F. (2015) *The Discourse of Race in Modern China*. Oxford: Oxford University Press.

Dittmer, J. (2014) Geopolitical assemblages and complexity, *Progress in Human Geography* 38(3), 385–401.

Dodds, K. (2009) *Geopolitics: A Short Introduction*. Oxford: Oxford University Press.

———. (2010) Flag planting and finger pointing: The Law of the Sea, the Arctic and the political geographies of the outer continental shelf, *Political Geography* 29(2), 63–73.

Doel, R. (2003) Constituting the postwar earth sciences: The military's influence on the environmental sciences in the USA after 1945, *Social Studies of Science* 33(5), 635–66.

Doel, R. E., Friedman, R. M. Lajus, J., Sörlin, S. and Wråkberg, U. (2014) Strategic Arctic science: national interests in building natural knowledge – interwar era through the Cold War, *Journal of Historical Geography* 44(April), 60–80.

Doherty, B. and Davidson H. (2015) Orange lifeboats used to return asylum seekers to be replaced by 'fishing boats'. *The Guardian*. Available from https://www.theguardian.com/australia-news/2015/mar/05/orange-lifeboats-used-to-return-asylum-seekers-to-be-replaced-by-fishing-boats. Last accessed on 6 January 2018.

Dohrn-van Rossum, G. (1996) *History of the Hour: Clocks and Modern Temporal Orders*. Chicago: University of Chicago Press.

Donne, J. (2001 [1624]) Meditation 17 – devotions upon emergent occasions. In Donoghue, D. (ed.) *The Complete Poetry and Selected Prose of John Donne*. New York: Modern Library.

Douglas, M. (2008) *Purity and Danger: An Analysis of Concepts of Pollution and Taboo*. London and New York: Routledge.

Doyle P. and Bennett, M. R. (2002) Terrain in military history: an introduction. In Doyle, P. and Bennett, M. R. (eds.) *Fields of Battle: Terrain in Military History*. Dordrecht: Kluwer, 1–7.

Duffield, M. (2007) *Development, Security and Unending War: Governing the World of Peoples*. Cambridge: Polity Press.

Dufresne, R. (2007) *Canada's Legal Claims Over Arctic Territories and Waters*. Ottawa: Parliamentary Information and Research Service.

Dulvy, N., et al. (2014) Extinction risk and conservation of the world's sharks and rays, *eLife 2014.3:e00590*. doi: 10.7554/eLife.00590 Last accessed on 14 June 2017.

Dumaine, C. and Mintzer, I. (2015) Confronting climate change and reframing security, *SAIS Review of International Affairs* 35(1), 5–16.

Dyson-Hudson, R. and Smith, E. A. (1978) Human territoriality: an ecological reassessment, *American Anthropologist*, 80(1), 21–41.

Easterling, K. (2014) Zone: the spatial softwares of extrastatecraft, *Places Journal* November. Available from https://goo.gl/c2zSFO. Last accessed on 21 August 2015.

EITI [Extractive Industries Transparency Initiative] (2013) *Progress Report 2013: Beyond Transparency*. Oslo: EITI Secretariat.

Elden, S. (2009) *Terror and Territory: The Spatial Extent of Sovereignty*. Minneapolis: University of Minnesota Press.

———. (2010) Land, terrain, territory, *Progress in Human Geography* 34(6), 799–817.

———. (2013a) *The Birth of Territory*, Chicago: University of Chicago Press.

———. (2013b) Secure the volume: vertical geopolitics and the depth of power, *Political Geography* 32(2), 35–51.

———. (2017a) A conversation with Stuart Elden: approaching territory [online]. *Kerb: Journal of Landscape Architecture*, 24, 18–23. Available from https://goo.gl/U79vBS. Last accessed on 17 May 2017.

———. (2017b) Foucault and geometrics. In Bonditti, P., Bigo, D. and Gros, F. (eds.) *Foucault and the Modern International: Silences and Legacies for the Study of World Politics*. London: Palgrave Macmillan, 295–311.

———. (2017c) Legal terrain: the political materiality of territory. *London Review of International Law*. doi: 10.1093/lril/lrx008

———. (forthcoming) *Shakespearean Territories*.

Ellis, E. C. and Ramankutty, N. (2008) Putting people in the map: anthropogenic biomes of the world, *Frontiers in Ecology and the Environment* 6(8), 439–47.

Emel J., Huber, M. T. and Makene, M. H. (2011) Extracting sovereignty: capital, territory and gold mining in Tanzania, *Political Geography* 30(2), 70–79.

Energy and Climate Intelligence Unit (2016) Asia's Tigers: reconciling coal, climate and energy demand. Available from https://goo.gl/4C1Cwe. Last accessed on 19 May 2016.

Engel, U. and Nugent, P. (2010) *Respacing Africa*. Leiden: Brill.

Engelmann, S. (2015) Toward a poetics of air: sequencing and surfacing breath, *Transactions of the Institute of British Geographers* 40(3), 430–44.

ERM [Environmental Resource Management] (2014) Tweneboa, Enyenra, Ntomme (TEN) Project, Ghana: Final Environmental Impact Statement. London: Tullow Oil.

Evans, J. (2009) Where lawlessness is law: the settler-colonial frontier as a legal space of violence, *Australian Feminist Law Journal* 30(1), 3–22.

Evans, R. and Thorpe, B. (1998) Commanding men: masculinities and the convict system, *Journal of Australian Studies* 22(56), 17–34.

The *Express Tribune* with the *International New York Times* (2015) Chinese court jails Muslim for 6 years for growing beard, wife gets 2 years for wearing veil. Available from https://goo.gl/R0ie9d. Last accessed on 11 July 2015.

FAA (2017) Overflight fees, *Federal Aviation Administration*, 23 February. Available from https://goo.gl/1grf2M. Last accessed on 29 March 2017.

Fabricant, N. and Postero, N. (2015) Sacrificing indigenous bodies and lands: the political-economic history of lowland Bolivia in light of the recent TIPNIS debate. *The Journal of Latin American and Caribbean Anthropology* 20(3), 452–74.

Fanon, F. (1961) *Les damnés de la terre*. Paris: François Maspero.

———. (1965) *The Wretched of the Earth*. Translated by C. Farrington. London: Penguin.

Farish, M. (2006) Frontier engineering: from the globe to the body in the Cold War Arctic, *The Canadian Geographer/Le Géographe Canadien* 50(2), 177–96.

———. (2013) The lab and the land: overcoming the Arctic in Cold War Alaska, *Isis: Journal of the History of Science Society* 104(1), 1–29.

Fatah, L. (2008) The impacts of coal mining on the economy and environment of South Kalimantan Province, Indonesia, *ASEAN Economic Bulletin* 25(1), 85–98.

Ferguson, J. (2005) Seeing like an oil company: space, security and global capital in neoliberal Africa, *American Anthropologist* 107(3), 377–82.

Field, A. (1985) *International Air Traffic Control: Management of the World's Airspace*. Oxford: Pergamon Press.

Fine, G. A. and Hallett, T. (2003) Dust: a study in sociological miniaturism, *The Sociological Quarterly* 44(1), 1–15.

Fletcher, J. O. (1997) Interview for the Polar History Program, 23 January, Boulder CO, interviewer: Brian Shoemaker, Available from https://goo.gl/awuSxb. Last accessed on 13 June 2017.

Flint, R. F. (1953) Snow, Ice and Permafrost in Military Operations. Special Report 15: Snow Ice and Permafrost Research Establishment. Washington, DC: US Army Corps of Engineers.

Flitton, D. (2014) Asylum seeker boat turn-backs supported by 71 per cent in poll, *Sydney Morning Herald*, 4 June. Available from https://goo.gl/NkSLrJ. Last accessed on 14 April 2017.

Forsyth, I. (2016) Desert journeys: from exploration to covert operations, *The Geographical Journal* 182(3), 226–35.

Forth, G. (2009) Heads under bridges or in mud: reflections on a Southeast Asian 'diving rumour', *Anthropology Today* 25(6), 3–6.

Foucault, M. (1980) Prison talk (interviewer J.J. Brochier). In Gordon, C. (ed.) *Power/Knowledge: Selected Interviews and Other Writings 1972–1977*. New York: Pantheon Books, 37–54.

———. (1986) Of other spaces, *Diacritics* 16(1), 22–27.

———. (1991 [1975]) *Discipline and Punish: The Birth of the Prison*. London: Penguin.

———. (2009) *Security, Territory, Population*. New York: Palgrave.

Franckx, E. (1993) *Maritime Claims in the Arctic: Canadian and Russian Perspectives*. Berlin: Springer.

Frodeman, R. (2003) *Geo-logic: Breaking Ground between Philosophy and the Earth Sciences*. Albany, NY: SUNY Press.

Fuller, T. (1850 [1622]) *History of the Worthies of England*. New edition with P. Austin Nuttall. London: Thomas Tegg.

Galli, C. (ed.) (2010) *Political Spaces and Global War*. A. Sitze. Translated by E. Fay. Minneapolis: University of Minnesota Press.

Garcia, M. E., Quintanilla, J., Ramos, O., Ormachea, M. and Niura, A. (2008) *Estudio de La Distribución de Metales Pesados En Aguas Superficiales Y Subterráneas En La Cuenca Del Lago Poopo*. La Paz, Bolivia: Instituto de Investigaciones Químicas, Universidad Mayor de San Andrés.

Ge, M., Johannes, F. and Damassa, T. (2014) 6 graphs explain the world's top 10 emitters. World Resources Institute. Available from https://goo.gl/8OBLoU. Last accessed on 19 May 2016.

Ghana Constitution (1992) Available from http://www.africanchildforum.org/clr/ Legislation%20Per%20Country/ghana/ghana_constitution_1992_en.pdf. Last accessed on 2 January 2018.

Ghana Maritime Authority (2011) Annual Report of the Ghana Maritime Authority. Accra: Government of the Republic of Ghana.

Ghana Shipping (Protection of Offshore Operations and Assets) Regulations 2012 (Legislative Instrument 2010). Accra: Government of Ghana.

Gibbs, L. and Warren, A. (2014) Thinking space – killing sharks: cultures and politics of encounter and the sea, *Australian Geographer* 45(2), 101–7.

Gibbs, L. and Warren, A. (2015) Transforming shark hazard policy: learning from ocean-users and shark encounter in Western Australia, *Marine Policy* 58(August), 116–24.

Gluckman, R. (2000) Beijing's Desert Storm. Originally published in *Asiaweek Inside Story*. Available from https://goo.gl/UriT7P. Last accessed on 10 July 2015.

Goehring, J. E. (2003) The dark side of landscape: ideology and power in the Christian myth of the desert, *Journal of Medieval and Early Modern Studies* 33(3), 437–51.

Goldammer, J. (2007) History of equatorial vegetation fires and fire research in Southeast Asia before the 1997–98 episode: a reconstruction of creeping environmental changes, *Mitigation and Adaptation Strategies for Global Change* 12(1), 13–32.

Goldammer J. G. and Crutzen P. J. (1993) Fire in the environment: scientific rationale and summary of results of Dahlem Workshop. In Goldammer J. G and Crutzen P. J. (eds.) *Fire in the Environment: The Ecological. Atmospheric, and Climatic Importance of Vegetation Fires*. Hoboken, NJ: John Wiley and Sons, 1–14.

Goldin, P. R. (2015) Representations of regional diversity during the Eastern Zhou Dynasty. In Pines, Y., Goldin, P. R. and Kern, M. (eds.) *Ideology of Power and Power of Ideology in Early China*. Leiden: Brill, 31–48.

Gordillo, G. (2013) Opaque zones of empire: notes toward a theory of terrain, Paper presented at the Association of American Geographers annual meeting, Los Angeles, 9 April.

———. (2014) The Opaque Planet. *Space and Politics. Blog on the spatial and affective rhythms of politics – Blog sobre los ritmos espaciales y afectivos de la política*. Available from https://goo.gl/PUhnj6. Last accessed on 11 April 2015.

———. (2015) Terrain as insurgent weapon: an affective geometry of warfare in the valley of death. Presented at Space, Materiality and Violence workshop, PWIAS-UBC, Vancouver, March 2015.

———. (forthcoming a) The metropolis: the infrastructure of empire. In Hetherington, K. (ed.) *Infrastructures: Environment and Life in the Anthropocene*. Durham, NC: Duke University Press.

————. (forthcoming b) The forests destroyed by bulldozers: an affective geometry of the Argentine soy boom, *American Ethologist*.

Gordon, H. S. (1954) The economic theory of a common property resource: the fishery, *Journal of Political Economy* 62(2), 124–42.

Gordon, J. S. (2002) *A Thread Across the Ocean: The Heroic Story of the Transatlantic Cable*. New York: Bloomsbury Publishing.

Gottmann, J. (1973) *The Significance of Territory*. Charlottesville: University of Virginia Press.

Goudie, A. S. (2009) Dust storms: recent developments, *Journal of Environmental Management* 90(1), 89–94.

Goudie, A. S. and Middleton, N. J. (2006) *Desert Dust in the Global System*. Heidelberg and New York: Springer.

Government of Ghana (2009) Submission by the Government of the Republic of Ghana for the Establishment of the Outer Limits of the Continental Shelf of Ghana Pursuant to Article 76, paragraph 8 of the United National Convention on the Law of the Sea. Executive Summary. New York: United Nations Office of Legal Affairs. Available from https://goo.gl/L5Hplc. Last accessed on 15 August 2015.

Graham, B. (1995) *Geography and Air Transport*. Hoboken, NJ: John Wiley and Sons.

Graham, S. (1998) The end of geography or the explosion of place? Conceptualizing space, place and information technology, *Progress in Human Geography* 22(2), 165–85.

————. (ed.) (2010) *Disrupted Cities: When Infrastructure Fails*. London and New York: Routledge.

Green, J. (2014) *Drawn from the Ground: Sound, Sign and Inscription in Central Australian Sand Stories*. Cambridge: Cambridge University Press.

Green, M., Ganassin, C. and Reid, D. (2009) Report into the NSW Shark Meshing (Bather Protection) Program. Sydney: New South Wales Department of Primary Industries, Fisheries Conservation and Aquaculture Branch.

Greenberg, G. (2008) *A Grain of Sand: Nature's Secret Wonder*. Minneapolis: Voyageur Press.

Gregory, D. (2011) From a view to a kill: drones and late modern war, *Theory, Culture and Society* 28(7–8), 188–215.

————. (2015) The natures of war, *Antipode* 48(1), 3–56.

Grewcock M. (2014) Australian border policing: regional 'solutions' and neo-colonialism, *Race & Class* 55(3), 71–78.

Griffin, D.W. (2007) Atmospheric movement of microorganisms in clouds of desert dust and implications for human health, *Clinical Microbiology Review* 20(3), 459–77.

Griffin, D.W. and Kellogg, C. A. (2004) Dust storms and their impact on ocean and human health: dust in Earth's atmosphere, *EcoHealth* I, 284–95.

Griffin, D. W., Kellogg, C. A., Garrison V. H. and Shinn, E. A. (2002) The global transport of dust: an intercontinental river of dust, microorganisms and toxic chemicals flows through the Earth's atmosphere, *American Scientist* 90(3), 228–35.

Grosz, E. (2005) *Time Travels: Feminism, Nature, Power*. Crow's Nest, AU: Allen & Unwin.

———. (2008) *Chaos, Territory, Art: Deleuze and the Framing of the Earth*. New York: Columbia University Press.

Grove, R. (1995) *Green Imperialism*. Cambridge: Cambridge University Press.

The Guardian (2014) China hopes to revive the Silk Road with bullet trains to Xinjiang. Available from https://goo.gl/snj9AI. Last accessed on 10 July 2016.

Guardian Staff (2014) Towbacks may breach international law, UN refugee agency cautions Abbott. *The Guardian*, 11 January. Available from https://goo.gl/wE2tmF. Last accessed on 14 April 2017.

Haglund, W. D. and Sorg, M. H. (2002) Human remains in water environments. In Haglund, W. D. and Sorg, M. H. (eds.) *Advances in Forensic Taphonomy: Method, Theory, and Archaeological Perspectives*. Boca Raton, FL: CRC Press, 201–18.

Hakim, C. (2016) A strange anomaly in management of airspace, *The Straits Times*, 21 March. Available from https://goo.gl/pA41vz. Last accessed on 21 March 2017.

Halloran, R. (1970) Technician charged in slaying on ice island in Arctic Ocean, *The New York Times* 31 July, 1, 18.

Hamblin, J. (2002) The Navy's 'sophisticated' pursuit of science: undersea warfare, the limits of internationalism, and the utility of basic research, 1945–1956, *Isis: Journal of the History of Science Society* 93(1), 1–27.

Hansen, T. B. and Stepputat, F. (2009) *Sovereign Bodies: Citizens, Migrants, and States in the Postcolonial World*. Princeton, NJ: Princeton University Press.

Hastrup, K. and Hastrup, F. (eds.) (2015) *Waterworlds: Anthropology in Fluid Environments*. Oxford: Berghahn Books.

Hau'ofa, E. (2008) *We Are the Ocean: Selected Writings*. Honolulu: University of Hawai'i Press.

Hayes, A. and Clarke, M. E. (eds.) (2016) *Inside Xinjiang: Space, Place and Power in China's Muslim Far Northwest*. London and New York: Routledge.

Hayes-Conroy, J. and Hayes-Conroy, A. (2010) Visceral geographies: mattering, relating, and defying, *Geography Compass* 4(9), 1273–1283.

Haynes, R. D. (1998) *Seeking the Centre: The Australian Desert in Literature, Art and Film*. Cambridge: Cambridge University Press.

Haynes, T. D. (2013) *Desert: Nature and Culture*. London: Reaktion Books.

Head, L., Atchison, J. and Phillips, C. (2015) The distinctive capacities of plants: re-thinking difference via invasive species, *Transactions of the Institute of British Geographers* 40(3), 399–413.

Heidegger, M. (2004) *What Is Called Thinking*. New York: Perennial, HarperCollins.

Hellwarth, B. (2012) *Sealab: America's Forgotten Quest to Live and Work on the Seafloor*. New York: Simon & Schuster.

Helmreich, R. (1967) Prolonged stress in SEALAB II: a field study of individual and group reactions, Department of Psychology, University of Texas, Psychological Branch, ONR.

Hendrix, C. S. and Salehyan, I. (2012) Climate change, rainfall, and social conflict in Africa, *Journal of Peace Research* 49(1), 35–50.

Henry, L. S., Kim, J. and Lee, D. (2012) From smelter fumes to silk road winds: exploring legal responses to transboundary air pollution over South Korea, *Washington University Global Studies Law Review* 11(3), 565–626.

Herawati, H. and Santoso, H. (2011) Tropical forest susceptibility to and risk of fire under changing climate: a review of fire nature, policy and institutions in Indonesia, *Forest Policy and Economics* 13(4), 227–33.

Hessler, V. P. (1966) On a floating island, *Science* 151(3716), 1360–62.

Heupel, M. and Simpfendorfer, C. (2008) Movement and distribution of young bull sharks *Carcharhinus leucas* in a variable estuarine environment, *Aquatic Biology* 1, 277–89.

Heynen, N., Kaika, M. and Swyngedouw, E. (2006) *In the Nature of Cities: Urban Political Ecology and the Politics of Urban Metabolism*. London: Routledge.

Higham, R. (1965) Government, companies, and national defense: British aeronautical experience, 1918–1945 as the basis for a broad hypothesis, *Business History Review* 39(3), 323–47.

Hinkelman, E. (2008) *Dictionary of International Trade: Handbook of the Global Trade Community*. Petaluma, CA: World Trade Press.

Hirsch, P. (2016) The shifting regional geopolitics of Mekong dams, *Political Geography* 51(March), 63–74.

Hobbes, T. (2016 [1624]) *Leviathan, or the matter forme and power of a commonwealth ecclesiastical and civil,* eBooks@Adelaide, The University of Adelaide Library, Adelaide. Available from https://goo.gl/AJIvf0. Last accessed on 17 May 2017.

———. (1986) *Leviathan*. New York: Penguin.

Hönke, J. (2010) New political topographies. Mining companies and indirect discharge in Southern Katanga (DRC), *Politique Africaine* 4(120), 105–27.

Horner, R. A. (2000) Interview for the Polar History Program, 18 August, University of Washington, interviewer: Brian Shoemaker, Available from https://goo.gl/raf8pO. Last accessed on 13 June 2017.

Howitt, R. (2001) Frontiers, borders, edges: liminal challenges to the hegemony of exclusion, *Australian Geographical Studies* 39(2), 233–45.

Hsiang, S. M. and Burke, M. (2014) Climate, conflict, and social stability: what does the evidence say? *Climatic Change* 123(1), 39–55.

Hulme, M. (2011) Reducing the future to climate: a story of climate determinism and reductionism. *OSIRIS* 26(1), 245–66.

Hyndman, J. and Mountz, A. (2008) Another brick in the wall? Neo-refoulement and the externalization of asylum in Australia and Europe, *Government and Opposition* 43(2), 249–69.

Idris, A. H., Berg, R. A., Bierens, J., Bossaert, L., Branche, C. M., Gabrielli, A. and Morley, P. T. (2003) Recommended guidelines for uniform reporting of data from drowning the 'Utstein style', *Circulation* 108(20), 2565–74.

Ingold, T. (2011) *Being Alive: Essays on Movement, Knowledge and Description*. London and New York: Routledge.

———. (2012). Toward an ecology of materials, *Annual Review of Anthropology* 41, 427–442.

International Civil Aviation Organisation (1974) *The Convention on International Civil Aviation: Annexes 1 to 18*. Montreal: ICAO.

———. (1984) *Air Traffic Services Planning Manual*. Montreal: ICAO.

International Civil Aviation Organisation (1998) *Manual on Airspace Planning Methodology for the Determination of Separation Minima*. Montreal: ICAO.

———. (2002) *Council – 164th Session: Summary Minutes with Subject Index* (Doc 9796-C/1140). Montreal: ICAO.

———. (2008) *Performance-Based Navigation Manual*. Montreal: ICAO.

ITLOS [International Tribunal on the Law of the Sea] (2015) Dispute concerning delimitation of the maritime boundary between the Republic of Ghana and the Republic of Côte D'Ivoire submitted to a Special Chamber of the Tribunal [Press release]. 22 January. Available from https://goo.gl/6VolKO. Last accessed on 18 August 2015.

Jabour, B. and Hurst, D. (2014) Nauru to increase visa cost for journalists from $200 to $8,000. *The Guardian*, 8 January. Available from https://goo.gl/6QtGLh. Last accessed on 14 April 2017.

Jackson, M. and Fannin, M. (2011) Letting geography fall where it may – aerographies address the elemental, *Environment and Planning D: Society and Space* 29(3), 435–44.

Jackson, S. E. (1995) The water is not empty: cross-cultural issues in conceptualising sea space, *The Australian Geographer* 26(1), 87–96.

Jasper, D. (2006) *The Sacred Desert: Religion, Literature, Art and Culture*. Oxford: Blackwell Publishing.

Jones, D. S. (2004) ASEAN initiatives to combat haze pollution: an assessment of regional cooperation in public policy-making, *Asian Journal of Political Science* 12(2), 59–77.

Jones, R. (2016) *Violent Borders: Refugees and the Right to Move*. London: Verso.

Jørgensen, D. (2009) An oasis in a watery desert? Discourses on an industrial ecosystem in the Gulf of Mexico Rigs-to-Reefs program, *History and Technology: An International Journal* 25(4), 343–64.

Kaldor Centre (2015) Turning back boats. Andrew and Renata Kaldor Centre for International Refugee Law. Available from https://goo.gl/GQ1Yee. Last accessed on 14 April 2017.

Kane, S. C. (2012a) *Where Rivers Meet the Sea: The Political Ecology of Water*. Philadelphia: Temple University Press.

———. (2012b) Water security in Buenos Aires and the Paraná-Paraguay Waterway, *Human Organization* 71(2), 211–21.

———. (2016) Reestablishing the fundamental bases for environmental health: infrastructure and the social topographies of surviving seismic disaster. In Singer, M. (ed.) *A Companion to Environmental Health: Anthropological Perspectives*. Hoboken, NJ: John Wiley & Sons, 348–72.

Kaplan, A. (2005) Where is Guantanamo?, *American Quarterly* 57(3), 831–58.

Kaplan, C. (1996) *Questions of Travel: Postmodern Discourses of Displacement*. Durham, NC: Duke University Press.

Kasarda, J. and Lindsay, G. (2011) *Aerotropolis: The Way We'll Live Next*. New York: Farrar, Straus and Giroux.

Keough, S.B (2010) The importance of place in community radio broadcasting: a case study of WDVX, Knoxville, Tennessee, *Journal of Cultural Geography* 27(1), 77–98.

Kim, I. (2014) Messages from a middle power: participation by the Republic of Korea in regional environmental cooperation on transboundary air pollution issues, *International Environmental Agreements: Politics, Law and Economics* 14(2), 147–62.

Kindervater, K. H. (2017) Drone strikes, ephemeral sovereignty, and changing conceptions of territory, *Territory, Politics, Governance* 5(2), 207–21.

Kitchin, R. M. (1998) Towards geographies of cyberspace, *Progress in Human Geography* 22(3), 385–406.

Klein, N. (2014) Assessing Australia's push back the boats policy under international law: legality and accountability for maritime interceptions of irregular migrants, *Melbourne Journal of International Law* 15(2), 1–31.

Klinger, J. M. (2015) A historical geography of rare earth elements: from discovery to the atomic age, *The Extractive Industries and Society* 2(3), 572–80.

Knowler, G. (2015) Countries along New Silk Road await Chinese money train, *The Journal of Commerce*. Available from https://goo.gl/ynl88X. Last accessed on 10 July 2016.

Koenig, L. S, Greenway, K. R., Dunbar, M. and Hattersley-Smith, G. (1952) Arctic ice islands, *Arctic* 5, 66–102.

Kratochwil, F. (1986) Of systems, boundaries, and territoriality: an inquiry into the formation of the state system, *World Politics* 39(1), 27–52.

Kuhlken, R. (1999) Settin' the woods on fire: rural incendiarism as protest, *The Geographical Review* 89(3), 343–63.

Kull, C. (2002) Madagascar aflame: landscape burning as peasant protest, resistance, or a resource management tool? *Political Geography* 21, 927–53.

La Patria (2012) Red Departamental de Carreteras, *La Patria*, 12 March, p. 3b.

———. (2013a) Hasta Julio de 2014 Se Concluye El Primer Tramo Del Toledo-Ancaravi, *La Patria*, 15 June, p. 4a.

———. (2013b) Se Pretende Consolidar a Belén Como Banco de Materiales Para Toledo-Culluri, *La Patria*, 4 July, p. 4a.

———. (2013c) Cruce Belén Proveerá Materiales Para Obras Del Tramo Toledo-Culluri, *La Patria*, 7 July, p. 4a.

———. (2013d) Tramo Toledo-Ancaravi Presenta Un Considerable Retraso En 10 Meses de Labor, *La Patria*, 18 August, p. 5b.

———. (2013e) Tramo Toledo-Ancaravi Tiene Un Avance Físico 'mínimo' del 6,5 % En Un Año, *La Patria*, 20 September, p. 5a.

———. (2013f) Pobladores de El Choro Liberan Banco de Materiales Del Tramo Toledo-Culluri, *La Patria*, 12 December, p. 6a.

———. (2015) Morales Promete Más Dobles Vías Para Diferentes Regiones Del País, *La Patria*, 3 February, p. 5a.

Lambert, D., Martins, L. and Ogborn, M. (2006) Currents, visions and voyages: historical geographies of the sea, *Journal of Historical Geography* 32(3), 479–93.

Lanphier, E. and Dwyer, J. (1954) Diving with self-contained underwater breathing apparatus, *EDU Special Report Series*, 1–54 to 11–54.

Lash, S. (2012) Deforming the figure: topology and the social imaginary, *Theory, Culture and Society* 29(4–5), 261–87.

Latour, B. (1993 [1991]) *We Have Never Been Modern.* Translated by C. Porter. Cambridge, MA: Harvard University Press.

Latour, B. (2005) *Reassembling the Social: An Introduction to Actor-Network-Theory.* Oxford: Oxford University Press.

Laughland, O. and Farrell, P. (2014) Asylum seekers across Australia launch legal appeals following data breach. *The Guardian*, 8 March. Available from https://goo.gl/JngazX. Last accessed on 14 April 2017.

Le Maître, A. (1682) *La metropolitée, ou, De l'êtablissement des villes capitales, de leur utilité passive & active, de l'union de leurs parties, & de leur anatomie, de leur commerce, &c.* Amsterdam: Chés Balthes Boekholt pour Jean van Gorp.

Leary, W. M. (1999) *Under Ice: Waldo Lyon and the Development of the Arctic Submarine.* College Station: Texas A&M University Press.

Lefebvre, H. (1991) *The Production of Space.* Oxford: Blackwell Publishing.

Lehman, G. (2017) Discussion about indigenous conceptions of land and water, January. Personal communication.

Lehman, J. (2013a) Volumes beyond volumetrics: a response to Simon Dalby's 'The Geopolitics of Climate Change', *Political Geography* 37(May), 51–52.

———. (2013b) Relating to the sea: enlivening the ocean as an actor in Eastern Sri Lanka, *Environment and Planning D: Society and Space* 31(3), 485–501.

———. (2016) A sea of potential: the politics of global ocean observations, *Political Geography* 55, 113–23.

Leschack, L. A. (1964) Long-period vertical oscillation of the ice recorded by continuous gravimeter measurements from drift station T-3, *Arctic* 17(4), 272–79.

Lewis, M. W. and Wigen, K. (1997) *The Myth of Continents: A Critique of Metageography.* Berkeley: University of California Press.

Lin, W. (2013) A geopolitics of (im)mobility? *Political Geography* 36(September), A1–A3.

———. (2016) Drawing lines in the sky: the emotional labours of airspace production, *Environment and Planning A* 48(6), 1030–46.

———. (2017a) Catering for flight: rethinking aeromobility as logistics, *Environment and Planning D: Society and Space*, doi: 10.1177/0263775817697977.

———. (2017b) Sky watching: vertical surveillance in civil aviation, *Environment and Planning D: Society and Space*, 35(3), 399–417.

Liu, J. and Diamond, J. (2005) China's environment in a globalizing world, *Nature* 435(7046) (30 June), 1179–86.

Livingstone, D. (2003) *Putting Science in Its Place: Geographies of Scientific Knowledge.* Chicago: University of Chicago Press.

Locke, J. (1823 [1689]) Two Treatises of Government *The Works of John Locke. A New Edition – Corrected. In Ten Volumes. Vol. V.* London: Printed for Thomas Tegg and others.

Lockhart, T. (2014) Comment on Dauntless at Sea blogpost [6 December 2014]. Available from https://goo.gl/1euBjF. Last accessed on 13 June 2017.

Long, J. C. (2006) Border anxiety in Palestine-Israel, *Antipode* 38(1), 107–27.

Lorenzo, G. A. (2011) Marcha Indígena Por El TIPNIS En Bolivia: Más Que Un Simple Problema?, *Revista Andina de Estudios Politicos* 9(August–September), 3–17.

Lövbrand, E. and Stripple, J. (2006) The climate as political space: on the territorialisation of the global carbon cycle, *Review of International Studies* 32, 217–35.

Lowry, S.T. (1974) The archaeology of the circulation concept in economic theory, *Journal of the History of Ideas* 35(3), 429–44.

Lynch, K. (1962) *Site Planning*. Cambridge, MA: MIT Press.

MacDonald, F. (2007) Anti-Astropolitik – outer space and the orbit of geography, *Progress in Human Geography* 31(5), 592–615.

MacKenzie, D. (2009) Making things the same: gases, emission rights and the politics of carbon markets, *Accounting, Organizations and Society* 34(3–4), 440–55.

Mackinnon, M. (1967) The design, construction, and outfitting of Sealab II. In Pauli, D. and Clapper, G. (eds.) *Project Sealab Report: An Experimental 45-Day Undersea Saturation Dive at 205 Feet*. Washington, DC: ONR, 67–87.

Mahony, M. (2014) The predictive state: science, territory and the future of the Indian climate, *Social Studies of Science* 44(1), 109–33.

Malecki, E. J. and Wei, H. (2009) A wired world: the evolving geography of submarine cables and the shift to Asia, *Annals of the Association of American Geographers* 99(2), 360–82.

Marder, M. (2015) *Pyropolitics: When the World Is Blaze*. London: Rowman & Littlefield International.

Martin, L., and Secor, A.J. (2014) Towards a post-mathematical topology. *Progress in Human Geography* 38(3), 420–438.

Massey, D. (1992) Politics and space/time, *New Left Review* 196, 65–84.

———. (2005) *For Space*. London: SAGE Publications Inc.

Massumi, B. (2015) *Politics of Affect*. Cambridge: Polity Press.

Maxwell-Stewart, H. (2016) The rise and fall of penal transportation. In Knepper, P. and Johansen, A. (eds.) *The Oxford Handbook of the History of Crime and Criminal Justice*. Oxford: Oxford University Press.

Mayer, J. (2006) Transboundary perspectives on managing Indonesia's fires, *Journal of Environment & Development* 15(2), 202–23.

Mazzone, W. (1967) Sealab II atmosphere control. In Pauli, D. and Clapper, G. (eds.) *Project Sealab Report: An Experimental 45-Day Undersea Saturation Dive at 205 Feet*. Washington, DC: ONR, 110–12.

Mbembe, A. (2008) *Necropolitics. Foucault in an Age of Terror*. Amsterdam: Springer.

McCormack, D. P. (2007) Molecular affects in human geographies, *Environment and Planning A* 39(2), 359–77.

———. (2009) Aerostatic spacing: on things becoming lighter than air, *Transactions of the Institute of British Geographers* 34(1), 25–41.

———. (2015) Envelopment, exposure, and the allure of becoming elemental, *Dialogues in Human Geography* 5(1), 85–89.

McDowell, S. D., Steinberg, P. E. and Tomasello, T. K. (2008) *Managing the Infosphere: Governance, Technology, and Cultural Practice in Motion*. Philadelphia: Temple University Press.

McNeish, J. (2013) Extraction, protest and indigeneity in Bolivia: the TIPNIS effect, *Latin American and Caribbean Ethnic Studies* 8(2), 221–42.

McNiven, I. (2004) Saltwater People: spiritscapes, maritime rituals and the archaeology of Australian indigenous seascapes, *World Archaeology* 35(3), 329–49.

Meng, Z. and Lu, B. (2007) Dust events as a risk factor for daily hospitalization for respiratory and cardiovascular diseases in Minqin, China, *Atmospheric Environment* 41(33), 7048–58.

Merchant, S. (2011a) Negotiating underwater space: the sensorium, the body and the practice of scuba diving, *Tourist Studies* 11(3), 215–34.

———. (2011b) The body and the senses: visual methods, videography and the submarine sensorium, *Body and Society* 17(1), 53–72.

———. (2014) Deep ethnography: witnessing the ghosts of SS Thistlegorm. In Anderson, J. and Peters, J. (eds), *Water Worlds: Human Geographies of the Ocean*. Aldershot: Ashgate, 119–35.

Merriman, P. (2007) *Driving Spaces: A Cultural-Historical Geography of England's M1 Motorway*. Oxford: Blackwell Publishing.

Merriman, P. (2012) *Mobility, Space, and Culture*. London and New York: Routledge.

Meserve, R. I. (1982) The inhospitable land of the barbarian, *Journal of Asian History* 16(1), 51–89.

Mezzadra, S., and Neilson, B. (2013) *Border as Method, or, the Multiplication of Labor*. Durham, NC: Duke University Press.

Mill, J. S. (1963 [1859]) *Collected Works of John Stuart Mill*, [J.M. Robson (ed.) Originally in On Liberty, published 1859]. Toronto: University of Toronto Press.

Millennium (2013). Special issue of *Millennium: Journal of International Studies* 41(3), 397–678.

Miller, J.W. Bowen, H. Radloff, R. and Helmreich, R. (1967) The Sealab II human behaviour program. In Pauli, D. and Clapper, G. (eds.) *Project Sealab Report: An Experimental 45-Day Undersea Saturation Dive at 205 Feet*. Washington, DC: ONR, 245–71.

Misselden, E. (1969 [1623]) *The Circle of Commerce or, The Ballance of Trade*. Paris and London: Da Capo Press – Hachette Book Group.

Mitchell, A. J. (2005) Heidegger and terrorism, *Research in Phenomenology* 35(1), 181–218.

Mitchell, C.W. (1991) *Terrain Evaluation: An Introductory Handbook to the History, Principles, and Methods of Practical Terrain Assessment*, 2nd edition. Harlow: Longman Scientific & Technical.

Mitchell, T. (1991) The limits of the state: beyond statist approaches and their critics, *American Political Science Review* 85(1), 77–96.

Mitchell, W. J. T. (2002) *Landscape and Power*. Chicago: University of Chicago Press.

MoEJ. (2006) Abstract of the special committee report on dust and sandstorm issues, Ministry of Environment in Japan. Available from https://goo.gl/Lpf6GU. Last accessed on 15 February 2016.

Mohan, G. (2013) Beyond the enclave: towards a critical political economy of China and Africa, *Development and Change* 44(6),1255–72.

Morgensen, S. L. (2011) The biopolitics of settler colonialism: right here, right now, *Settler Colonial Studies* 1(1), 52–76.

Mountz, A. (2004) Embodying the nation-state: Canada's response to human smuggling, *Political Geography* 23(3), 323–45.

———. (2010) *Seeking Asylum: Human Smuggling and Bureaucracy at the Border* Minneapolis: University of Minnesota Press.

Mountz, A., Coddington, K., Catania, R.T. and Loyd, J. M. (2013) Conceptualizing detention: mobility, containment, bordering, and exclusion, *Progress in Human Geography* 37(4), 522–41.

Moxley, M. (2010) China's great green wall grows in climate fight, *The Guardian*. Available from https://goo.gl/qhURJj. Last accessed on 15 July 2016.

Mukerji, C. (2009) *Impossible Engineering: Technology and Territoriality on the Canal du Midi*. Princeton, NJ: Princeton University Press.

Mulrennan, M. and Scott, C. (2000) Mare nullius: indigenous rights in saltwater environments, *Development and Change* 31(3), 681–708.

Murdocca, C. (2010) 'There is something in that water': race, nationalism and legal violence, *Law & Social Inquiry* 35(2), 369–402.

Murray, E. Inman, D. and Koontz, W. (1967) Sealab II underwater weather station. In Pauli, D. and Clapper, G. (eds), *Project Sealab Report: An Experimental 45-Day Undersea Saturation Dive at 205 Feet*. Washington, DC: ONR, 369–84.

Myers, F. R. (1991) *Pintupi Country, Pintupi Self: Sentiment, Place, and Politics Among Western Desert Aborigines*. Berkeley: University of California Press.

Natural Resources Canada (2015) Atlas of Canada, 15 April 2015 release: Canada (map MCR102). Available from https://goo.gl/WeqRB9. Last accessed on 13 June 2017.

Needham, J., Wang, L. and de Solla Price, D. J. (1986) *Heavenly Clockwork: The Great Astronomical Clocks of Medieval China (No. 1)*. Cambridge: University of Cambridge.

Neff, C. (2012) Australian beach safety and the politics of shark attacks, *Coastal Management* 40(1), 88–106.

Nethery, A., Rafferty-Brown, B. and Taylor, S. (2013) Exporting detention: Australia-funded immigration detention in Indonesia, *Journal of Refugee Studies* 26(1), 88–109.

Newland, K. (2003) Troubled waters: rescue of asylum seekers and refugees at sea, Migration Information Source. Available from https://goo.gl/tmkb8d. Last accessed on 14 April 2017.

Newman, D. and Paasi, A. (1998) Fences and neighbours in the postmodern world: boundary narratives in political geography, *Progress in Human Geography* 22(2), 186–207.

Nicolaysen, L. (2013) Japan calls for action of China air zone. *The Australian*, 1 December. Available from https://goo.gl/U4clRp. Last accessed on 28 March 2017.

Nicolson, M. (1960) *The Breaking of the Circle: Studies in the Effect of the 'New Science' upon Seventeenth-Century Poetry*. New York: Columbia University Press.

Nietzsche, F. (2001 [1882]) *The Gay Science*. Edited by B.A.O. Williams. Translated by J. Nauckhoff and A. Del Caro. Cambridge: Cambridge University Press.

Nilsson, L. (1965) Drama of life before birth, *Life* 58(17), April 30.

Nitze, P. (1967) Foreword. In Pauli, D. and Clapper, G. (eds.) *Project Sealab Report: An Experimental 45-Day Undersea Saturation Dive at 205 Feet*. Washington, DC: ONR, i.

NOAA. (n.d.) What is the great Pacific garbage patch? Available from https://ocean-service.noaa.gov/facts/garbagepatch.html. Last accessed on 23 July 2017.

Norboo, T., Angchuk, P.T., Yahya, M., Kamat, S.R., Pooley, F.D., Corrin, B., Kerr, I.H., Bruce, N. and Ball, K.P. (1991) Silicosis in a Himalayan village population: role of environmental dust, *Thorax* 46(5), 861–63.

Office of Environment and Heritage NSW (2011) Death or injury to marine species following capture in shark control programs on ocean beaches – key threatening process listing. NSW Scientific Committee final determination. Available from https://goo.gl/ueJEVv. Last accessed on 7 April 2016.

O'Kelly, M. E. (1998) A geographer's analysis of hub-and-spoke networks, *Journal of Transport Geography* 6(3), 171–86.

Oldenziel, R. (2011) Islands: the United States as a networked empire, In G. Hecht (ed.) *Entangled Geographies: Empire and Technopolitics in the Global Cold War*, Cambridge, MA: MIT Press, 13–41.

O'Neal, H., Bond, G., Lanphear, R. and Odum, T. (1967) *Project Sealab Summary Report: An Experimental Eleven-Day Undersea Saturation Dive at 193 Feet.* Sealab, I Project Group, ONR Report ACR – 108.

Ong, A. and Collier, S. (eds.) (2005) *Global Assemblages: Technology, Politics and Ethics as Anthropological Problems.* Oxford: Blackwell Publishing.

ONR [United States Office of Naval Research] (1967) Project Sealab Report: an experimental underseasaturation dive at 205 feet Sealab Project Group. In: Pauli, D. and Clapper, P., eds, Report ACR-124. (https://archive.org/stream/projectsealabrep00paul#page/n0/mode/1up). Accessed 18 February 2016.

Oreskes, N. (2003) A context of motivation: US Navy oceanographic research and the discovery of sea-floor hydrothermal vents, *Social Studies of Science* 33(5), 697–742.

Ó Tuathail, G. (1996) *Critical Geopolitics: The Politics of Writing Global Space.* Minneapolis: University of Minnesota Press.

Oum, T. H. (1998) Overview of regulatory change in international air transport and Asian strategies towards the US open skies initiative, *Journal of Air Transport Management* 4(3), 127–34.

Paasi, A. (1998) Boundaries as social processes: territoriality in the world of flows, *Geopolitics*, 3(1), 69–88.

———. (2012) Border studies reanimated: going beyond the territorial/relational divide, *Environment and Planning A* 44(10), 2303–9.

Pagel, W. (1951) William Harvey and the purpose of circulation, *Isis: Journal of the History of Science Society* 42(1), 22–38.

Painter, J. (2010) Rethinking territory, *Antipode* 42(5), 1090–118.

———. (2011) Territory and network: a false dichotomy? In Vanier, M. (ed.) *Territoires, Territorialité, Territorialisation: Controverses et Perspectives.* Rennes: Presses Universitaires de Rennes, 57–66.

Pampín, J. B. and López-Abajo Rodríguez, B. A. (2001) Surprising drifting of bodies along the coast of Portugal and Spain, *Legal Medicine* 3(3), 177–82.

Pascoe, D. (2001) *Airspaces.* London: Reaktion Books.

Perera, S. (2002) A line in the Sea, *Australian Humanities Review* (September), 1–8.

———. (2009) *Australia and the Insular Imagination: Beaches, Borders, Boats, and Bodies.* New York: Palgrave Macmillan.

Perera, S. (2013) Oceanic corpo-graphies, refugee bodies and the making and unmaking of waters, *Feminist Review* 103(1), 58–79.

Peters, K. (2010) Future promises for contemporary social and cultural geographies of the sea, *Geography Compass* 4(9), 1260–72.

———. (2012) Manipulating material hydro-worlds: rethinking human and more-than-human relationality through offshore radio piracy, *Environment and Planning A* 44(5), 1241–54.

———. (2014) Tracking (im)mobilities at sea: ships, boats and surveillance strategies, *Mobilities* (9)3, 414–31.

———. (2015) Drifting: towards mobilities at sea, *Transactions of the Institute of British Geographers* 40(2), 262–72.

———. (2017) *Rebel Radio: Sound, Space, Society*. Basingstoke: Palgrave.

———. and Turner, J. (2015) Between crime and colony: interrogating (im) mobilities aboard the convict ship, *Social & Cultural Geography* 16(7), 844–62.

Pettijohn, F. J., Potter, P. E. and Siever, R. (1987) *Sand and Sandstone*. New York and Heidelberg: Springer Science and Business Media.

Pharand, D. (1969) The legal status of ice shelves and ice islands in the Arctic, *Les Cahiers de droit* 103, 461–75.

———. (1971) State jurisdiction over Ice Island T-3: the Escamilla case, *Arctic* 24(2), 83–89.

———. (2009) *Canada's Arctic Waters in International Law*. Cambridge: Cambridge University Press.

Phillips, J., Hailwood, E. and Brooks, A. (2016) Sovereignty, the 'resource curse' and the limits of good governance: a political economy of oil in Ghana, *Review of African Political Economy* 43(147), 26–42.

Picon, A. (1992) *French Architects and Engineers in the Age of Enlightenment*. Cambridge: Cambridge University Press.

———. (2002) *Les saint-simoniens: raison, imaginaire et utopie*. Paris: Belin.

Pieraccini, M. (2015) Democratic legitimacy and new commons: examples from English protected areas, *International Journal of the Commons* 9(2), 552–72.

Platoff, A. M. (2014) Flags in space: NASA symbols and flags in the US manned space program, *The Flag Bulletin: The International Journal of Vexillology* 46(5–6), 143–221.

Polunin, N. (1958) The botany of ice-island T-3, *Journal of Ecology* 46(2), 323–47.

Powell, R. C. (2007) 'The rigours of an arctic experiment': the precarious authority of field practices in the Canadian High Arctic, 1958–1970, *Environment and Planning A* 39(8) 1794–1811.

Pratt, G. (2005) Abandoned women and spaces of exception, *Antipode* 37(5), 1052–78.

Pritchard, S.B. (2011) *Confluence: The Nature of Technology and the Remaking of the Rhone*. Cambridge, MA: Harvard University Press.

Protevi, J. (2009) *Political Affect: Connecting the Social and the Somatic*. Minneapolis: University of Minnesota Press.

Pugliese, J. (2007) Geocorpographies of torture, *ACRAWSA* e-journal 3(1), 1–18.

Putz, C. (2015) Will all roads in Central Asia eventually lead to China? *The Diplomat.* Available from https://goo.gl/Si6tKe. Last accessed on 10 July 2016.

Pyne, S. (1987) *The Ice: A Journey to Antarctica.* Iowa City: University of Iowa Press.

———. (1994) Maintaining focus: an introduction to anthropogenic fire, *Chemosphere* 29(5), 889–911.

———. (1997a) *World Fire: The Culture of Fire on Earth.* Seattle: University of Washington Press.

———. (1997b) *Vestal Fire.* Seattle: University of Washington Press.

———. (2001) *Fire: A Brief History.* Seattle: University of Washington Press.

———. (2014) Moved by fire: history's Promethean moment, *The Appendix* 2(4). Available from https://goo.gl/3XBfTl. Last accessed on 20 May 2016.

Quintanilla, J., Coudrain-Ribstein, A., Martinez, J. and Camacho, V. (1995) Hidroquímica de las aguas del altiplano de Bolivia, *Bulletin de L'Institut Francais D'Etudes Andines* 24(3), 461–71.

Rademacher, A. M. (2011) *Reigning the River: Urban Ecologies and Political Transformation in Kathmandu.* Durham, NC: Duke University Press.

Raguraman, K. (1986) Capacity and route regulation in international scheduled air transportation: a case study of Singapore, *Singapore Journal of Tropical Geography* 7(1), 53–67.

Ramos, O. E. R. Cáceres, L. F., Ormachea Muñoz, M. R., Bhattacharya, P., Quino, I., Quintanilla, J., Sracek, O., Thunvik, R., Bundschuh, J. and García, M.E. (2012) Sources and behavior of arsenic and trace elements in groundwater and surface water in the Poopó lake basin, Bolivian Altiplano, *Environmental Earth Sciences* 66(3), 793–807.

Randall, J. (1992) Review of the biology of the tiger shark (*Galeocerdor cuvier*), *Australian Journal of Marine and Freshwater Research* 43(1), 21–31.

Rappler.com (2015) Indonesia steps up commitment to fight climate change at #COP21. Available from https://goo.gl/3FXjRy. Last accessed on 19 May 2016.

Rediker, M. (2004) The Red Atlantic; or, 'a terrible blast swept over the heaving sea'. In Klein, B. and Mackenthun, G. (eds) *Sea Changes. Historicizing the Ocean.* London and New York: Routledge, 111–30.

Reid, D., Robbins, W. and Peddemors, V. (2011) Decadal trends in shark catches and effort from the New South Wales, Australia, Shark Meshing Program 1950–2010, *Marine and Freshwater Research* 62(6), 676–93.

Robinson, N. A. (2001) Forest fires as a common international concern: precedents for the progressive development of international environmental law, *Pace Environmental Law Review* 18, 459–504.

Rockström, J., Steffen, W., Noone, K., Chapin, F., Lambin, E., Lenton, T., Scheffer, M., Folke, C., Schellnhuber, H., Nykvist, B., De Wit, C., Hughes, T., van der Leeuw, S., Rodhe, H., Sörlin, S., Snyder, P., Costanza, R., Svedin, U., Falkenmark, M., Karlberg, L., Corell, R., Fabry, V., Hansen, J., Walker, B., Liverman, D., Richardson, K., Crutzen, P. and Foley, J. (2009) Planetary boundaries: exploring the safe operating space for humanity, *Ecology and Society* 14(2), 32. Available from https://goo.gl/2i9nHt. Last accessed on 23 May 2016.

Romero, A.M., et al. (2017) Chemical geographies, *GeoHumanities* 3(1), 158–77.

Rosaviatsia (2016) EASA SIB 2015–16R2 Simferopol Flight Information Region (FIR), dated 17 February 2016, *Russian Federal Air Transport Agency*, 19 February. Available from https://goo.gl/ESclt9. Last accessed on 29 March 2017.

Rose, E. P. F. and Paul, N. C. (eds.) 2000 *Geology and Warfare: Examples of the Influence of Terrain and Geologists on Military Operations*. Bath: The Geological Society.

Rose, G. and Tolia-Kelly, D. P. (2012) Visuality/materiality: introducing a manifesto for practise. In Rose, G. and Tolia-Kelly, D. P. (eds.) *Visuality/Materiality: Images, Objects and Practices*. Aldershot: Ashgate, 1–12.

Rose, N. (2007) *The Politics of Life Itself: Biomedicine, Power, and Subjectivity in the Twenty-First Century*. Princeton, NJ: Princeton University Press.

Rosen, E. (1910) *In the Foreign Legion*. London: Duckworth and Co.

Rossell Arce, P. (2011) 'El Parteaguas Del Evismo' Bolivia Despues Del Conflicto Del Tipnis. *Nueva Sociedad* 237(January–February), 4–16.

Rothwell, D. (1996) *The Polar Regions and the Development of International Law*. Cambridge: Cambridge University Press.

Rowan, R. (2017) Cosmic legal geographies: asteroid mining, new space and the contested sovereignty in extra-planetary space, Annual Association of American Geographers Conference, Boston.

Rozwadowski, H. (2010) Ocean depths, *Environmental History* 15(3), 520–25.

———. (2012) Arthur C. Clarke and the Limitations of the Ocean as a Frontier, *Environmental History* 17(3), 578–602.

Ruggie, J. G. (1993) Territoriality and beyond: problematizing modernity in international relations, *International organization* 47(1), 139–74.

Russell, F. (2004) *Mistehay Sakahegan, The Great Lake: The Beauty and Treachery of Lake Winnipeg*. Winnipeg: Heartland Associates.

Russia Today (2015) 'Sand-ageddon': Chinese capital hit by worst sand storm in decade, *Russia Today*. Available from https://goo.gl/ULQ8kY. Last accessed on 10 July 2016.

Sack, R. (1986) *Human Territory*. Cambridge: Cambridge University Press.

Sage, D. (2008) Framing space: a popular geopolitics of American manifest destiny in outer space, *Geopolitics* 13(1), 27–53.

———. (2014) *How Outer Space Made America: Geography, Organisation, and the Cosmic Sublime*. Aldershot: Ashgate.

Sallis, J. (2000) *Force of Imagination: The Sense of the Elemental*. Bloomington: Indiana University Press.

Salter, M. (2013) To make move and let stop: mobility and the assemblage of circulation, *Mobilities* 8(1), 7–19.

Sammler, K. (2015) Subsuming the submerged: producing seabeds as political territories. Paper presented at the Annual Meeting of the Association of American Geographers, Hyatt Regency Hotel, Chicago, 21–25 April.

Sandano, I. A. (2013) Kashgar: the next economic booming hub – analysis, *Eurasia Review*. Available from https://goo.gl/S52Bbi. Last accessed on 10 July 2015.

Schmitt, C. (1997) *Land and Sea*. Washington, DC: Plutarch Press.

———. (2006 [1950]) *The Nomos of the Earth in the International Law of the Jus Publicum Europaeum.* Translated by G.L. Ulmen. New York: Telos Press.

———. (2008) *The Leviathan in the State Theory of Thomas Hobbes: Meaning and Failure of a Political Symbol.* Translated by G. Schwab and E. Hilfstein. Chicago: University of Chicago Press.

———. (2011) *Writings on War.* Ed. T. Nunan. Cambridge: Polity Press.

Science (2016) Rover reveals puzzling sand dunes on Mars, *American Association for the Advancement of Science.* Available from https://goo.gl/cccj4Y. Last accessed on 10 November 2016.

Scott, H. (2012) The contested spaces of the subterranean: colonial governmentality, mining, and the mita in early Spanish Peru, *Journal of Latin American Geography* 11(S), 7–33.

Scott, J. C. (1999) *Seeing Like a State: How Certain Schemes to Improve the Human Condition Have Failed.* New Haven, CT: Yale University Press.

———. (1987) Everyday forms of resistance, *The Copenhagen Journal of Asian Studies* (July), 33–62.

Scott, W. (1996 [1820]) *Ivanhoe.* Edited by I. Duncan. Oxford: Oxford University Press.

Seiler, W., and Crutzen, P.J. (1980) Estimates of gross and net fluxes of carbon between the biosphere and the atmosphere from biomass burning, *Climatic Change* 2(3), 207–247.

Selby, J., and Hoffmann. C. (2014) Beyond scarcity: rethinking water, climate change and conflict in the Sudans, *Global Environmental Change* 29(November), 360–70.

Sermier, C. (2002) *Mongolia: Empire of the Steppes.* New York: W.W. Norton.

Serres, M. (2000) *The Birth of Physics.* Manchester: Clinamen Press.

SF Gate (2016) What's up with the black sand at Ocean Beach? Available from https://goo.gl/7LNB3W. Last accessed on 10 November 2016.

Shaw, I. G. (2013) Predator empire: the geopolitics of US drone warfare, *Geopolitics* 18(3), 536–59.

Sikor, T. (ed.) (2013) *The Justices and Injustices of Ecosystem Services.* London and New York: Routledge.

Simpfendorfer, C. and Heupel, M. (2012) Assessing habitat use and movement. In Carrier, J., Musick, J. and Heithaus, M. (eds.) *Biology of Sharks and their Relatives.* London: CRC Press, 579–601.

Skaff, J. K. (2012) *Sui-Tang China and Its Turko-Mongol Neighbors: Culture, Power, and Connections, 580–800.* Oxford: Oxford University Press.

Sloterdijk, P. (2013) *In the World Interior of Capital.* Translated by W. Hoban, Cambridge: Polity Press.

Sloterdijk, P. and Heinrichs, H. J. (2011) *Neither Sun Nor Death.* Los Angeles: Semiotext(e).

Small, R. (1983) Nietzsche and a Platonist tradition of the cosmos: center everywhere and circumference nowhere, *Journal of the History of Ideas* 44(1), 89–104.

Smith, A. (2015) Risky bodies offshore: spatialisation, securitisation and visual regimes of migration, Master's Thesis, Center for Migration and Refugee Studies, American University in Cairo.

Smith, D. D. (1960) Scientific Report No.4: Development of Surface Morphology on Fletcher's Ice Island, T-3, Cambridge, MA: US Air Force Cambridge Research Center.

Smith, G.W. (1966) Sovereignty in the North: the Canadian aspect of an international problem. In Macdonald, R. St J. (ed.) *The Arctic Frontier*. Toronto: University of Toronto Press, 194–255.

Smith, S. (1957) Not waving but drowning. *Collected Poems of Stevie Smith*. Available from https://goo.gl/78B2H2. Last accessed on 17 May 2017.

Smith, S., Swanson, N.W. and Gökarıksel, B. (2016) Territory, bodies and borders, *Area* 48(3), 258–61.

Smoothey, A., Gray, C., Kennelly, S., Masens, O., Peddemores, V. and Robinson, W. (2016) Patterns of occurrence of sharks in Sydney Harbour, a large urbanised estuary, *PLoS ONE* 11(1) e0146911. doi:10.1371/journal.pone.0146911

Sneddon, C. (2007) Nature's materiality and the circuitous paths of accumulation: dispossession of freshwater fisheries in Cambodia, *Antipode* 39(1), 167–93.

Soja, E. (1971). *The Political Organization of Space*. Washington, DC: Association of American Geographers.

Soll, D. (2013) *Empire of Water: An Environmental and Political History of the New York City Water Supply*. Ithaca, NY: Cornell.

Spence, E. (2014) Towards a more-than-sea geography: exploring the relational geographies of superrich mobility between sea, superyacht and shore in the Cote d'Azur, *Area* 46(2), 203–9.

Spinoza, B. (1677) *The Ethics*. Translated by R. H. M. Elwes, 1883. Available from https://goo.gl/MgXeJa. Last accessed on 5 January 2016.

Squire, R. (2016a) Rock, water, air, fire: foregrounding the elements in the Gibraltar-Spain dispute, *Environment and Planning D: Society and Space* 34(3), 3545–63.

———. (2016b) Immersive terrain: living and working on the seafloor in SEALAB II, *Area* 48(3), 332–38.

Squire, V. (2014) Desert 'trash': posthumanism, border struggles, and humanitarian politics, *Political Geography* 39, 11–21.

Staeheli, L., Marshall, D. and Maynard, N. (2016) Circulations and the entanglements of citizenship formation, *Annals of the American Association of Geographers* 106(2), 377–84.

Starosielski, N. (2015) *The Undersea Network*. Durham, NC: Duke University Press.

Steedman, C. (2001) *Dust*. Manchester: Manchester University Press.

Steffen, W., Sanderson, R.A., Tyson, P.D., Jäger, J., Matson, P.A., Moore III, B., Oldfield, F., Richardson, K., Schellnhuber, H.-J., Turner, B.L. and Wasson, R.J. (2004) *Global Change and the Earth System: A Planet Under Pressure*. Berlin: Springer/International Geosphere-Biosphere Programme.

Steinberg, P. E. (1999) Navigating to multiple horizons: toward a geography of ocean-space, *The Professional Geographer* 51(3), 366–75.

———. (2001) *The Social Construction of the Ocean*. Cambridge: Cambridge University Press.

———. (2005) Insularity, sovereignty and statehood: the representation of islands on Portolan Charts and the construction of the territorial state, *Geografiska Annaler: Series B, Human Geography* 87(4), 253–65.

————. (2009) Sovereignty, territory, and the mapping of mobility: a view from the outside, *Annals of the Association of American Geographers* 99(3), 467–95.

Steinberg, P. E. and Kristoffersen, B. (2017) 'The ice edge is lost . . . nature moved it': mapping ice as state practice in the Canadian and Norwegian north, *Transactions of the Institute of British Geographers* 42(4), 625–41.

————. and McDowell, S. D. (2003) Mutiny on the bandwidth: the semiotics of statehood in the internet domain name registries of Pitcairn Island and Niue, *New Media and Society* 5(1), 47–67.

————. Nyman, E. and Caraccioli, M. J. (2012) Atlas swam: freedom, capital, and floating sovereignties in Seasteading vision, *Antipode* 44(4), 1532–50.

————. and Peters, K. (2015) Wet ontologies, fluid spaces: giving depth to volume through oceanic thinking, *Environment and Planning D: Society and Space* 33(2), 247–64.

————. Tasch, J. and Gerhardt, H. (2015) *Contesting the Arctic: Politics and Imaginaries in the Circumpolar North*. London: I.B. Tauris.

Strandsbjerg, J. (2010) *Territory, Globalization and International Relations: The Cartographic Reality of Space*. London: Palgrave Macmillan.

Stratford, E. (1998a) A biopolitics of population decline: the *Australian Women's Sphere* as a discourse of resistance, *Australian Geographer* 29(3), 357–70.

————. (1998b) Health and nature in the 19th century Australian women's popular press, *Health & Place* 4(2), 101–12.

————. (2015) *Geographies, Mobilities, and Rhythms over the Life-Course: Adventures in the Interval*. New York and London: Routledge.

————. (2016) *Island Geographies: Essays and Conversations*. London: Routledge.

————. (2017) Imagining the archipelago. In Stephens, M. A. and Roberts, B. R. (eds) *Archipelagic American Studies: Decontinentalizing the Study of American Culture*. Durham, NC: Duke University Press, 74–94.

Stratford, E., Baldacchino, G., McMahon, E., Farbotko, C. and Harwood, A. (2011) Envisioning the archipelago, *Island Studies Journal* 6(2), 113–30.

Stratford, E., Farbotko, C. and Lazrus, H. (2013) Tuvalu, sovereignty and climate change: considering fenua, the archipelago and emigration, *Island Studies Journal* 8(1), 67–83.

Stratford, E., McMahon, E., Farbotko, C., Jackson, M. and Perera, S. (2011) Review Forum. Reading Suvendrini Perera's 'Australia and the Insular Imagination', *Political Geography* 30(6), 329–38.

Straughan, E. (2012) Touched by water: the body in scuba diving, *Emotion, Space and Society* 5(1), 19–26.

Sullivan, W. (1961) *Assault on the Unknown: The International Geophysical Year*. New York: McGraw-Hill.

Swanton, M. (ed.) (1978) *Beowulf*. Manchester: Manchester University Press.

Swyngedouw, E. (2010) Apocalypse forever? Post-political populism and the spectre of climate change, *Theory, Culture & Society* 27(2–3), 213–32.

Szpilman, D., Bierens, J., Handley, A. J. and Orlowski, J. P. (2012) Review Article. Current Concepts. Drowning, *The New England Journal of Medicine* 366(22), 2101–10.

Tang, A. (2015) Amnesty calls for inquiry into Australia paying asylum boat crew to turn back. Reuters. 28 October. Available from https://goo.gl/nXkH97. Last accessed on 14 April 2017.

Taylor, K. (ed.) (1975) *Henri Saint-Simon (1760–1825): Selected Writings on Science, Industry, and Social Organisation.* London: Taylor and Francis.

Taylor, R. (2002) Human property: threat or saviour? *Murdoch University Electronic Journal of Law* 9(4). Available from https://goo.gl/K5C5gQ. Last accessed on 17 May 2017.

Tazreiter, C. (2015) Lifeboat politics in the Pacific: affect and the ripples and shimmers of a migrant saturated future, *Emotion, Space and Society* 16(August), 99–107.

Tech Times (2016) Aliens on Google Earth? UFO Fanatics Spot Futuristic Structures in Egypt. Available from https://goo.gl/4yDbSP. Last accessed on 10 November 2016.

Tedmanson, S. (2012) Western Australia – 'shark attack capital of the world', *The Times,* 2 April. Available from https://goo.gl/36bhJL. Last accessed on 28 April 2016.

Ten Bos, R. (2009) Towards an amphibious anthropology: water and Peter Sloterdijk, *Environment and Planning D: Society and Space* 27(1), 73–86.

Teo, H-M. (2012) *Desert Passions Orientalism and Romance Novels.* Austin: University of Texas Press.

Thiessen, K. (2010) Stabilization of natural clay riverbanks with rockfill columns: a full-scale field test and numerical verification. PhD thesis, Department of Civil Engineering, University of Manitoba, Winnipeg.

Thompson, C. (2013) *Shipwreck in Art And Literature: Images and Interpretations from Antiquity to the Present Day.* London and New York: Routledge.

Thrift, N. (2009) *Shaping the Day: A History of Timekeeping in England and Wales 1300–1800.* Oxford: Oxford University Press.

Time (2009) The Cultural Demolition of Kashgar, China. Available from https://goo.gl/ljkNzm. Last accessed on 10 July 2015.

Toh, R. S. (1998) Toward an international open skies regime: advances, impediments, and impacts, *Journal of Air Transportation World Wide* 3(1), 61–71.

Topolovic, M. (2014) *Constructed Land: Singapore 1924–2012.* Zuirch: ETH Zurich DArch/Future Cities Laboratory.

Tormes, F. and Guedry, F. (1974) Disorientation phenomena in naval helicopter pilots, Naval Aerospace Medical Research Laboratory, Pensacola, Florida.

Tratt, D. M., Frouin, R. J. and Westphal, D. L. (2001) April 1998 Asian dust event: a southern California perspective, *Journal of Geophysical Research* 16(16),18.371–18.379.

Truman, H. (1945) Policy of the United States with respect to the natural resources of the subsoil and sea bed of the continental shelf, proclamation 2667. Available from https://goo.gl/KWy7av. Last accessed on 14 June 2017.

Tsing, A. L. (2005) *Friction: An Ethnography of Global Connection.* Princeton, NJ: Princeton University Press.

———. (2015) *The Mushroom at the End of the World: On the Possibility of Life in Capitalist Ruins.* Princeton, NJ: Princeton University Press.

Tuan, Y. F. (2013) *Romantic Geography: In Search of the Sublime Landscape*. London and Madison: University of Wisconsin Press.

Tuck, E., McKenzie, M. and McCoy, K. (2014) Land education: indigenous, postcolonial, and decolonizing perspectives on place and environmental education research, *Environmental Education Research* 20(1), 1–23.

Tullow Oil (2013) *Corporate Responsibility Report: Creating Shared Prosperity Through Partnership*. London: Tullow Oil.

Turner, A. J. (1982) 'The accomplishment of many years': three notes towards a history of the sand-glass, *Annals of Science* 39(2), 161–72.

Turner, J. F. (1893) *The significance of the frontier in American history*, A paper read at the meeting of the American Historical Association in Chicago, 12 July 1893, during the World Columbian Exposition.

Turner, J. and Peters, K. (2016) Rethinking mobility in criminology: beyond horizontal mobilities of prisoner transportation, *Punishment & Society* 19(1), 96–114.

Tutton, R. (n.d.) The Conversation. Available from https://theconversation.com/pro files/richard-tutton-303551. Last accessed on 29 August 2017.

Udden, J. A. (1914) Mechanical composition of clastic sediment, *Bulletin of Geological Society of America* 25(1), 655–744.

Ugolini, L. (2014) War-stained: British combatants and uniforms, 1914–18, *War & Society* 33(3), 155–71.

UN Convention on the Continental Shelf (1958) [Online]. 499 UNTS 312, opened for signature 29 April 1958, entered into force 10 June 1964. Available from https://goo.gl/6mv7XB. Last accessed on 13 August 2015.

UNCLOS [United Nations Convention on the Law of the Sea] (1982) [Online]. 1833, 1834, 1835 UNTS 3, opened for signature 10 December 1982, entered into force 16 November 1994. Available from https://goo.gl/hMU0HU. Last accessed on 13 August 2015.

Underdown, R. B. (1995) *Aviation Law for Pilots*. Oxford: Blackwell Publishing.

UNFCCC [United Nations Framework Convention on Climate Change] (2012) Clean Development Mechanism Project Design Document Form (CDM-PDD): Jubilee Oil Field Associated Gas Recovery & Utilization Project v3.5. Bonn: UNFCCC.

United States Code (n.d.) Chapter 18, section 7: Special maritime and territorial jurisdiction of the United States defined. Available from https://goo.gl/zSvxjb. Last accessed on 13 June 2017.

United States v. Escamilla (1972) Case No. 71–1575, United States Court of Appeals, Fourth Circuit, 467 F.2d 341.

Urry, J. (2014) *Offshoring*. Hoboken, NJ and London: John Wiley and Sons.

US Navy (1965) SEALAB I, Command Information Bureau. Available from https://goo.gl/NcVnln. Last accessed on 14 June 2017.

US Navy (1966) SEALAB II Man in the Sea, Command Information Bureau. Available from https://goo.gl/zEhYrg. Last accessed on 14 June 2017.

USA Today (2014) China hopes trade, tourism can calm Silk Road terror, republished by Uyghur Human Rights Project (UHRP). Available from https://goo.gl/yB3Z7h. Last accessed on 10 July 2015.

Valdivia, C., Seth, A., Gilles, J.L., Garcia, M., Jimenez, E., Cusicanqui, J., Navia, F. and Yucra, E. (2010) Adapting to climate change in Andean ecosystems:

landscapes, capitals, and perceptions shaping rural livelihood strategies and linking knowledge systems, *Annals of the Association of American Geographers* 100(4), 818–34.

Valdivia, C., Thibeault, J., Gilles, J. L., García, M. and Seth, A. (2013) Climate trends and projections for the Andean Altiplano and strategies for adaptation, *Advances in Geosciences* 33(April), 69–77.

van Dooren, T. (2014) *Flight Ways: Life and Loss at the Edge of Extinction.* New York: Columbia University Press.

Varkkey, H. (2012) The ASEAN way and haze mitigation efforts, *Journal of International Studies* 8, 77–97.

———. (2013) Patronage politics, plantation fires and transboundary haze, *Environmental Hazards* 12(3–4), 200–221.

Veracini, L. (2007) Historylessness: Australia as a settler colonial collective, *Postcolonial Studies* 10(3), 271–85.

Vermeesch, P., Fenton, C.R., Kober, F., Wiggs, G.F.S., Bristow, C.S. and Xu, S. (2010) Sand residence times of one million years in the Namib Sand Sea from cosmogenic nuclides, *Nature Geoscience* 3(12), 862–65.

Waitt, G. and Warren, A. (2008) Talking shit over a brew after a good session with your mates': surfing, space and masculinity, *Australian Geographer* 39(3), 353–65.

Walcott, D. (2007) The sea is history. In *Collected Poems*. New York: Farrar, Straus and Giroux, 364–67. Available from https://goo.gl/Ll5LrO. Last accessed on 17 May 2017.

Wang, S., Wang, J., Zhou, Z. and Shang, K. (2005) Regional characteristics of three kinds of dust storm events in China, *Atmospheric Environment* 39(3), 509–20.

Wangkiat, P. (2015) Asean nations vow to be haze-free by 2020, *Bangkok Post*. Available from https://goo.gl/Fygwqv. Last accessed on 20 May 2016.

Warkentin, J. (1961) Manitoba settlement patterns. In Kemp, D. (ed.) *Transactions Series III, No. 16*, Winnipeg: Manitoba Historical Society.

Watch the Med (2016) The sea as frontier. Available from https://goo.gl/xA3gmE. Last accessed on 14 April 2017.

Watson, C. (1997) Re-embodying sand drawing and re-evaluating the status of the camp: the practice and iconography of women's public sand drawing in Balgo, WA, *Australian Journal of Anthropology* 8(2), 104–24.

Weizman, E. (2002) Control in the air, *Open democracy*. Available from https://goo.gl/DSrnAA. Last accessed on 14 June 2017.

Well, D. E. and Slover, N. L. (1962) *Ice Runway Investigations on the Ellesmere Ice Shelf.* Port Hueneme: US Naval Civil Engineering Laboratory.

Welland, M. (2009) *Sand: The Never-Ending Story.* Berkeley and Los Angeles: University of California Press.

———. (2015) *The Desert: Lands of Lost Borders.* London: Reaktion Books.

Wentworth, C. K. (1922) A scale of grade and class terms for clastic sediments, *Journal of Geology* 30(5), 377–92.

West, J. (2011) Changing patterns of shark attacks in Australian waters, *Marine and Freshwater Research* 62(6), 744–54.

Whatmore, S. (2006) Materialist returns: practicing cultural geography in and for a more-than-human world, *Cultural Geographies* 13(4), 600–609.

White, R. (1995) *The Organic Machine: The Remaking of the Columbia River*. New York: Hill and Wang.

Whitehead, M. (2009) *State, Science and the Skies: Governmentalities of the British Atmosphere*. Hoboken, NJ and Oxford: John Wiley and Sons.

———. (2014) *Environmental Transformations: A Geography of the Anthropocene*. Abingdon: Routledge.

Whitehouse, A. and Mulyana, A. (2004) Coal fires in Indonesia, *International Journal of Coal Geology* 59(1), 91–97.

Whitlock, G. (2015) The hospitality of cyberspace: mobilising asylum seeker testimony online, *Bibliography* 38(2), 245–66.

Wilkening, K. (2006) Dragon dust: atmospheric science and cooperation on desertification in the Asia and Pacific Region, *Journal of East Asian Studies* 6(3), 433–61.

Wilkes, D. (1972) Law for special environments: ice islands and questions raised by the T-3 case, *Polar Record* 16(100), 23–27.

———. (1973) Law for special environments: jurisdiction over polar activities, *Polar Record* 16(104), 701–5.

Williams, A. J. (2013) Re-orientating vertical geopolitics, *Geopolitics* 18(1), 225–46.

Williams, R. (1983 [1976]) *Keywords: A Vocabulary of Culture and Society, Revised Edition*. New York: Oxford University Press.

Wilson, J. P. and Gallant, J. C. (2000) *Terrain Analysis: Principles and Applications*. Hoboken, NJ: John Wiley and Sons.

Winter, T. (2013) An uncomfortable truth: air-conditioning and sustainability in Asia, *Environment and Planning A* 45(3), 517–31.

Winters, H. A. with Galloway, Jr, G., Reynolds, W. J. and Rhyne, D. W. (1998) *Battling the Elements: Weather and Terrain in the Conduct of War*. Baltimore: The Johns Hopkins University Press.

Wise, M. L. (1978) *Ice Islands of the Arctic: Alaskan Air Command's Arctic Experience*. Elmendorf: Alaskan Air Command.

Wolfe, P. (2006) Settler colonialism and the elimination of the native, *Journal of Genocide Research* 8(4), 387–409.

Wood, C. E. (2006) *Mud: A Military History*. Washington, DC: Potomac Books.

Woodhouse, H. (1920) *Textbook of Aerial Laws and Regulations for Aerial Navigation, International, National and Municipal, Civil and Military*. New York: Frederick A. Stokes Company.

Woodroffe, C. (2002) *Coasts: Form, Process and Evolution*. Cambridge: Cambridge University Press.

Woon C.Y. and Dodds, K. (2017) Dredging up the volume: China, earthly engineering and the projection of geopower in the South China Sea, Annual Association of American Geographers Conference, Boston.

Worm, B., Davis, B., Kettemer, L., Ward-Paige, C., Chapman, D., Heithaus, M., Kessel, S. and Gruber, S. (2013) Global catches, exploitation rates, and rebuilding options for sharks, *Marine Policy* 40(July), 194–204.

Wyatt, R. (1990) *Death from the Skies: The Zeppelin Raids over Norfolk 19 January 1915*. Norwich: Gliddon Books.

Xinhua (2015) Full Text: Vision and actions on jointly building Belt and Road, National Development and Reform Commission, Ministry of Foreign Affairs, and Ministry of Commerce of the People's Republic of China, with State Council authorization. Available from https://goo.gl/NNoHqj. Last accessed on 10 July 2015.

Yusoff, K. (2014) Fathoming the unfathomable. In Lee, R. (ed.) *That Oceanic Feeling*. Southampton: John Hansard Gallery, 43–51.

Zalasiewicz, J. (2008) *The Earth After Us*. Oxford: Oxford University Press.

Zalasiewicz, J., Steffen, W., Leinfelder, R., Williams, M. and Waters, C. (2017) Petrifying Earth process: the stratigraphic imprint of key Earth system parameters in the Anthropocene, *Theory, Culture & Society* 34(2–3), 83–104.

Zheng, Z. (2009) *Mechanics of Wind-Blown Sand Movements*. Dordrecht and Heidelberg: Springer Verlag.

Ziegler, A., Phelps, J., Yuen, J.Q., Webb, E., Lawrence, D., Fox, J., Bruun, T., Leisz, S., Ryan, C., Dressler, W., Mertz, O., Pascual, U., Padochkk, C. and Koh, L.P. (2012) Carbon outcomes of major land-cover transitions in SE Asia: great uncertainties and REDD + policy implications, *Global Change Biology* 18(10), 3087–99.

Index

About the Authors

Ross Exo Adams is an architect, urbanist, and historian whose research focuses on the historical and political intersection of circulation and urbanisation. He is currently an Assistant Professor in Architecture at Iowa State University, USA. Ross has published and presented widely on the relations among architecture, geography, political theory, and ecology, and is author of *Circulation and Urbanization* (forthcoming).

Johanne Bruun is a doctoral candidate in the Department of Geography at Durham University, UK. Her research is at the intersection between scientific practice, material politics and spatialised governance, and her particular emphasis is on questions of terrain and territory. Current work explores the role of science in constructing territory across a range of geologic volumes in Cold War Greenland.

Nigel Clark is Chair of Social Sustainability at the Lancaster Environment Centre, Lancaster University, UK. He is the author of *Inhuman Nature: Sociable Life on a Dynamic Planet* (2011) and co-editor of *Atlas* (2012), *Material Geographies* (2008) and *Extending Hospitality* (2009). Nigel recently edited (with Kathryn Yusoff) a special issue of *Theory, Culture & Society* (2017) on 'Geosocial Formations and the Anthropocene' and is working on a book (with Bron Szerszynski) entitled *Anthropocene and Society*.

Kate Coddington is an Assistant Professor in the Geography Department at Durham University, UK. She studies approaches to public policy dealing with migrants and postcolonial governance that influence processes of bordering and citizenship. Recent work includes a co-edited special issue of *Emotion,*

Space, and Society, as well as publications in *The Professional Geographer* and *Gender, Place and Culture*.

Stuart Elden is Professor of Political Theory and Geography at the University of Warwick, UK. He works on various historical, political and conceptual aspects of the question of territory, and on twentieth-century French thought, especially Georges Canguilhem, Michel Foucault and Henri Lefebvre. Among his books are *Terror and Territory: The Spatial Extent of Sovereignty* (2009) and *The Birth of Territory* (2013).

Leah Gibbs is a Geographer and Senior Lecturer at the University of Wollongong, Australia. Her work considers human relations with nature, non-human others and materials. She is especially interested in people's interactions with water in the landscape. She regularly works with colleagues across the disciplines and is intrigued by the possibilities of interdisciplinary research. Her current major project examines the cultures and politics of human – shark encounter.

Stephanie C. Kane is Professor of International Studies at Indiana University, USA, where she writes and teaches the political ecology of water. From port cities in Brazil, Argentina and Singapore to the Canadian prairies, Kane's current ethnography explores how river and coastal city inhabitants embed themselves into the planetary crust and negotiate water disasters such as flooding, pollution and dispossession. *Where Rivers Meet the Sea* (2012) is her most recent book and 'Enclave Ecology', in *Human Organization* (2017), her most recent article.

Weiqang Lin is Assistant Professor at the Department of Geography, National University of Singapore. His research interests lie at the intersection of mobilities, (air) transport, infrastructure and transnational geopolitics. He has published in a wide range of peer-reviewed journals, including *Environment and Planning D* and *Transactions of the Institute of British Geographers*. His current research examines food logistics and their infrastructures in China and Singapore, as well as their related politics.

Thérèse Murray studied geography and philosophy at the University of Tasmania. She is interested in geographies of place and understanding in how specific places are felt and experienced. Murray is also interested in the material effects of geographic imaginaries – island and ocean – on human lives and inequity with particular regard to asylum seeking.

Marijn Nieuwenhuis is currently Teaching Fellow in International Relations and East Asia at the University of Warwick, UK. He works at the intersection of political geography and international relations. His current research focuses on the elemental politics of sand, gas and wind.

Kimberley Peters teaches human geography in the Department of Geography and Planning at University of Liverpool, UK, where her research seeks to better understand the governance of maritime space. She is co-editor of the volumes *Water Worlds: Human Geographies of the Ocean* (2014), *The Mobilities of Ships* (2015), and *Carceral Mobilities* (2017). She has written over twenty-five peer reviewed articles and book chapters, as well as the discipline-wide textbook *Your Human Geography Dissertation: Doing, Designing, Delivering* (2017) and the monograph, *Rebel Radio* (2018).

Jon Phillips is a Postdoctoral Research Associate in the Department of Geography at the University of Exeter, UK. His research interests are focused on energy and resource politics in the South, particularly in sub-Saharan Africa. The chapter in this volume draws from his doctoral research on the territories and materialities of offshore oil and gas in Ghana.

Rachael Squire is a Lecturer in Human Geography at Royal Holloway, University of London, UK. She is working on the critical geopolitics of undersea spaces, exploring the function of concepts such as territory and terrain beyond terra, the interplay between the human body and extreme environments, and the role of the non-human in characterising territorial volumes. Her work has been published in *Area* and *Environment and Planning D*.

Philip Steinberg is Professor of Political Geography and Director of IBRU: Centre for Borders Research at Durham University, UK. He has published widely on governance and political practice in extraterritorial spaces, including, most recently, *Contesting the Arctic: Politics and Imaginaries in the Circumpolar North* (2015). He is also editor-in-chief of *Political Geography*.

Elaine Stratford is Professor in the Institute for the Study of Social Change at the University of Tasmania, Australia. Research most recently captured in *Geographies, Mobilities and Rhythms Over the Life-Course* (2015), is motivated by trying to understand the conditions in which people flourish in place, in their movements, in daily life, and over the life-course, she is editor-in-chief of *Geographical Research* journal and lead editor for Rowman & Littlefield International's series *Rethinking the Island*.

Clayton Whitt is a sociocultural anthropologist who studied at the University of British Columbia, Canada. His primary research investigates how people in the highlands of western Bolivia manage and respond to climate change and other environmental problems, and how spatial transformations related to such phenomena are refracted into local politics.

CPSIA information can be obtained
at www.ICGtesting.com
Printed in the USA
LVHW011454270121
677651LV00002B/247